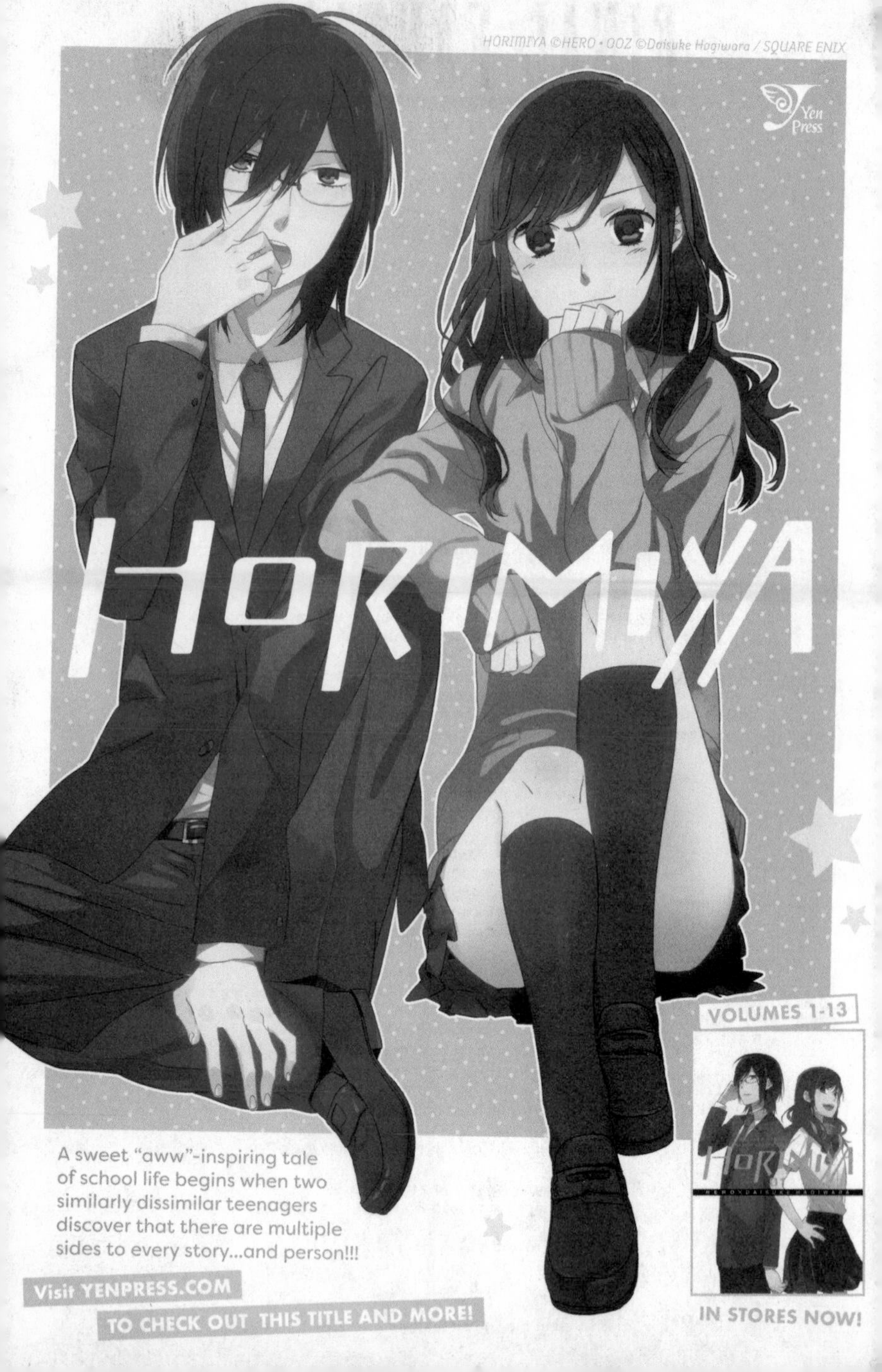

HORIMIYA ©HERO • OOZ ©Daisuke Hagiwara / SQUARE ENIX
Yen Press
HORIMIYA
VOLUMES 1-13
A sweet "aww"-inspiring tale of school life begins when two similarly dissimilar teenagers discover that there are multiple sides to every story...and person!!!
Visit YENPRESS.COM
TO CHECK OUT THIS TITLE AND MORE!
IN STORES NOW!

# FINAL FANTASY®

ファイナルファンタジー　ロスト・ストレンジャー

# LOST STRANGER

Story: Hazuki Minase　　Art: Itsuki Kameya

## VOLUME 5

Translation: Melody Pan　Lettering: Bianca Pistillo

FINAL FANTASY LOST STRANGER Volume 5 ©2020 Hazuki Minase, Itsuki Kameya/SQUARE ENIX CO., LTD. ©2020 SQUARE ENIX CO., LTD. All Rights Reserved. First published in Japan in 2020 by SQUARE ENIX CO., LTD. English translation rights arranged with SQUARE ENIX CO., LTD. and Yen Press, LLC through Tuttle-Mori Agency, Inc., Tokyo.

English translation © 2020 by SQUARE ENIX CO., LTD.

Yen Press
150 West 30th Street, 19th Floor
New York, NY 10001

Visit us at yenpress.com
facebook.com/yenpress
twitter.com/yenpress
yenpress.tumblr.com
instagram.com/yenpress

First Yen Press Edition: October 2020
The chapters in this volume were originally published as ebooks by Yen Press.

Yen Press is an imprint of Yen Press, LLC.
The Yen Press name and logo are trademarks of Yen Press, LLC.

Library of Congress Control Number: 2018948073

ISBNs: 978-1-9753-1679-2 (paperback)
978-1-9753-1680-8 (ebook)

10 9 8 7 6 5 4 3 2 1

BVG

Printed in the United States of America

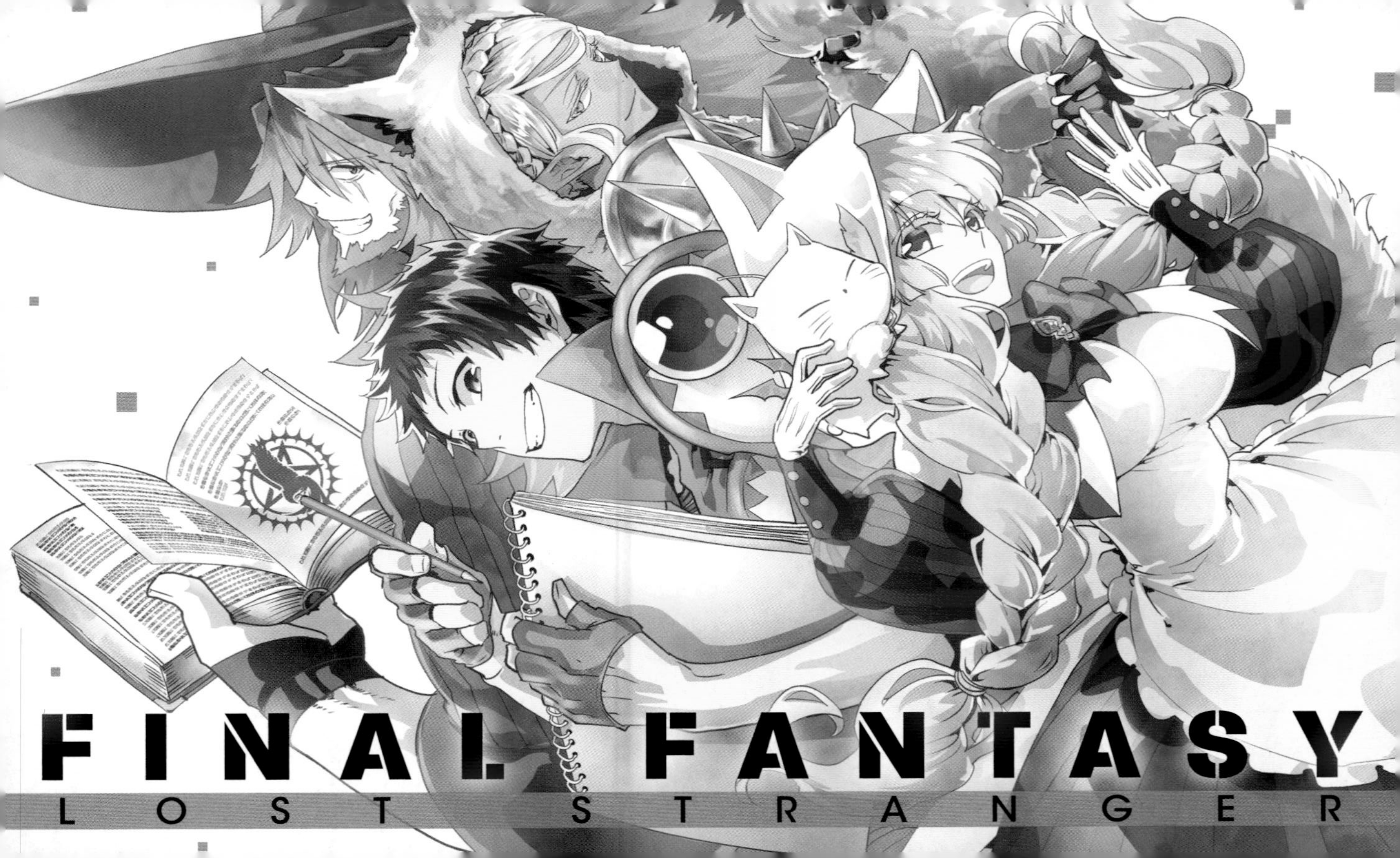
FINAL FANTASY
LOST STRANGER

# FINAL FANTASY

ファイナルファンタジー　　ロスト・ストレンジャー

## LOST STRANGER

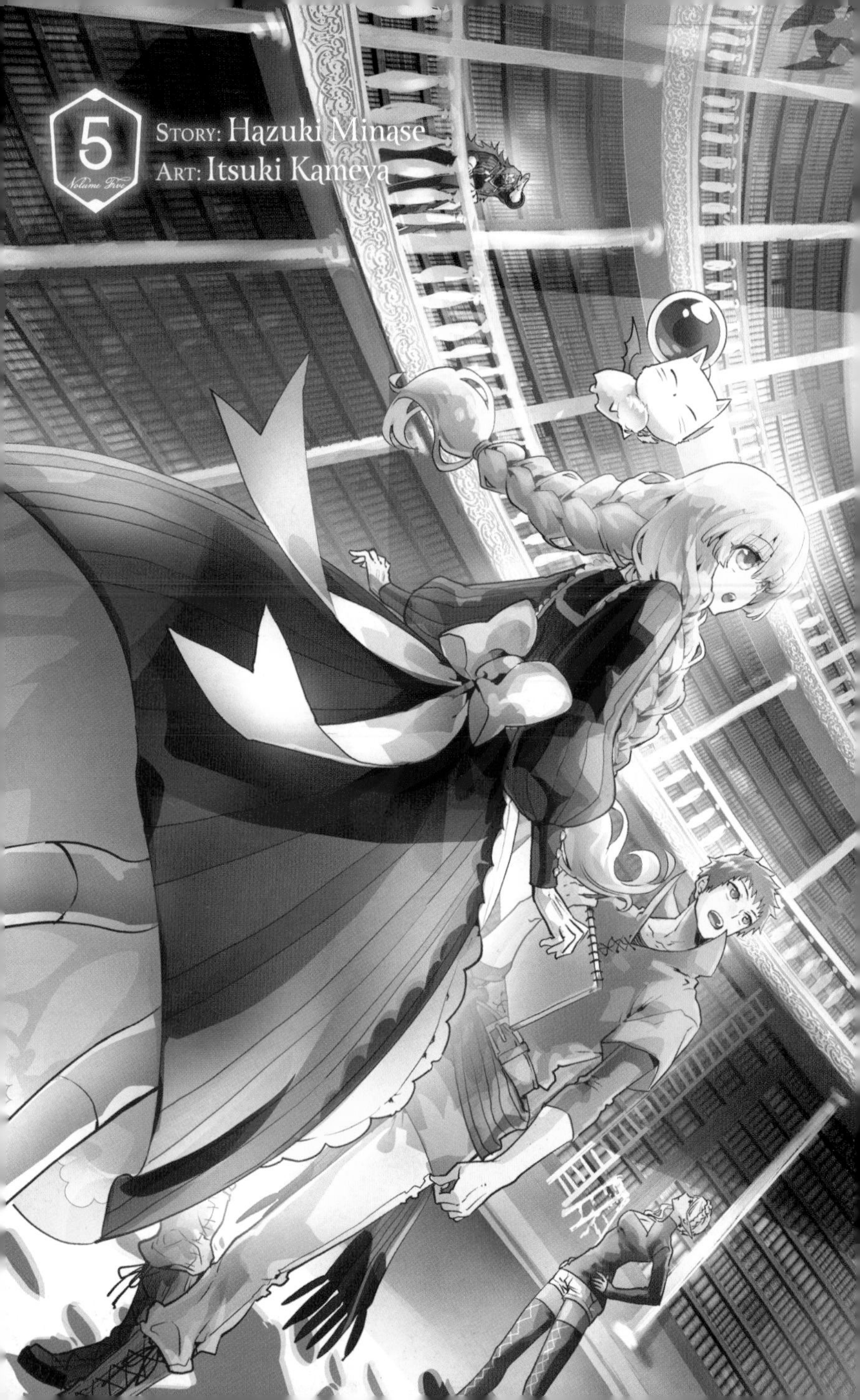
5
Volume Five
STORY: Hazuki Minase
ART: Itsuki Kameya

# FINAL FANTASY®

ファイナルファンタジー　ロスト・ストレンジャー

# LOST STRANGER

## STORY & CHARACTERS

Shogo and his little sister Yuko are SE employees. After awakening from their run-in with a truck, they found themselves in the *FF* world they'd always longed for...! Much like in the games, Shogo and Yuko had fun exploring the area, but tragedy would soon befall them. The ultimate fantasy awaits——a forbidden tale of reincarnation in another world with an *FF* twist!!

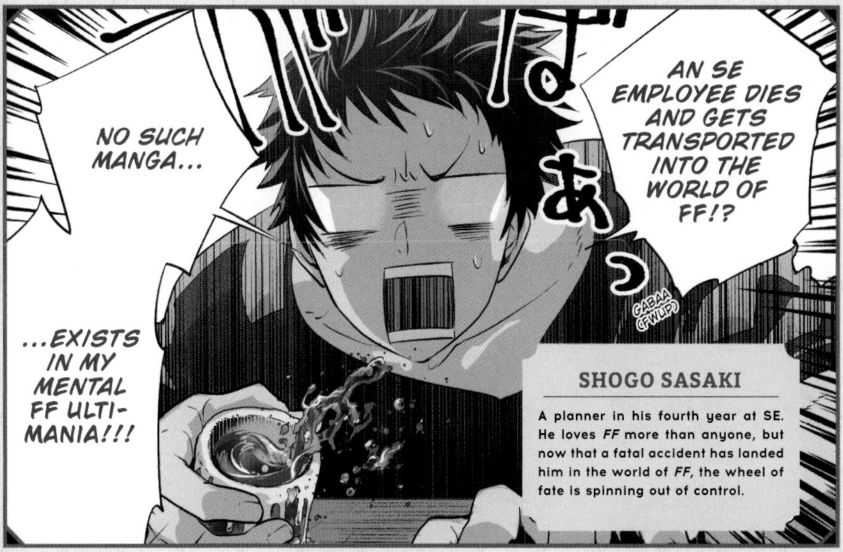
AN SE EMPLOYEE DIES AND GETS TRANSPORTED INTO THE WORLD OF FF!?
ばぁっ
GABAA (FWUP)
NO SUCH MANGA...
...EXISTS IN MY MENTAL FF ULTI-MANIA!!!

### SHOGO SASAKI

A planner in his fourth year at SE. He loves *FF* more than anyone, but now that a fatal accident has landed him in the world of *FF*, the wheel of fate is spinning out of control.

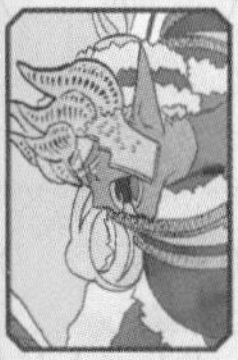

### REI HAGAKURE

An Elrein Warrior who is loyal to Sharu to a fault.

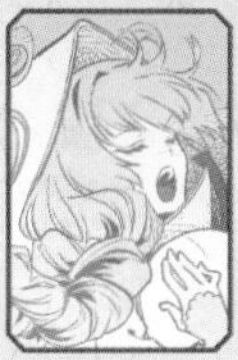

### SHARURU LINKINGFEATHER

A kindhearted White Mage who eagerly treats all who are injured.

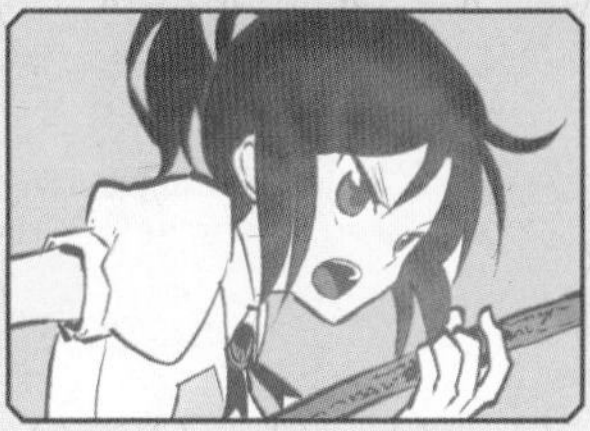

### YUKO SASAKI

A second-year sales department employee at SE. She was transported alongside her brother Shogo but was killed saving a little girl from a dragon. Her soul was turned into a crystal.

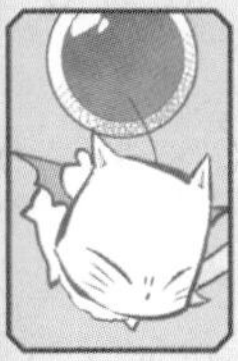

### MOG MOGCAN

A moogle who travels with Sharuru's party.

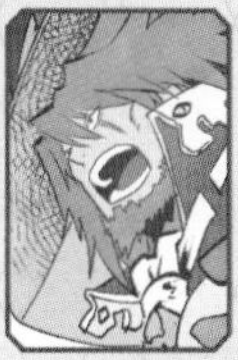

### DUSTON VOLTA

A burly Black Mage of the Hyuuj race who also cooks.

## THE STORY SO FAR

Shogo's party is in the magical kingdom of Mysidia in search of the "Raise" spell to resurrect Yuko. As the conflict with the Magus Sisters—who seek to overthrow the monarchy—reaches a boiling point, Shogo's "Libra" ability gains new powers. Shogo hears a voice coming from the tattered Mantle of Mysidia, an item that enables him to create the magically imbued Reflect Mail. He recalls that in *FF*, any spell that's already been bounced back will go through the next "Reflect" barrier it hits. He uses this knowledge to corner the Magus Sisters...but then the eldest sister, Cindy, loses control of her magic, which now threatens to consume her. Shogo and Sara come to her aid, but just how will this intense battle end...?

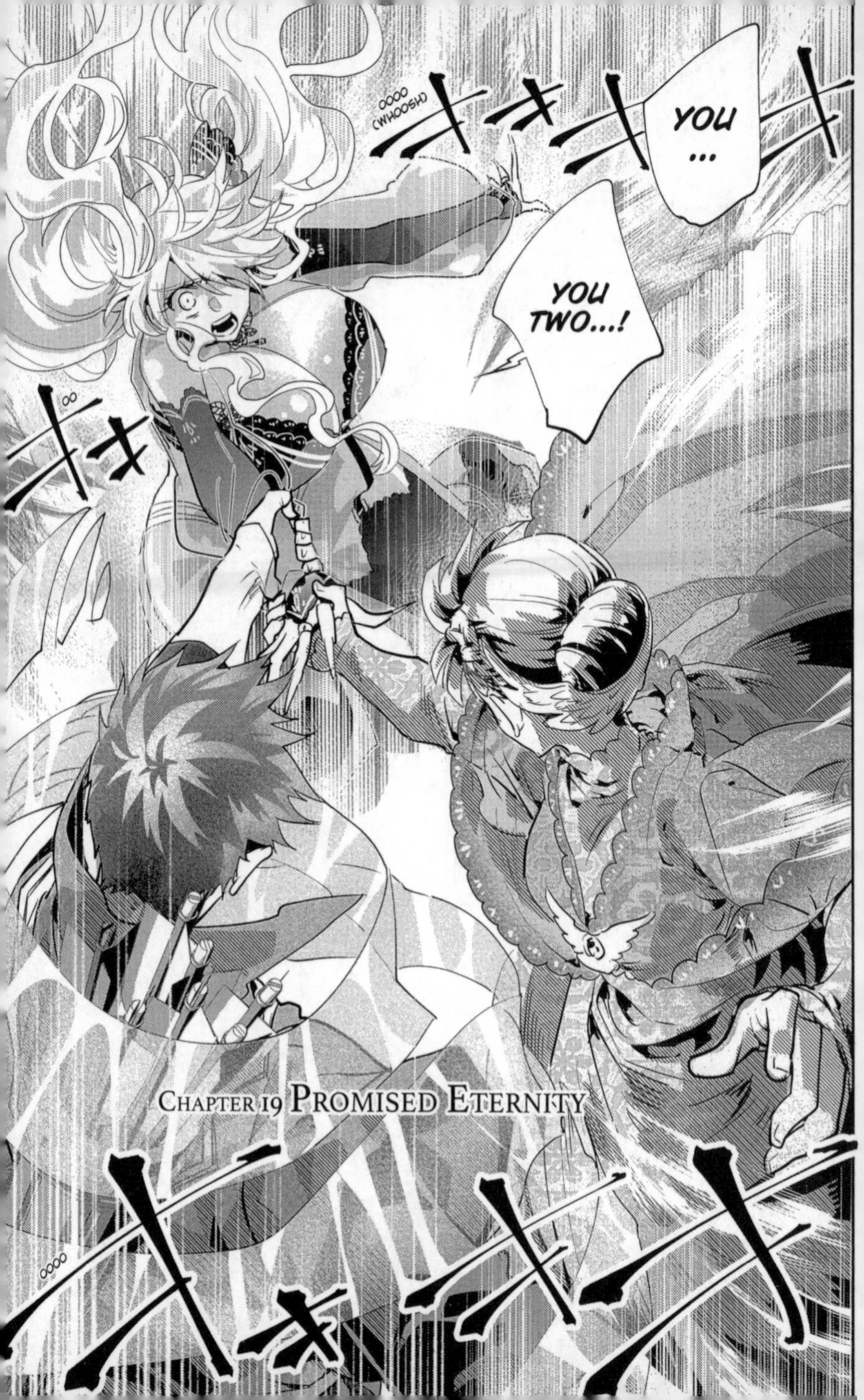
OOOO (WHOOSH)
YOU ...
YOU TWO...!
CHAPTER 19 PROMISED ETERNITY
OOOO

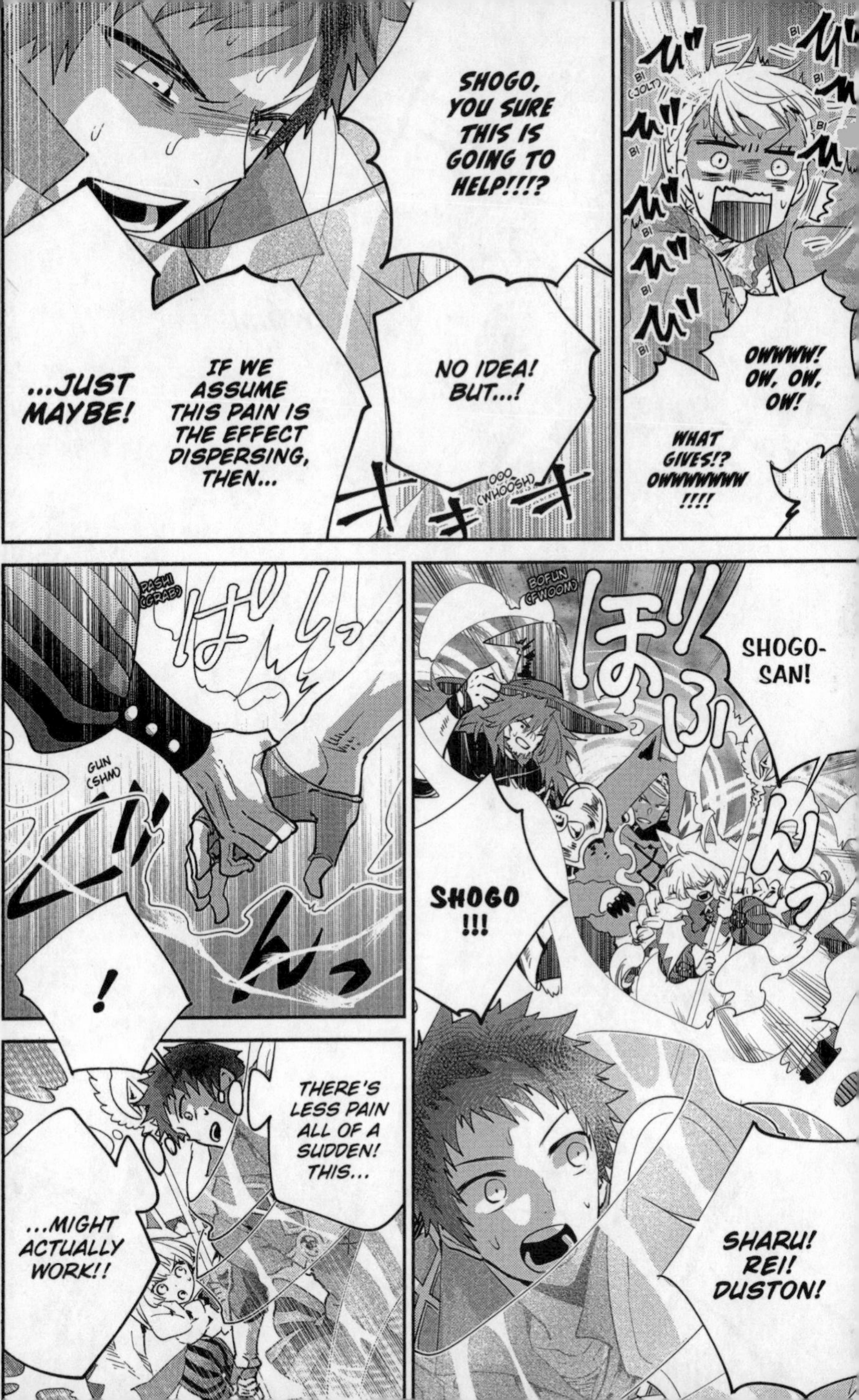

BI (JOLT)
BI
OWWWW! OW, OW, OW!
WHAT GIVES!? OWWWWWWW!!!!
SHOGO, YOU SURE THIS IS GOING TO HELP!!!?
NO IDEA! BUT...!
OOO (WHOOSH)
IF WE ASSUME THIS PAIN IS THE EFFECT DISPERSING, THEN...
...JUST MAYBE!
BOFUN (FWOOM)
SHOGO-SAN!
SHOGO!!!
SHARU! REI! DUSTON!
PASHI (GRAB)
GUN (SHM)
!
THERE'S LESS PAIN ALL OF A SUDDEN! THIS...
...MIGHT ACTUALLY WORK!!

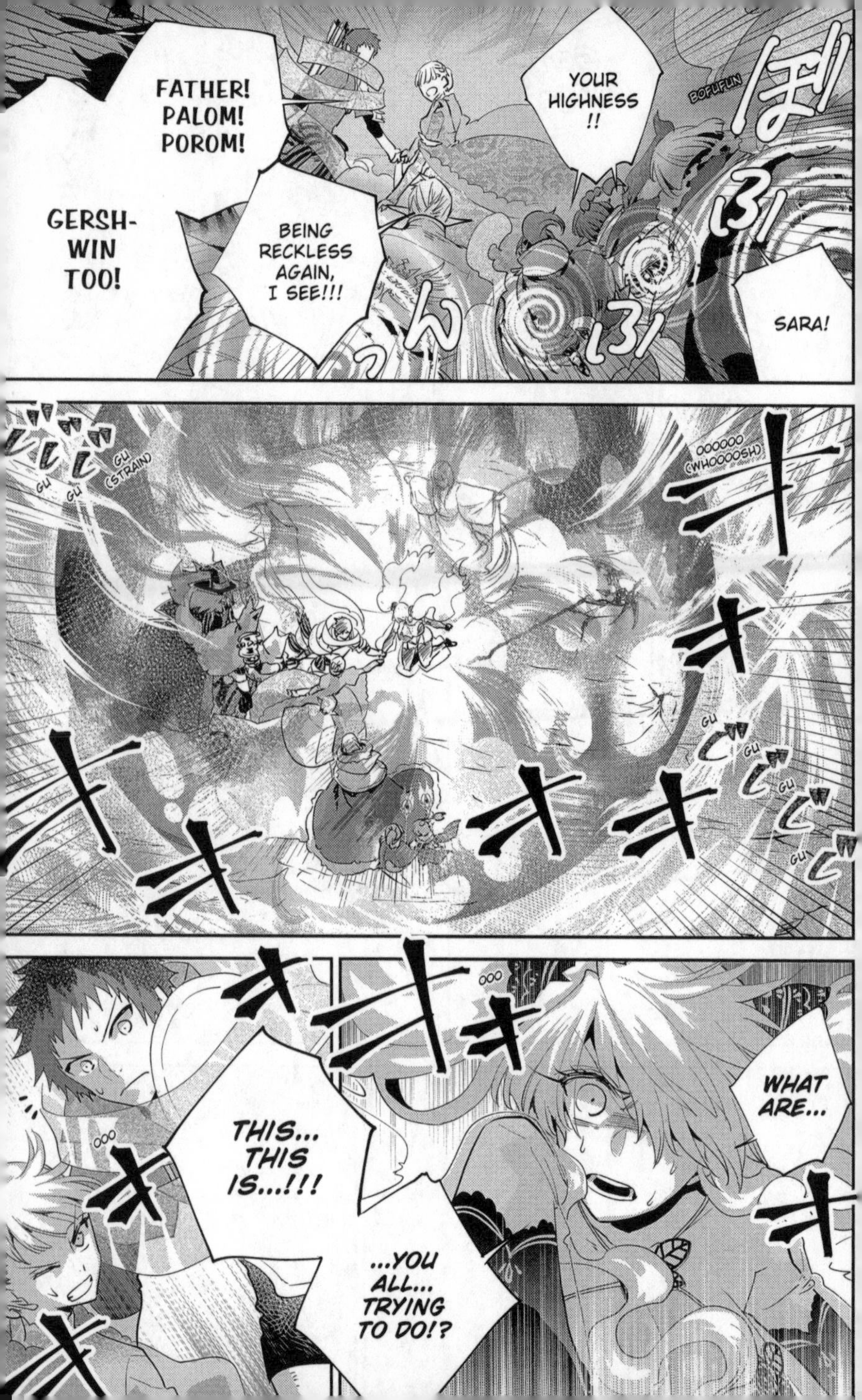
BOFUFUN
YOUR HIGHNESS !!
SARA!
FATHER! PALOM! POROM!
BEING RECKLESS AGAIN, I SEE!!!
GERSH-WIN TOO!
OOOOOO (WHOOOOSH)
GU
GU
GU
GU
GU GU GU (STRAIN)
OOO
WHAT ARE...
...YOU ALL... TRYING TO DO!?
THIS... THIS IS...!!!
OOO

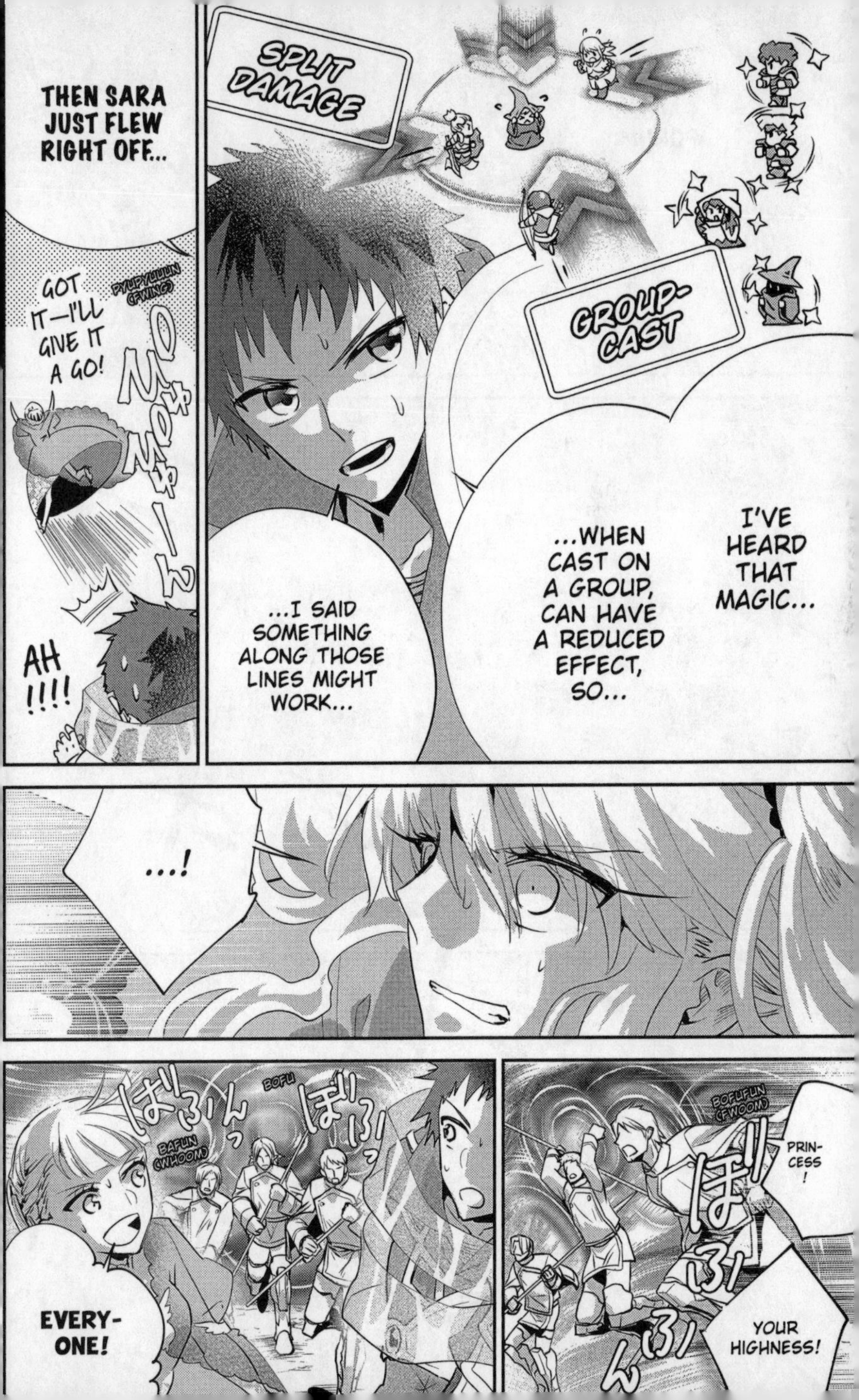
SPLIT DAMAGE
GROUP-CAST
I'VE HEARD THAT MAGIC...
...WHEN CAST ON A GROUP, CAN HAVE A REDUCED EFFECT, SO...
...I SAID SOMETHING ALONG THOSE LINES MIGHT WORK...
THEN SARA JUST FLEW RIGHT OFF...
GOT IT—I'LL GIVE IT A GO!
PYUPYUUUN (FWING)
AH!!!!
...!
BOFUFUN (FWOOM)
PRIN-CESS!
YOUR HIGHNESS!
BOFU
BAFUN (WHOOM)
EVERY-ONE!

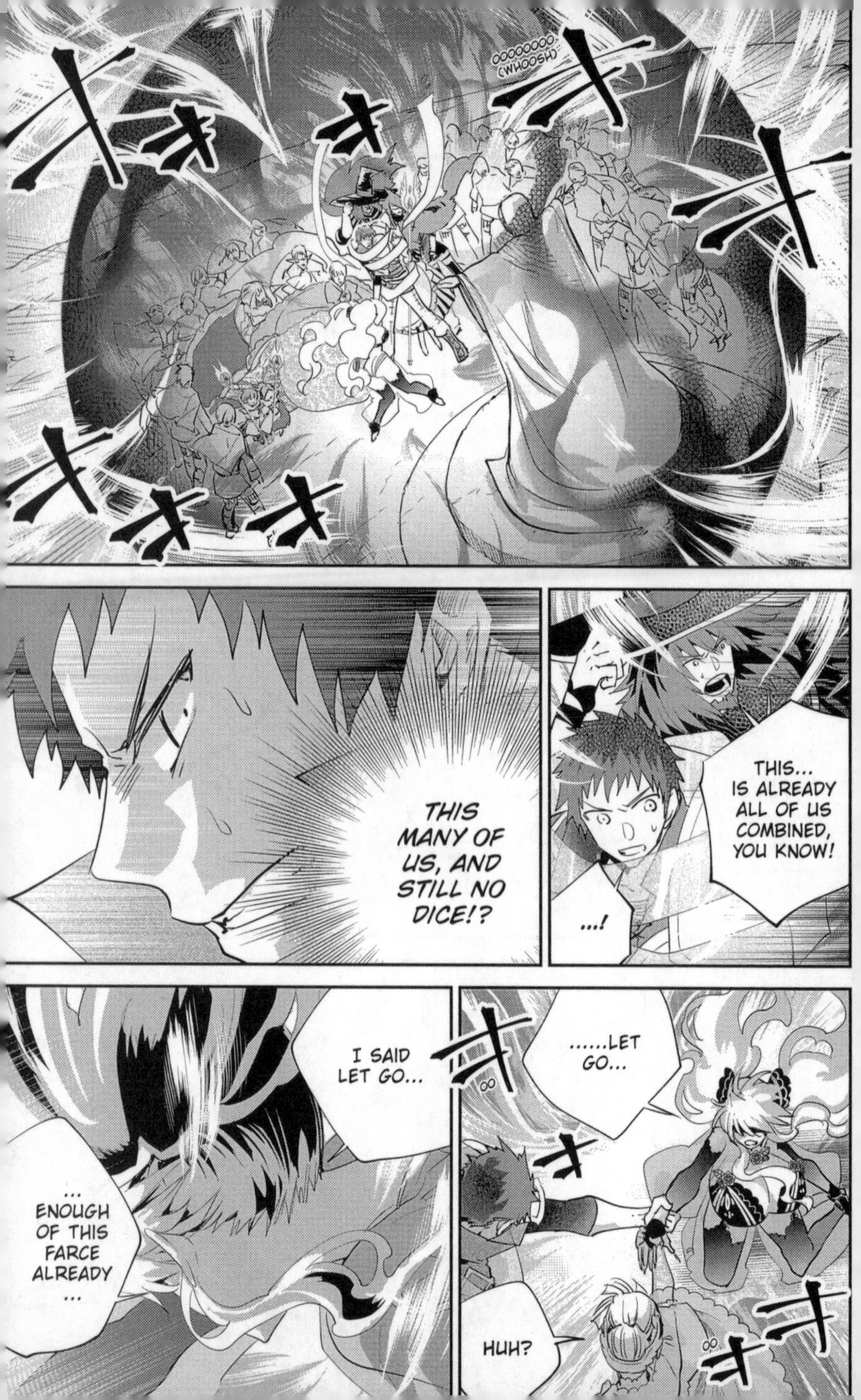
(WHOOSH)
THIS... IS ALREADY ALL OF US COMBINED, YOU KNOW!
...!
THIS MANY OF US, AND STILL NO DICE!?
......LET GO...
HUH?
I SAID LET GO...
... ENOUGH OF THIS FARCE ALREADY ...

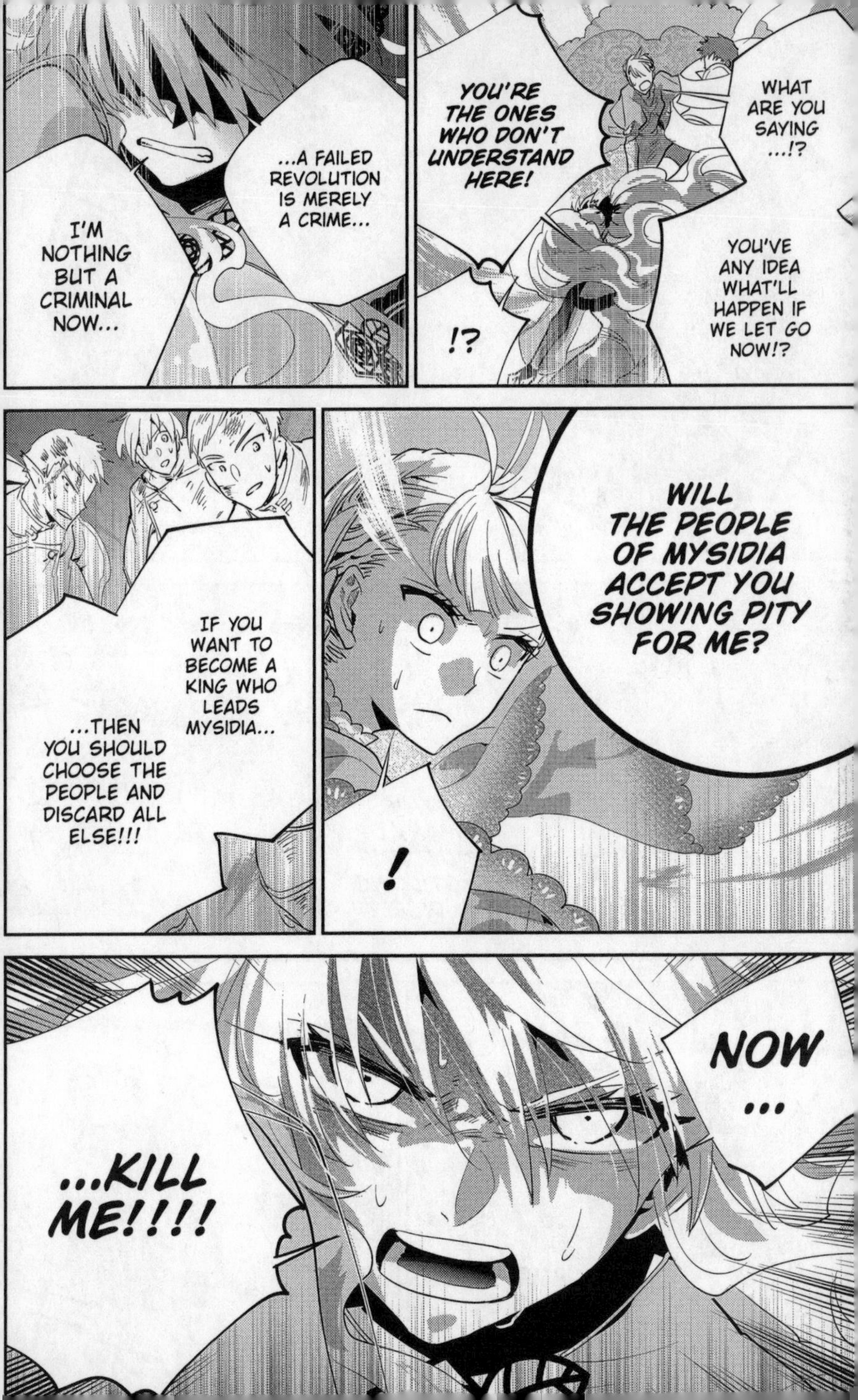
WHAT ARE YOU SAYING ...!?
YOU'RE THE ONES WHO DON'T UNDERSTAND HERE!
YOU'VE ANY IDEA WHAT'LL HAPPEN IF WE LET GO NOW!?
!?
...A FAILED REVOLUTION IS MERELY A CRIME...
I'M NOTHING BUT A CRIMINAL NOW...
WILL THE PEOPLE OF MYSIDIA ACCEPT YOU SHOWING PITY FOR ME?
!
IF YOU WANT TO BECOME A KING WHO LEADS MYSIDIA...
...THEN YOU SHOULD CHOOSE THE PEOPLE AND DISCARD ALL ELSE!!!
NOW ...
...KILL ME!!!!

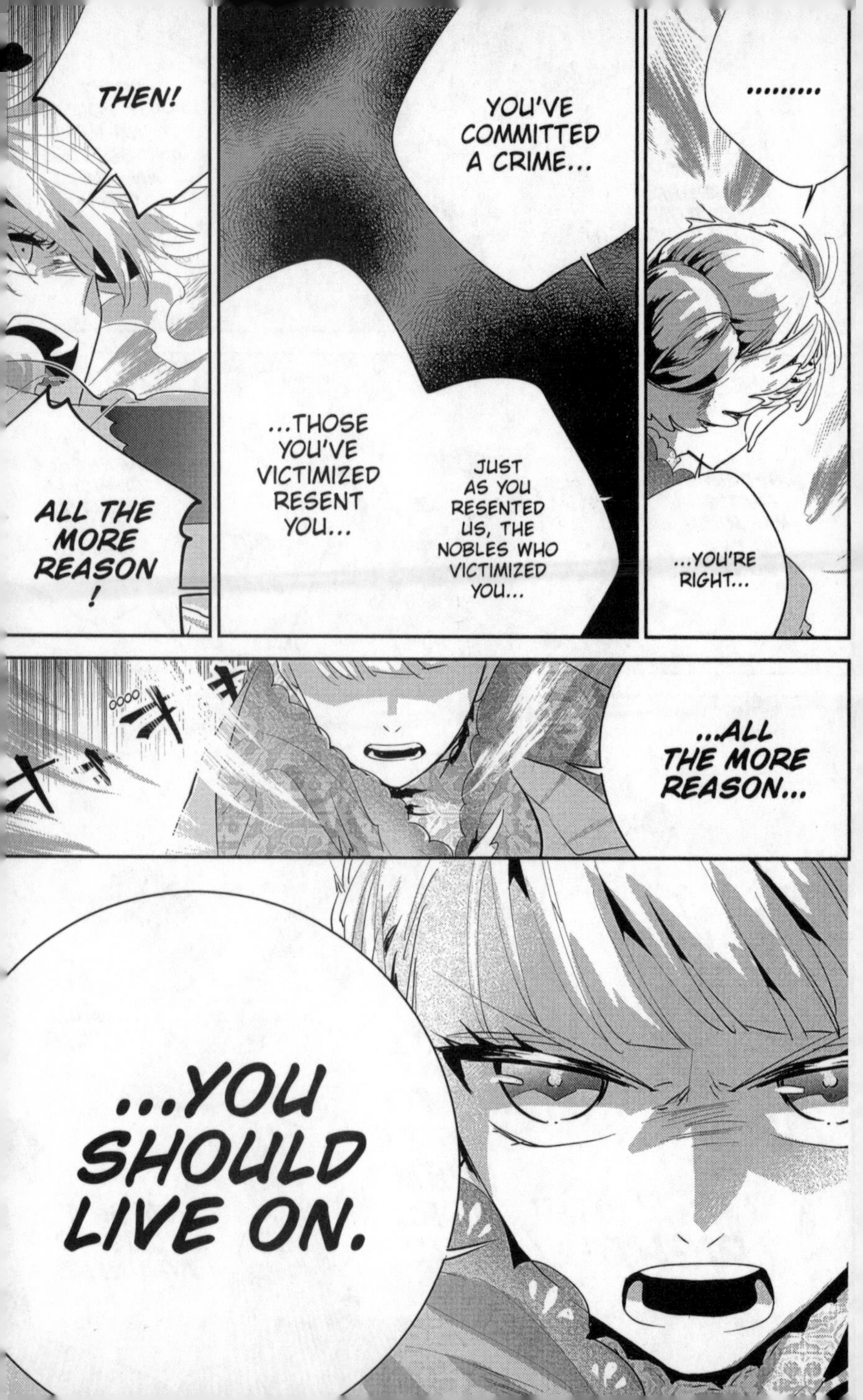
.........
...YOU'RE RIGHT...
YOU'VE COMMITTED A CRIME...
JUST AS YOU RESENTED US, THE NOBLES WHO VICTIMIZED YOU...
...THOSE YOU'VE VICTIMIZED RESENT YOU...
THEN!
ALL THE MORE REASON!
...ALL THE MORE REASON...
...YOU SHOULD LIVE ON.

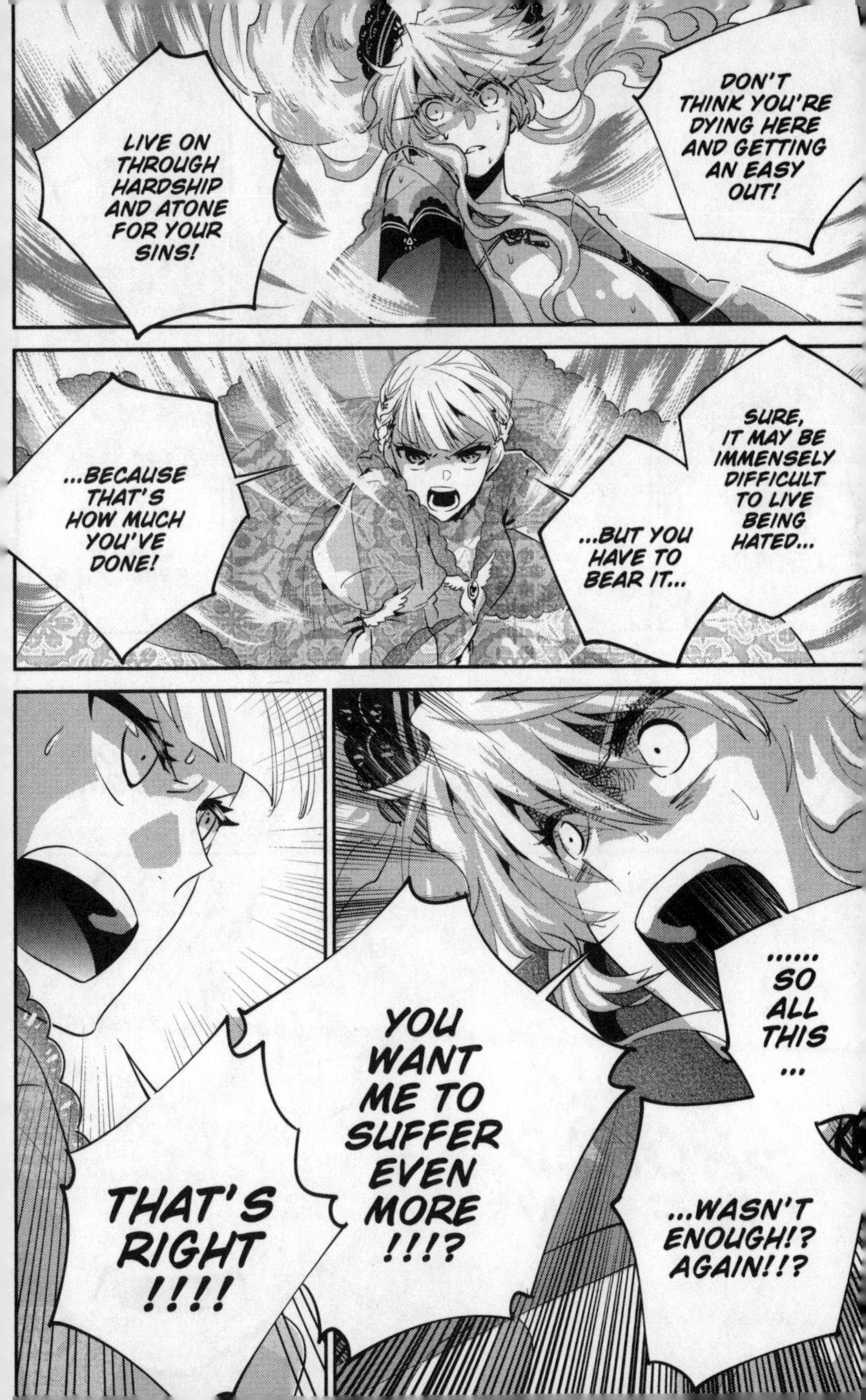
DON'T THINK YOU'RE DYING HERE AND GETTING AN EASY OUT!
LIVE ON THROUGH HARDSHIP AND ATONE FOR YOUR SINS!
SURE, IT MAY BE IMMENSELY DIFFICULT TO LIVE BEING HATED...
...BUT YOU HAVE TO BEAR IT...
...BECAUSE THAT'S HOW MUCH YOU'VE DONE!
...... SO ALL THIS ...
...WASN'T ENOUGH!? AGAIN!!?
YOU WANT ME TO SUFFER EVEN MORE !!!?
THAT'S RIGHT !!!!

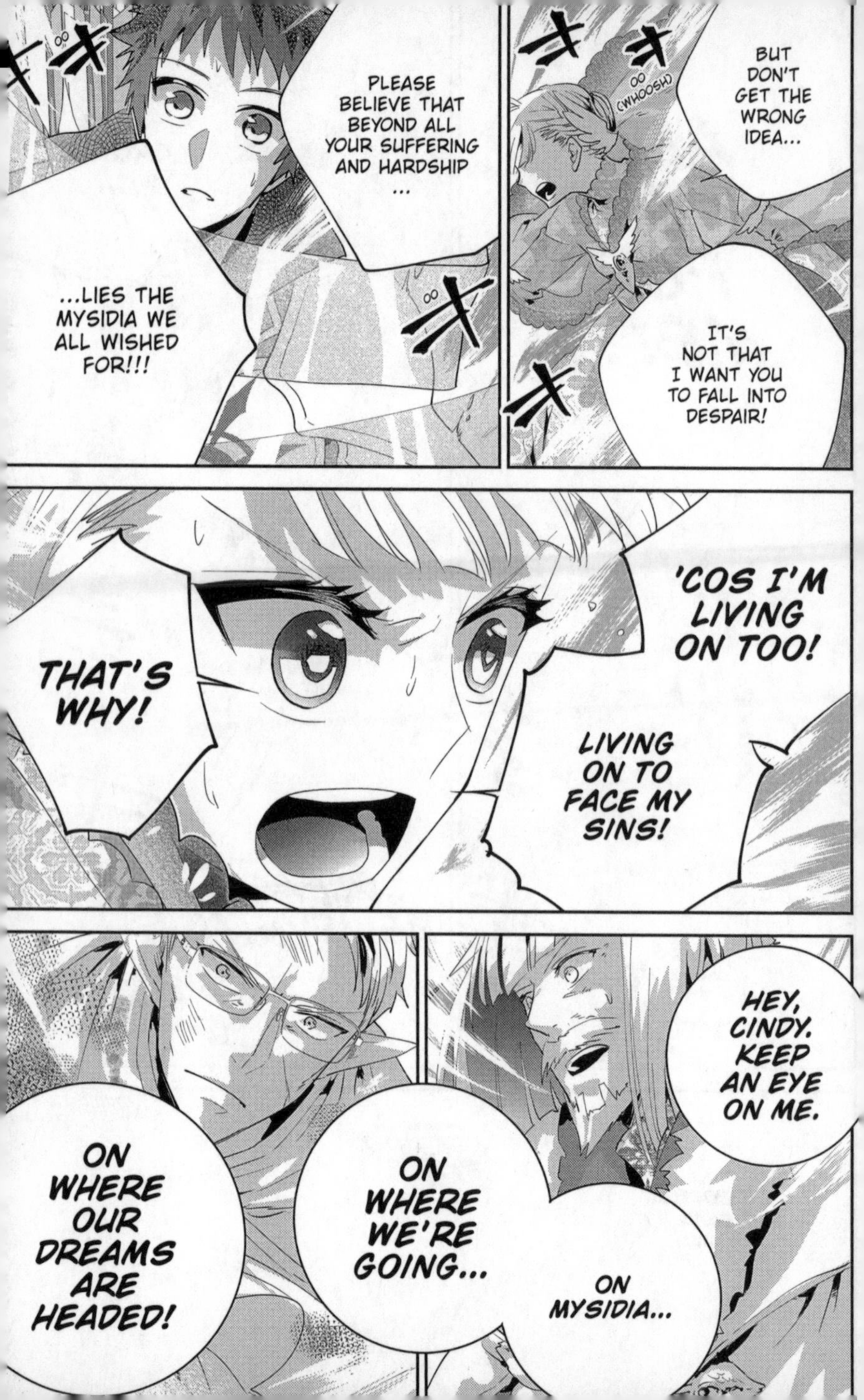
BUT DON'T GET THE WRONG IDEA...
(WHOOSH)
IT'S NOT THAT I WANT YOU TO FALL INTO DESPAIR!
PLEASE BELIEVE THAT BEYOND ALL YOUR SUFFERING AND HARDSHIP ...
...LIES THE MYSIDIA WE ALL WISHED FOR!!!
'COS I'M LIVING ON TOO!
LIVING ON TO FACE MY SINS!
THAT'S WHY!
HEY, CINDY. KEEP AN EYE ON ME.
ON MYSIDIA...
ON WHERE WE'RE GOING...
ON WHERE OUR DREAMS ARE HEADED!

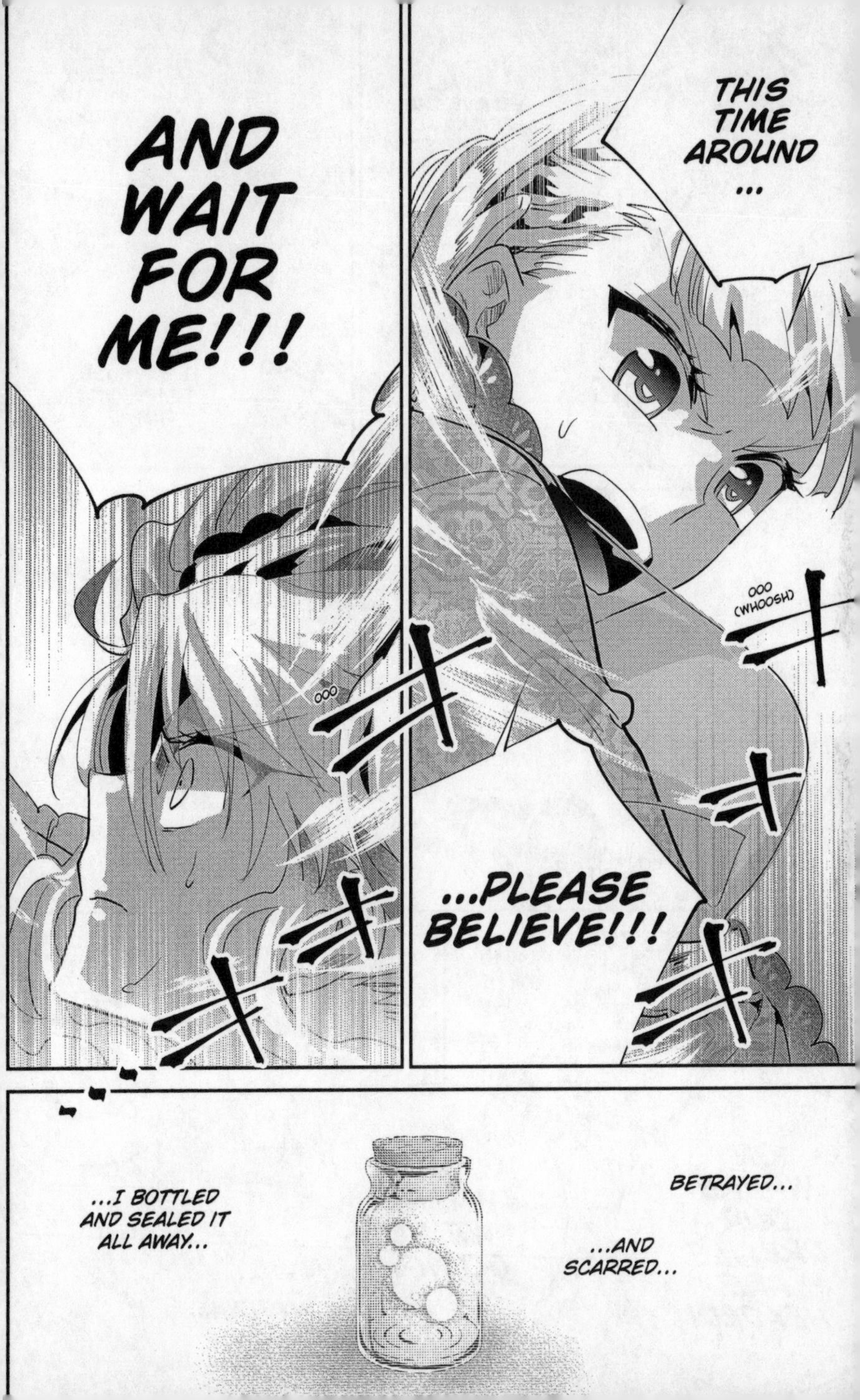
THIS TIME AROUND ...
OOO (WHOOSH)
...PLEASE BELIEVE!!!
AND WAIT FOR ME!!!
OOO
BETRAYED...
...AND SCARRED...
...I BOTTLED AND SEALED IT ALL AWAY...

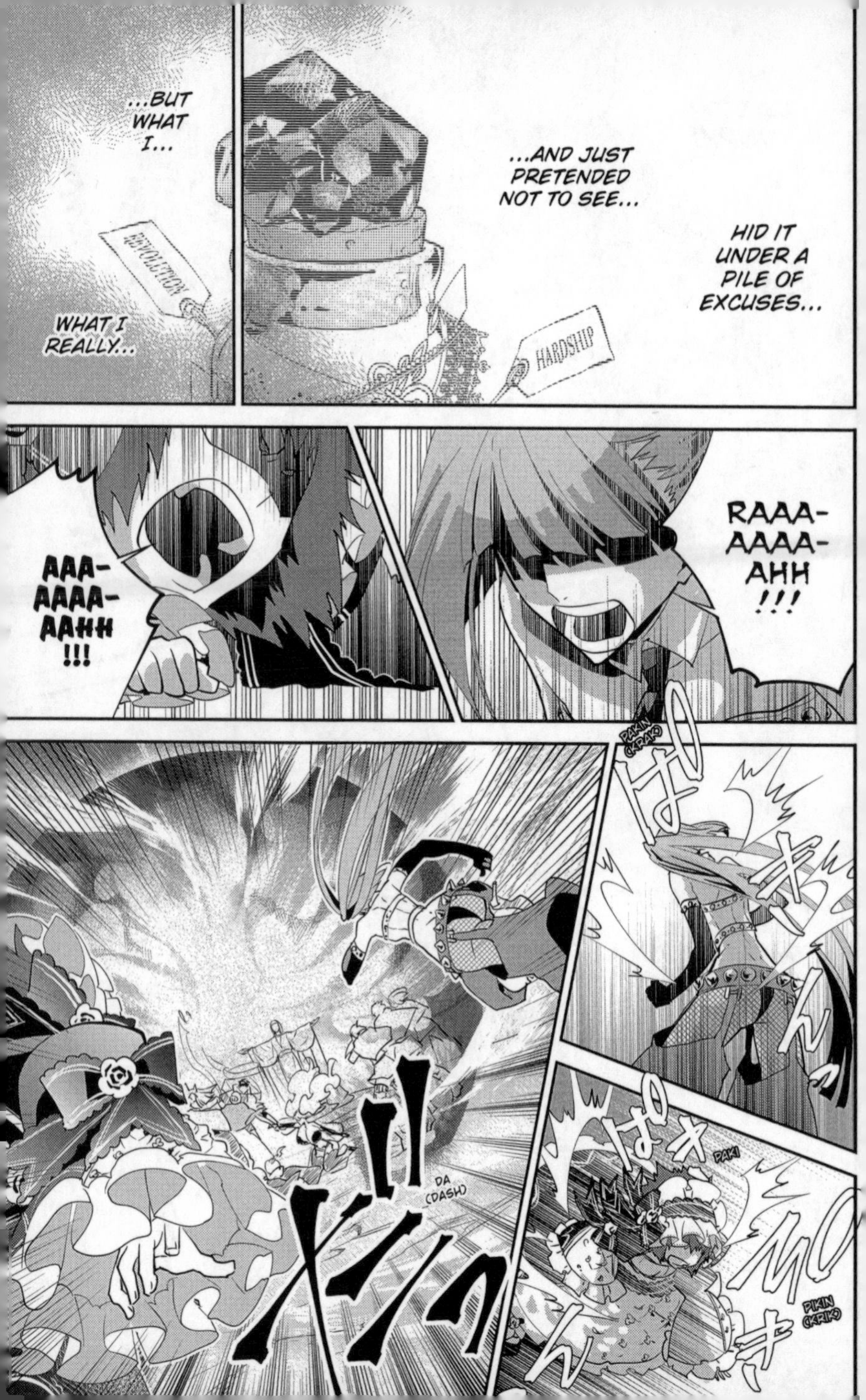
HID IT UNDER A PILE OF EXCUSES...
...AND JUST PRETENDED NOT TO SEE...
HARDSHIP
...BUT WHAT I...
REVOLUTION
WHAT I REALLY...
RAAAAAAA-AHH!!!
AAA-AAAA-AAHH!!!
PAKIN (KRAK)
PAKI
PIKIN (KRIK)
DA (DASH)

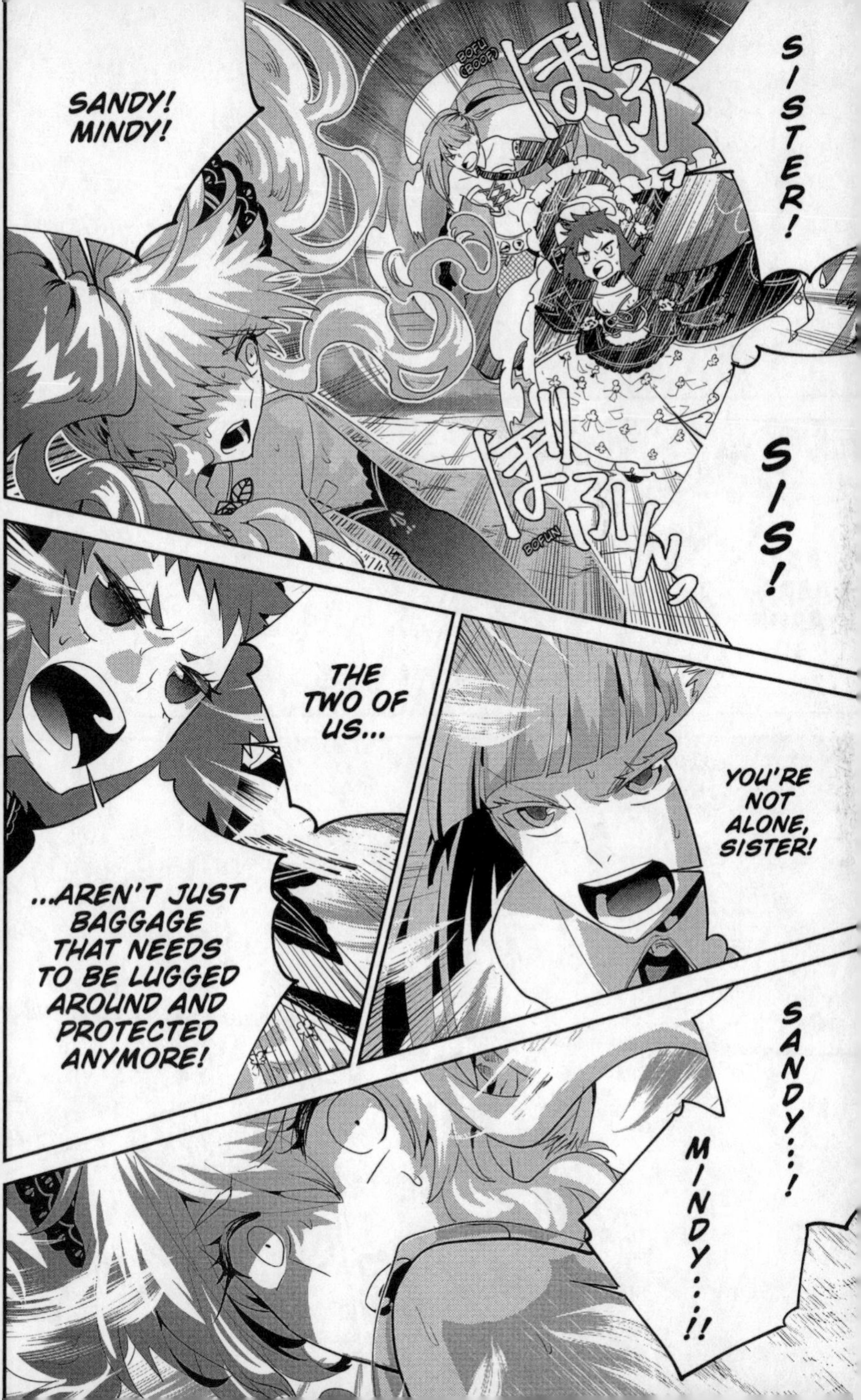
SISTER!
BOFU (BOOP)
SIS!
BOFUN
SANDY! MINDY!
YOU'RE NOT ALONE, SISTER!
THE TWO OF US...
...AREN'T JUST BAGGAGE THAT NEEDS TO BE LUGGED AROUND AND PROTECTED ANYMORE!
SANDY...!
MINDY...!!

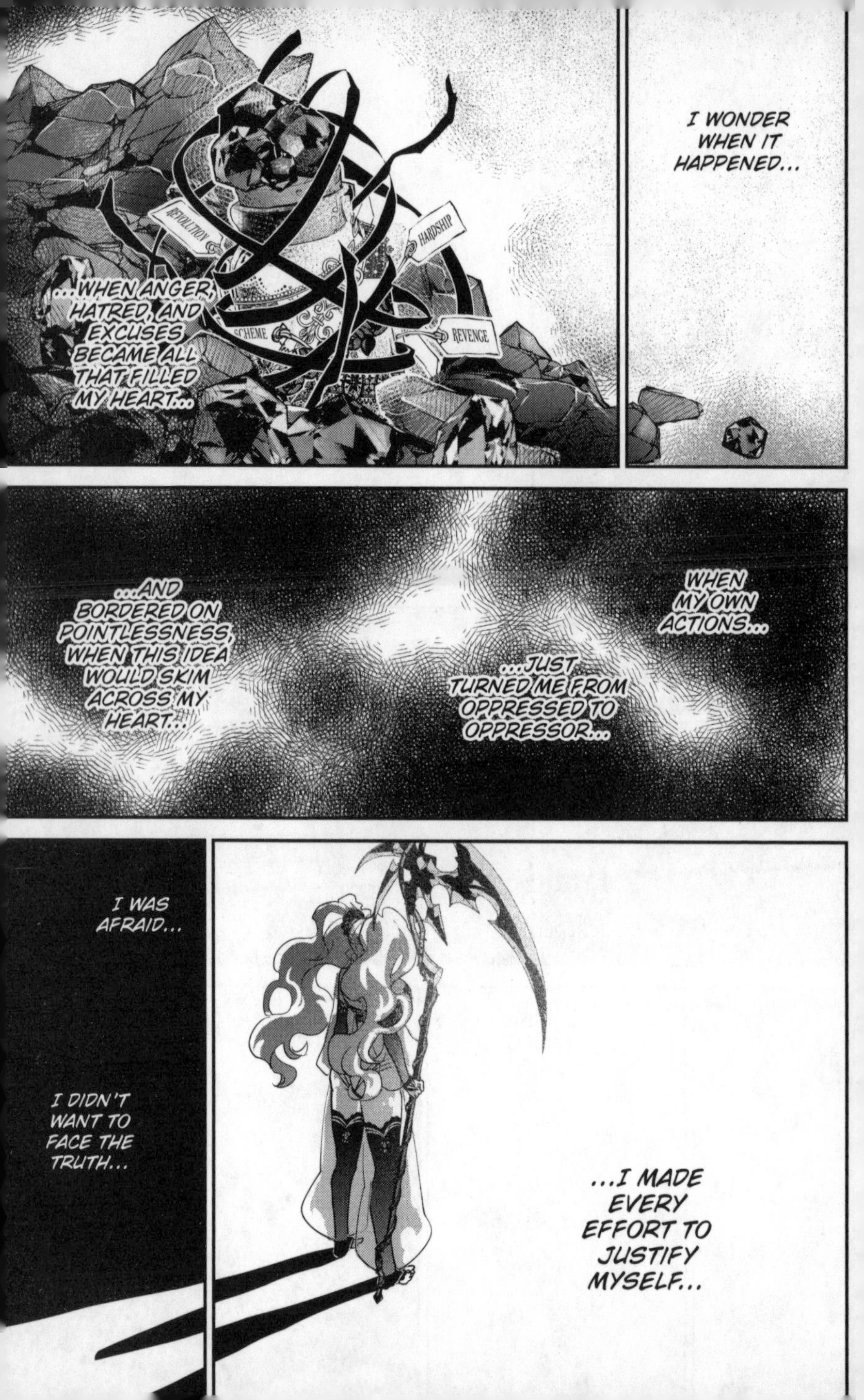
I WONDER WHEN IT HAPPENED...
HARDSHIP
REVOLUTION
REVENGE
SCHEME
...WHEN ANGER, HATRED, AND EXCUSES BECAME ALL THAT FILLED MY HEART...
WHEN MY OWN ACTIONS...
...JUST TURNED ME FROM OPPRESSED TO OPPRESSOR...
...AND BORDERED ON POINTLESSNESS, WHEN THIS IDEA WOULD SKIM ACROSS MY HEART...
...I MADE EVERY EFFORT TO JUSTIFY MYSELF...
I WAS AFRAID...
I DIDN'T WANT TO FACE THE TRUTH...

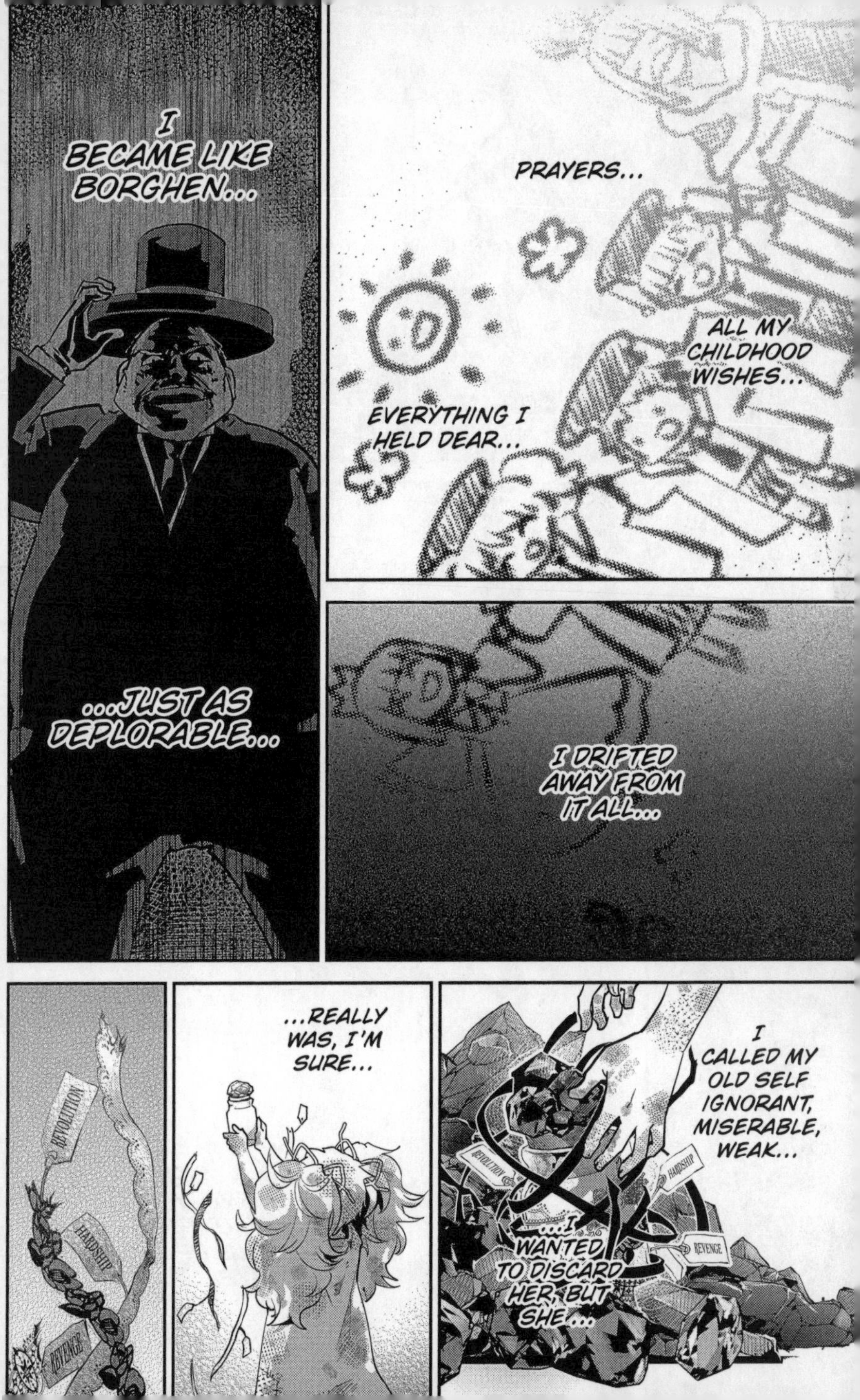
PRAYERS...
ALL MY CHILDHOOD WISHES...
EVERYTHING I HELD DEAR...
I DRIFTED AWAY FROM IT ALL...
I BECAME LIKE BORGHEN...
...JUST AS DEPLORABLE...
I CALLED MY OLD SELF IGNORANT, MISERABLE, WEAK...
REVOLUTION
HARDSHIP
REVENGE
...I WANTED TO DISCARD HER, BUT SHE...
...REALLY WAS, I'M SURE...
REVOLUTION
HARDSHIP
REVENGE

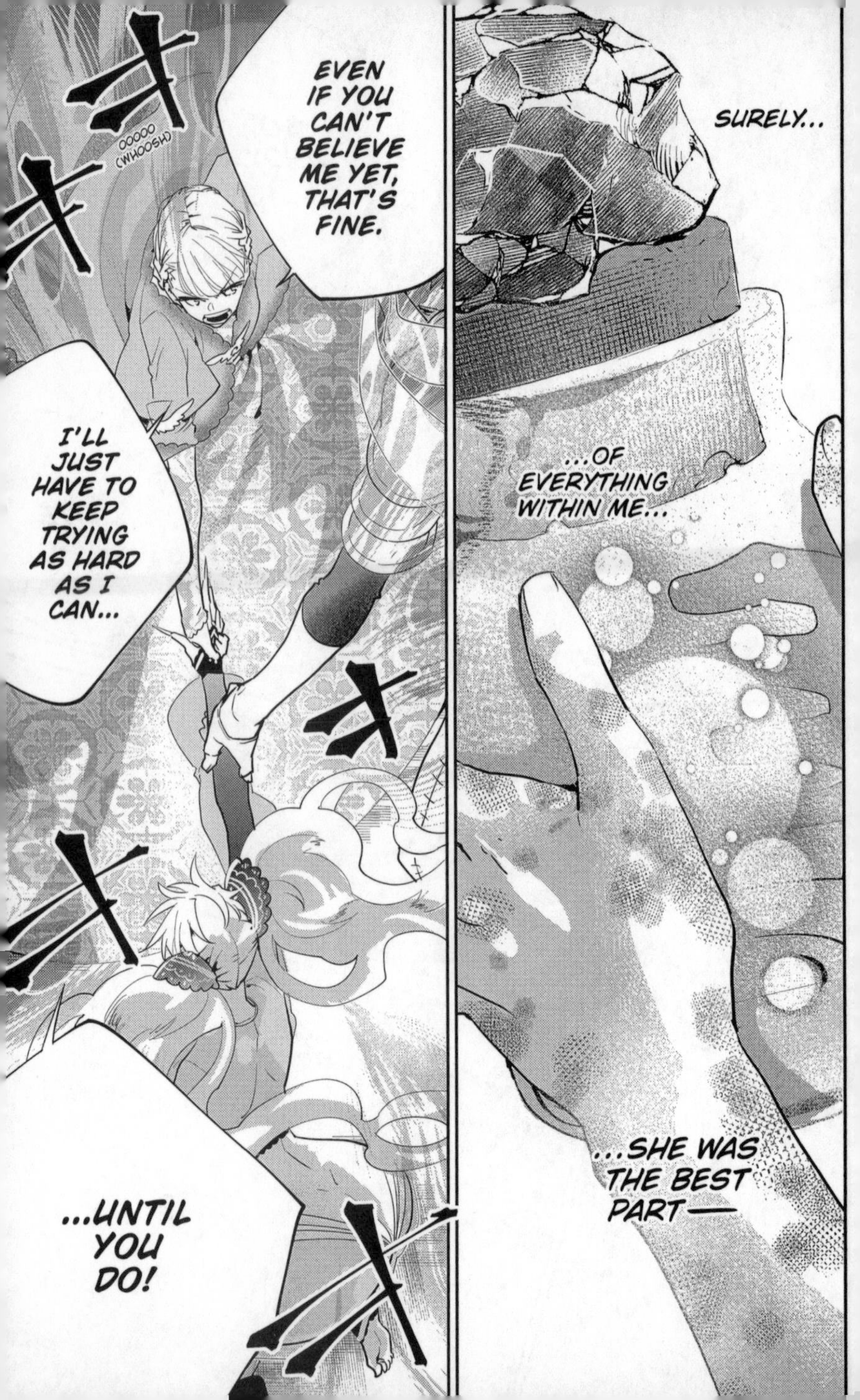
SURELY...
...OF EVERYTHING WITHIN ME...
...SHE WAS THE BEST PART—
EVEN IF YOU CAN'T BELIEVE ME YET, THAT'S FINE.
(WHOOSH)
I'LL JUST HAVE TO KEEP TRYING AS HARD AS I CAN...
...UNTIL YOU DO!

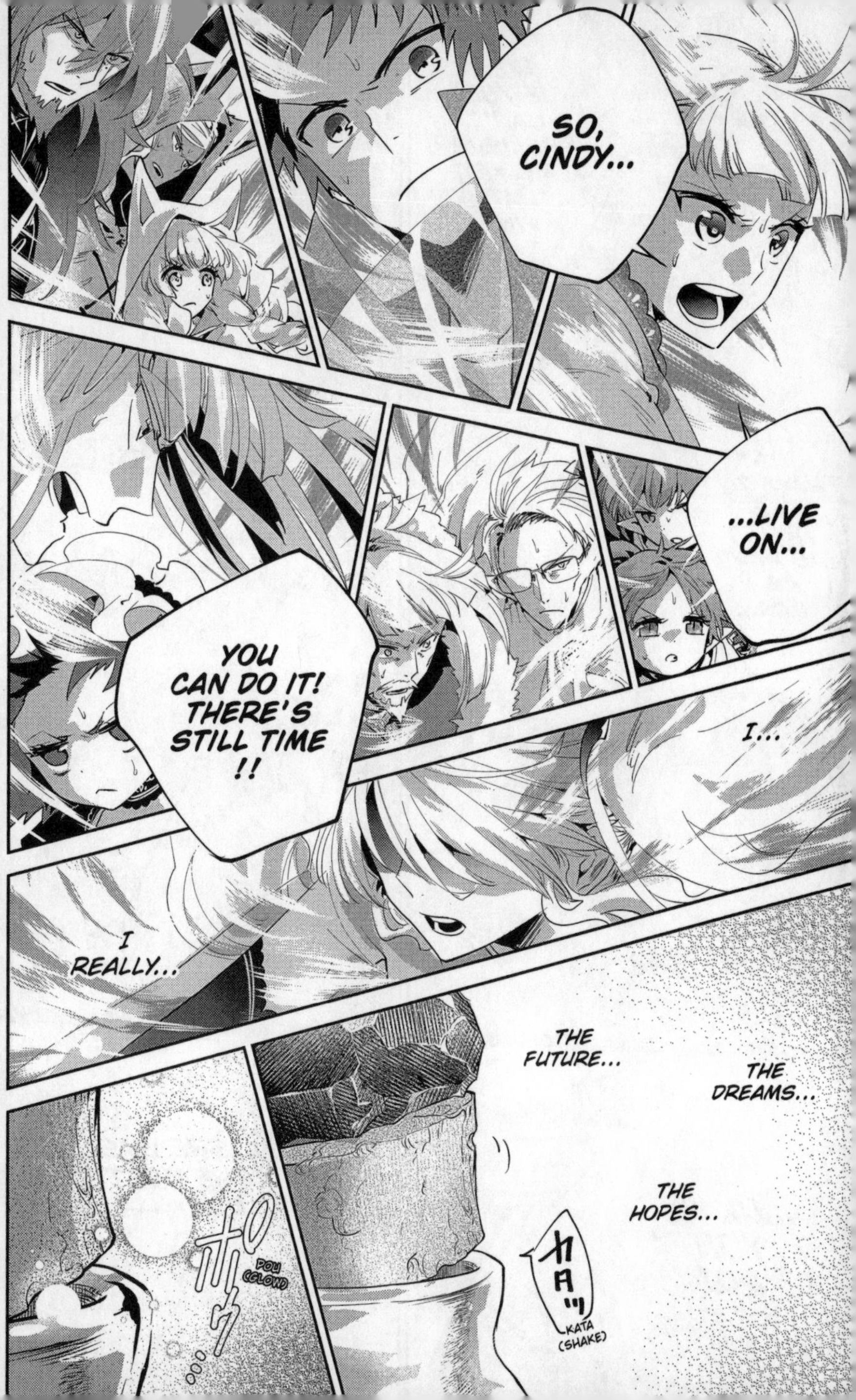
SO, CINDY...
...LIVE ON...
YOU CAN DO IT! THERE'S STILL TIME!!
I...
I REALLY...
THE FUTURE...
THE DREAMS...
THE HOPES...
カタッ
KATA (SHAKE)
POU (GLOW)

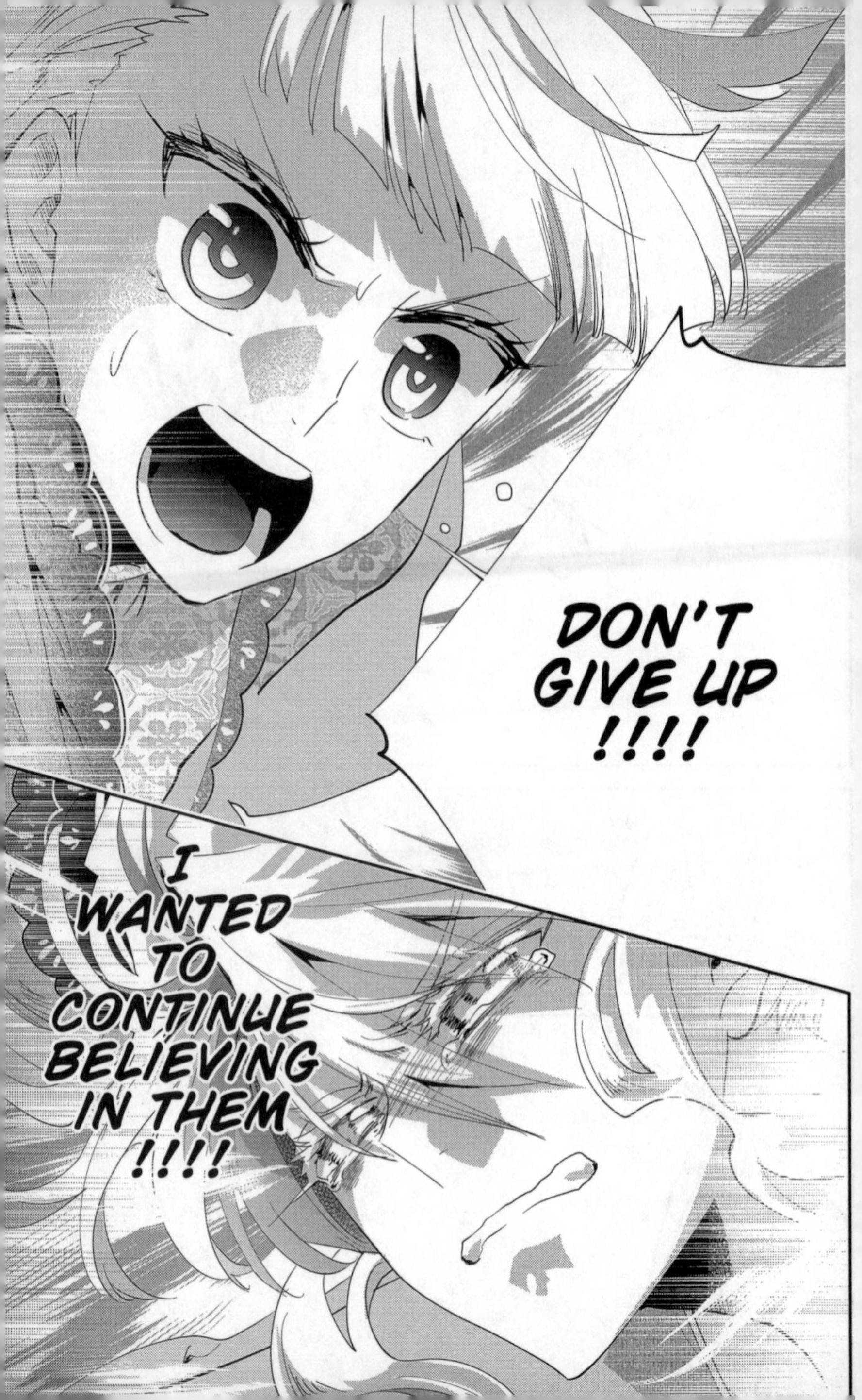
DON'T GIVE UP !!!!
I WANTED TO CONTINUE BELIEVING IN THEM !!!!

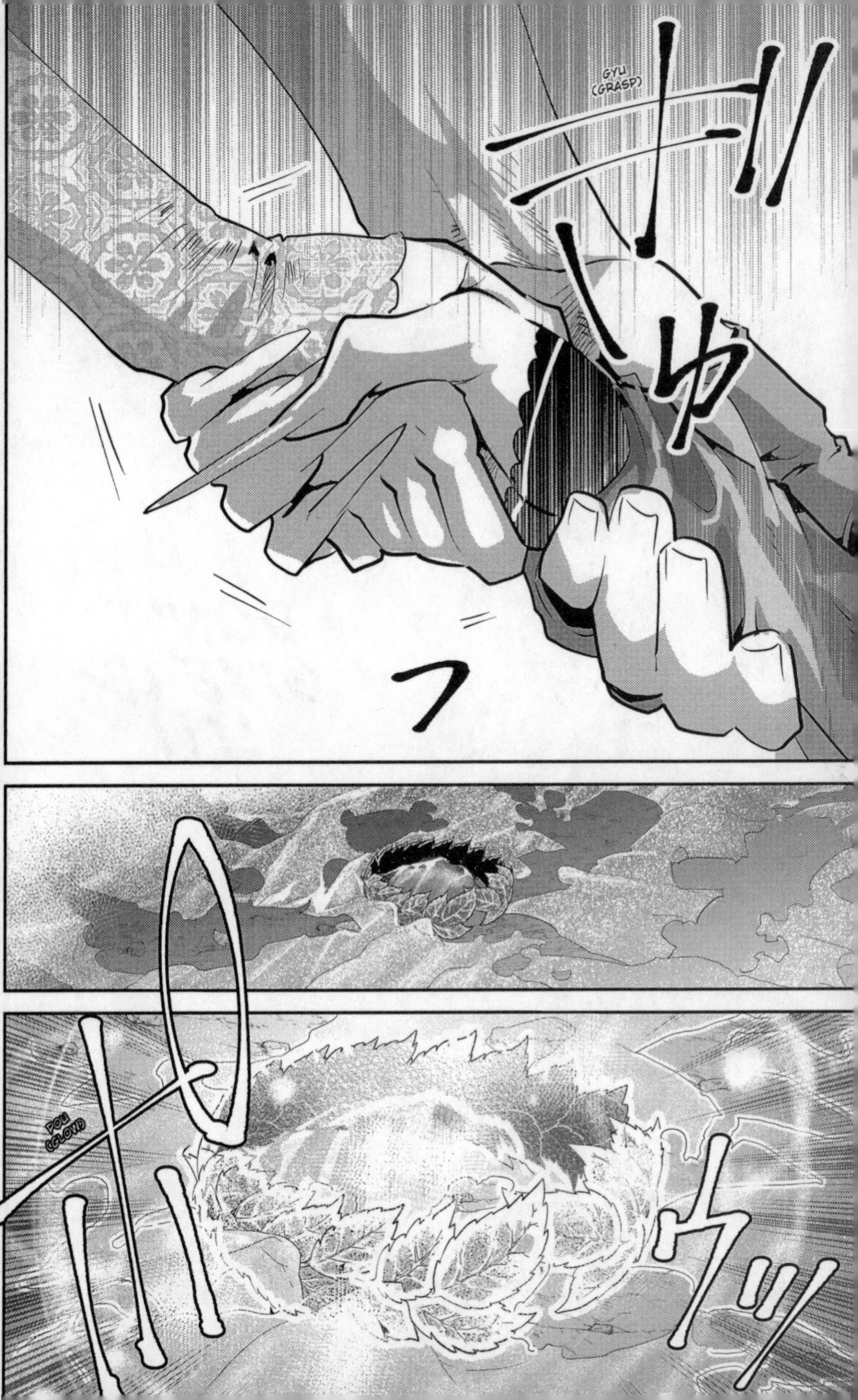
GYU
(GRASP)
ぎゅっ
POU
(GLOW)
ポウッ

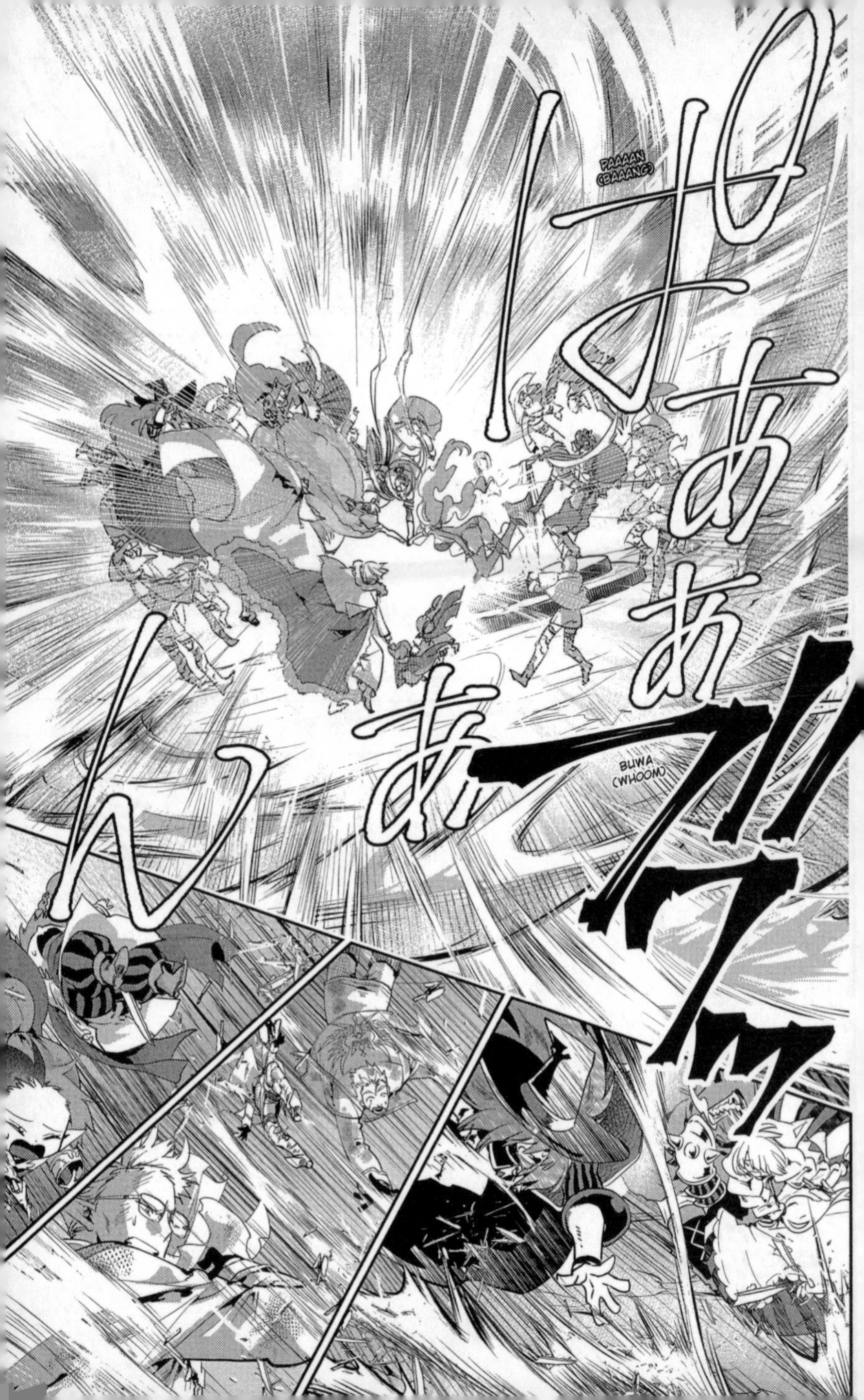
PAAAAN (BAAANG)
BUWA (WHOOM)

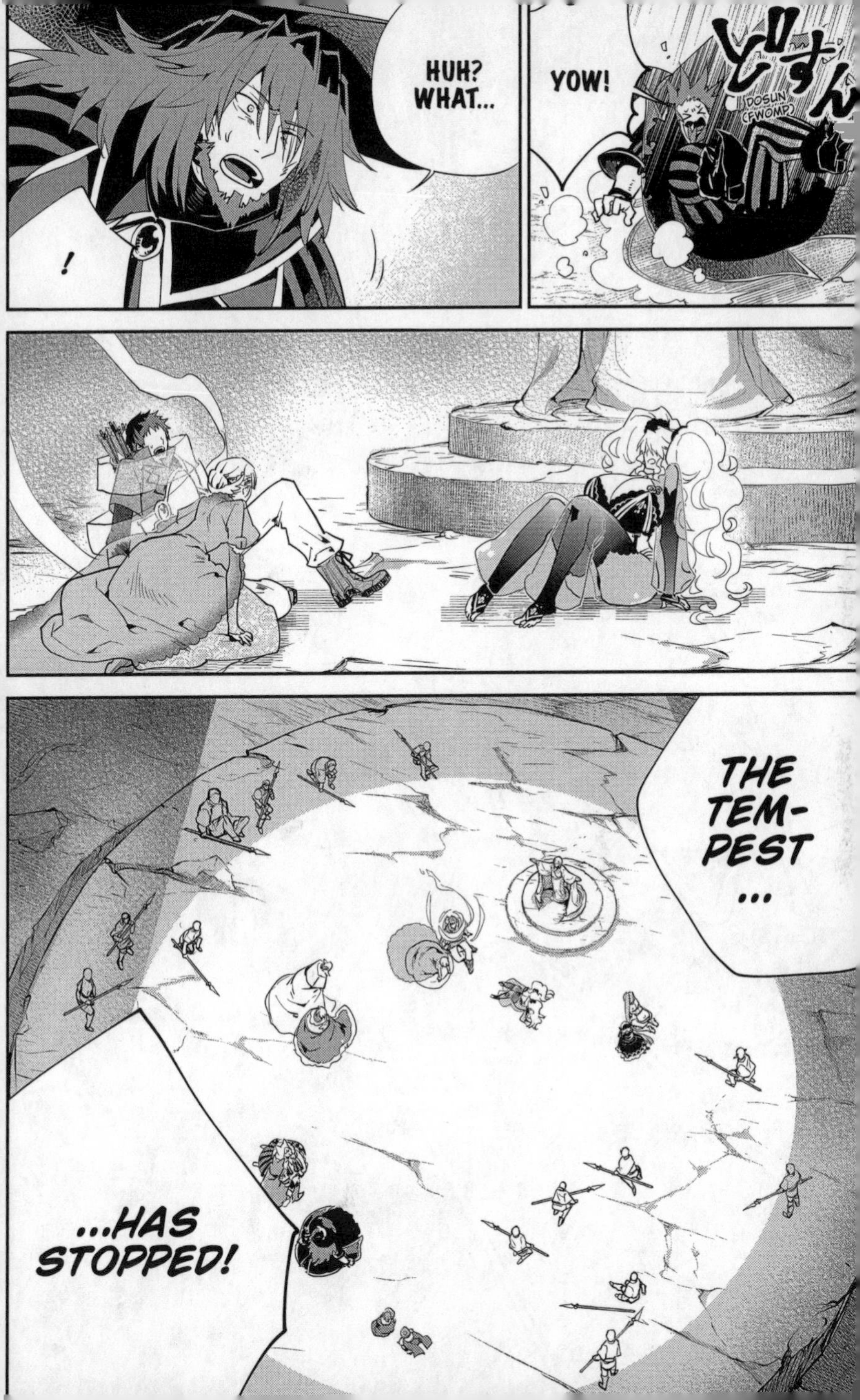
どすん
DOSUN (FWOMP)
YOW!
HUH? WHAT...
!
THE TEM-PEST ...
...HAS STOPPED!

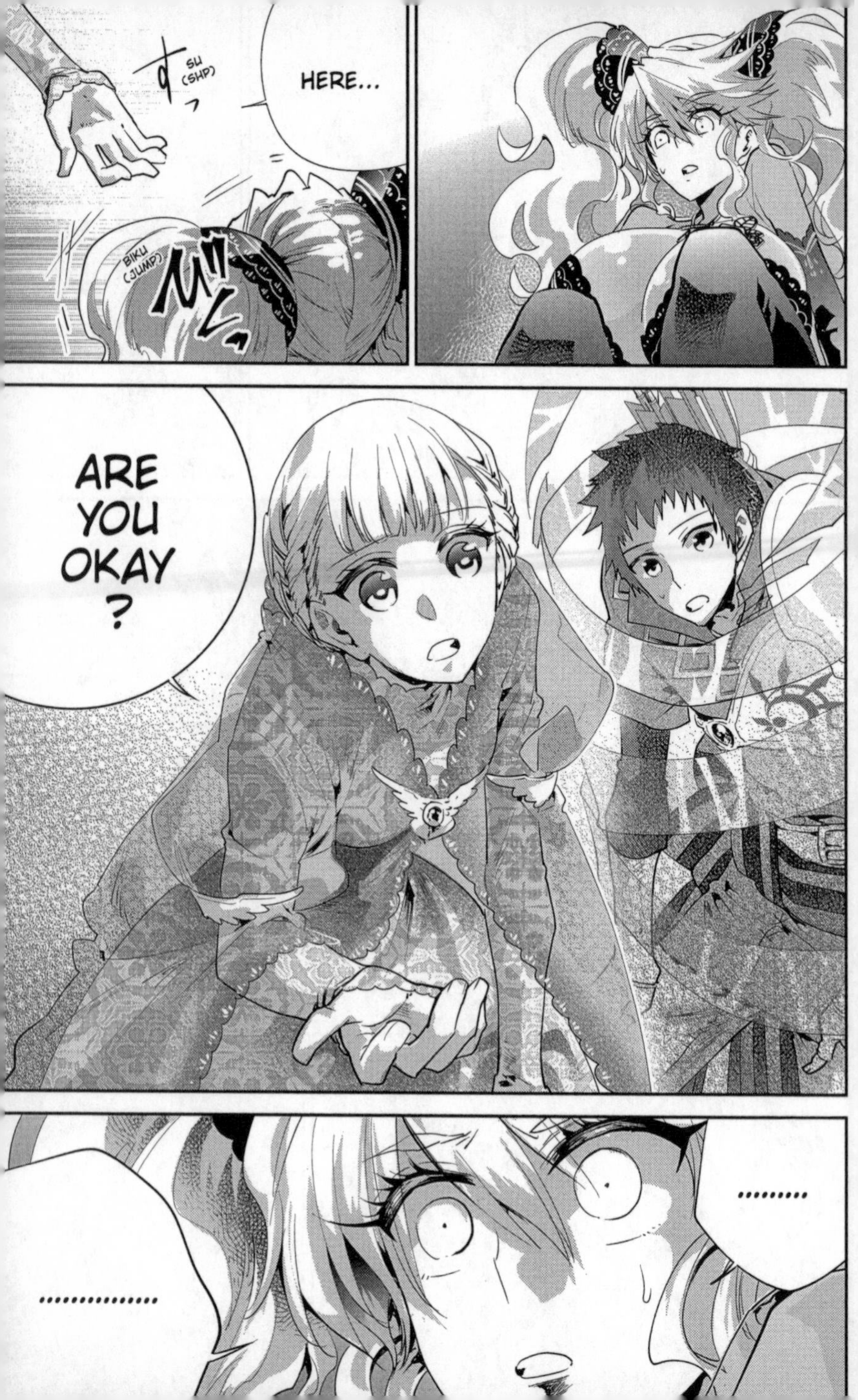
HERE...
SU (SHP)
BIKU (JUMP)
ARE YOU OKAY?
.........
..............

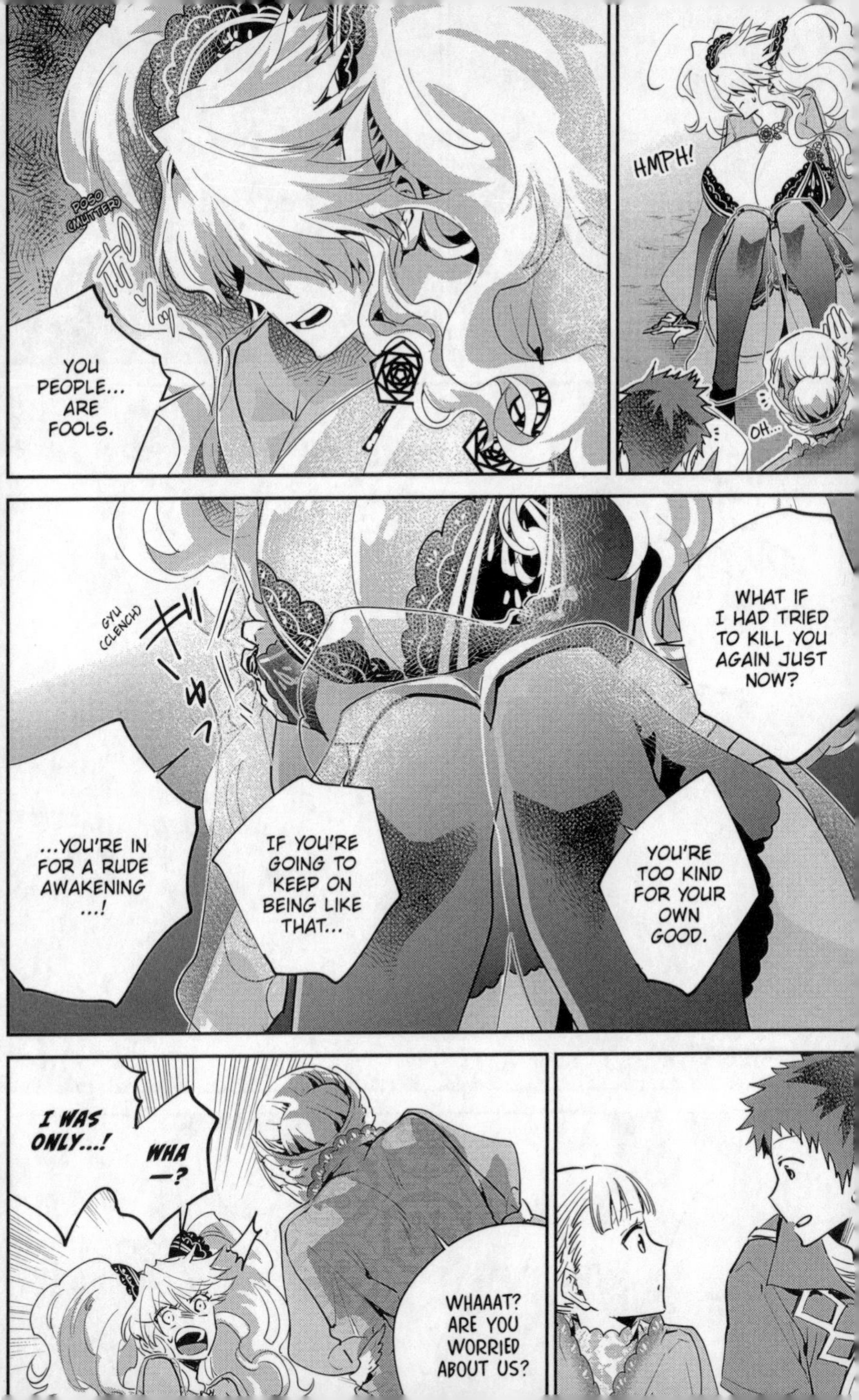
HMPH!
OH...
POSO (MUTTER)
YOU PEOPLE... ARE FOOLS.
WHAT IF I HAD TRIED TO KILL YOU AGAIN JUST NOW?
YOU'RE TOO KIND FOR YOUR OWN GOOD.
GYU (CLENCH)
IF YOU'RE GOING TO KEEP ON BEING LIKE THAT...
...YOU'RE IN FOR A RUDE AWAKENING...!
WHAAAT? ARE YOU WORRIED ABOUT US?
WHA—?
I WAS ONLY...!

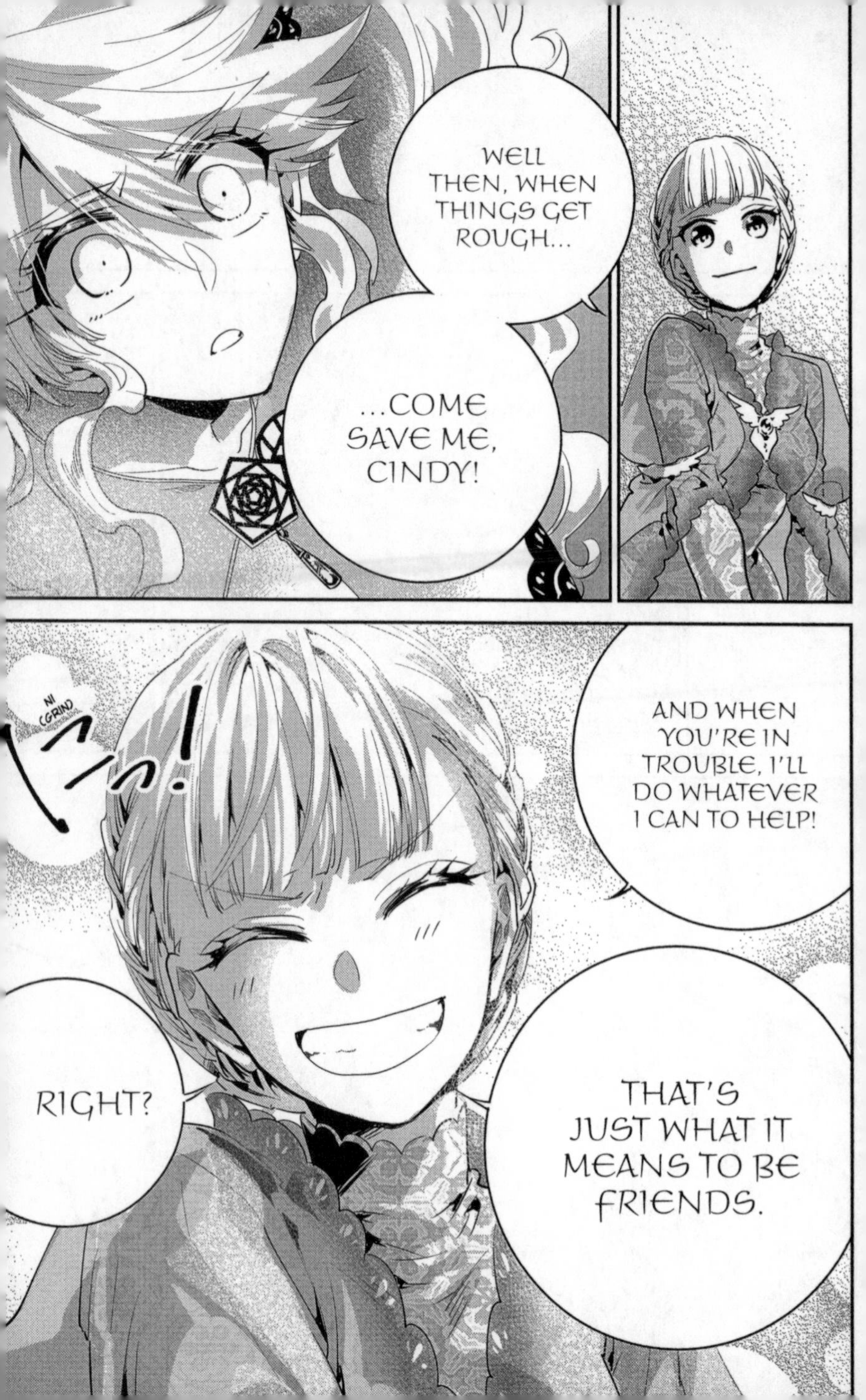
WELL THEN, WHEN THINGS GET ROUGH...
...COME SAVE ME, CINDY!
AND WHEN YOU'RE IN TROUBLE, I'LL DO WHATEVER I CAN TO HELP!
NI GRIN
THAT'S JUST WHAT IT MEANS TO BE FRIENDS.
RIGHT?

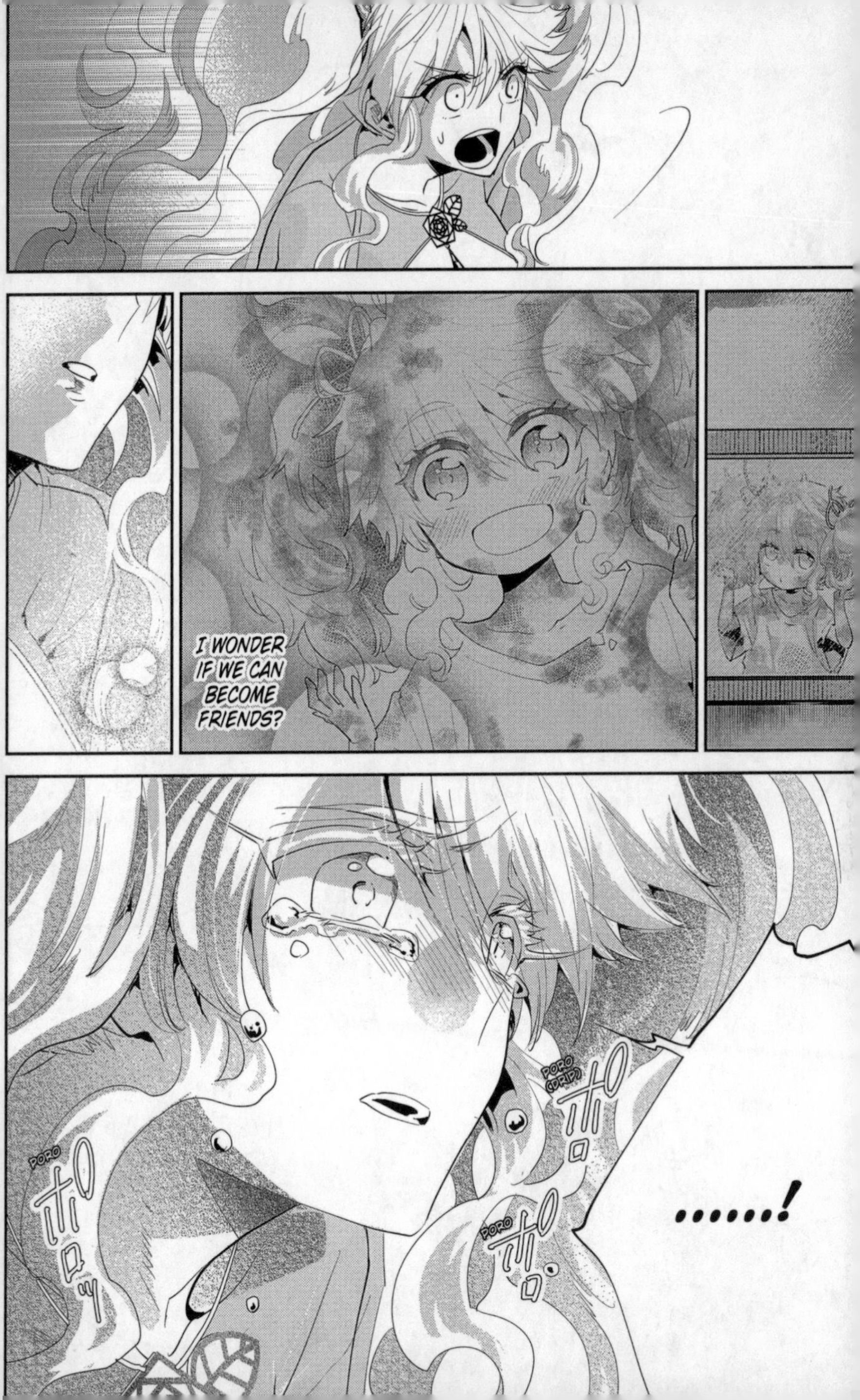
I WONDER IF WE CAN BECOME FRIENDS?
......!
PORO (DRIP)
ポロ
PORO
ポロ
PORO
ポロッ

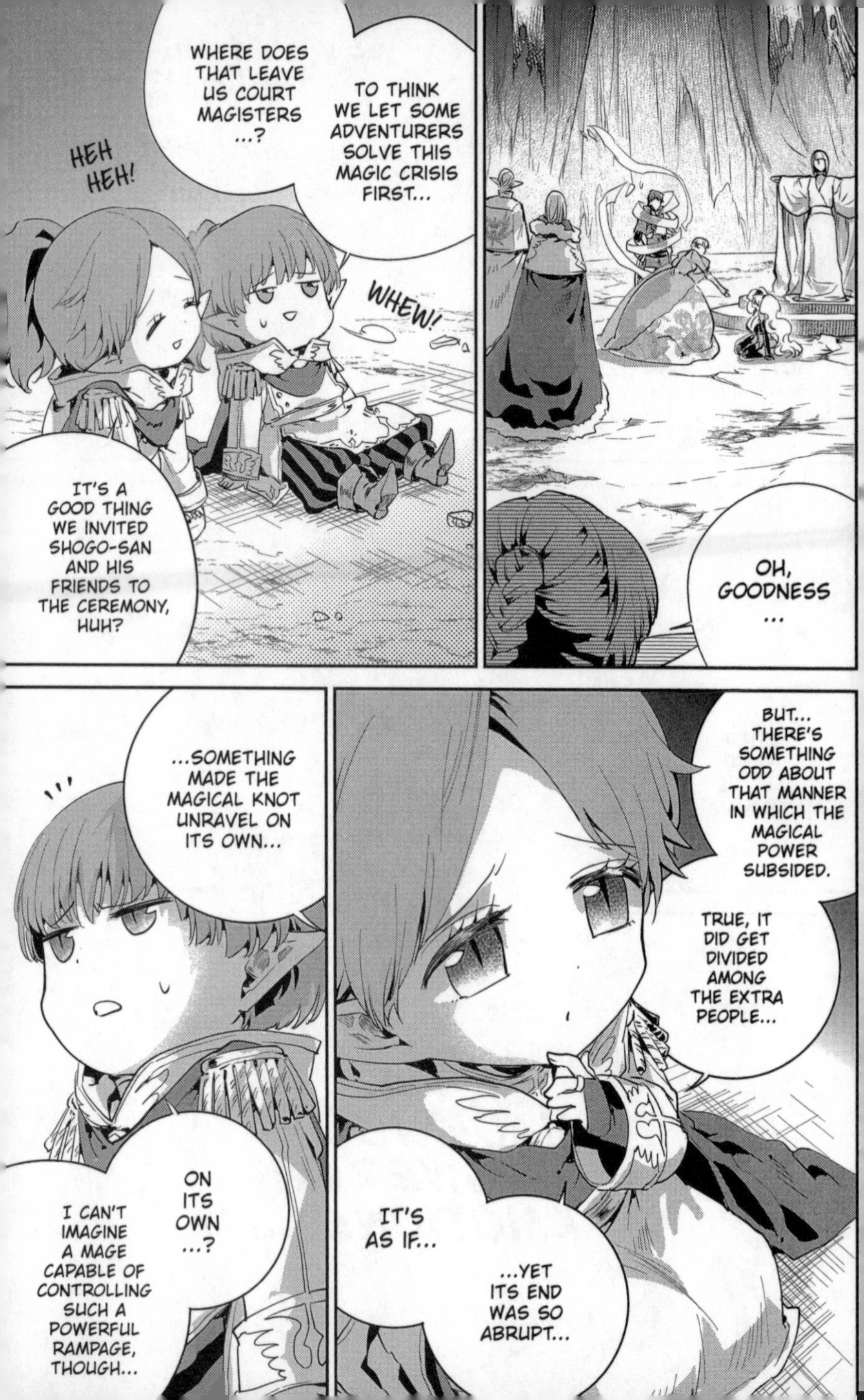
OH, GOODNESS...
TO THINK WE LET SOME ADVENTURERS SOLVE THIS MAGIC CRISIS FIRST...
WHERE DOES THAT LEAVE US COURT MAGISTERS...?
WHEW!
HEH HEH!
IT'S A GOOD THING WE INVITED SHOGO-SAN AND HIS FRIENDS TO THE CEREMONY, HUH?
BUT... THERE'S SOMETHING ODD ABOUT THAT MANNER IN WHICH THE MAGICAL POWER SUBSIDED.
TRUE, IT DID GET DIVIDED AMONG THE EXTRA PEOPLE...
...YET ITS END WAS SO ABRUPT...
IT'S AS IF...
...SOMETHING MADE THE MAGICAL KNOT UNRAVEL ON ITS OWN...
ON ITS OWN...?
I CAN'T IMAGINE A MAGE CAPABLE OF CONTROLLING SUCH A POWERFUL RAMPAGE, THOUGH...

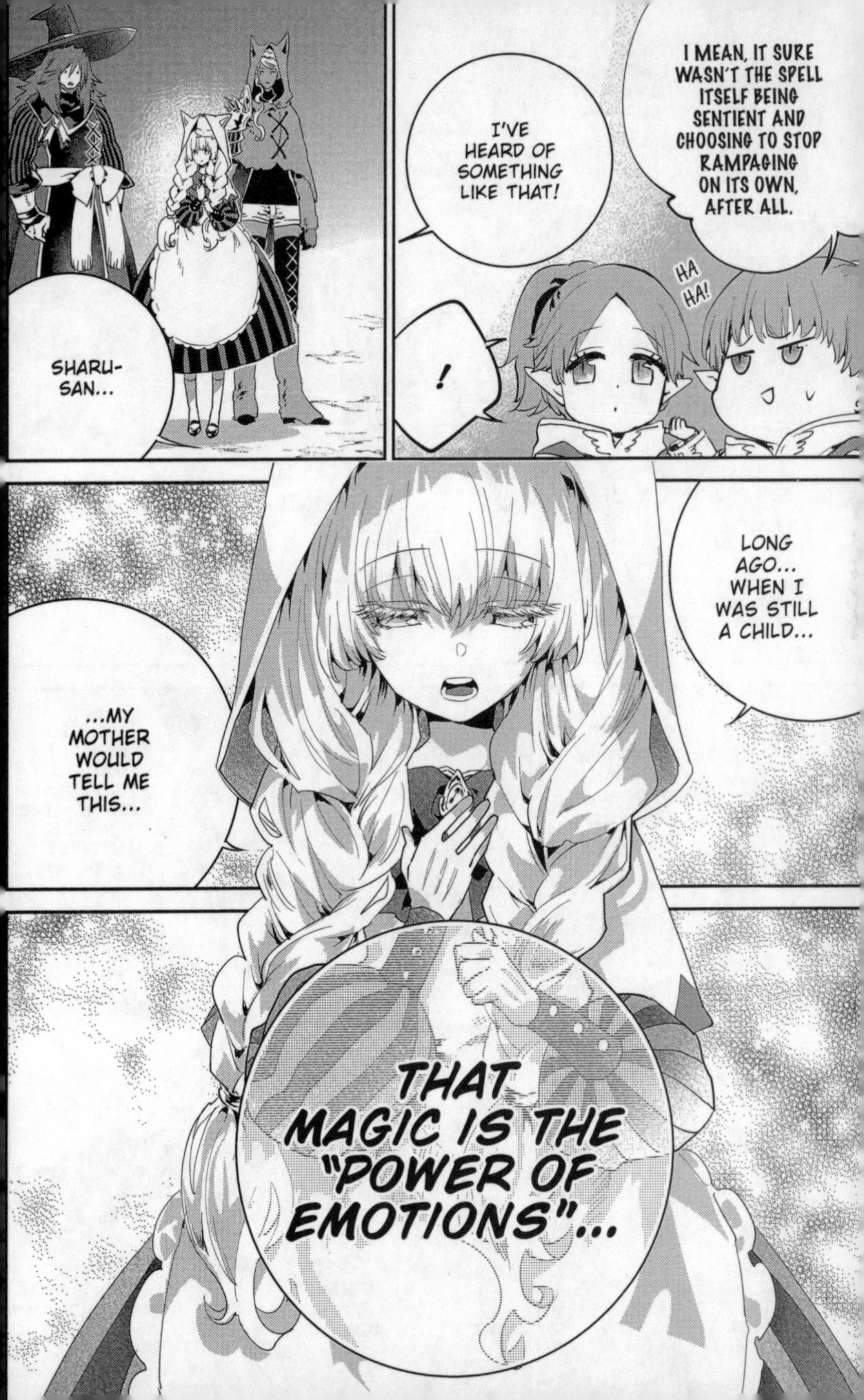
I MEAN, IT SURE WASN'T THE SPELL ITSELF BEING SENTIENT AND CHOOSING TO STOP RAMPAGING ON ITS OWN, AFTER ALL.
I'VE HEARD OF SOMETHING LIKE THAT!
HA HA!
!
SHARU-SAN...
LONG AGO... WHEN I WAS STILL A CHILD...
...MY MOTHER WOULD TELL ME THIS...
THAT MAGIC IS THE "POWER OF EMOTIONS"...

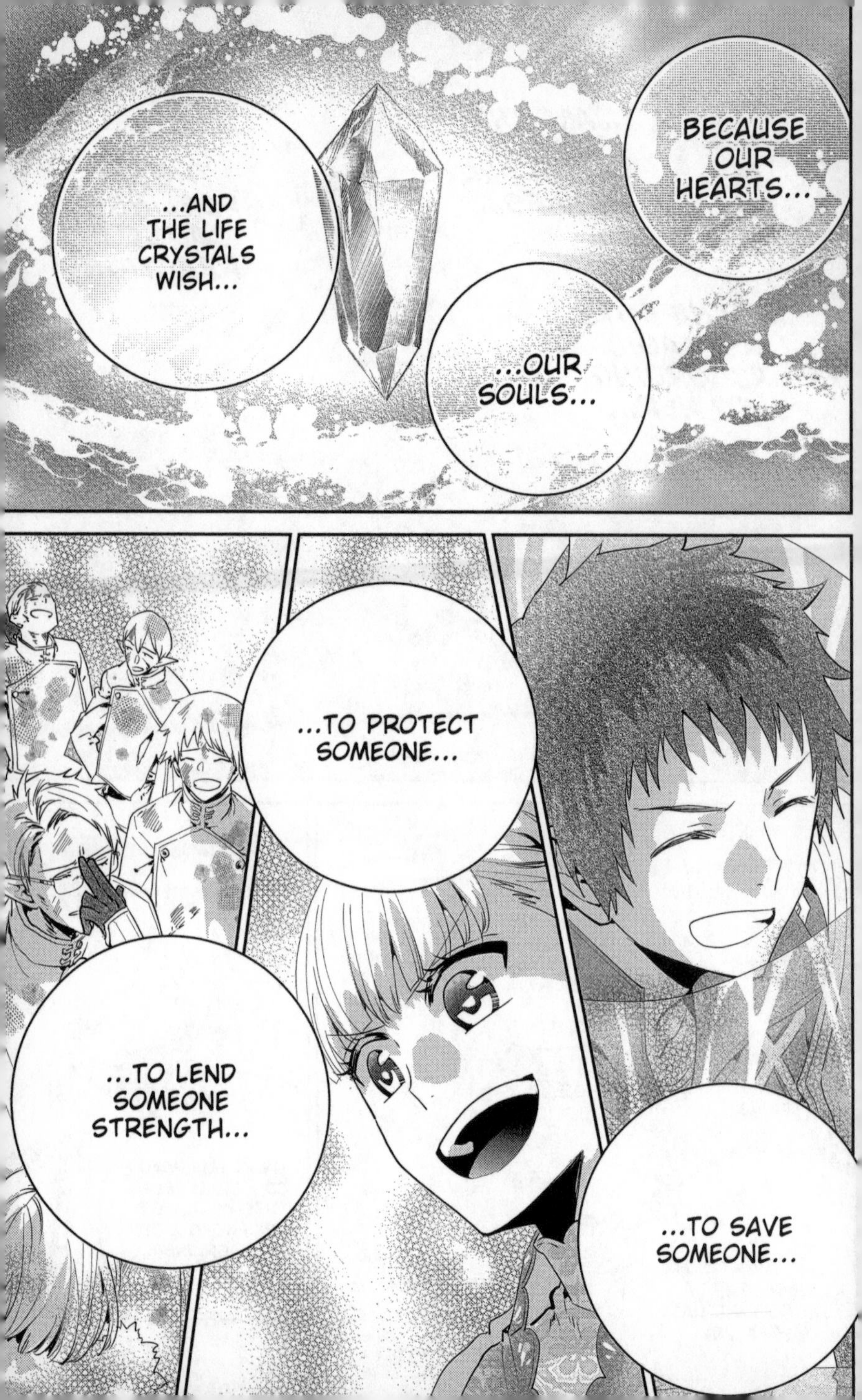
BECAUSE OUR HEARTS...
...OUR SOULS...
...AND THE LIFE CRYSTALS WISH...
...TO PROTECT SOMEONE...
...TO SAVE SOMEONE...
...TO LEND SOMEONE STRENGTH...

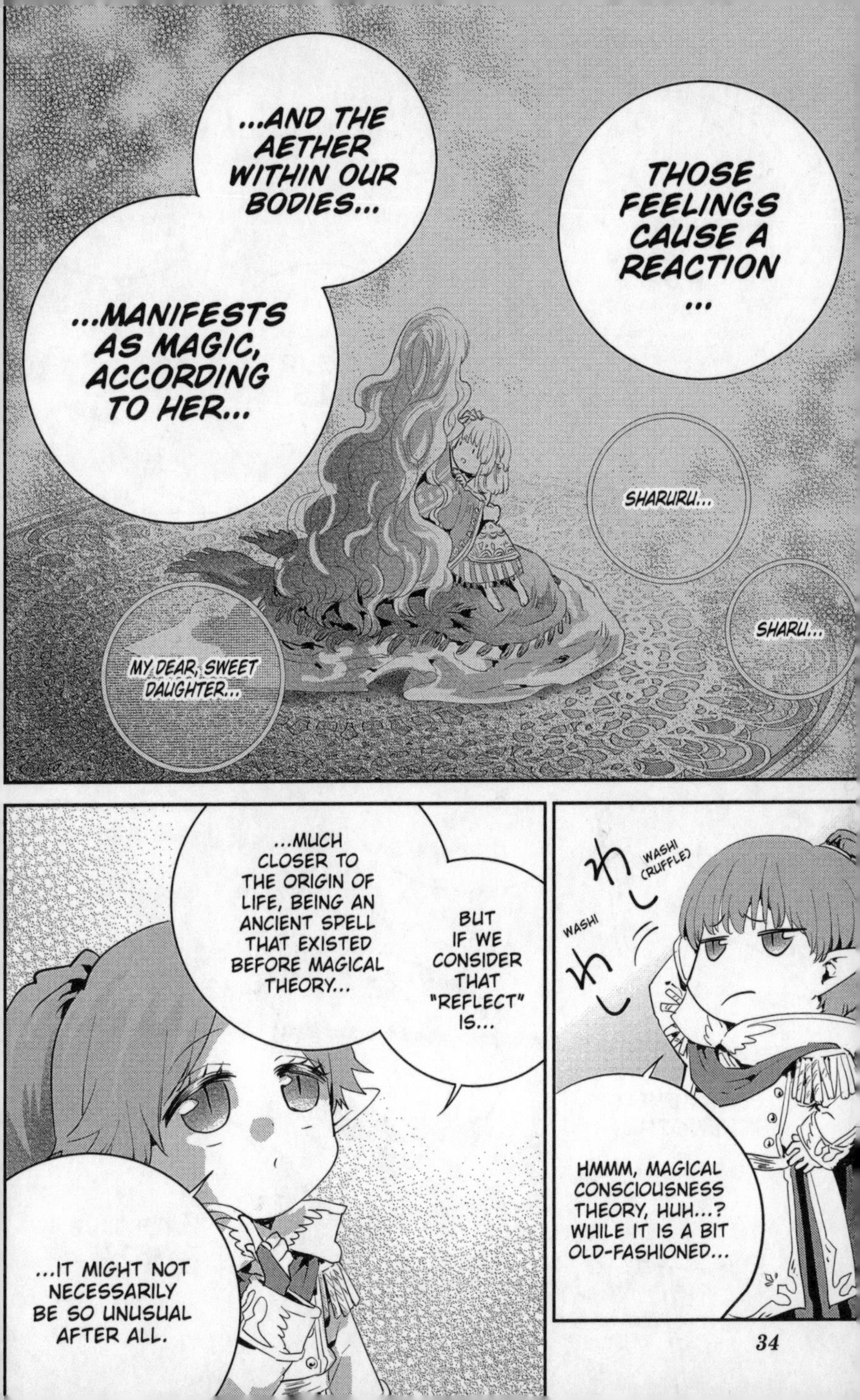
THOSE FEELINGS CAUSE A REACTION...
...AND THE AETHER WITHIN OUR BODIES...
...MANIFESTS AS MAGIC, ACCORDING TO HER...
SHARURU...
SHARU...
MY DEAR, SWEET DAUGHTER...
WASHI (RUFFLE)
WASHI
HMMM, MAGICAL CONSCIOUSNESS THEORY, HUH...? WHILE IT IS A BIT OLD-FASHIONED...
BUT IF WE CONSIDER THAT "REFLECT" IS...
...MUCH CLOSER TO THE ORIGIN OF LIFE, BEING AN ANCIENT SPELL THAT EXISTED BEFORE MAGICAL THEORY...
...IT MIGHT NOT NECESSARILY BE SO UNUSUAL AFTER ALL.

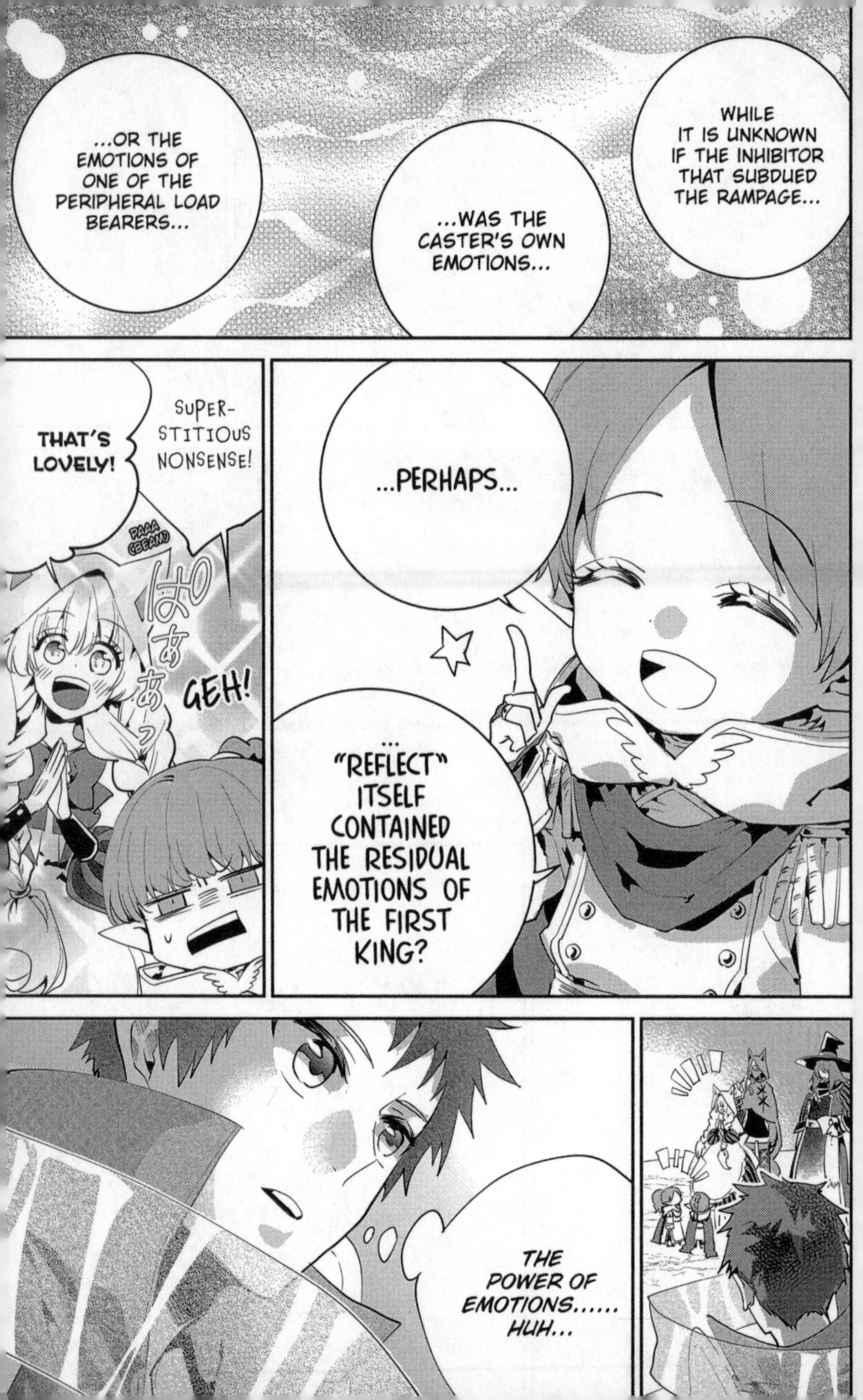
WHILE IT IS UNKNOWN IF THE INHIBITOR THAT SUBDUED THE RAMPAGE...
...WAS THE CASTER'S OWN EMOTIONS...
...OR THE EMOTIONS OF ONE OF THE PERIPHERAL LOAD BEARERS...
...PERHAPS...
... "REFLECT" ITSELF CONTAINED THE RESIDUAL EMOTIONS OF THE FIRST KING?
SUPER-STITIOUS NONSENSE!
THAT'S LOVELY!
PAAA (BEAM)
ぱあぁっ
GEH!
THE POWER OF EMOTIONS...... HUH...

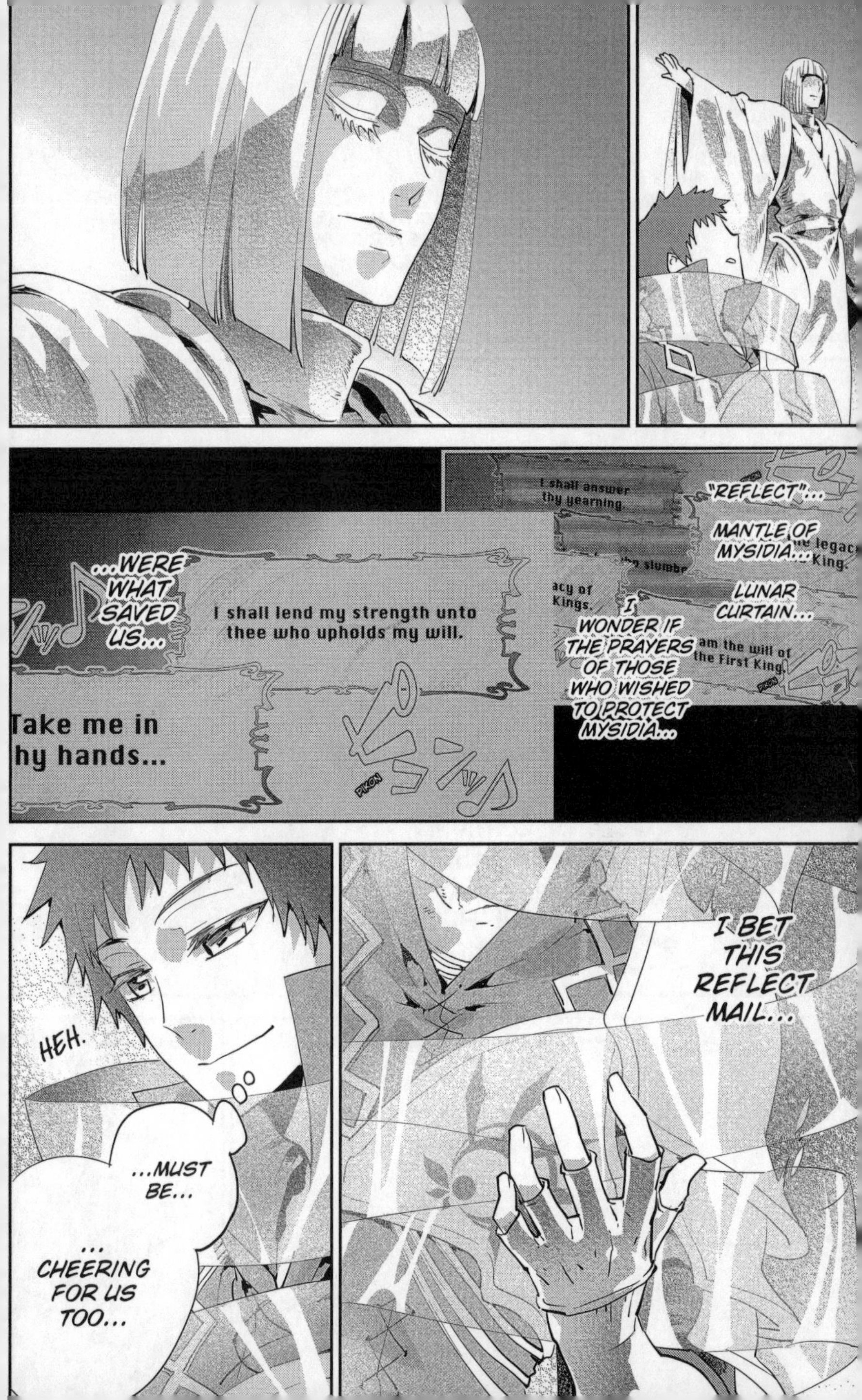
"REFLECT"...
MANTLE OF MYSIDIA...
LUNAR CURTAIN...
I shall answer thy yearning.
I WONDER IF THE PRAYERS OF THOSE WHO WISHED TO PROTECT MYSIDIA...
am the will of the First King.
PIKON
...WERE WHAT SAVED US...
I shall lend my strength unto thee who upholds my will.
Take me in
hy hands...
PIKON
I BET THIS REFLECT MAIL...
HEH.
...MUST BE...
...CHEERING FOR US TOO...

...FOR
SARA...

...FOR
EVERYONE...

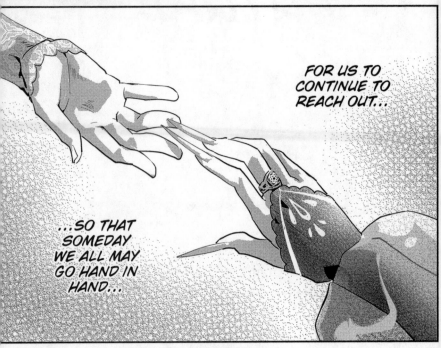

FOR US TO
CONTINUE TO
REACH OUT...

...SO THAT
SOMEDAY
WE ALL MAY
GO HAND IN
HAND...

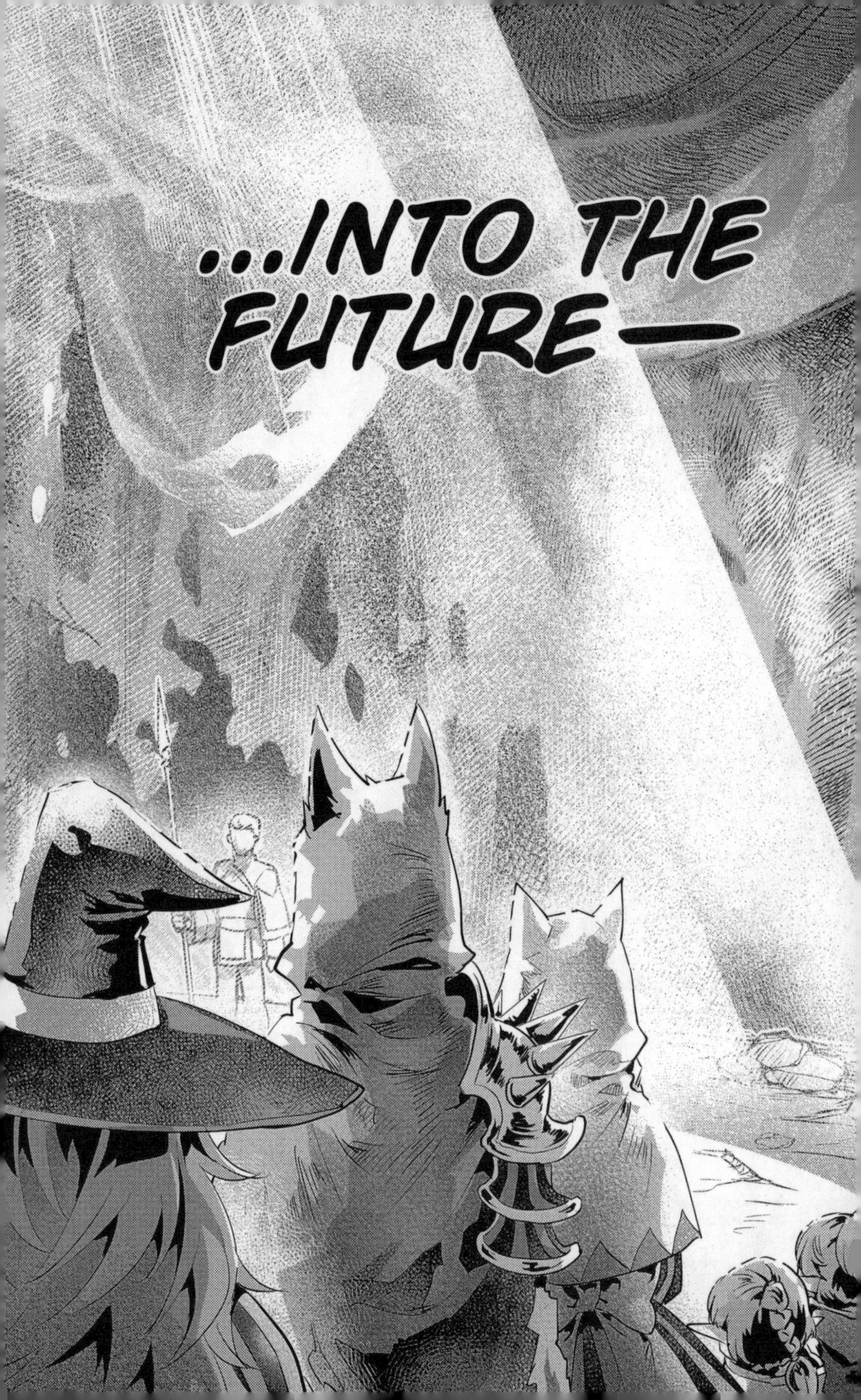
...INTO THE FUTURE—

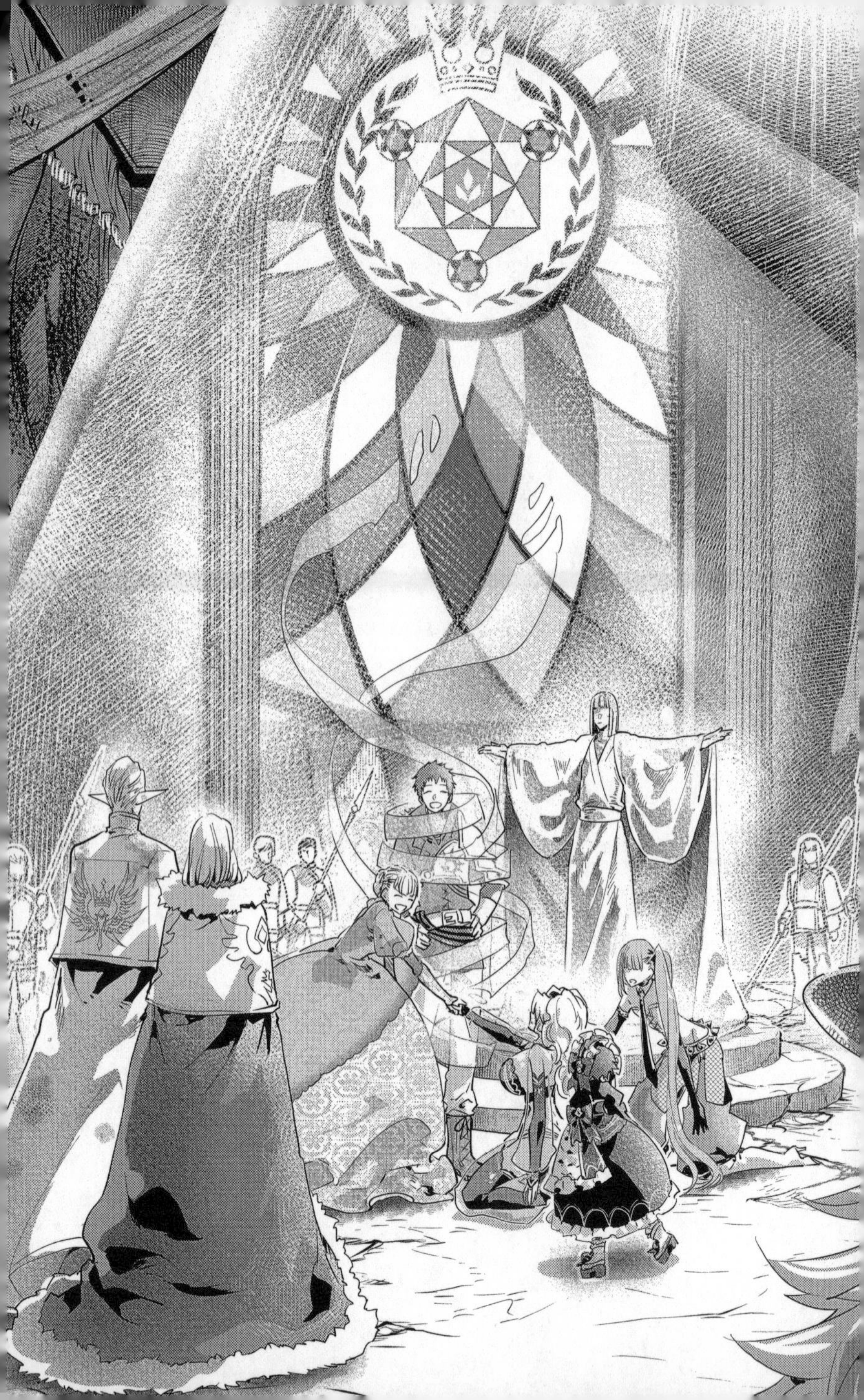

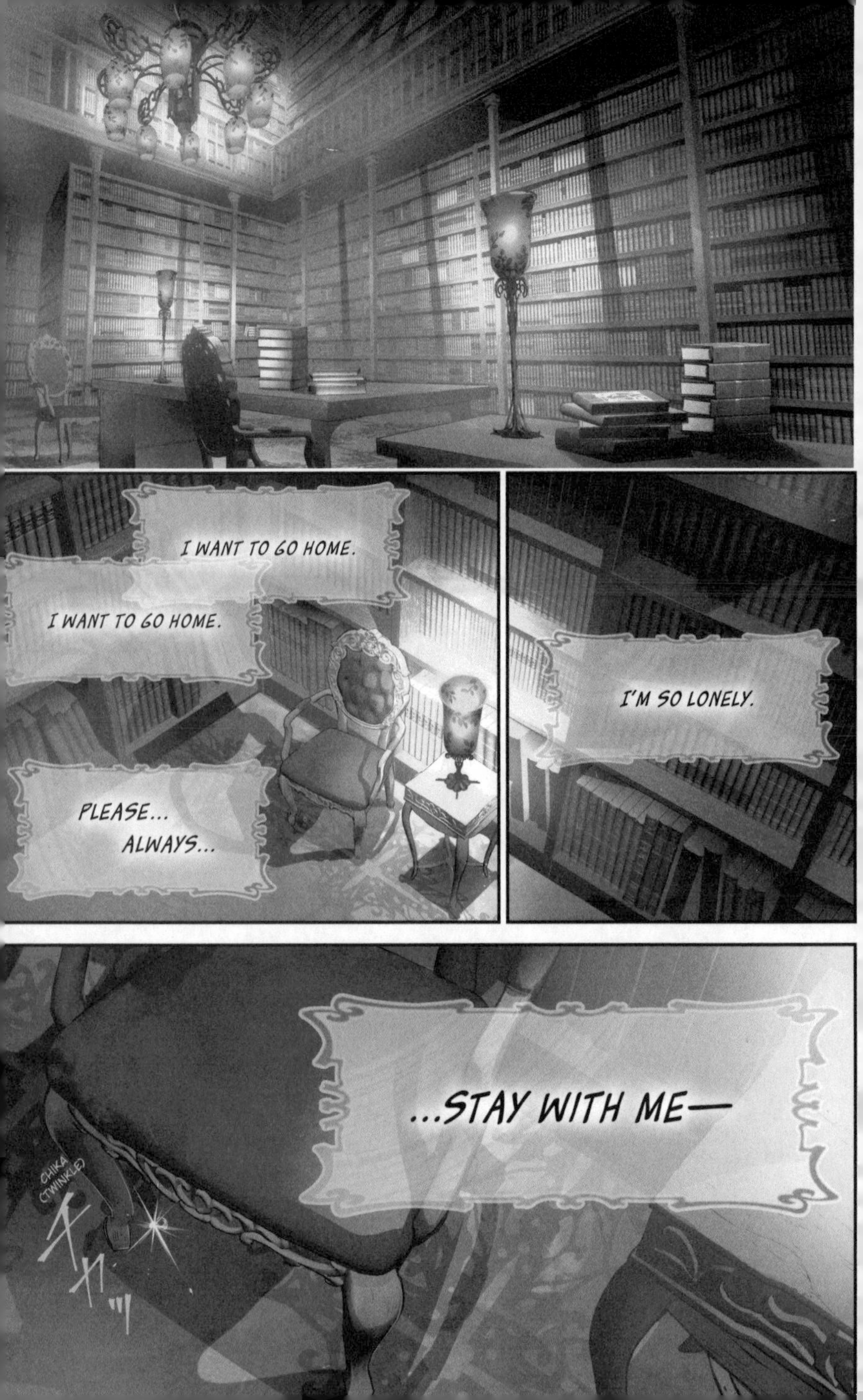
I'M SO LONELY.
I WANT TO GO HOME.
I WANT TO GO HOME.
PLEASE... ALWAYS...
...STAY WITH ME—
CHIKA (TWINKLE)

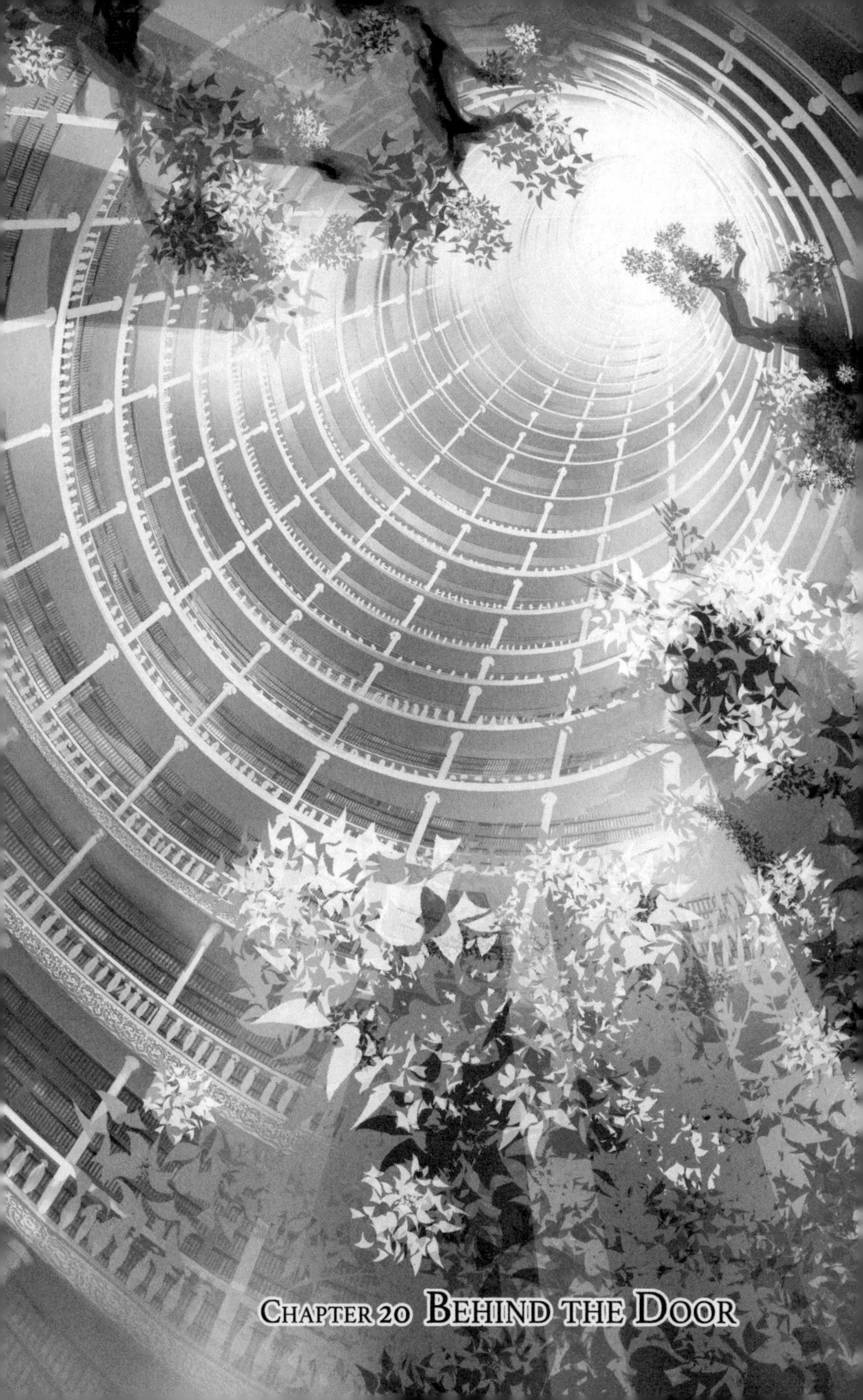

# Chapter 20 Behind the Door

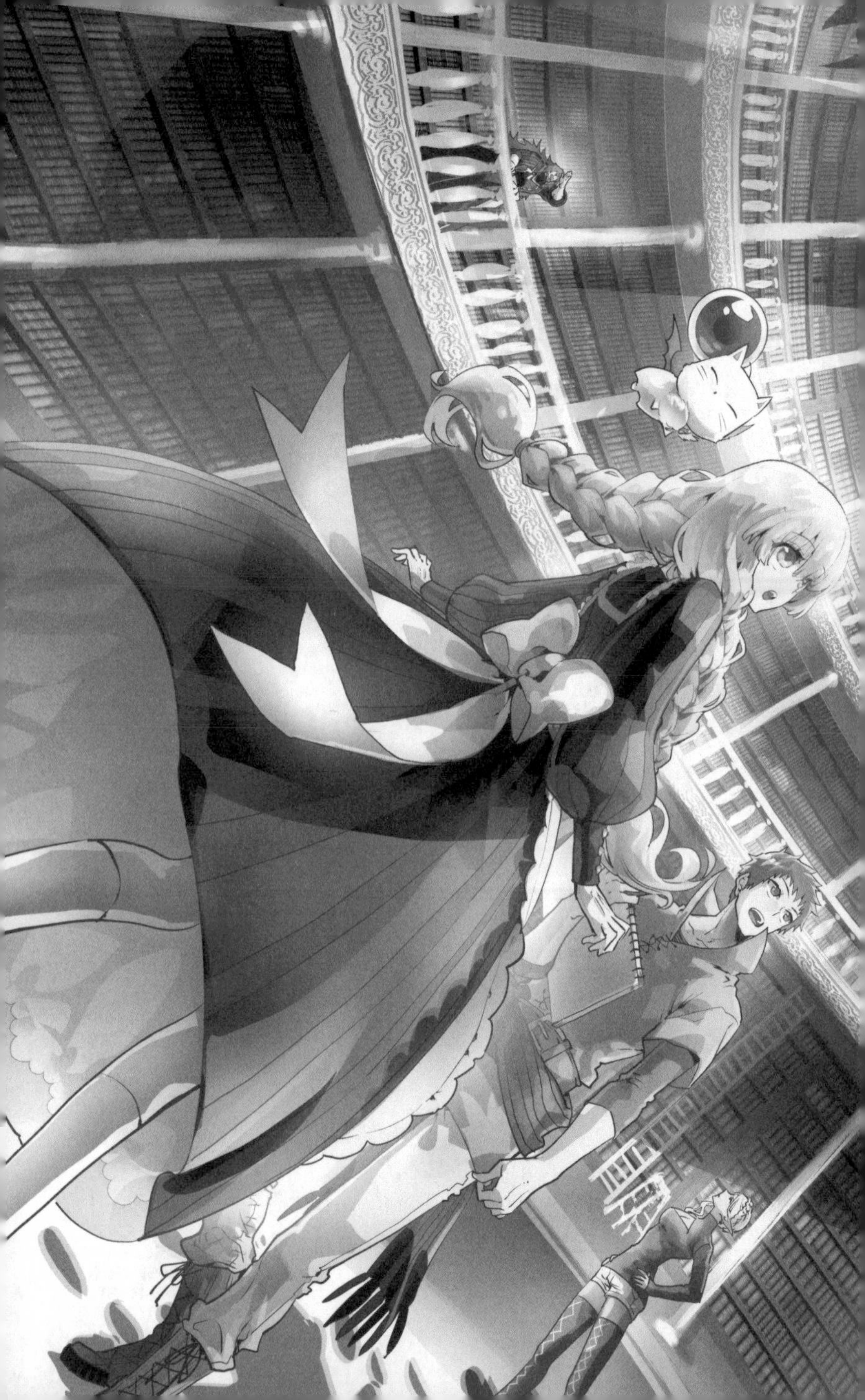

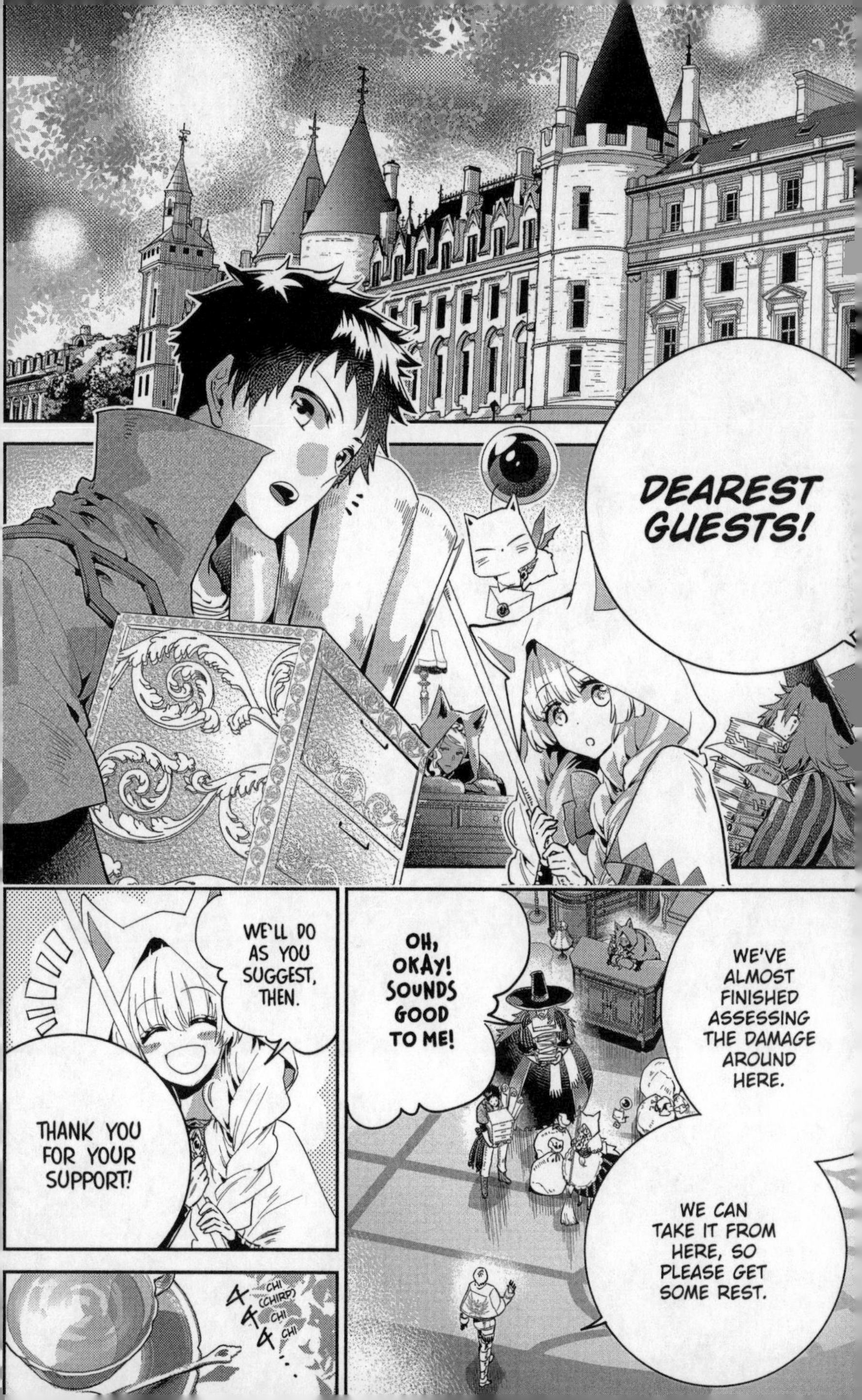
DEAREST GUESTS!
WE'VE ALMOST FINISHED ASSESSING THE DAMAGE AROUND HERE.
WE CAN TAKE IT FROM HERE, SO PLEASE GET SOME REST.
OH, OKAY! SOUNDS GOOD TO ME!
WE'LL DO AS YOU SUGGEST, THEN.
THANK YOU FOR YOUR SUPPORT!
CHI (CHIRP) CHI CHI

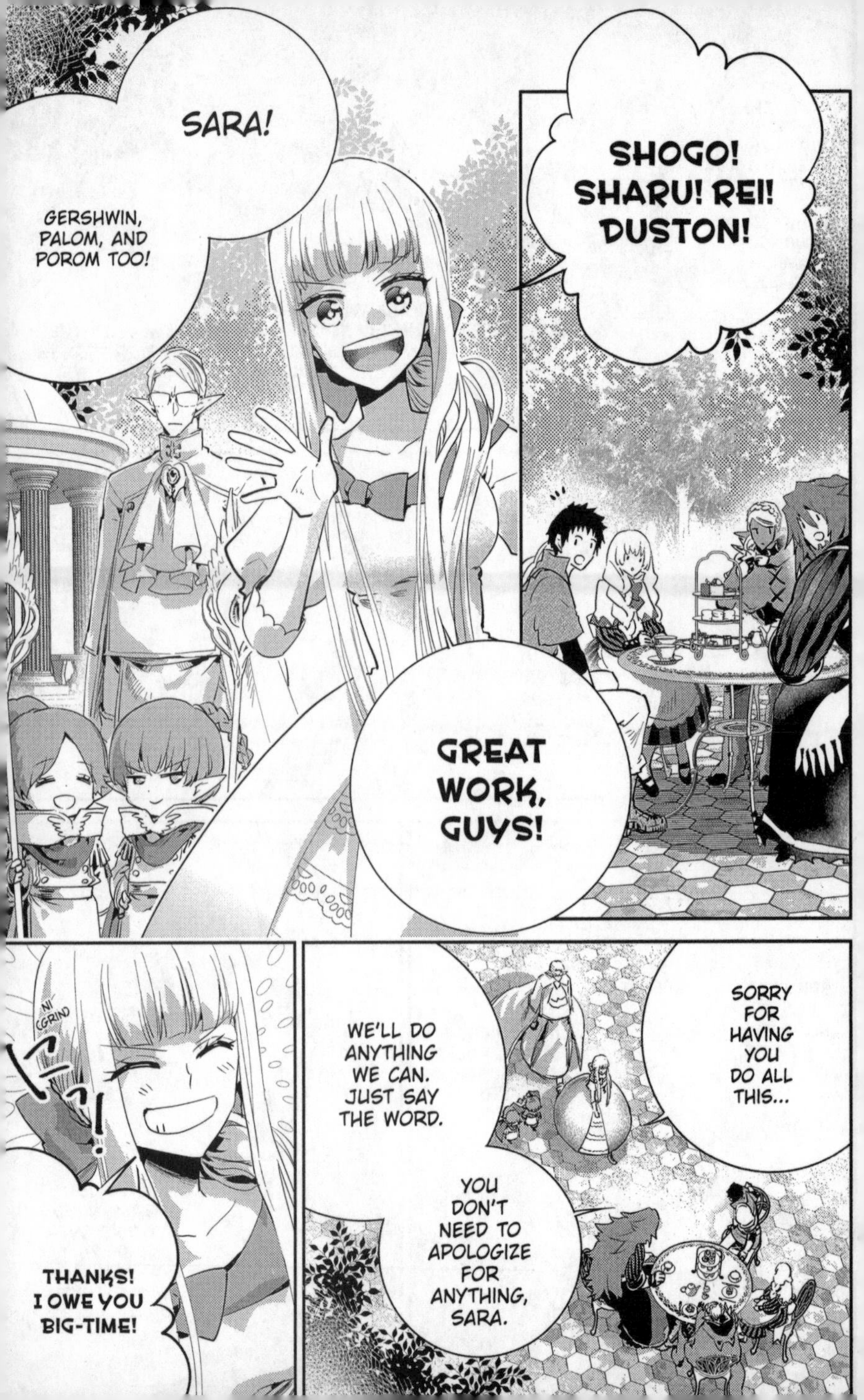
SHOGO! SHARU! REI! DUSTON!
SARA!
GERSHWIN, PALOM, AND POROM TOO!
GREAT WORK, GUYS!
SORRY FOR HAVING YOU DO ALL THIS...
WE'LL DO ANYTHING WE CAN. JUST SAY THE WORD.
YOU DON'T NEED TO APOLOGIZE FOR ANYTHING, SARA.
NI (GRIN)
THANKS! I OWE YOU BIG-TIME!

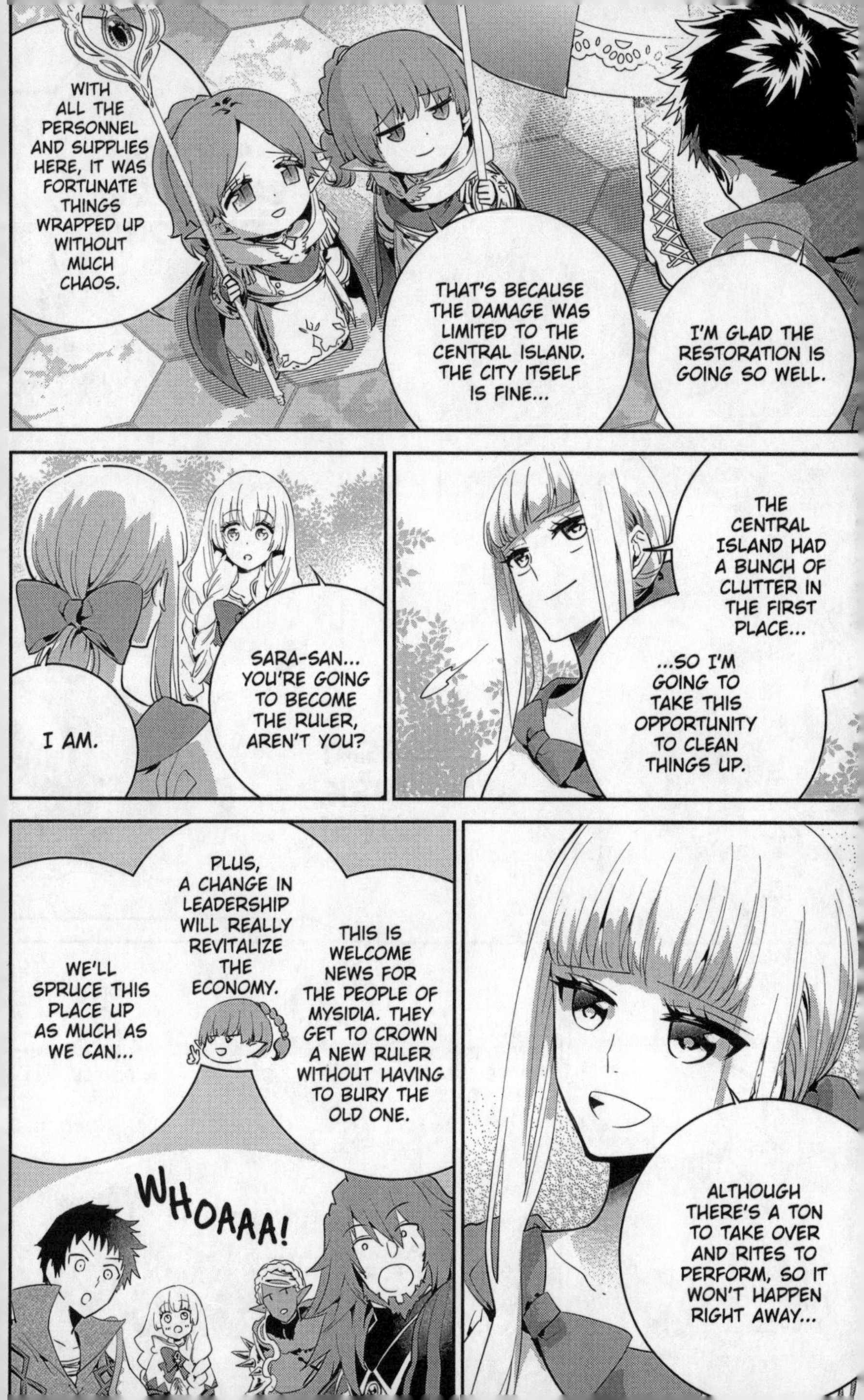
I'M GLAD THE RESTORATION IS GOING SO WELL.
THAT'S BECAUSE THE DAMAGE WAS LIMITED TO THE CENTRAL ISLAND. THE CITY ITSELF IS FINE...
WITH ALL THE PERSONNEL AND SUPPLIES HERE, IT WAS FORTUNATE THINGS WRAPPED UP WITHOUT MUCH CHAOS.
THE CENTRAL ISLAND HAD A BUNCH OF CLUTTER IN THE FIRST PLACE...
...SO I'M GOING TO TAKE THIS OPPORTUNITY TO CLEAN THINGS UP.
SARA-SAN... YOU'RE GOING TO BECOME THE RULER, AREN'T YOU?
I AM.
ALTHOUGH THERE'S A TON TO TAKE OVER AND RITES TO PERFORM, SO IT WON'T HAPPEN RIGHT AWAY...
THIS IS WELCOME NEWS FOR THE PEOPLE OF MYSIDIA. THEY GET TO CROWN A NEW RULER WITHOUT HAVING TO BURY THE OLD ONE.
PLUS, A CHANGE IN LEADERSHIP WILL REALLY REVITALIZE THE ECONOMY.
WE'LL SPRUCE THIS PLACE UP AS MUCH AS WE CAN...
WHOAAA!

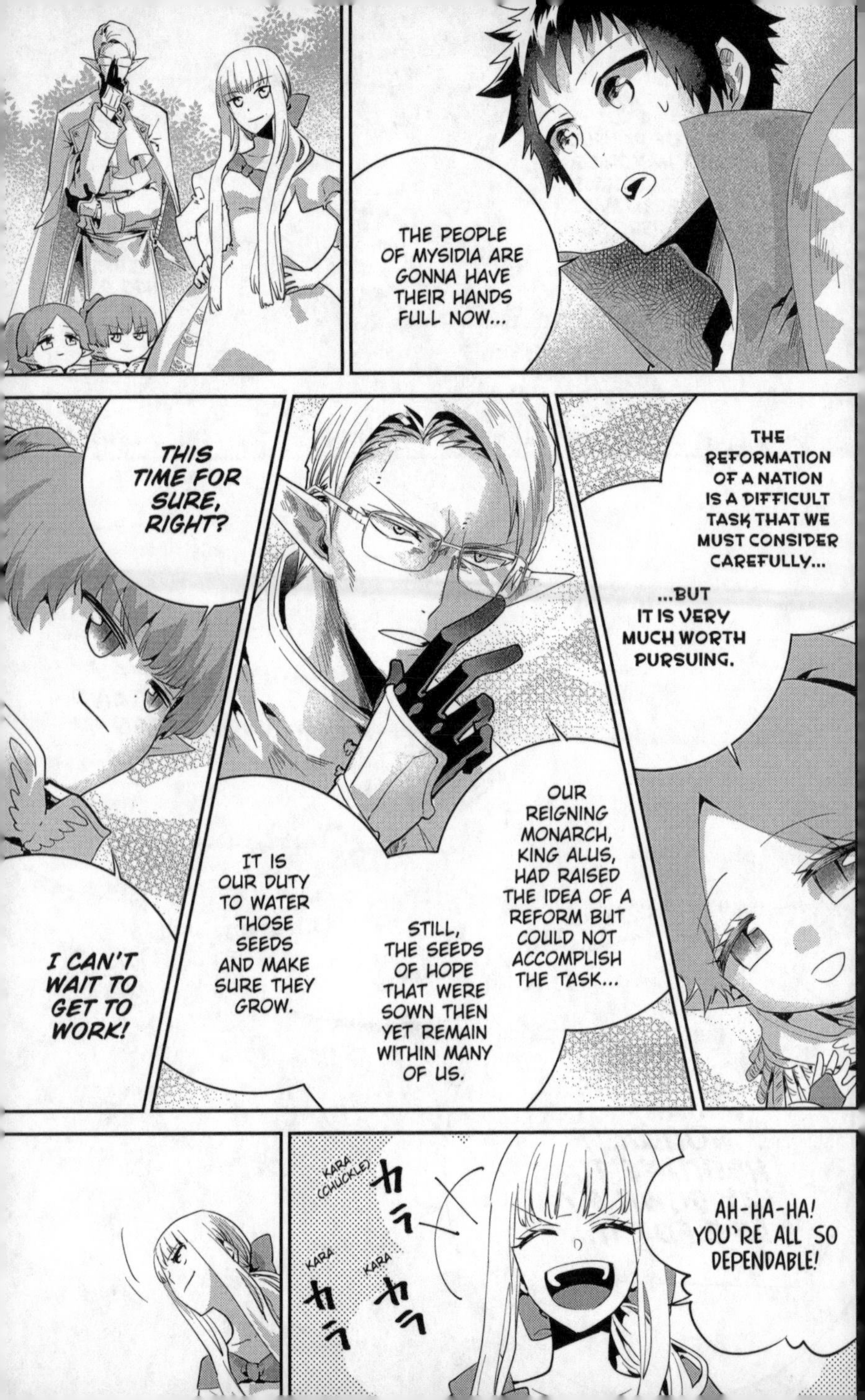
THE PEOPLE OF MYSIDIA ARE GONNA HAVE THEIR HANDS FULL NOW...
THE REFORMATION OF A NATION IS A DIFFICULT TASK THAT WE MUST CONSIDER CAREFULLY...
...BUT IT IS VERY MUCH WORTH PURSUING.
OUR REIGNING MONARCH, KING ALUS, HAD RAISED THE IDEA OF A REFORM BUT COULD NOT ACCOMPLISH THE TASK...
STILL, THE SEEDS OF HOPE THAT WERE SOWN THEN YET REMAIN WITHIN MANY OF US.
IT IS OUR DUTY TO WATER THOSE SEEDS AND MAKE SURE THEY GROW.
THIS TIME FOR SURE, RIGHT?
I CAN'T WAIT TO GET TO WORK!
AH-HA-HA! YOU'RE ALL SO DEPENDABLE!
カラ KARA (CHUCKLE)
カラ KARA
カラ KARA

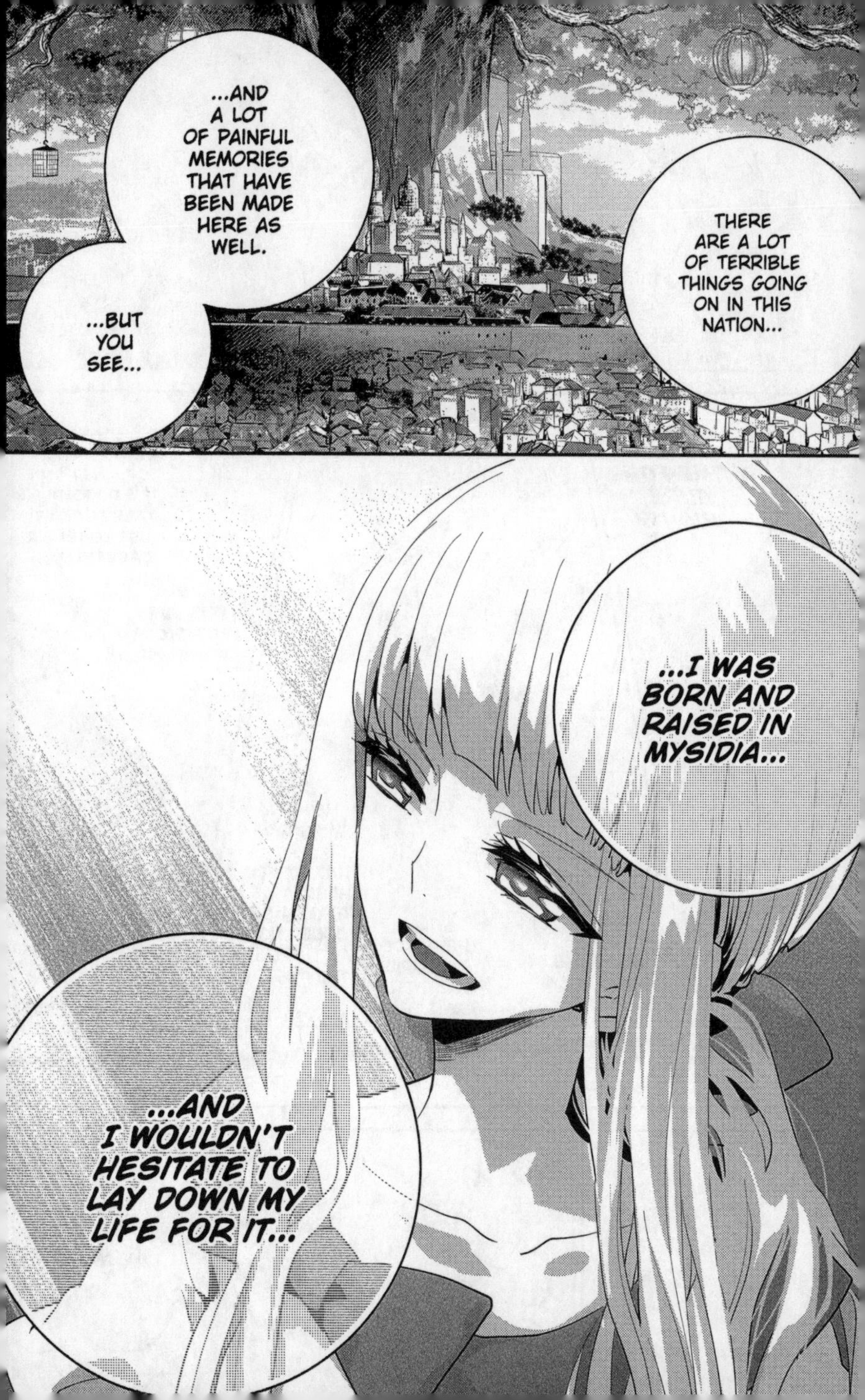
THERE ARE A LOT OF TERRIBLE THINGS GOING ON IN THIS NATION...
...AND A LOT OF PAINFUL MEMORIES THAT HAVE BEEN MADE HERE AS WELL.
...BUT YOU SEE...
...I WAS BORN AND RAISED IN MYSIDIA...
...AND I WOULDN'T HESITATE TO LAY DOWN MY LIFE FOR IT...

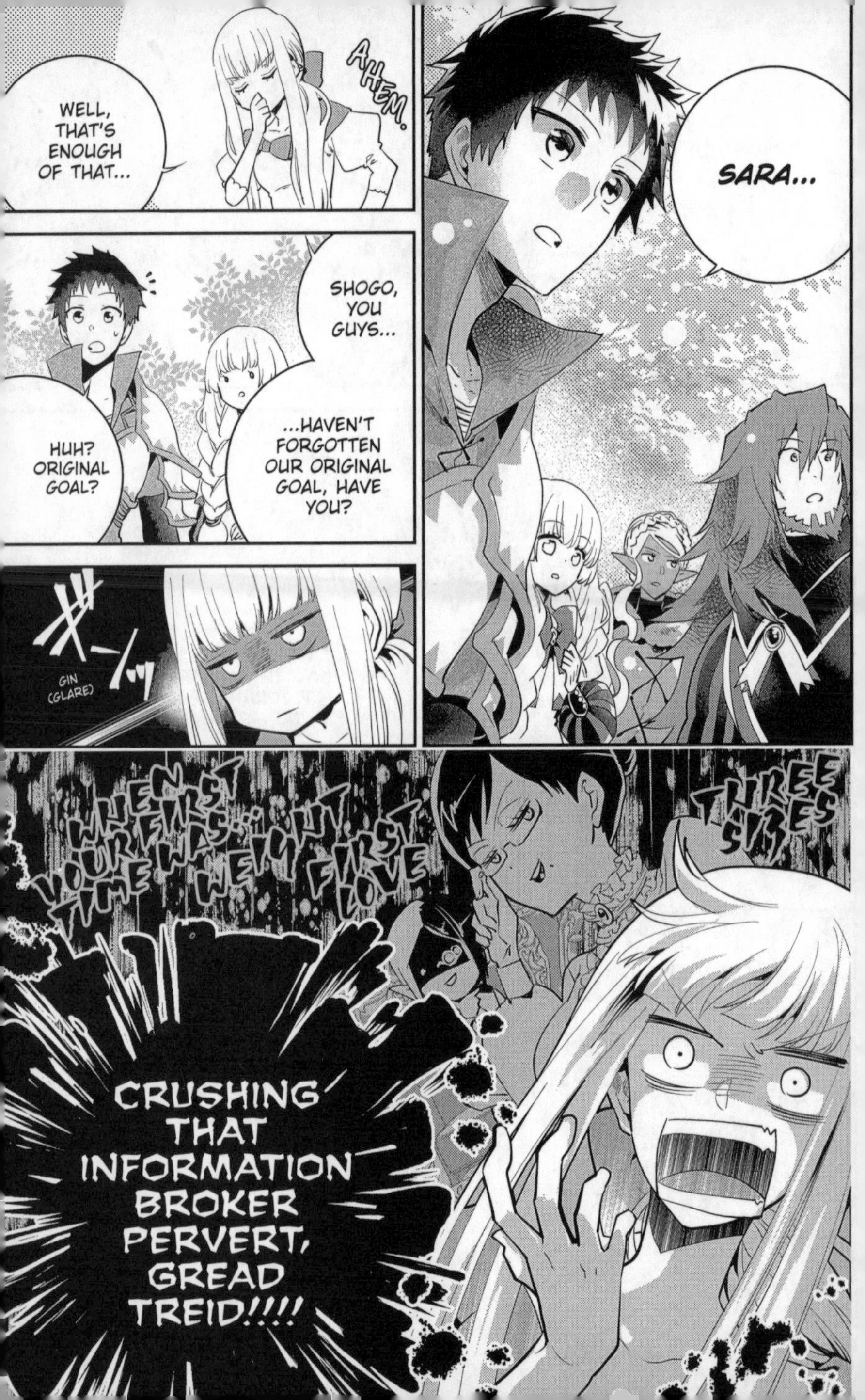
SARA...
AHEM.
WELL, THAT'S ENOUGH OF THAT...
SHOGO, YOU GUYS...
...HAVEN'T FORGOTTEN OUR ORIGINAL GOAL, HAVE YOU?
HUH? ORIGINAL GOAL?
GIN (GLARE)
THREE SIZES
CRUSHING THAT INFORMATION BROKER PERVERT, GREAD TREID!!!!

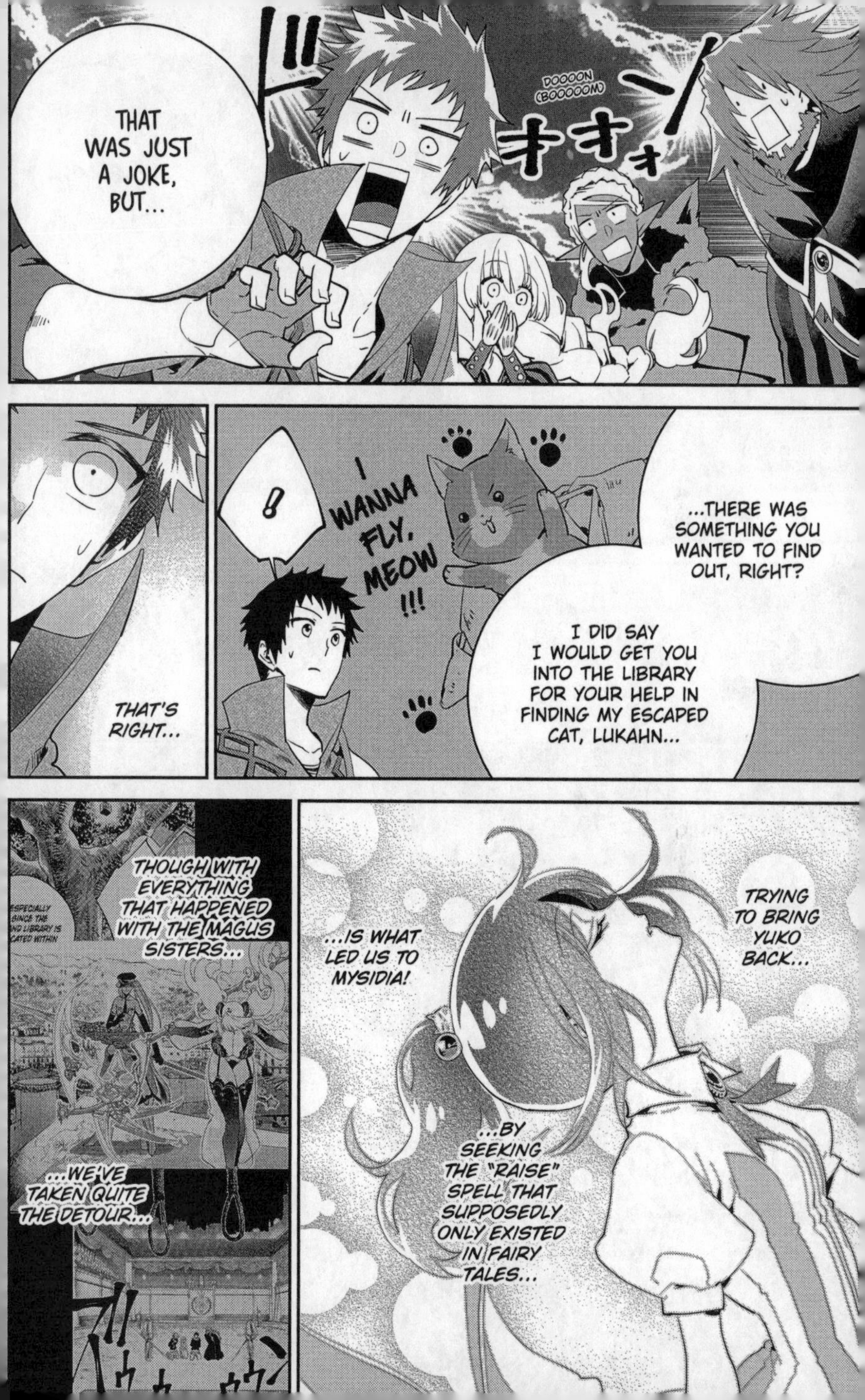
DOOOON (BOOOOOM)
THAT WAS JUST A JOKE, BUT...
...THERE WAS SOMETHING YOU WANTED TO FIND OUT, RIGHT?
I DID SAY I WOULD GET YOU INTO THE LIBRARY FOR YOUR HELP IN FINDING MY ESCAPED CAT, LUKAHN...
I WANNA FLY, MEOW!!!
!
THAT'S RIGHT...
TRYING TO BRING YUKO BACK...
...BY SEEKING THE "RAISE" SPELL THAT SUPPOSEDLY ONLY EXISTED IN FAIRY TALES...
...IS WHAT LED US TO MYSIDIA!
THOUGH WITH EVERYTHING THAT HAPPENED WITH THE MAGUS SISTERS...
...WE'VE TAKEN QUITE THE DETOUR...

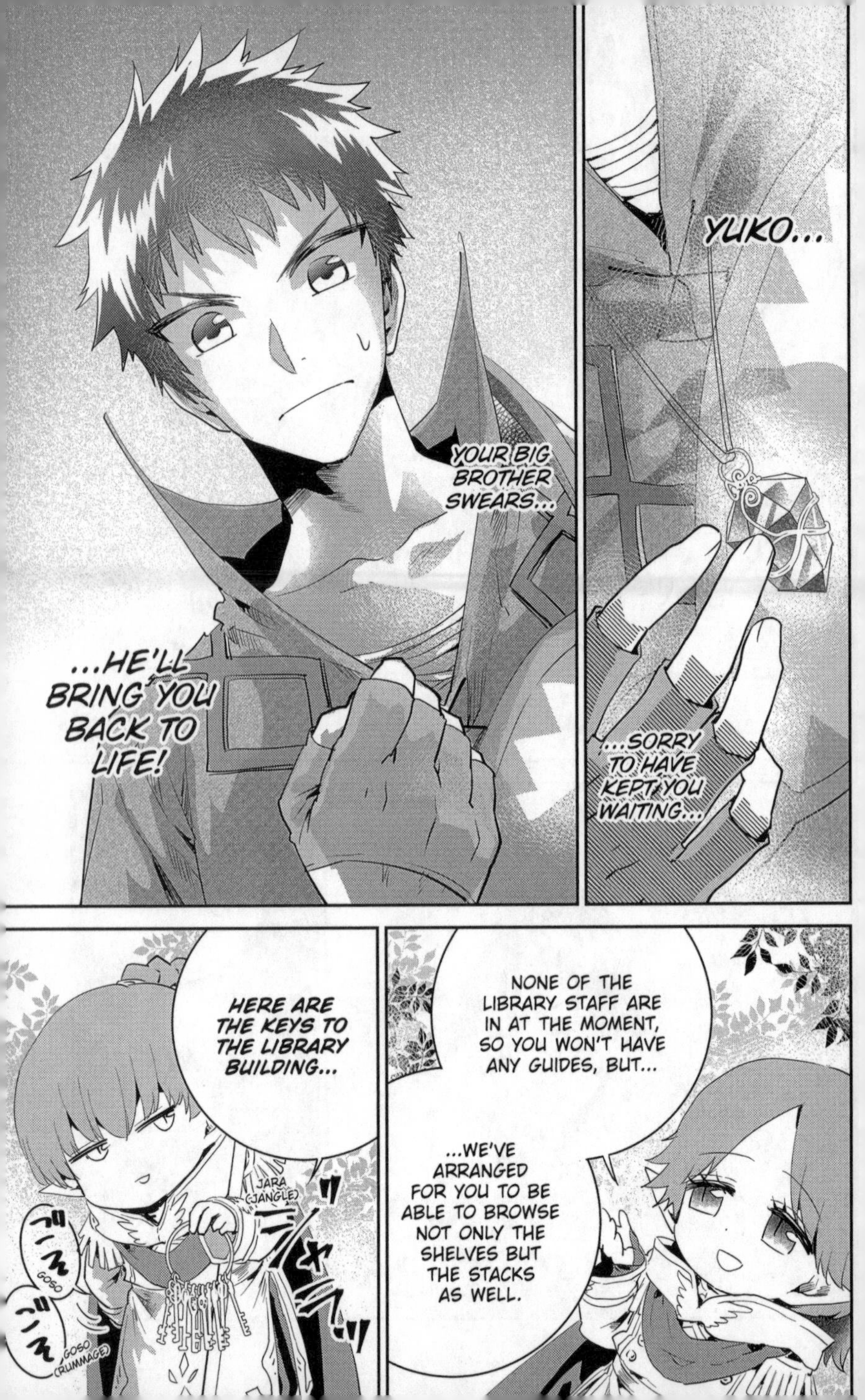
YUKO...
...SORRY TO HAVE KEPT YOU WAITING...
YOUR BIG BROTHER SWEARS...
...HE'LL BRING YOU BACK TO LIFE!
NONE OF THE LIBRARY STAFF ARE IN AT THE MOMENT, SO YOU WON'T HAVE ANY GUIDES, BUT...
...WE'VE ARRANGED FOR YOU TO BE ABLE TO BROWSE NOT ONLY THE SHELVES BUT THE STACKS AS WELL.
HERE ARE THE KEYS TO THE LIBRARY BUILDING...
JARA (JANGLE)
GOSO
GOSO (RUMMAGE)

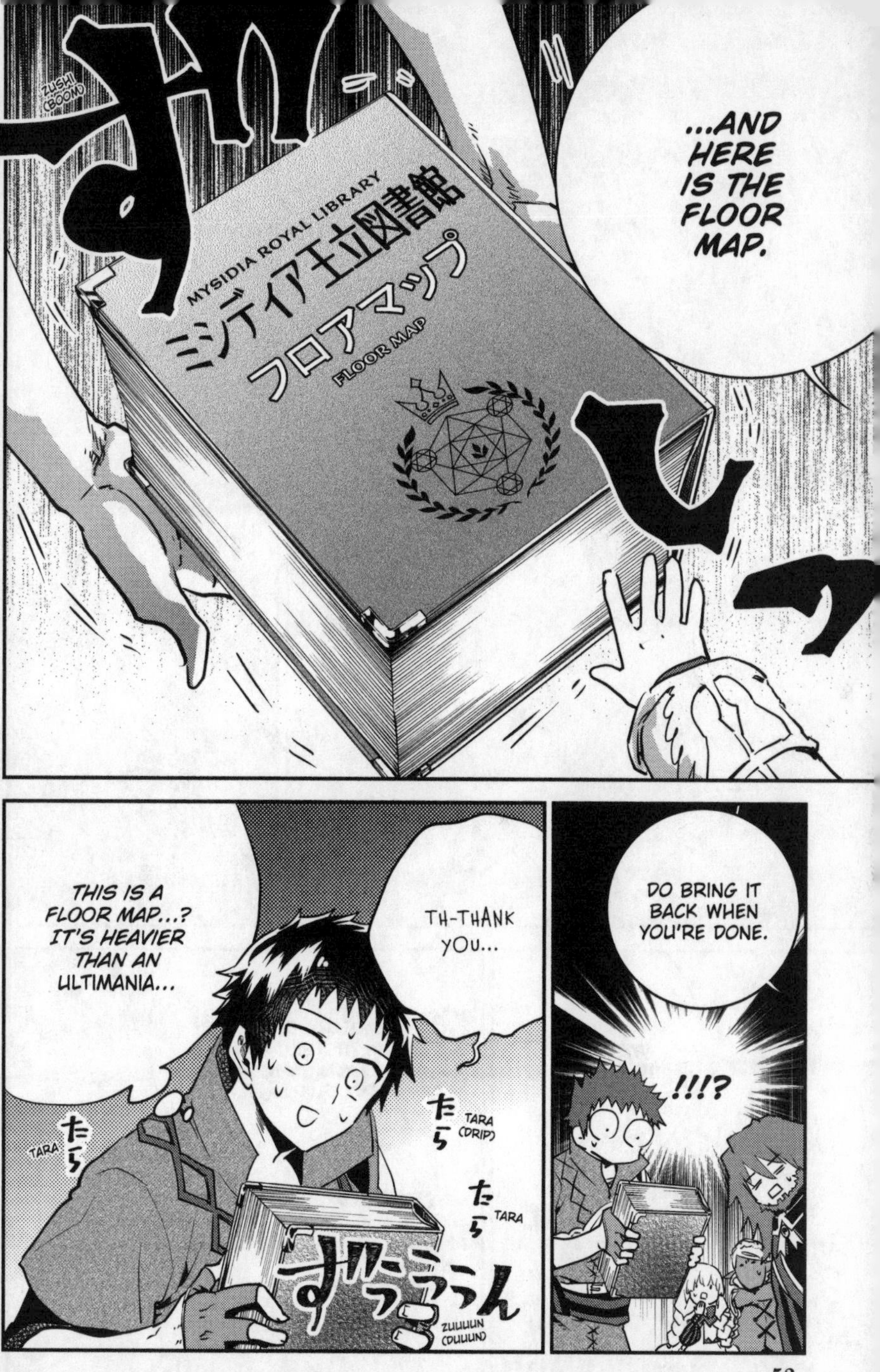
...AND HERE IS THE FLOOR MAP.
MYSIDIA ROYAL LIBRARY
ミシディア王立図書館
フロアマップ
FLOOR MAP
ZUSHI (BOOM)
DO BRING IT BACK WHEN YOU'RE DONE.
!!!?
TH-THANK YOU...
THIS IS A FLOOR MAP...? IT'S HEAVIER THAN AN ULTIMANIA...
たら
TARA (DRIP)
たら
TARA
たら
TARA
ZUUUUN (DUUUN)

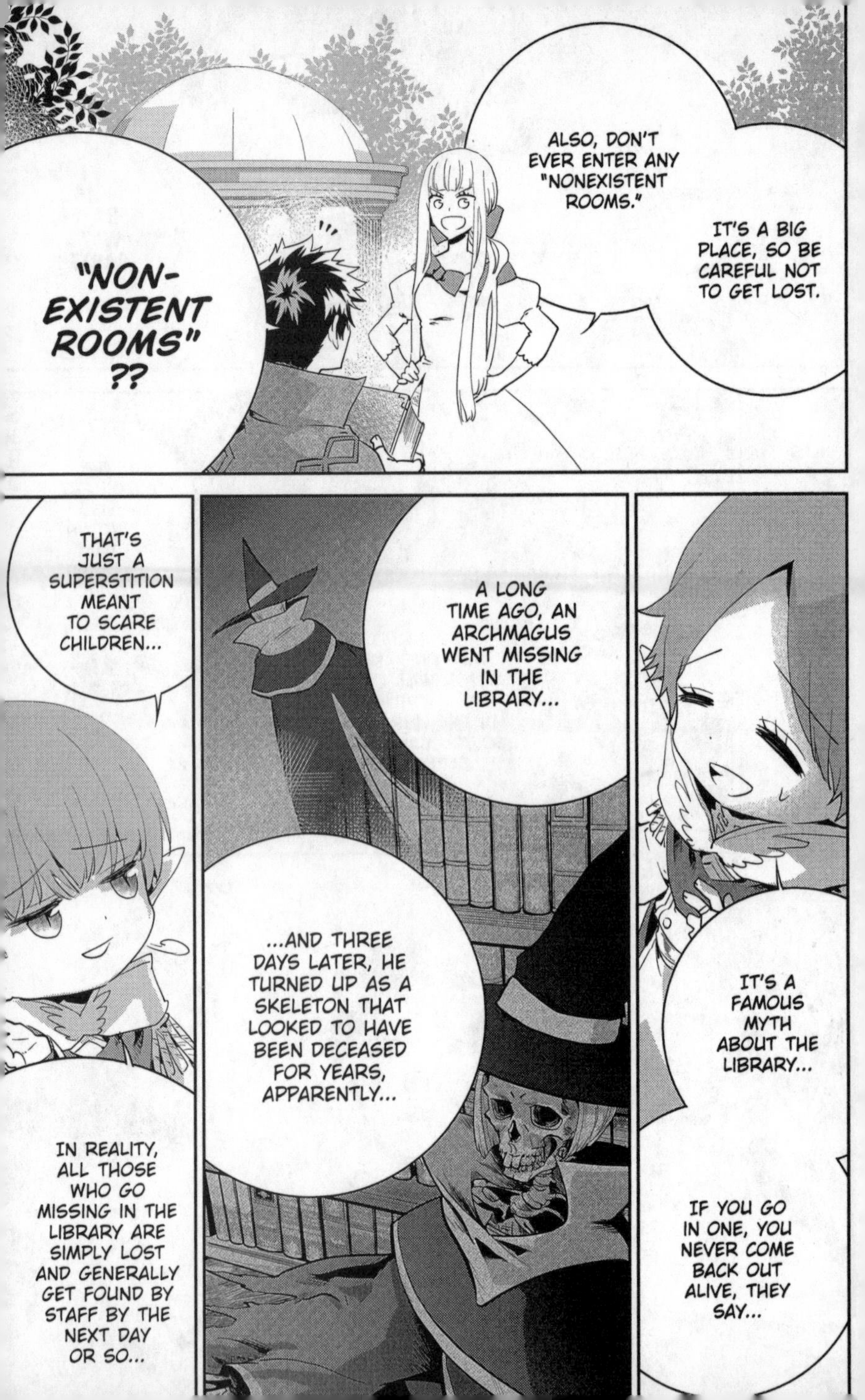

IT'S A BIG PLACE, SO BE CAREFUL NOT TO GET LOST.
ALSO, DON'T EVER ENTER ANY "NONEXISTENT ROOMS."
"NON-EXISTENT ROOMS" ??
IT'S A FAMOUS MYTH ABOUT THE LIBRARY...
IF YOU GO IN ONE, YOU NEVER COME BACK OUT ALIVE, THEY SAY...
A LONG TIME AGO, AN ARCHMAGUS WENT MISSING IN THE LIBRARY...
...AND THREE DAYS LATER, HE TURNED UP AS A SKELETON THAT LOOKED TO HAVE BEEN DECEASED FOR YEARS, APPARENTLY...
THAT'S JUST A SUPERSTITION MEANT TO SCARE CHILDREN...
IN REALITY, ALL THOSE WHO GO MISSING IN THE LIBRARY ARE SIMPLY LOST AND GENERALLY GET FOUND BY STAFF BY THE NEXT DAY OR SO...

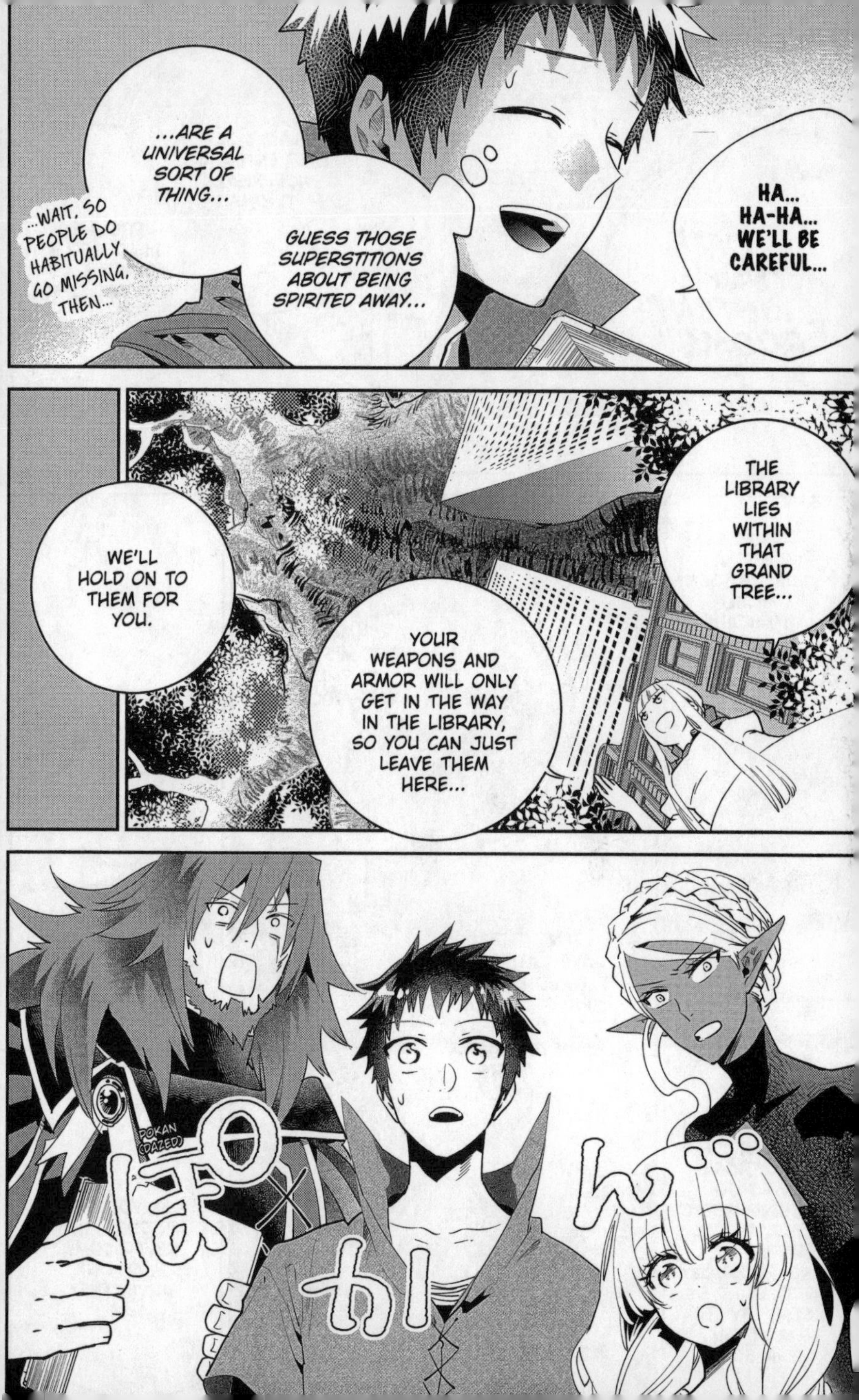
HA... HA-HA... WE'LL BE CAREFUL...
GUESS THOSE SUPERSTITIONS ABOUT BEING SPIRITED AWAY...
...ARE A UNIVERSAL SORT OF THING...
...WAIT, SO PEOPLE DO HABITUALLY GO MISSING, THEN...
THE LIBRARY LIES WITHIN THAT GRAND TREE...
YOUR WEAPONS AND ARMOR WILL ONLY GET IN THE WAY IN THE LIBRARY, SO YOU CAN JUST LEAVE THEM HERE...
WE'LL HOLD ON TO THEM FOR YOU.
ぽかーん…
POKAN (DAZED)

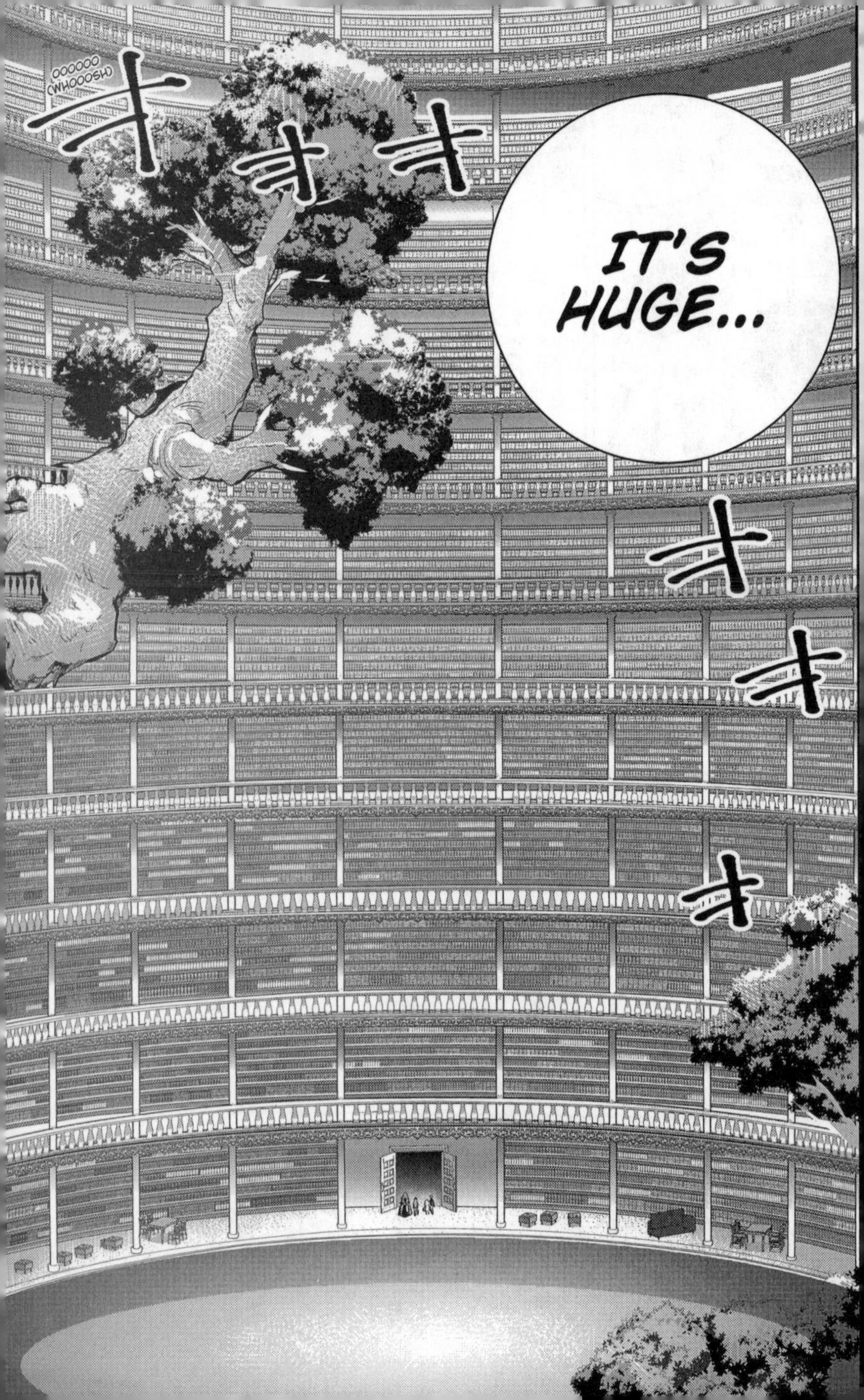
OOOOOO (WHOOOSH)
IT'S HUGE...

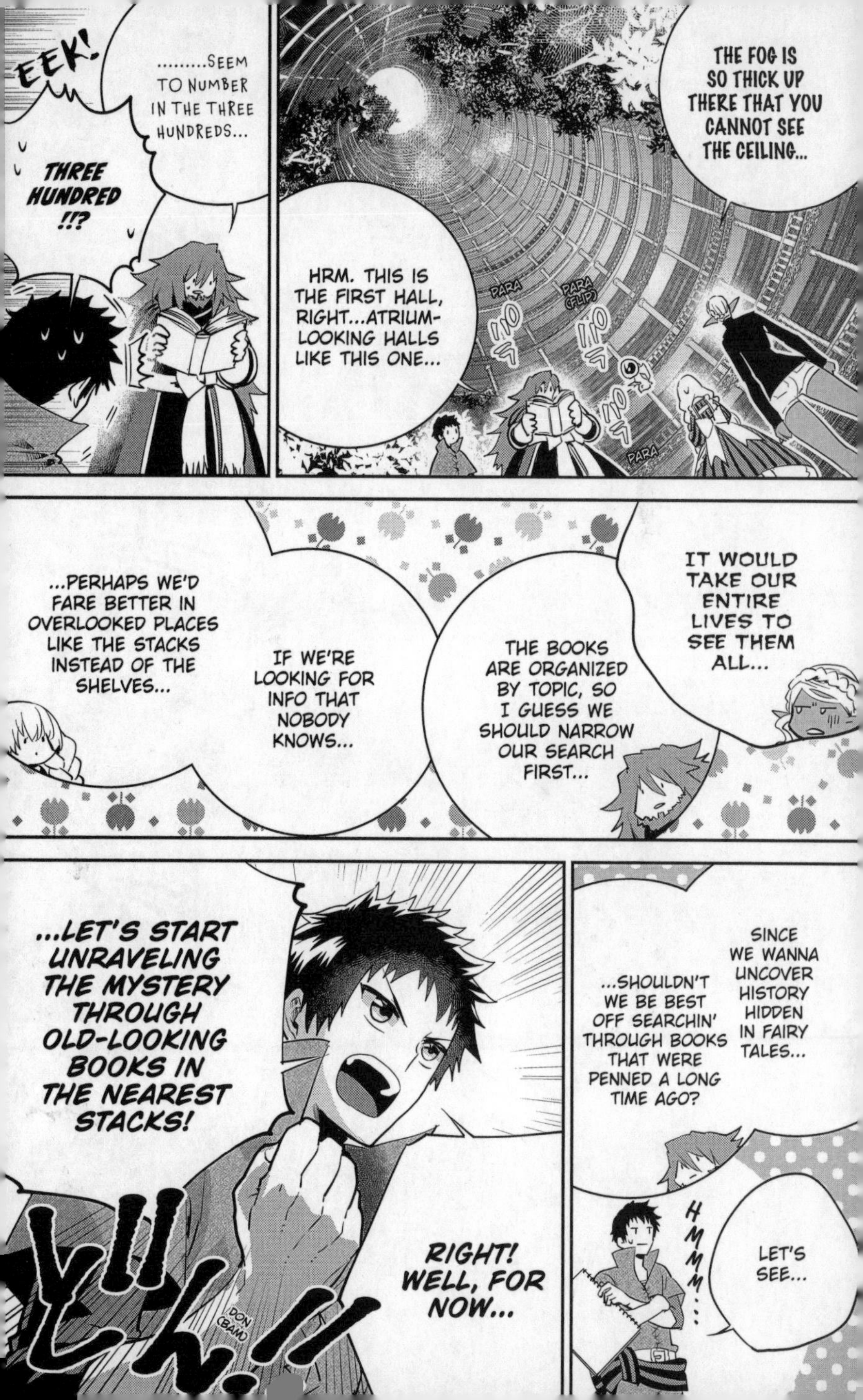
THE FOG IS SO THICK UP THERE THAT YOU CANNOT SEE THE CEILING...
HRM. THIS IS THE FIRST HALL, RIGHT...ATRIUM-LOOKING HALLS LIKE THIS ONE...
PARA
PARA (FLIP)
PARA
.........SEEM TO NUMBER IN THE THREE HUNDREDS...
EEK!
THREE HUNDRED !!?
IT WOULD TAKE OUR ENTIRE LIVES TO SEE THEM ALL...
THE BOOKS ARE ORGANIZED BY TOPIC, SO I GUESS WE SHOULD NARROW OUR SEARCH FIRST...
IF WE'RE LOOKING FOR INFO THAT NOBODY KNOWS...
...PERHAPS WE'D FARE BETTER IN OVERLOOKED PLACES LIKE THE STACKS INSTEAD OF THE SHELVES...
SINCE WE WANNA UNCOVER HISTORY HIDDEN IN FAIRY TALES...
...SHOULDN'T WE BE BEST OFF SEARCHIN' THROUGH BOOKS THAT WERE PENNED A LONG TIME AGO?
HMMM...
LET'S SEE...
RIGHT! WELL, FOR NOW...
...LET'S START UNRAVELING THE MYSTERY THROUGH OLD-LOOKING BOOKS IN THE NEAREST STACKS!
DON (BAM)

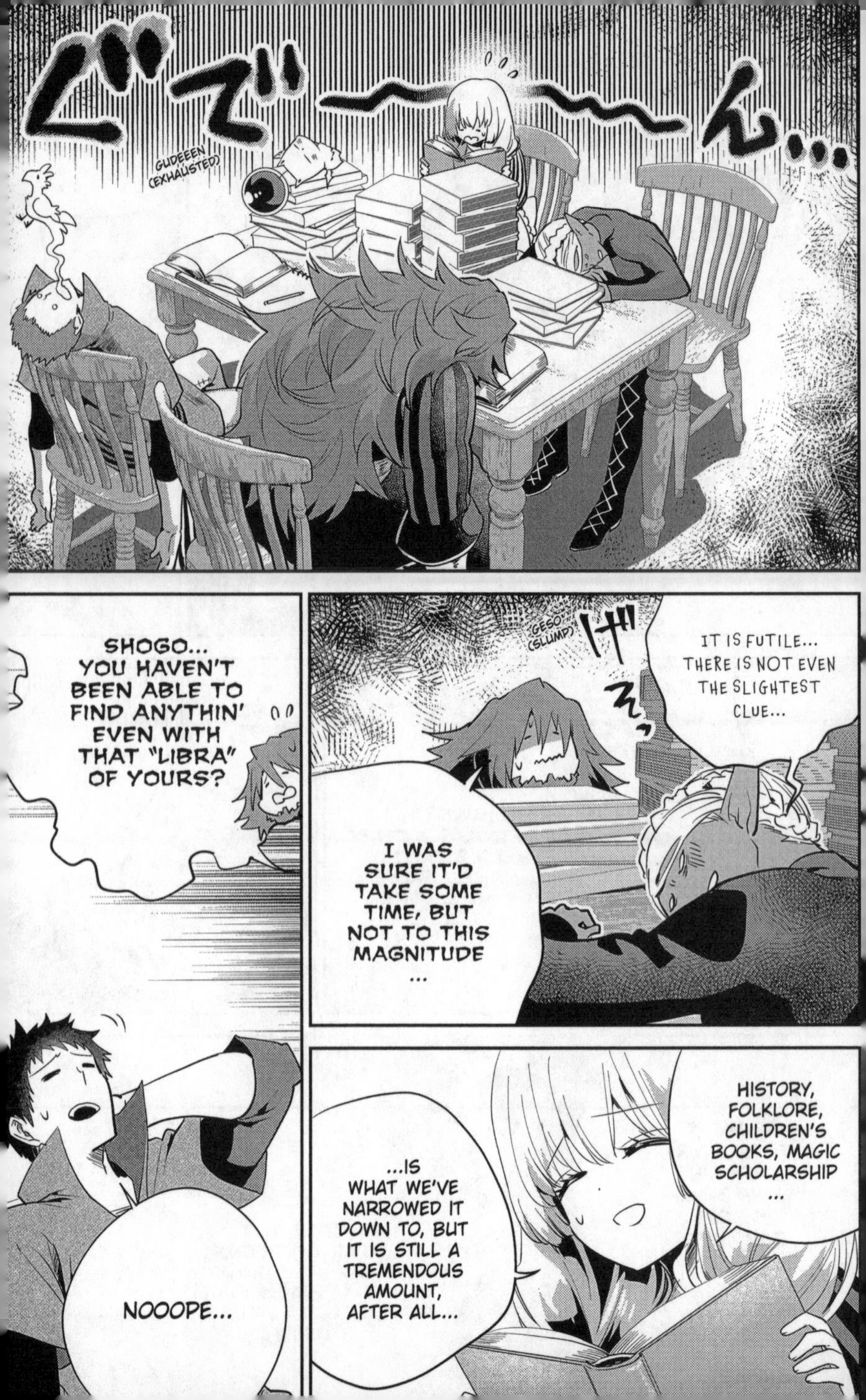
ぐでーーん…
GUDEEEN (EXHAUSTED)
GESO (SLUMP)
IT IS FUTILE... THERE IS NOT EVEN THE SLIGHTEST CLUE...
I WAS SURE IT'D TAKE SOME TIME, BUT NOT TO THIS MAGNITUDE ...
SHOGO... YOU HAVEN'T BEEN ABLE TO FIND ANYTHIN' EVEN WITH THAT "LIBRA" OF YOURS?
HISTORY, FOLKLORE, CHILDREN'S BOOKS, MAGIC SCHOLARSHIP ...
...IS WHAT WE'VE NARROWED IT DOWN TO, BUT IT IS STILL A TREMENDOUS AMOUNT, AFTER ALL...
NOOOPE...

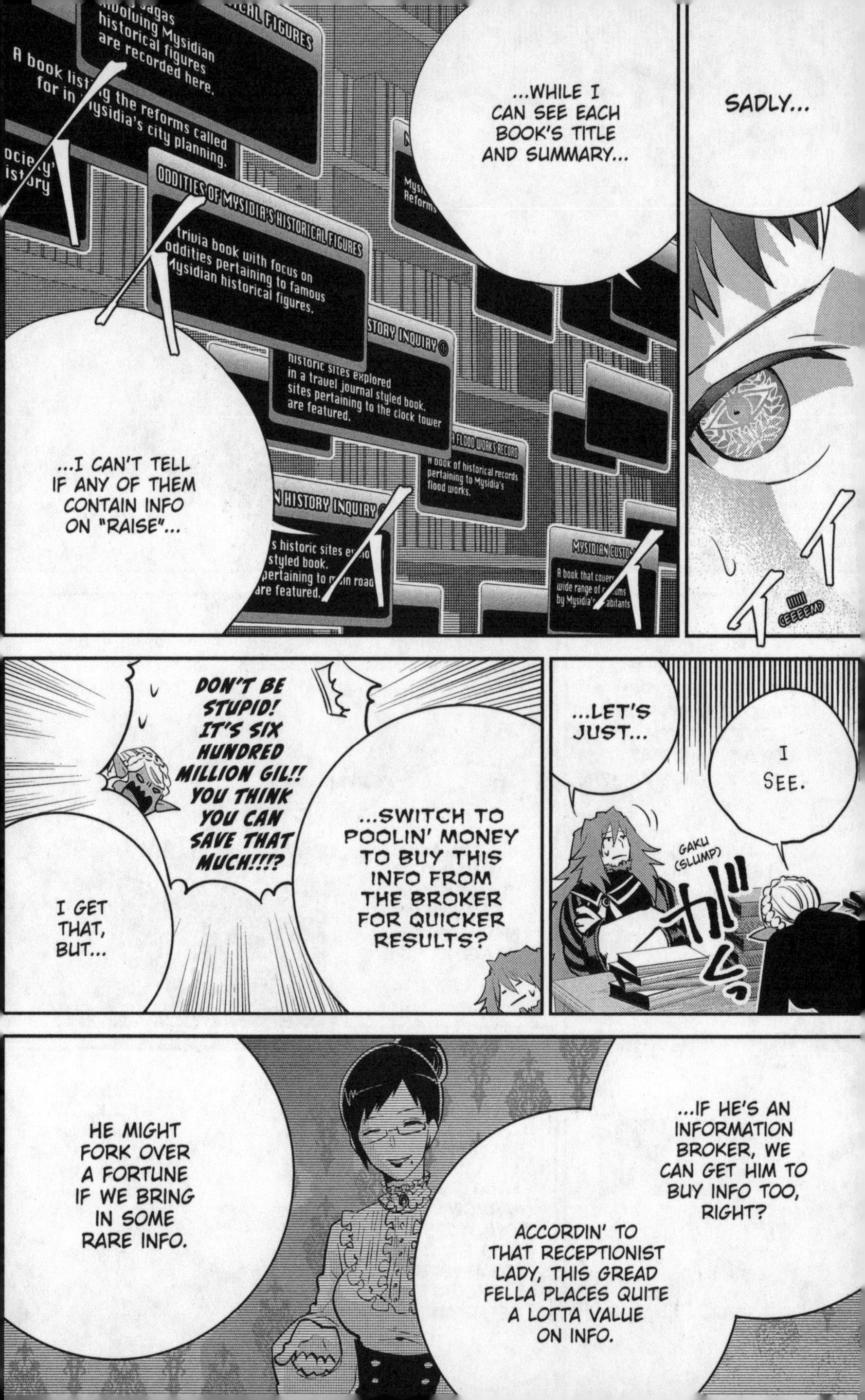
SADLY...
IIIII (EEEEEM)
...WHILE I CAN SEE EACH BOOK'S TITLE AND SUMMARY...
...volving Mysidian historical figures are recorded here.
A book listing the reforms called for in Mysidia's city planning.
ODDITIES OF MYSIDIA'S HISTORICAL FIGURES
trivia book with focus on oddities pertaining to famous Mysidian historical figures.
historic sites explored in a travel journal styled book. sites pertaining to the clock tower are featured.
FLOOD WORKS RECORD
A book of historical records pertaining to Mysidia's flood works.
...I CAN'T TELL IF ANY OF THEM CONTAIN INFO ON "RAISE"...
I SEE.
...LET'S JUST...
GAKU (SLUMP)
...SWITCH TO POOLIN' MONEY TO BUY THIS INFO FROM THE BROKER FOR QUICKER RESULTS?
DON'T BE STUPID! IT'S SIX HUNDRED MILLION GIL!! YOU THINK YOU CAN SAVE THAT MUCH!!!?
I GET THAT, BUT...
...IF HE'S AN INFORMATION BROKER, WE CAN GET HIM TO BUY INFO TOO, RIGHT?
ACCORDIN' TO THAT RECEPTIONIST LADY, THIS GREAD FELLA PLACES QUITE A LOTTA VALUE ON INFO.
HE MIGHT FORK OVER A FORTUNE IF WE BRING IN SOME RARE INFO.

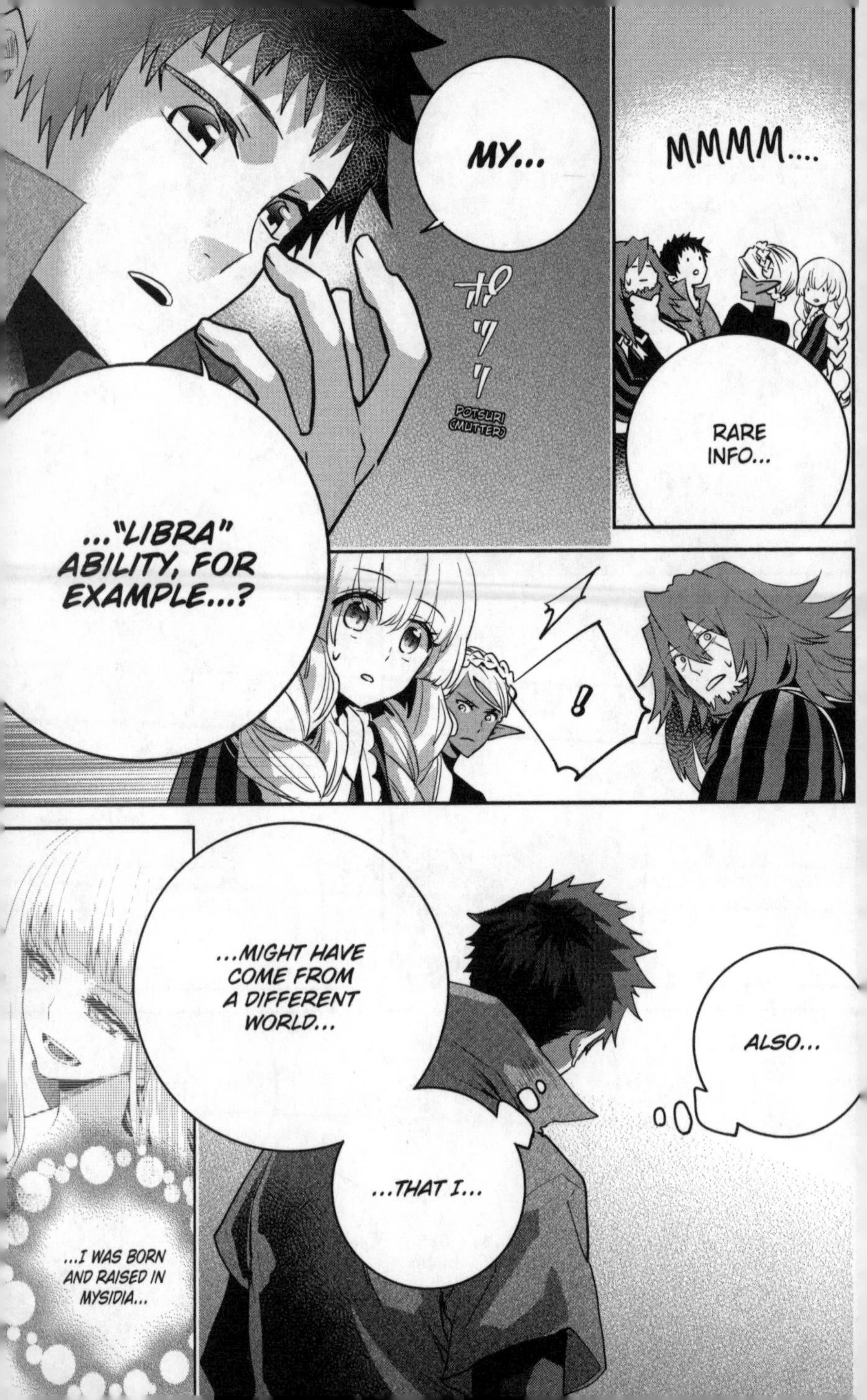
MMMM....
RARE INFO...
MY...
POTSURI (MUTTER)
..."LIBRA" ABILITY, FOR EXAMPLE...?
!
ALSO...
...MIGHT HAVE COME FROM A DIFFERENT WORLD...
...THAT I...
...I WAS BORN AND RAISED IN MYSIDIA...

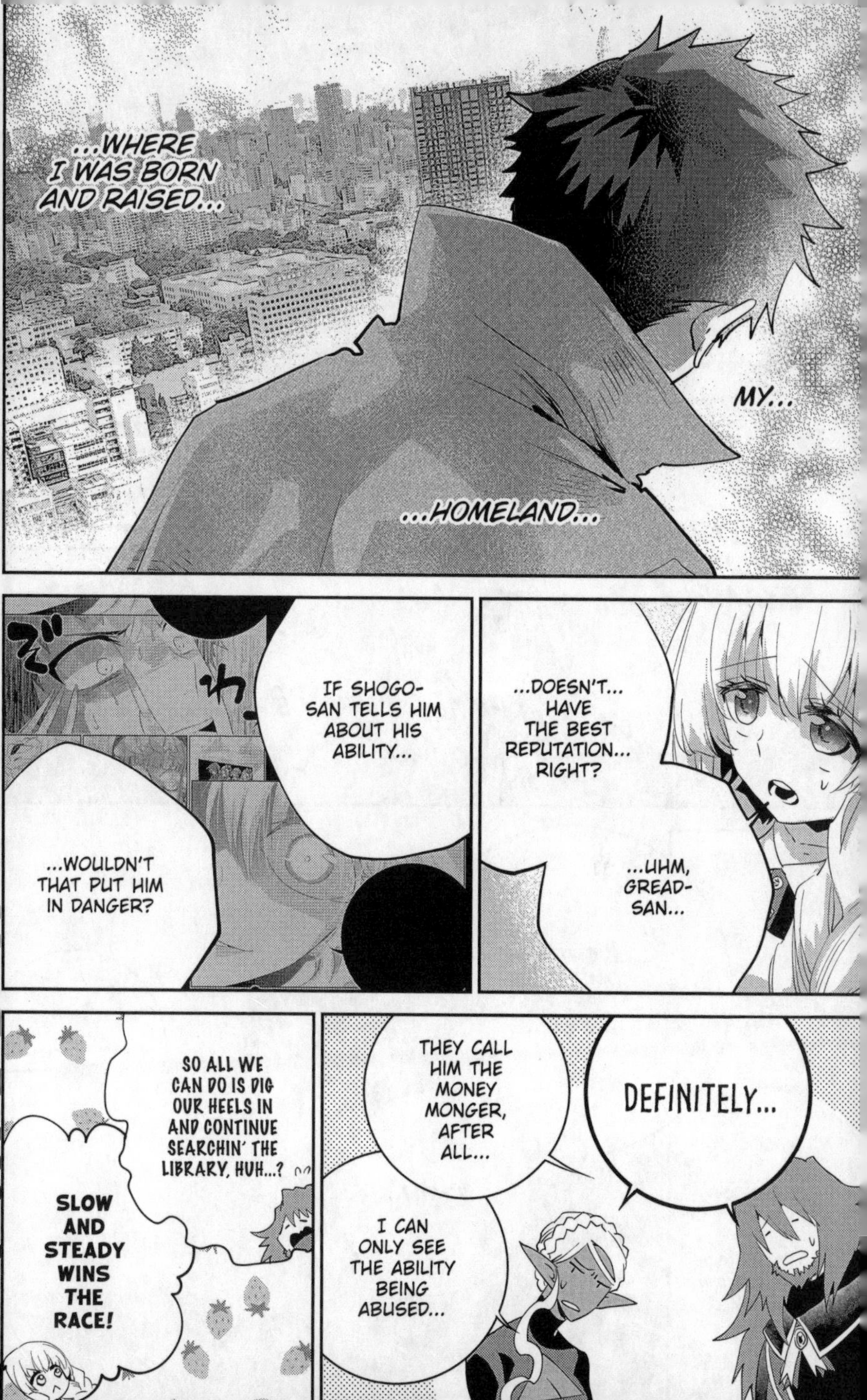
MY...
...HOMELAND...
...WHERE I WAS BORN AND RAISED...
...DOESN'T... HAVE THE BEST REPUTATION... RIGHT?
...UHM, GREAD-SAN...
IF SHOGO-SAN TELLS HIM ABOUT HIS ABILITY...
...WOULDN'T THAT PUT HIM IN DANGER?
DEFINITELY...
THEY CALL HIM THE MONEY MONGER, AFTER ALL...
I CAN ONLY SEE THE ABILITY BEING ABUSED...
SO ALL WE CAN DO IS DIG OUR HEELS IN AND CONTINUE SEARCHIN' THE LIBRARY, HUH...?
SLOW AND STEADY WINS THE RACE!

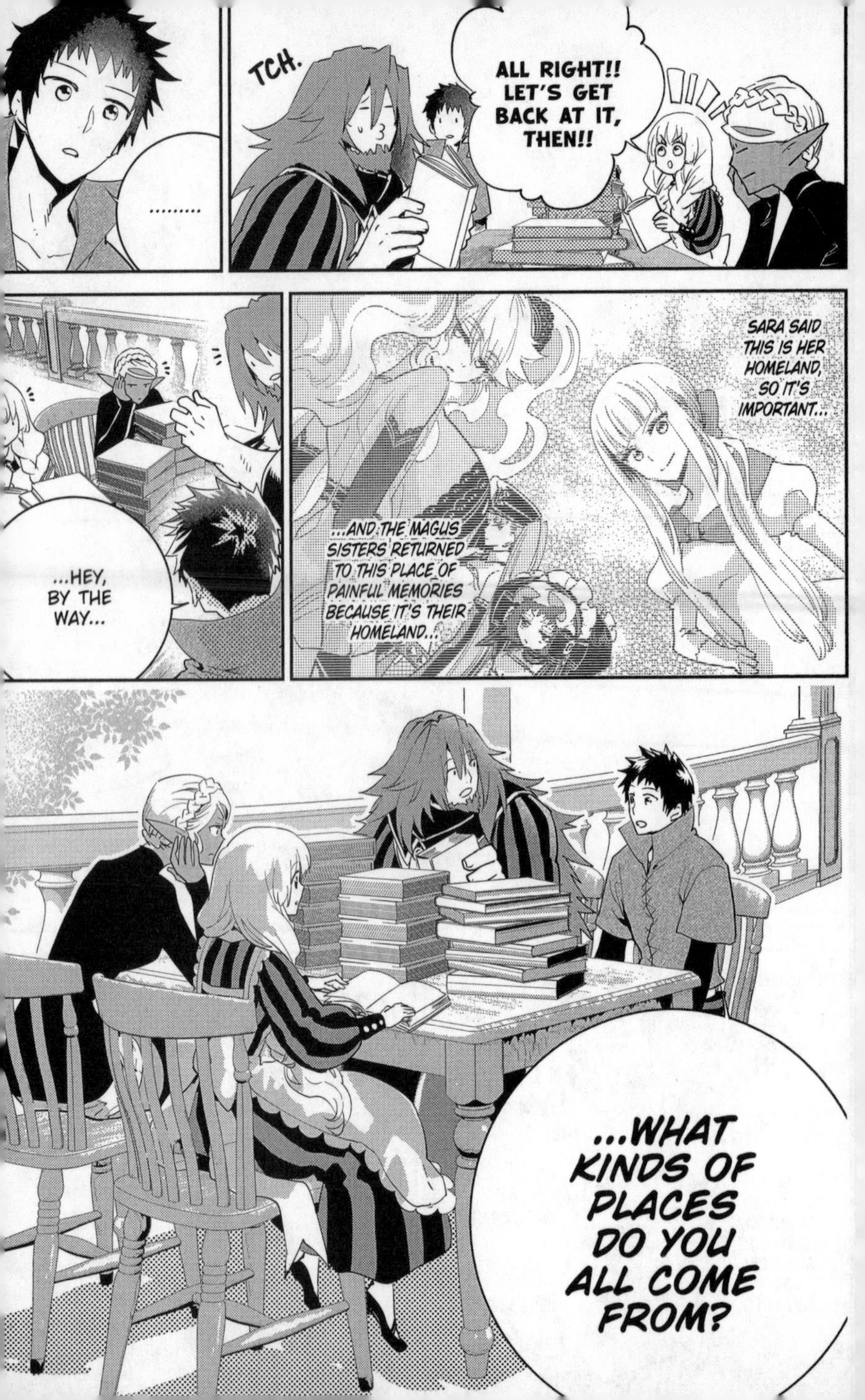
ALL RIGHT!! LET'S GET BACK AT IT, THEN!!
TCH.
.........
SARA SAID THIS IS HER HOMELAND, SO IT'S IMPORTANT...
...AND THE MAGUS SISTERS RETURNED TO THIS PLACE OF PAINFUL MEMORIES BECAUSE IT'S THEIR HOMELAND...
...HEY, BY THE WAY...
...WHAT KINDS OF PLACES DO YOU ALL COME FROM?

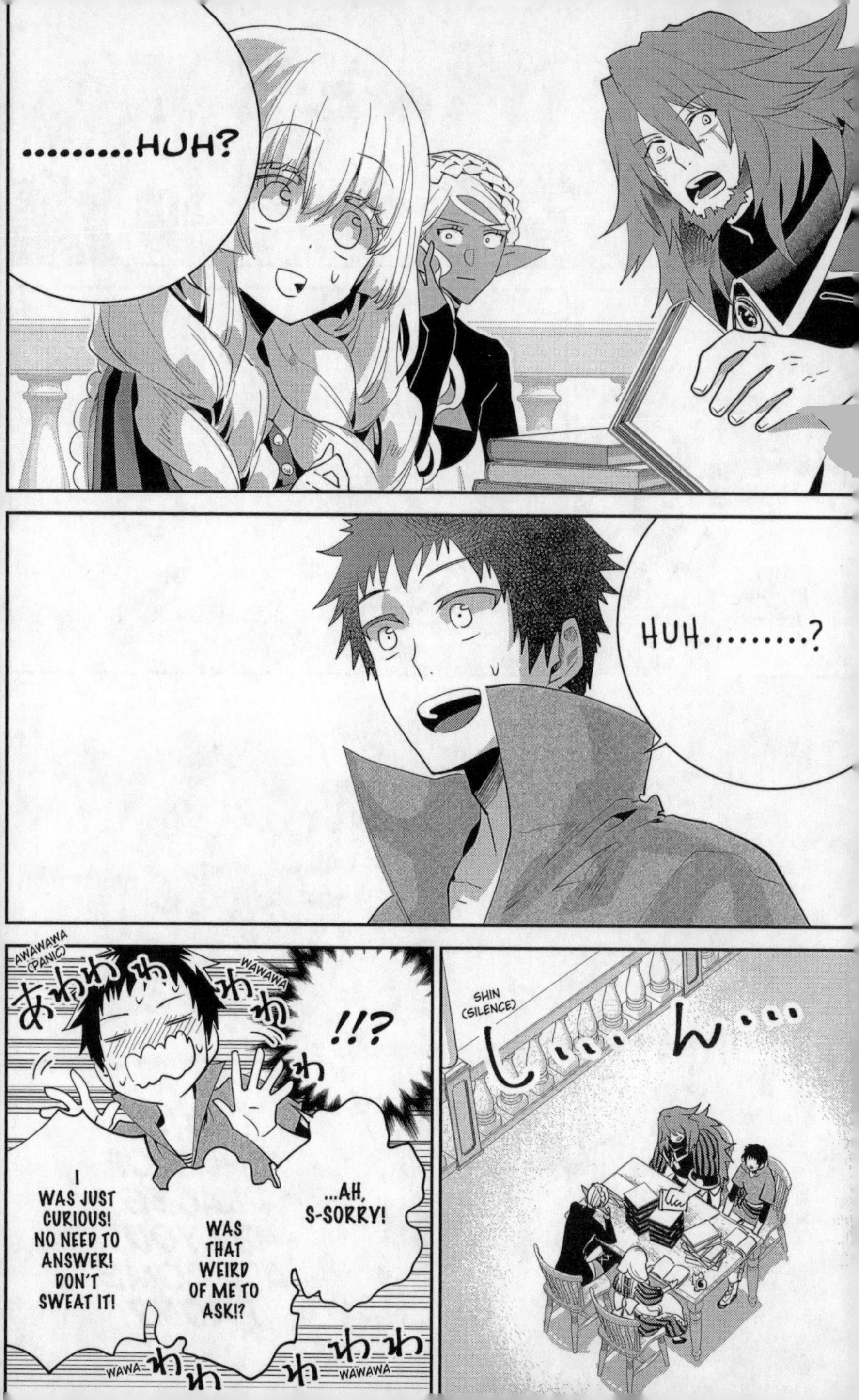
.........HUH?
HUH.........?
SHIN (SILENCE)
AWAWAWA (PANIC)
WAWAWA
!!?
...AH, S-SORRY!
WAS THAT WEIRD OF ME TO ASK!?
I WAS JUST CURIOUS! NO NEED TO ANSWER! DON'T SWEAT IT!
WAWAWA
WAWA

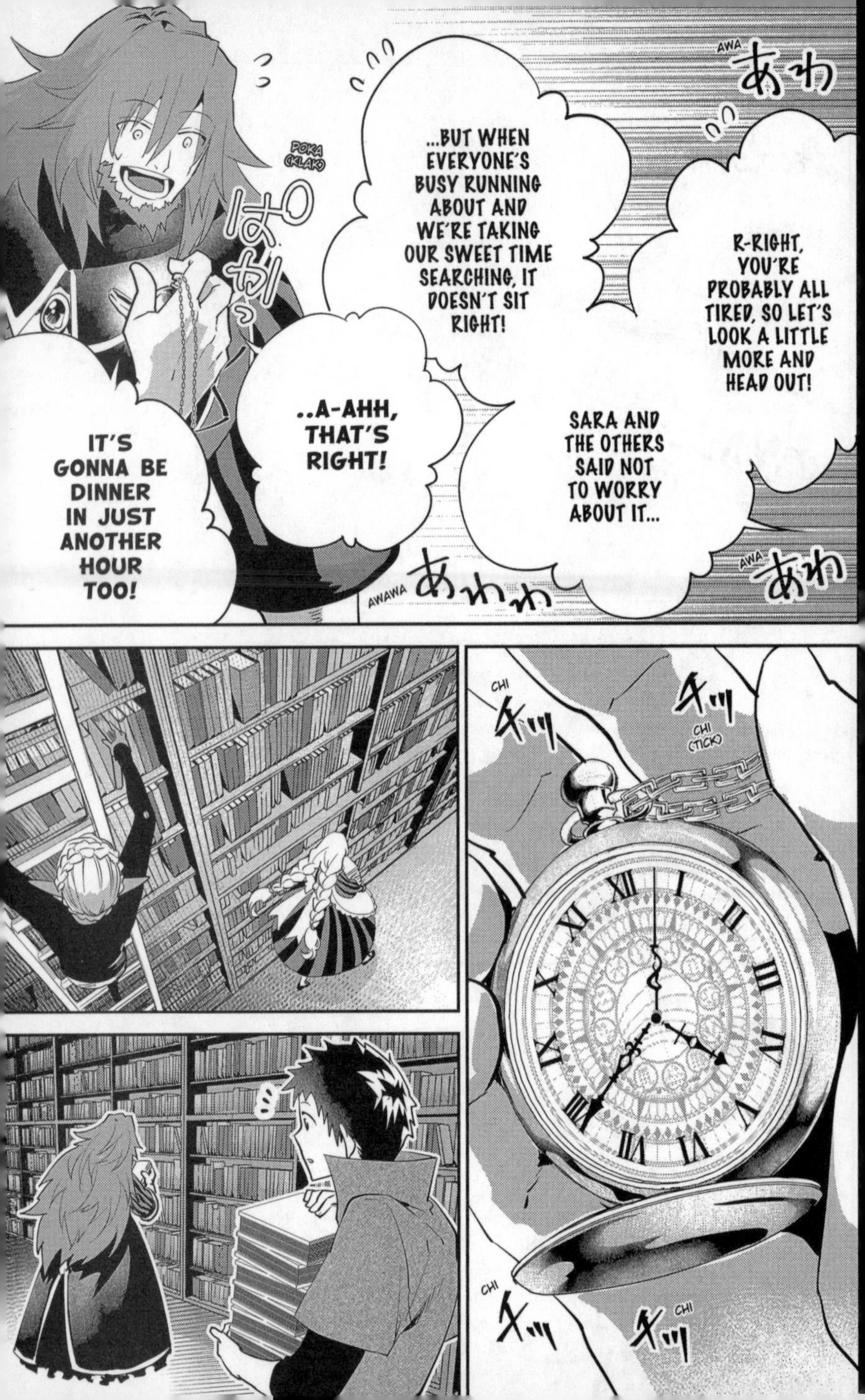
AWA あわ
R-RIGHT, YOU'RE PROBABLY ALL TIRED, SO LET'S LOOK A LITTLE MORE AND HEAD OUT!
...BUT WHEN EVERYONE'S BUSY RUNNING ABOUT AND WE'RE TAKING OUR SWEET TIME SEARCHING, IT DOESN'T SIT RIGHT!
POKA (KLAK) ぱかっ
SARA AND THE OTHERS SAID NOT TO WORRY ABOUT IT...
AWA あわ
AWAWA あわわ
..A-AHH, THAT'S RIGHT!
IT'S GONNA BE DINNER IN JUST ANOTHER HOUR TOO!
CHI チッ
CHI (TICK) チッ
CHI チッ
CHI チッ

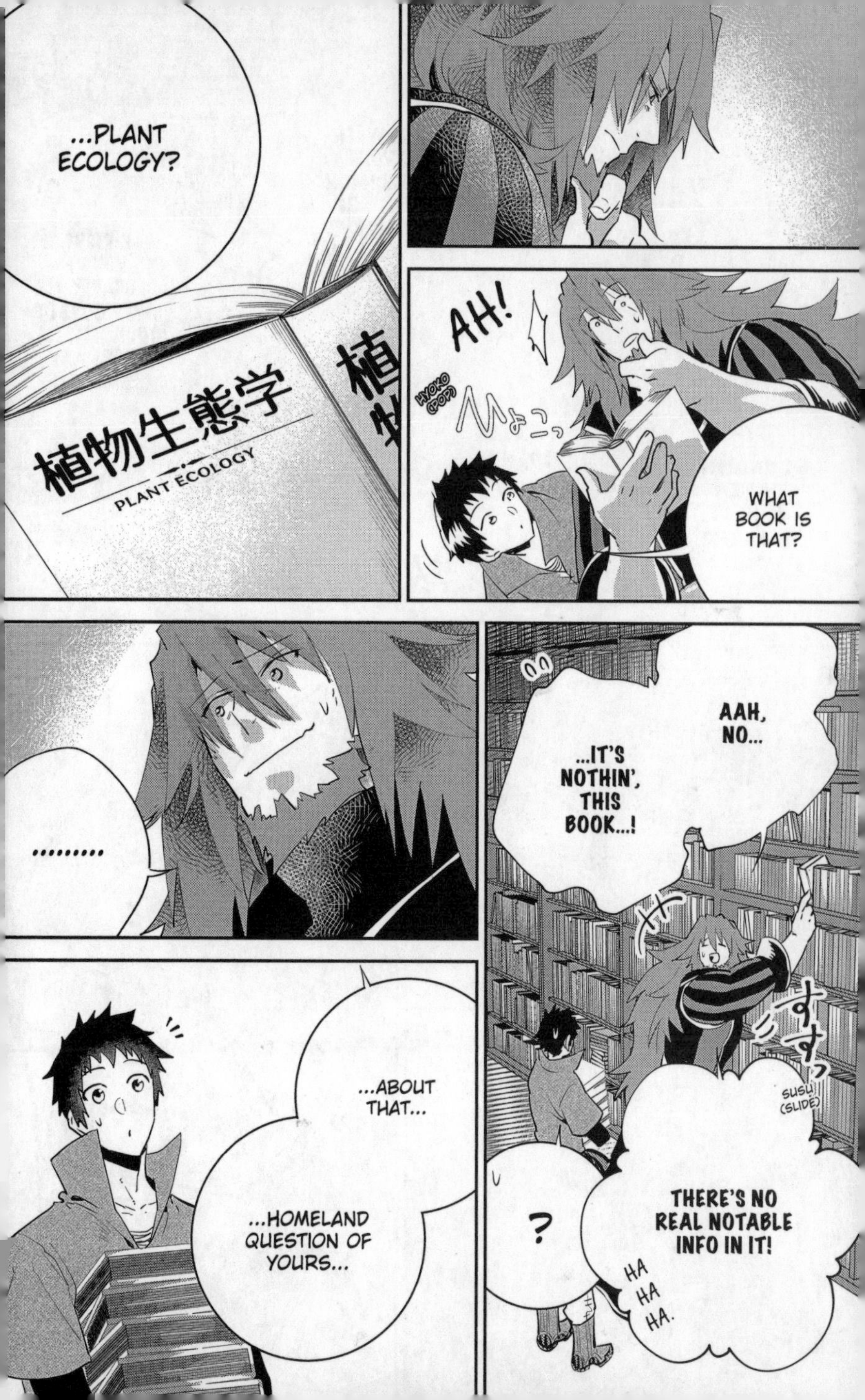

AH!
WHAT BOOK IS THAT?
HYOKO (POP)
...PLANT ECOLOGY?
植物生態学
PLANT ECOLOGY
AAH, NO...
...IT'S NOTHIN', THIS BOOK...!
SUSU (SLIDE)
THERE'S NO REAL NOTABLE INFO IN IT!
HA HA HA.
?
.........
...ABOUT THAT...
...HOMELAND QUESTION OF YOURS...

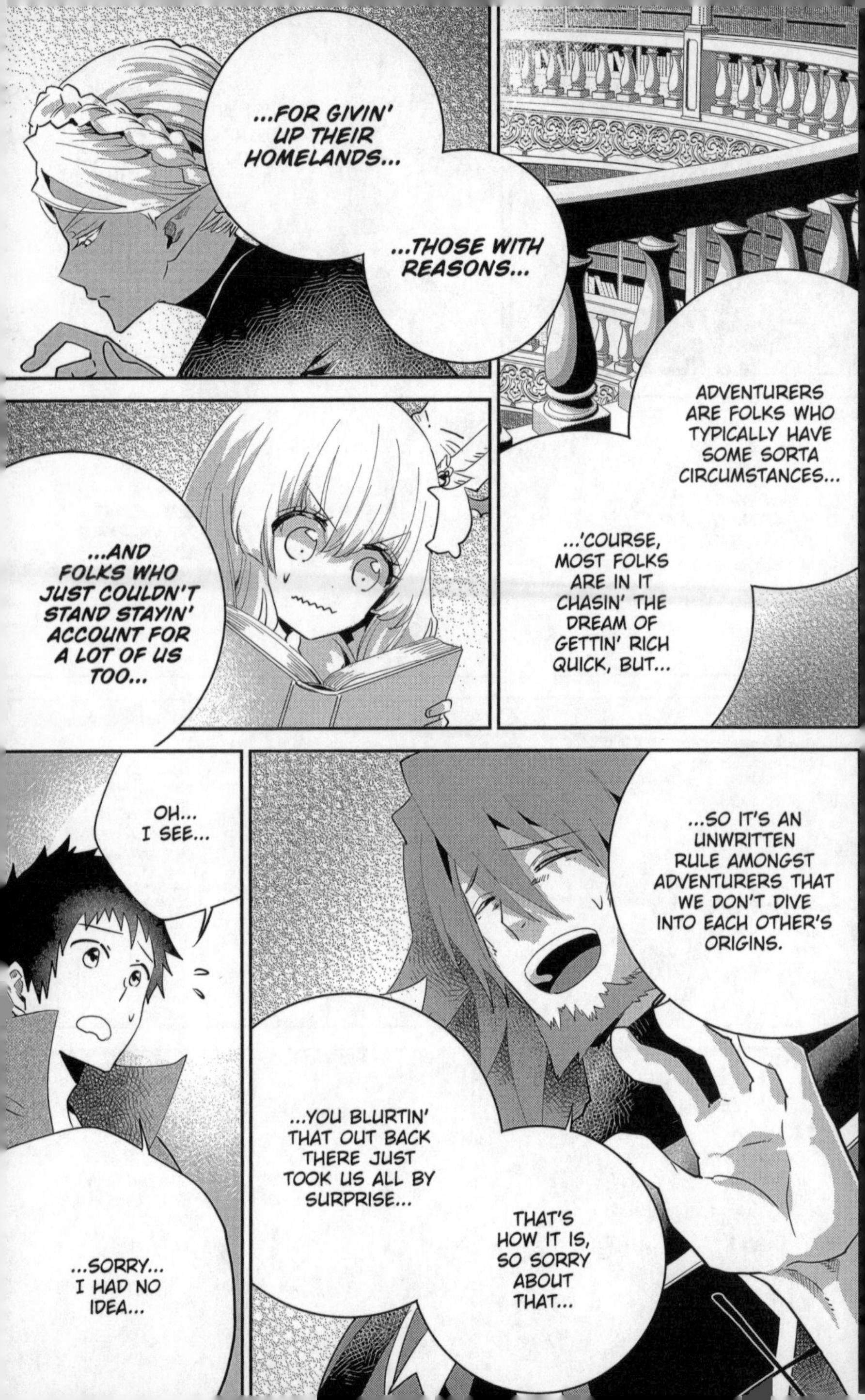
ADVENTURERS ARE FOLKS WHO TYPICALLY HAVE SOME SORTA CIRCUMSTANCES...
...'COURSE, MOST FOLKS ARE IN IT CHASIN' THE DREAM OF GETTIN' RICH QUICK, BUT...
...THOSE WITH REASONS...
...FOR GIVIN' UP THEIR HOMELANDS...
...AND FOLKS WHO JUST COULDN'T STAND STAYIN' ACCOUNT FOR A LOT OF US TOO...
...SO IT'S AN UNWRITTEN RULE AMONGST ADVENTURERS THAT WE DON'T DIVE INTO EACH OTHER'S ORIGINS.
THAT'S HOW IT IS, SO SORRY ABOUT THAT...
...YOU BLURTIN' THAT OUT BACK THERE JUST TOOK US ALL BY SURPRISE...
OH... I SEE...
...SORRY... I HAD NO IDEA...

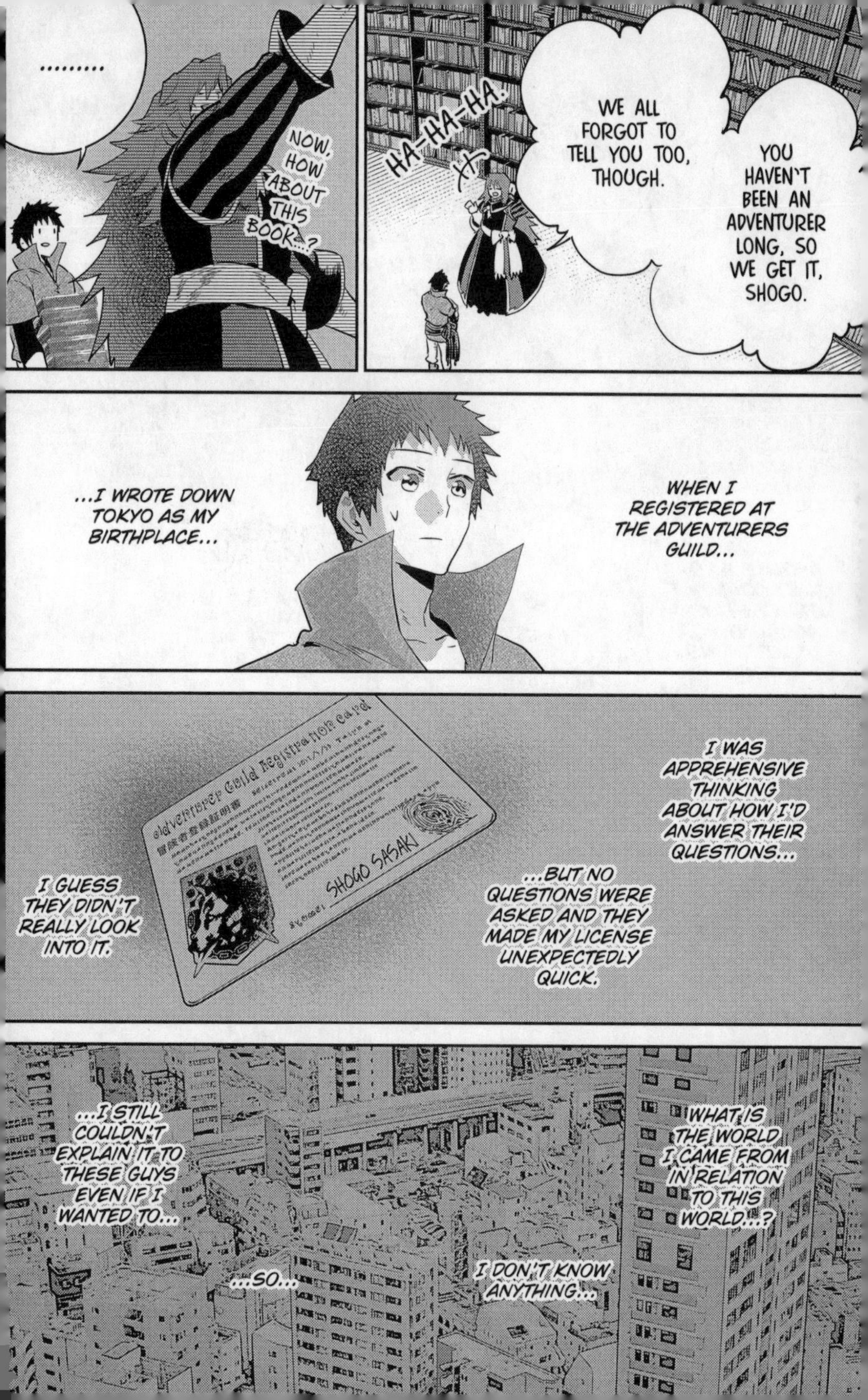
YOU HAVEN'T BEEN AN ADVENTURER LONG, SO WE GET IT, SHOGO.
WE ALL FORGOT TO TELL YOU TOO, THOUGH.
HA-HA-HA.
........
NOW, HOW ABOUT THIS BOOK...?
WHEN I REGISTERED AT THE ADVENTURERS GUILD...
...I WROTE DOWN TOKYO AS MY BIRTHPLACE...
Adventurer Guild Registration Card
SHOGO SASAKI
I WAS APPREHENSIVE THINKING ABOUT HOW I'D ANSWER THEIR QUESTIONS...
...BUT NO QUESTIONS WERE ASKED AND THEY MADE MY LICENSE UNEXPECTEDLY QUICK.
I GUESS THEY DIDN'T REALLY LOOK INTO IT.
WHAT IS THE WORLD I CAME FROM IN RELATION TO THIS WORLD...?
I DON'T KNOW ANYTHING...
...SO...
...I STILL COULDN'T EXPLAIN IT TO THESE GUYS EVEN IF I WANTED TO...

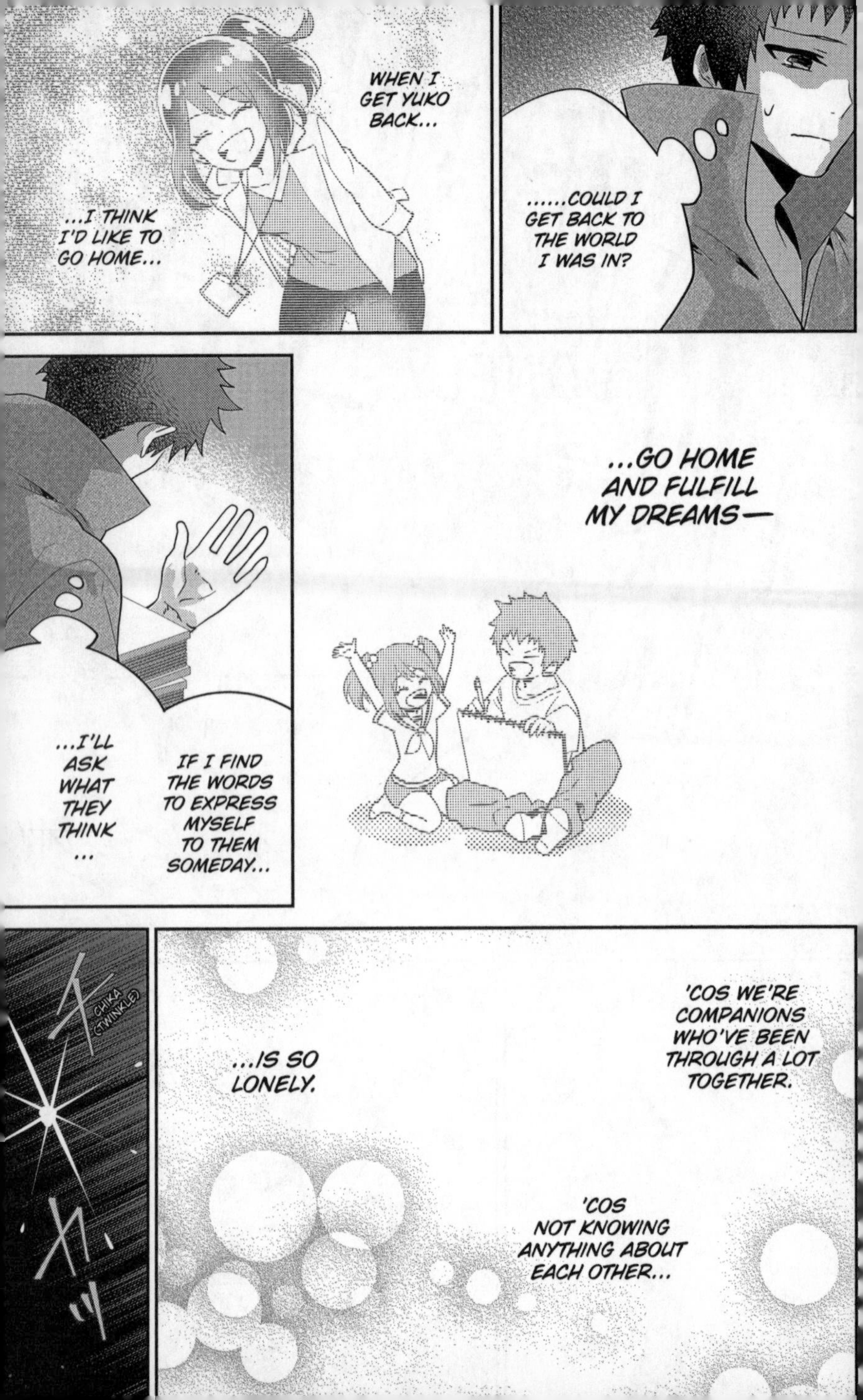
......COULD I GET BACK TO THE WORLD I WAS IN?
WHEN I GET YUKO BACK...
...I THINK I'D LIKE TO GO HOME...
...GO HOME AND FULFILL MY DREAMS—
IF I FIND THE WORDS TO EXPRESS MYSELF TO THEM SOMEDAY...
...I'LL ASK WHAT THEY THINK...
'COS WE'RE COMPANIONS WHO'VE BEEN THROUGH A LOT TOGETHER.
'COS NOT KNOWING ANYTHING ABOUT EACH OTHER...
...IS SO LONELY.
CHIKA (TWINKLE)

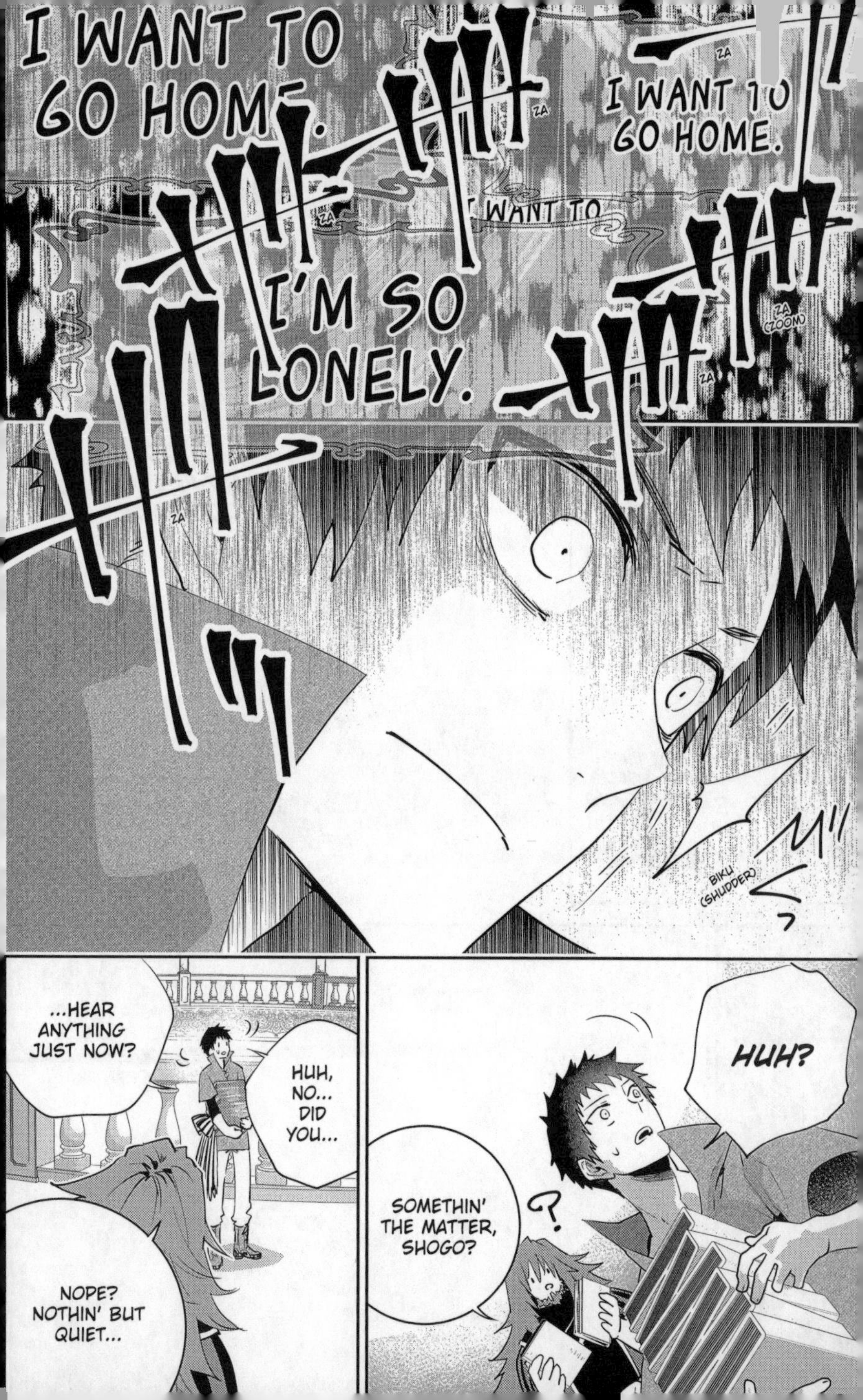
ZA
I WANT TO GO HOME.
ZA
I WANT TO
ZA
I'M SO LONELY.
ZA
I WANT TO GO HOME.
ZA (ZOOM)
ZA
ZA
BIKU (SHUDDER)
HUH?
SOMETHIN' THE MATTER, SHOGO?
HUH, NO... DID YOU...
...HEAR ANYTHING JUST NOW?
NOPE? NOTHIN' BUT QUIET...

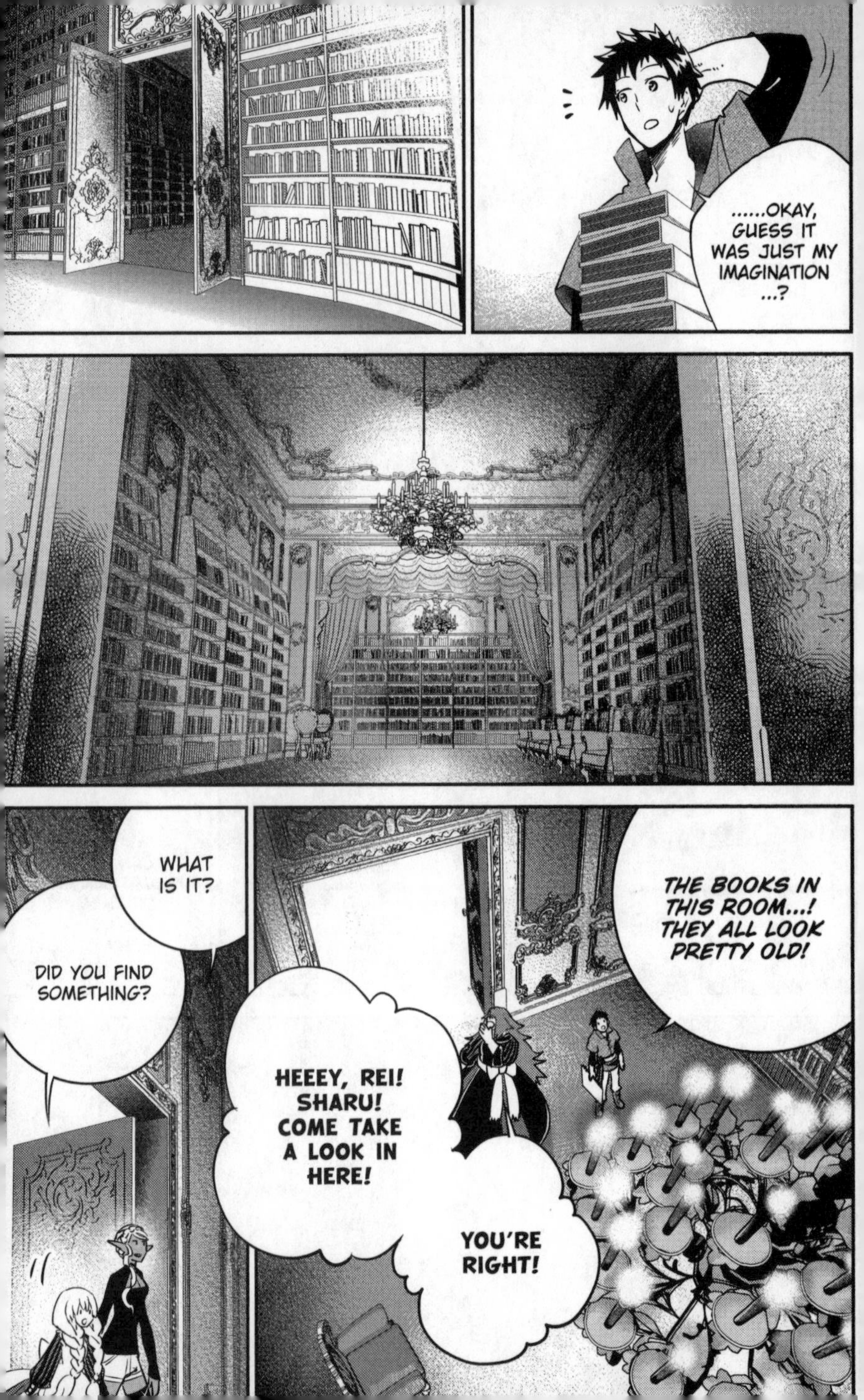
......OKAY, GUESS IT WAS JUST MY IMAGINATION ...?
THE BOOKS IN THIS ROOM...! THEY ALL LOOK PRETTY OLD!
HEEEY, REI! SHARU! COME TAKE A LOOK IN HERE!
YOU'RE RIGHT!
WHAT IS IT?
DID YOU FIND SOMETHING?

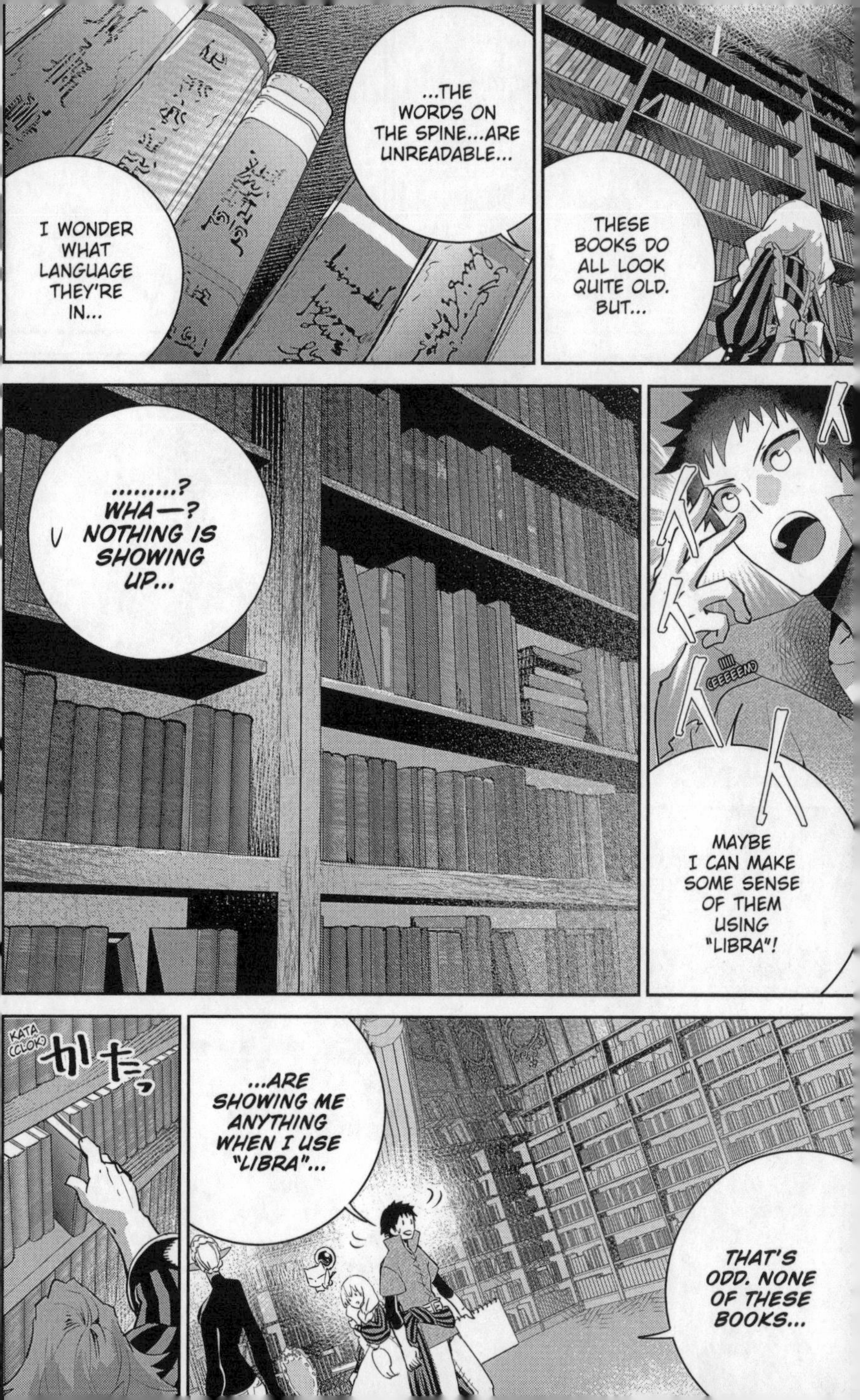
THESE BOOKS DO ALL LOOK QUITE OLD. BUT...
...THE WORDS ON THE SPINE...ARE UNREADABLE...
I WONDER WHAT LANGUAGE THEY'RE IN...
MAYBE I CAN MAKE SOME SENSE OF THEM USING "LIBRA"!
.........? WHA—? NOTHING IS SHOWING UP...
THAT'S ODD. NONE OF THESE BOOKS...
...ARE SHOWING ME ANYTHING WHEN I USE "LIBRA"...
KATA (CLOK)
かたっ

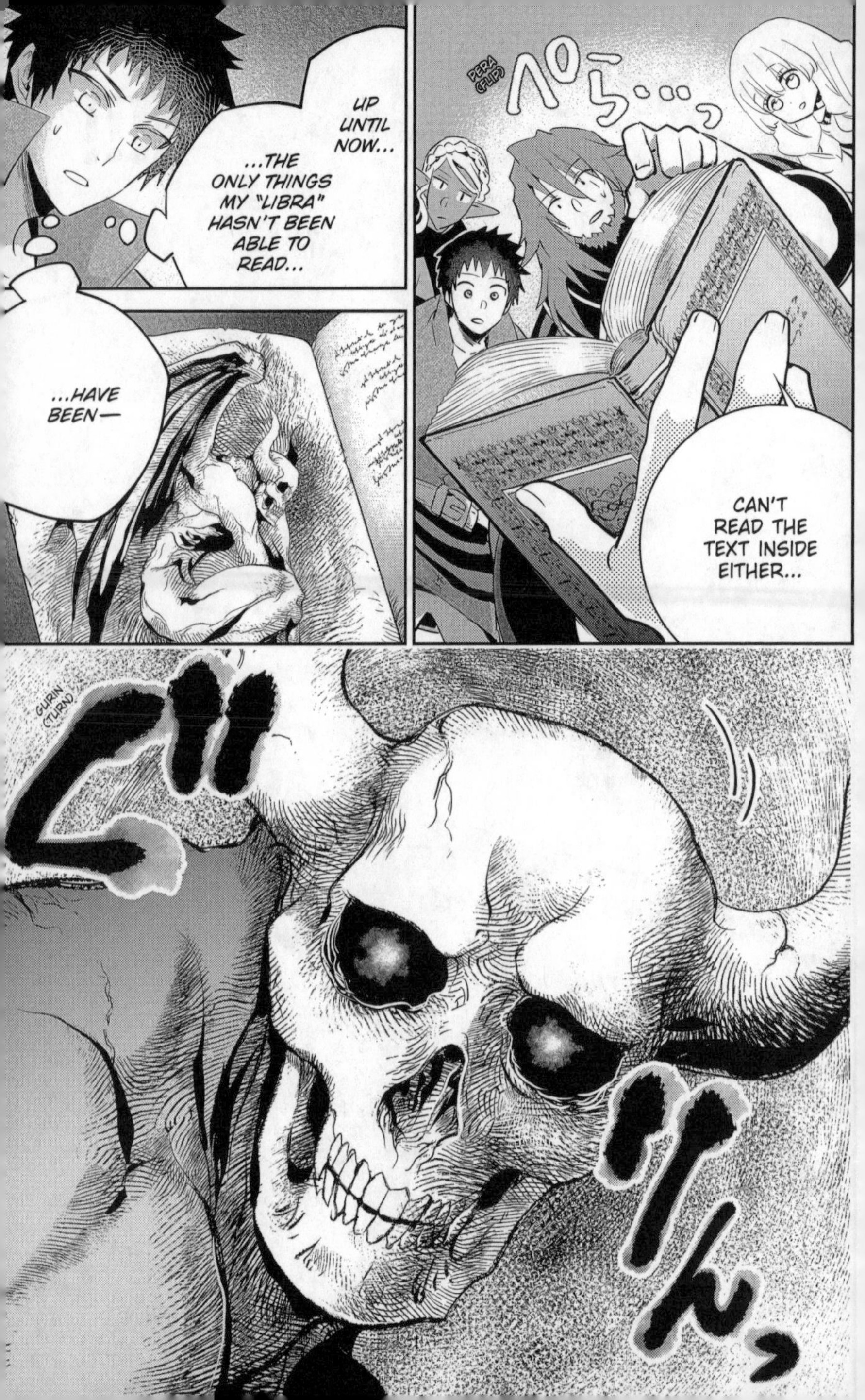
PERA (FLIP)
CAN'T READ THE TEXT INSIDE EITHER...
UP UNTIL NOW...
...THE ONLY THINGS MY "LIBRA" HASN'T BEEN ABLE TO READ...
...HAVE BEEN—
GURIN (TURN)

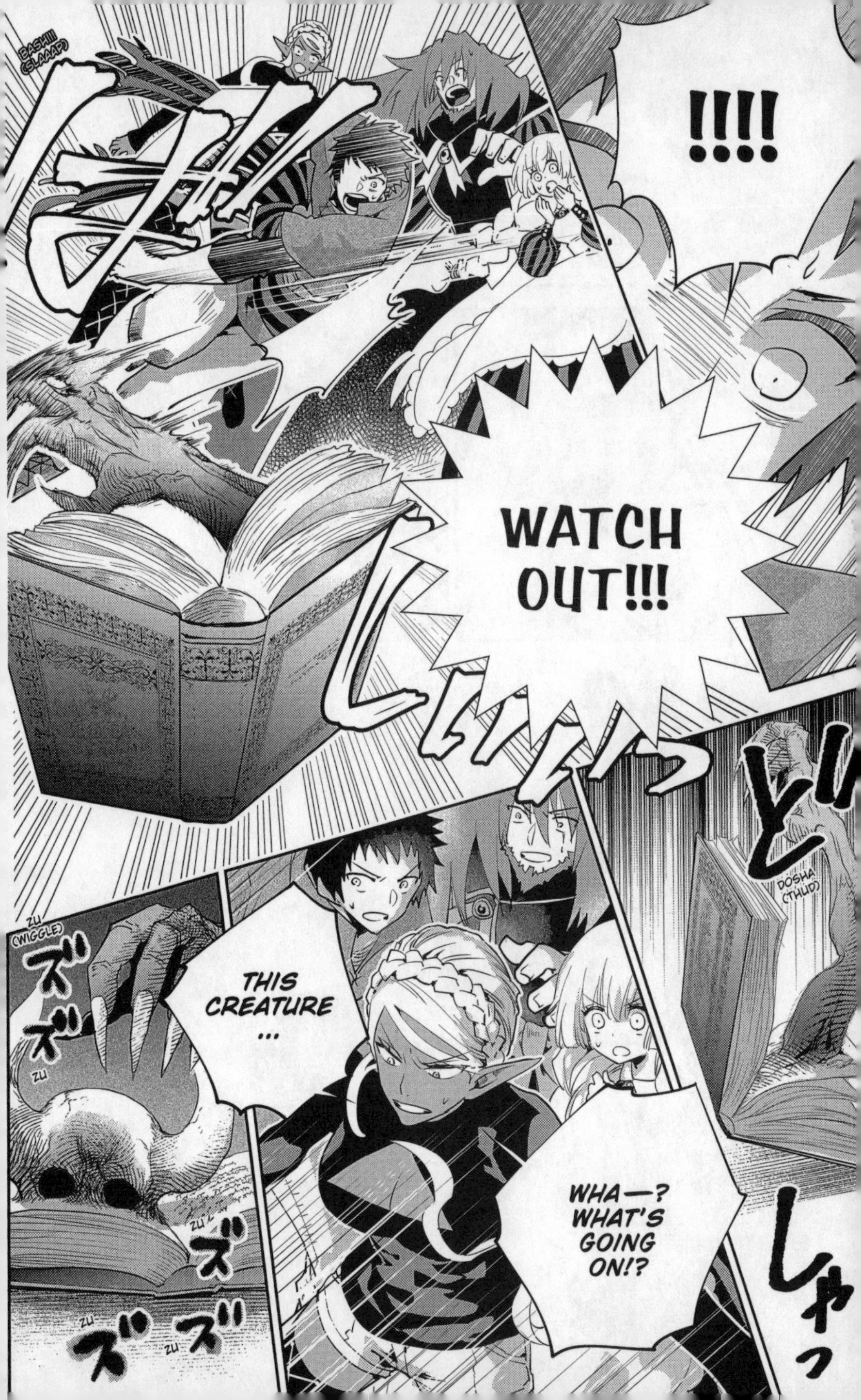
!!!!
WATCH OUT!!!
BASHIII (SLAAAP)
DOSHA (THUD)
WHA—? WHAT'S GOING ON!?
THIS CREATURE ...
ZU (WIGGLE)
ZU
ZU
ZU
ZU

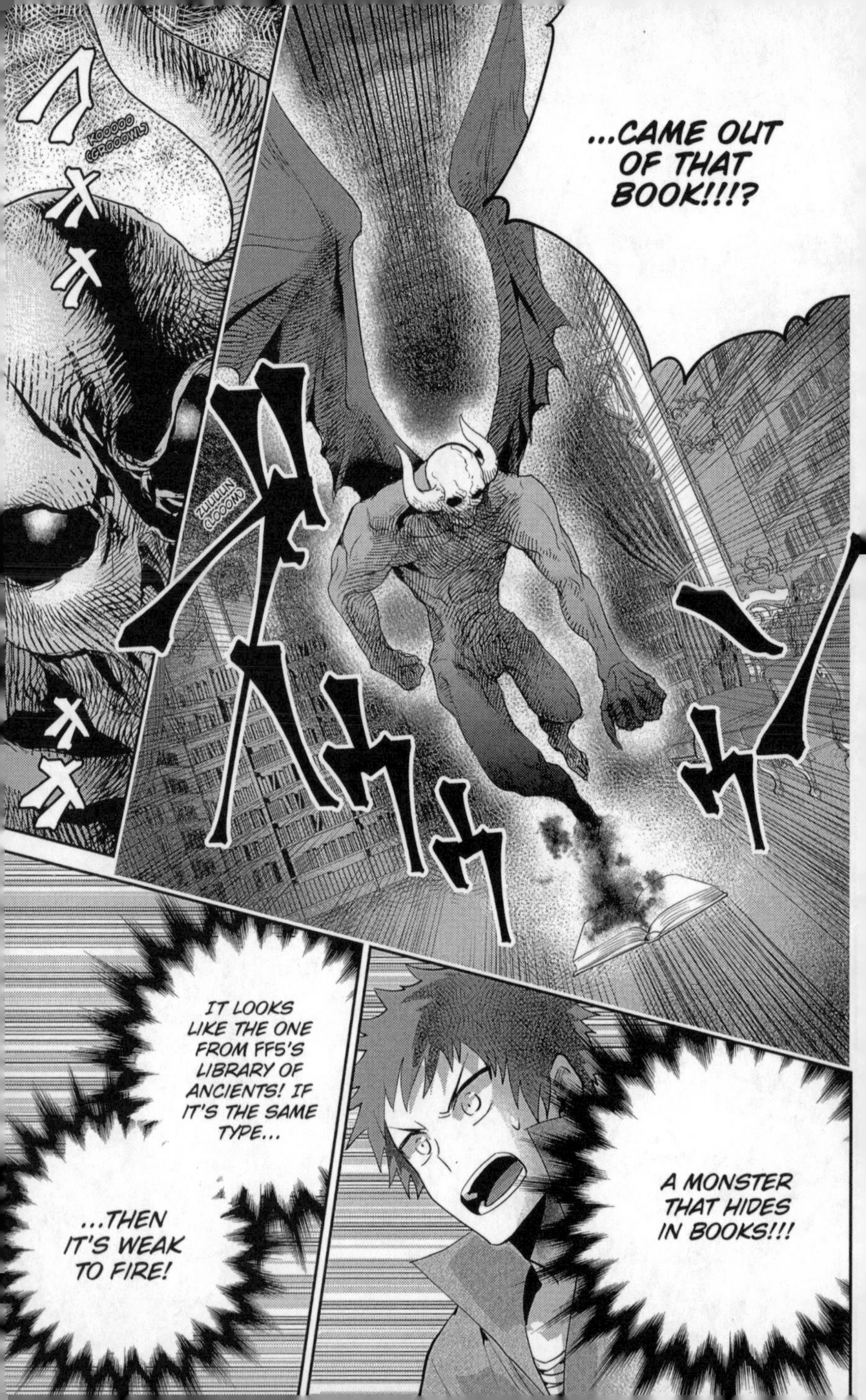
...CAME OUT OF THAT BOOK!!!?
ZUUUUN (LOOOM)
KOOOOO (GROOOWL)
A MONSTER THAT HIDES IN BOOKS!!!
IT LOOKS LIKE THE ONE FROM FF5'S LIBRARY OF ANCIENTS! IF IT'S THE SAME TYPE...
...THEN IT'S WEAK TO FIRE!

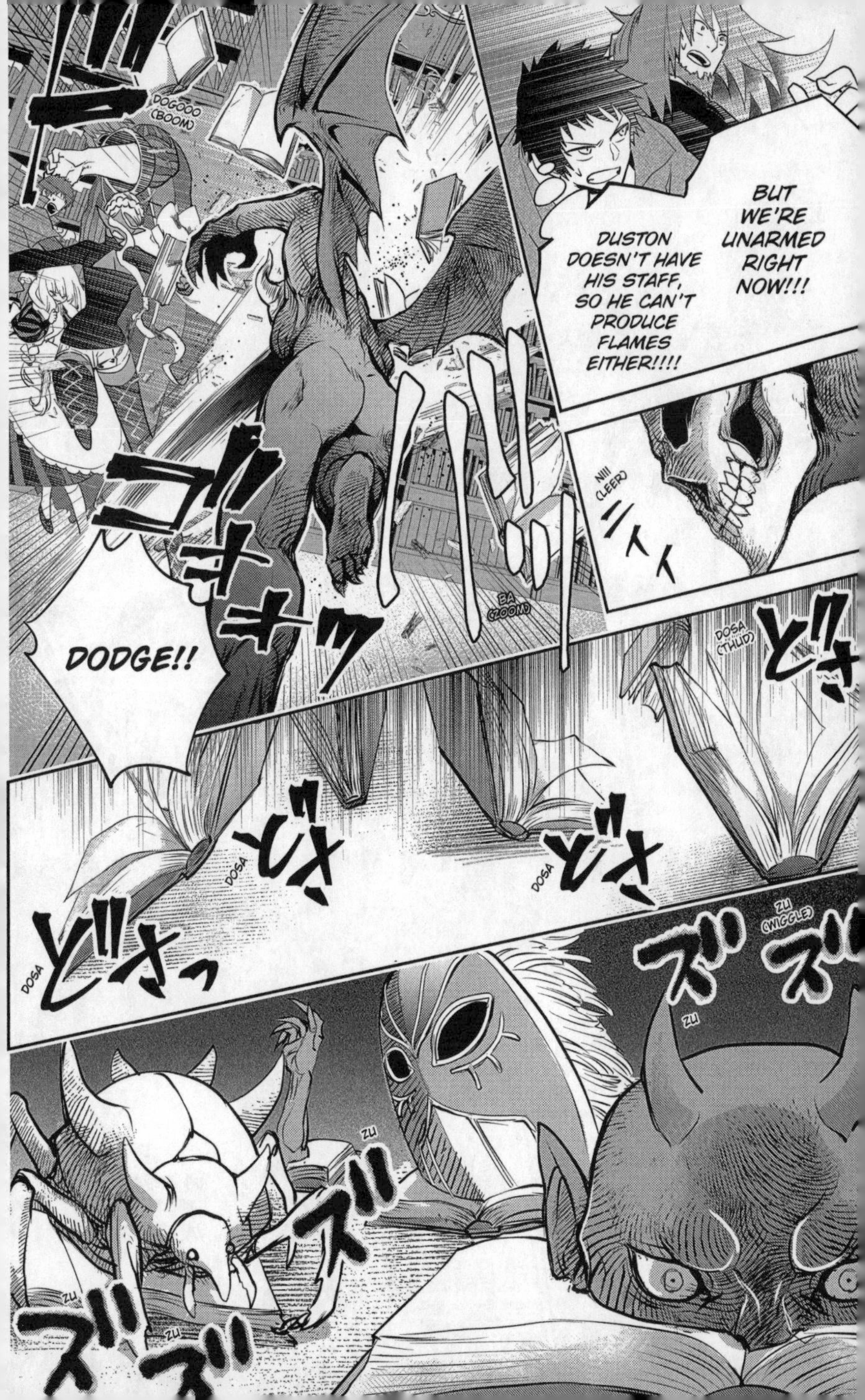
BUT WE'RE UNARMED RIGHT NOW!!!
DUSTON DOESN'T HAVE HIS STAFF, SO HE CAN'T PRODUCE FLAMES EITHER!!!!
NIII (LEER)
DOGOOO (BOOM)
DODGE!!
BA (ZOOM)
DOSA (THUD)
DOSA
DOSA
DOSA
ZU (WIGGLE)
ZU
ZU
ZU
ZU

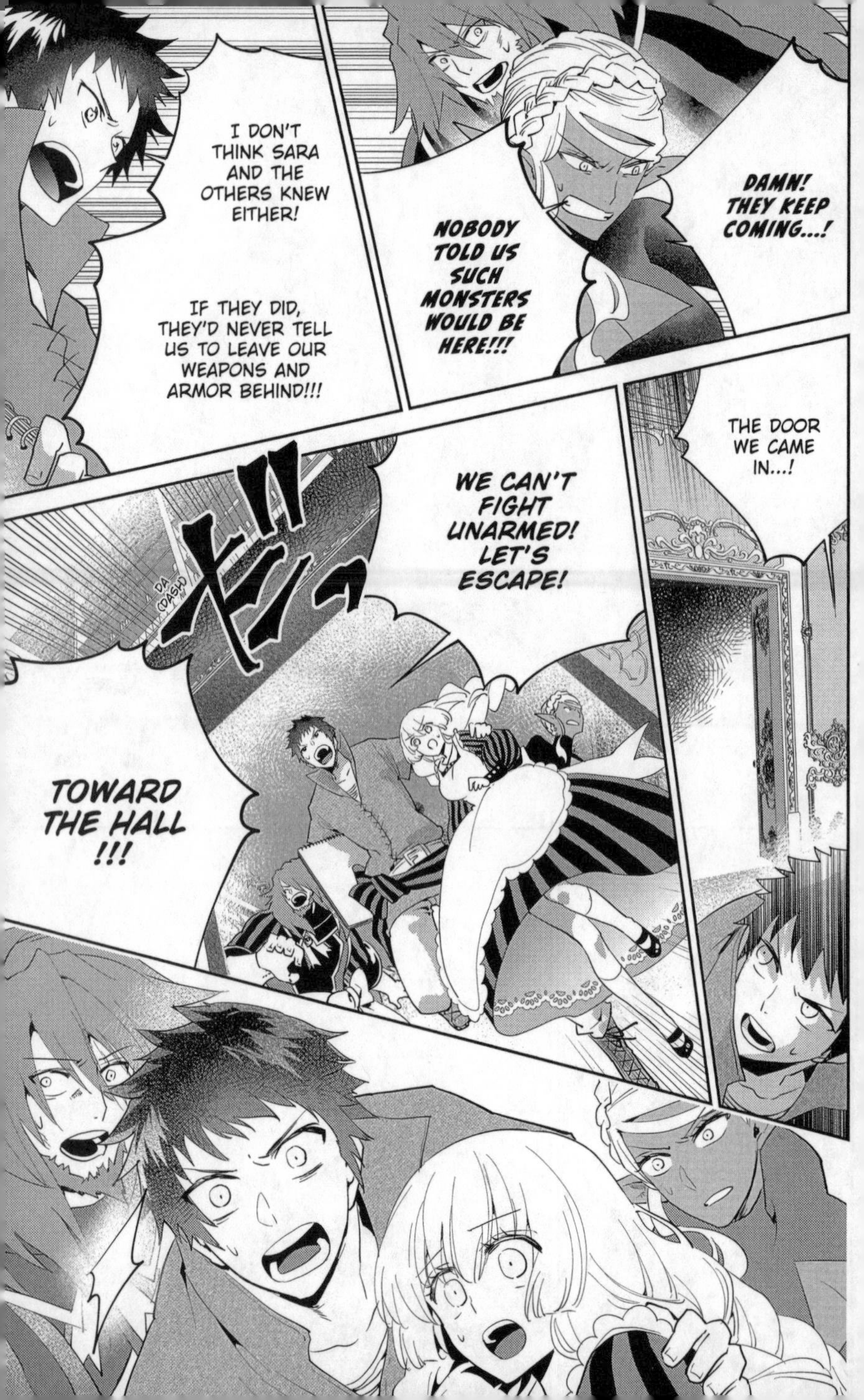
DAMN! THEY KEEP COMING...!
NOBODY TOLD US SUCH MONSTERS WOULD BE HERE!!!
I DON'T THINK SARA AND THE OTHERS KNEW EITHER!
IF THEY DID, THEY'D NEVER TELL US TO LEAVE OUR WEAPONS AND ARMOR BEHIND!!!
THE DOOR WE CAME IN...!
WE CAN'T FIGHT UNARMED! LET'S ESCAPE!
DA (DASH)
TOWARD THE HALL !!!

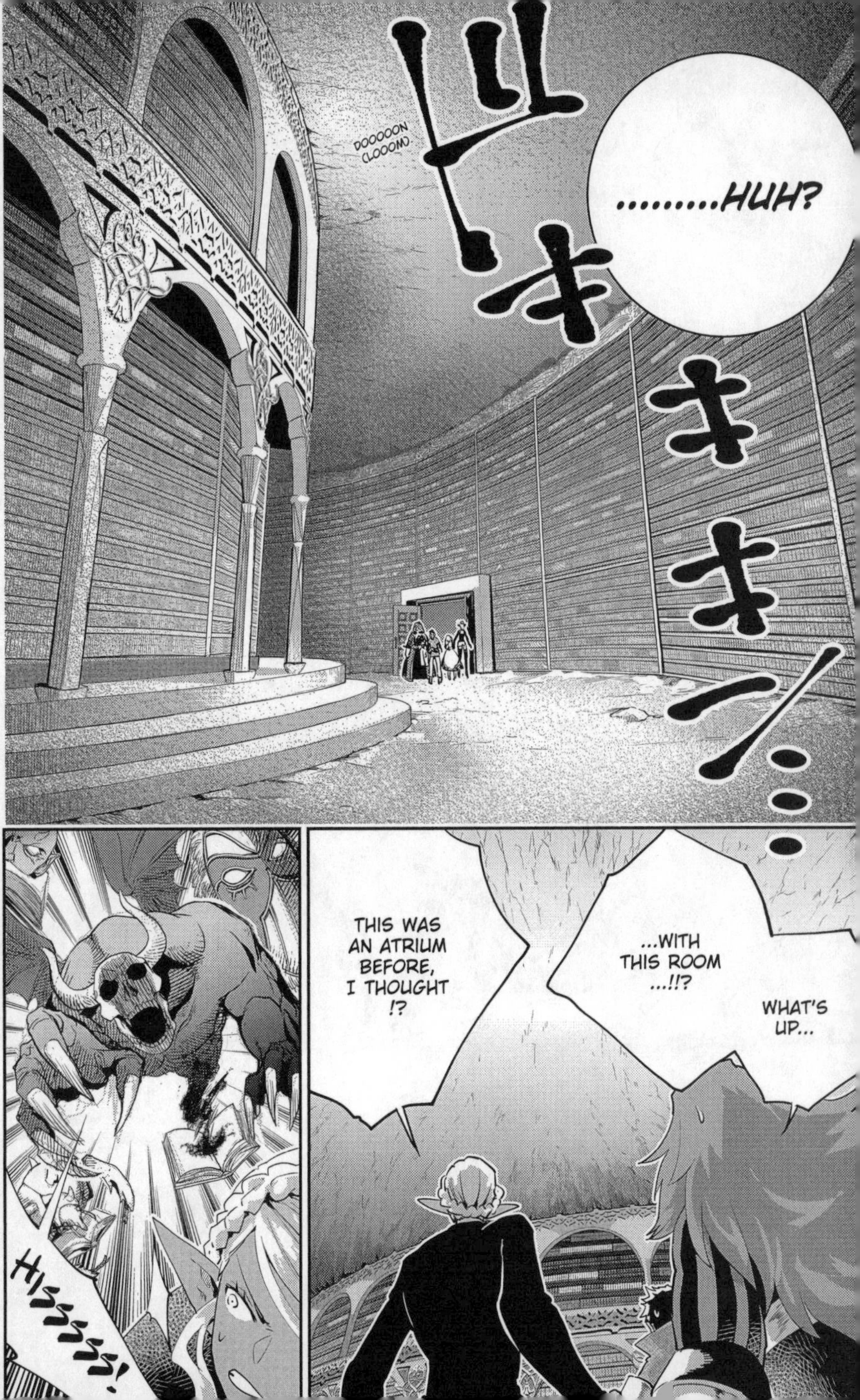
DOOOOON (LOOOM)
.........HUH?
WHAT'S UP...
...WITH THIS ROOM ...!!?
THIS WAS AN ATRIUM BEFORE, I THOUGHT !?
HISSSSS!

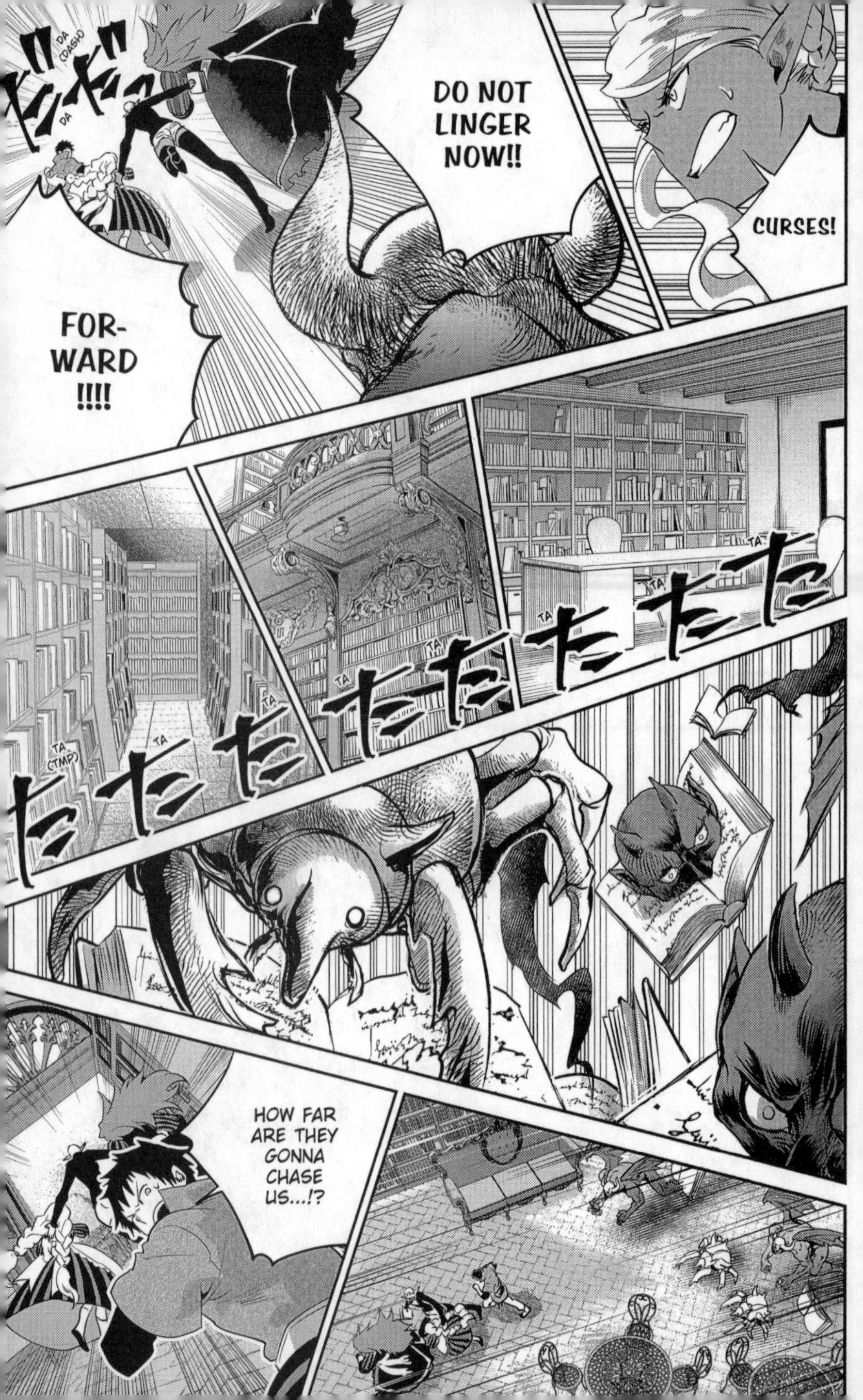
CURSES!
DO NOT LINGER NOW!!
DA (DASH) DA
FOR-WARD!!!!
TA TA TA TA TA TA
TA (TMP)
HOW FAR ARE THEY GONNA CHASE US...!?

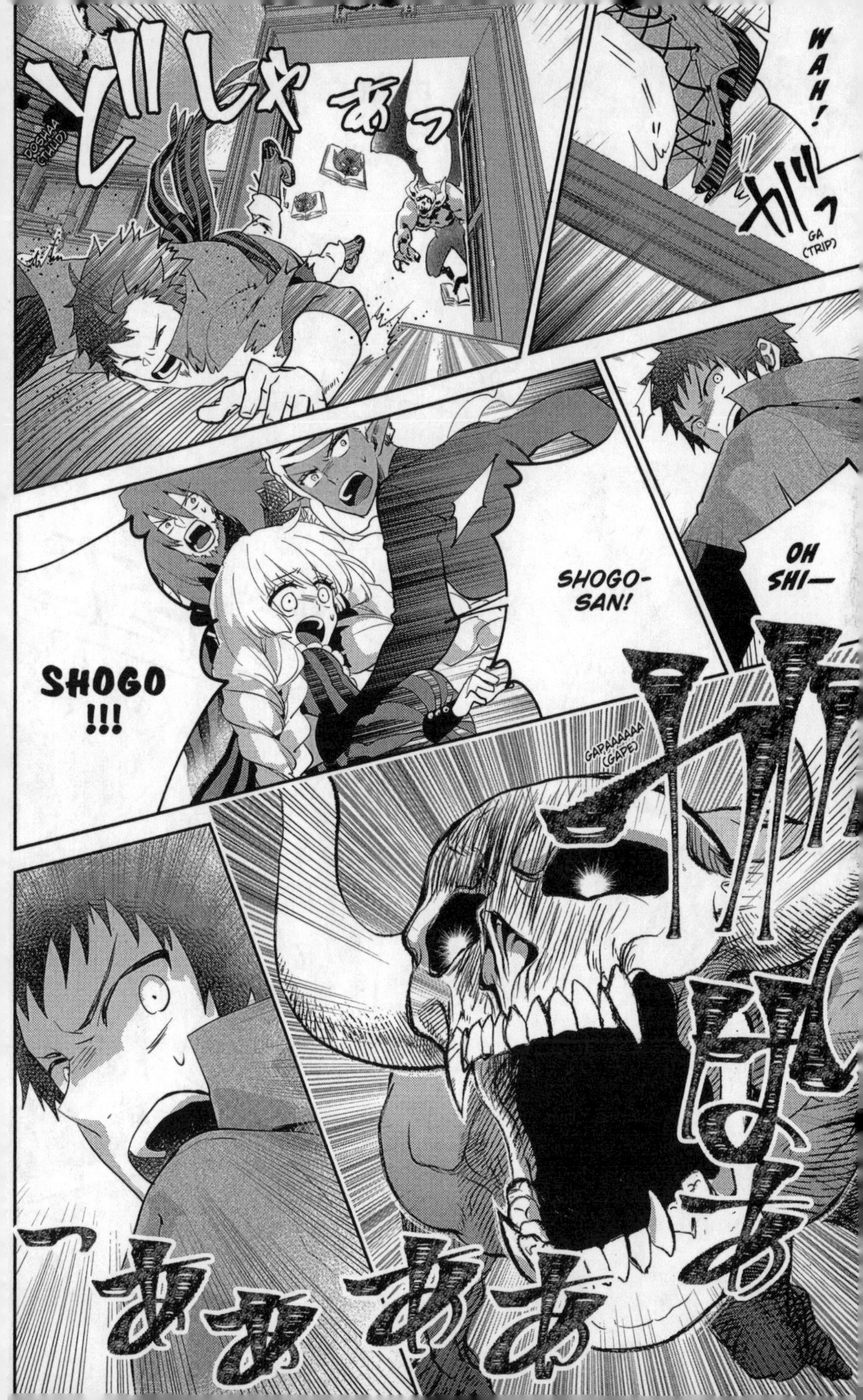
WAH!
ガリッ
GA (TRIP)
どしゃあっ
DOSHAA (THUD)
OH SHI—
SHOGO-SAN!
SHOGO !!!
GAPAAAAAA (GAPE)

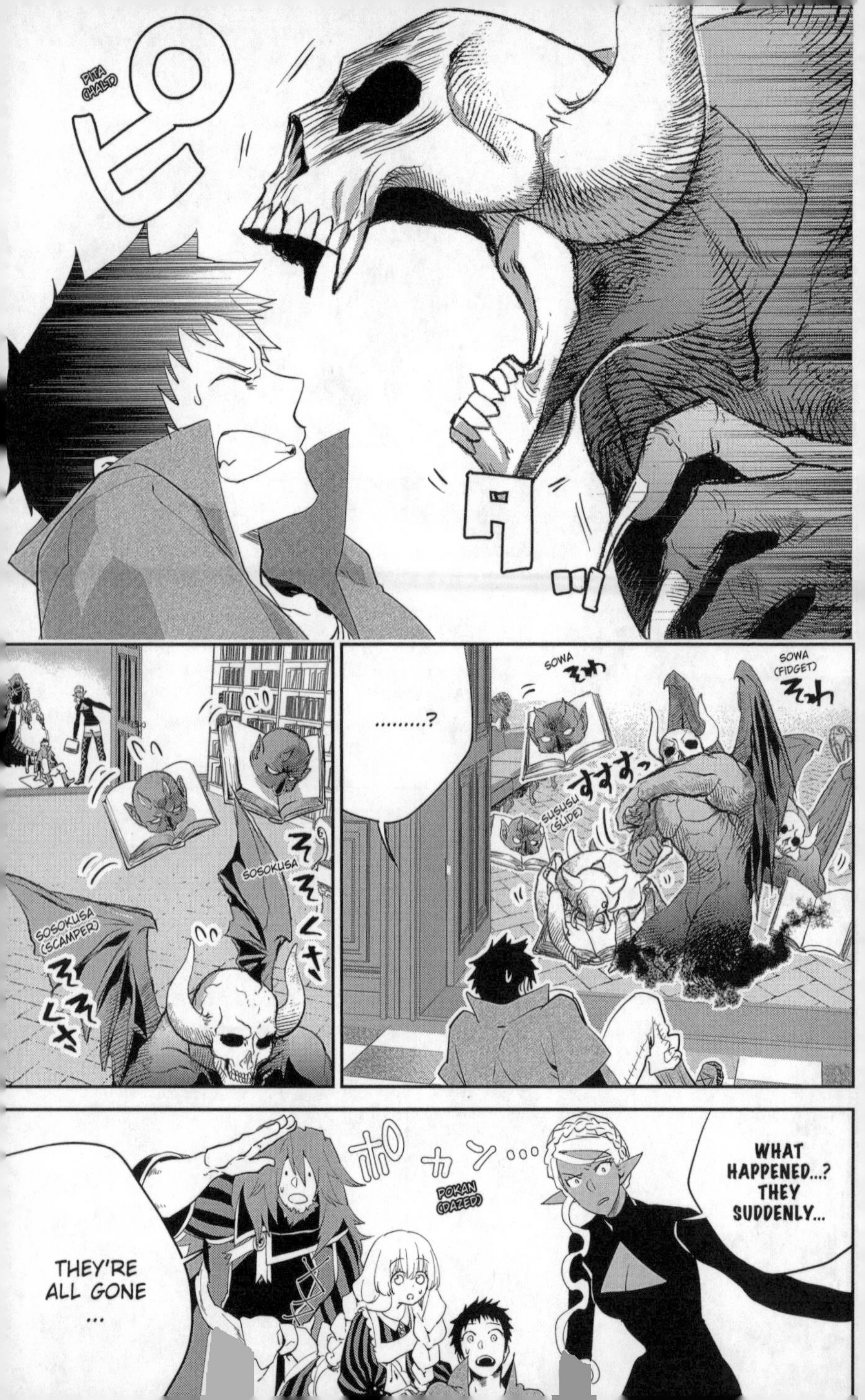
ピタ
PITA (HALT)
SOWA
そわ
SOWA (FIDGET)
そわ
すすすっ
SUSUSU (SLIDE)
.........?
SOSOKUSA
そそくさ
SOSOKUSA (SCAMPER)
そそくさ
WHAT HAPPENED...? THEY SUDDENLY...
ポカン…
POKAN (DAZED)
THEY'RE ALL GONE ...

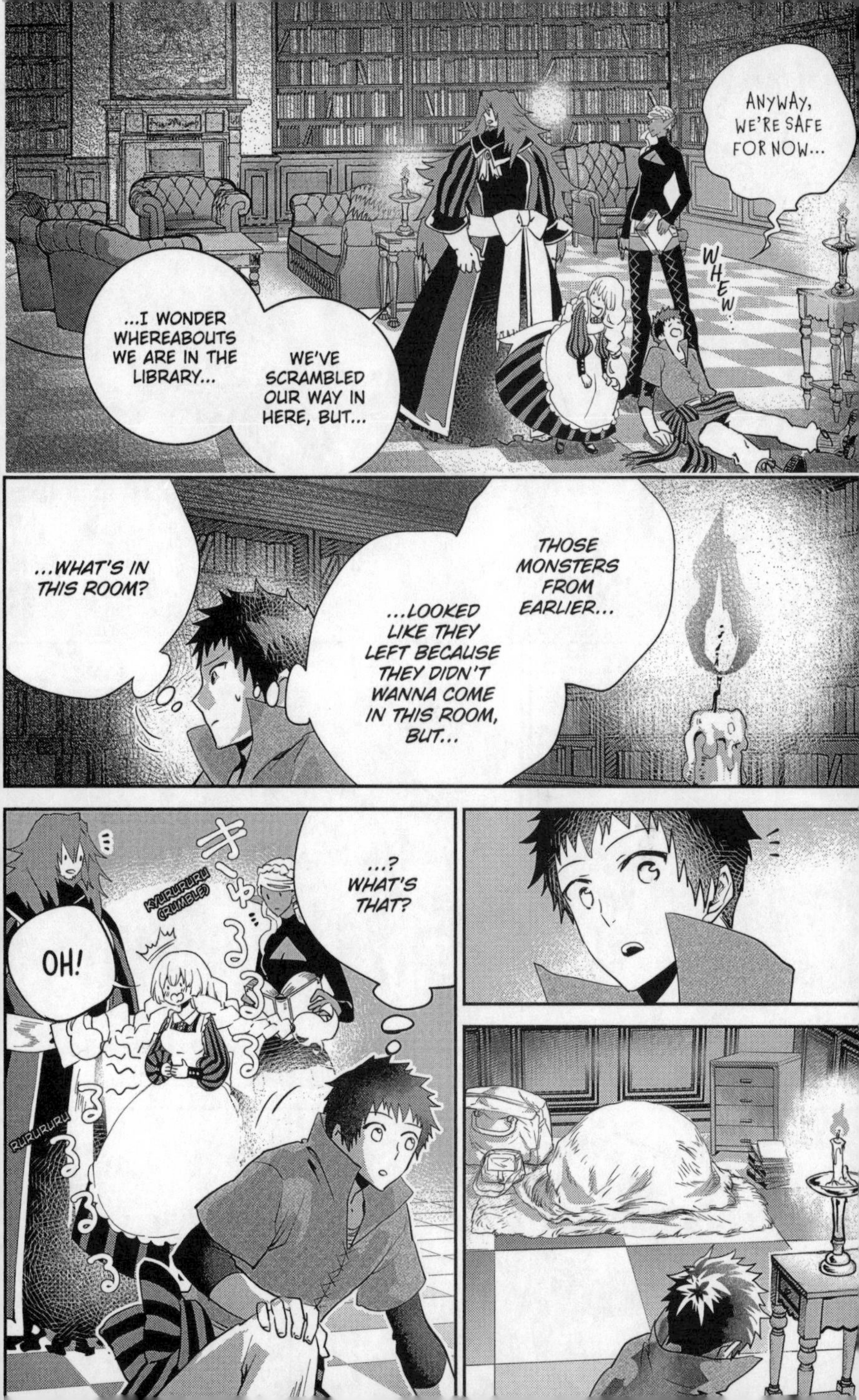
ANYWAY, WE'RE SAFE FOR NOW...
WHEW...
WE'VE SCRAMBLED OUR WAY IN HERE, BUT...
...I WONDER WHEREABOUTS WE ARE IN THE LIBRARY...
THOSE MONSTERS FROM EARLIER...
...LOOKED LIKE THEY LEFT BECAUSE THEY DIDN'T WANNA COME IN THIS ROOM, BUT...
...WHAT'S IN THIS ROOM?
...? WHAT'S THAT?
KYURURURU (RUMBLE)
OH!
RURURURU

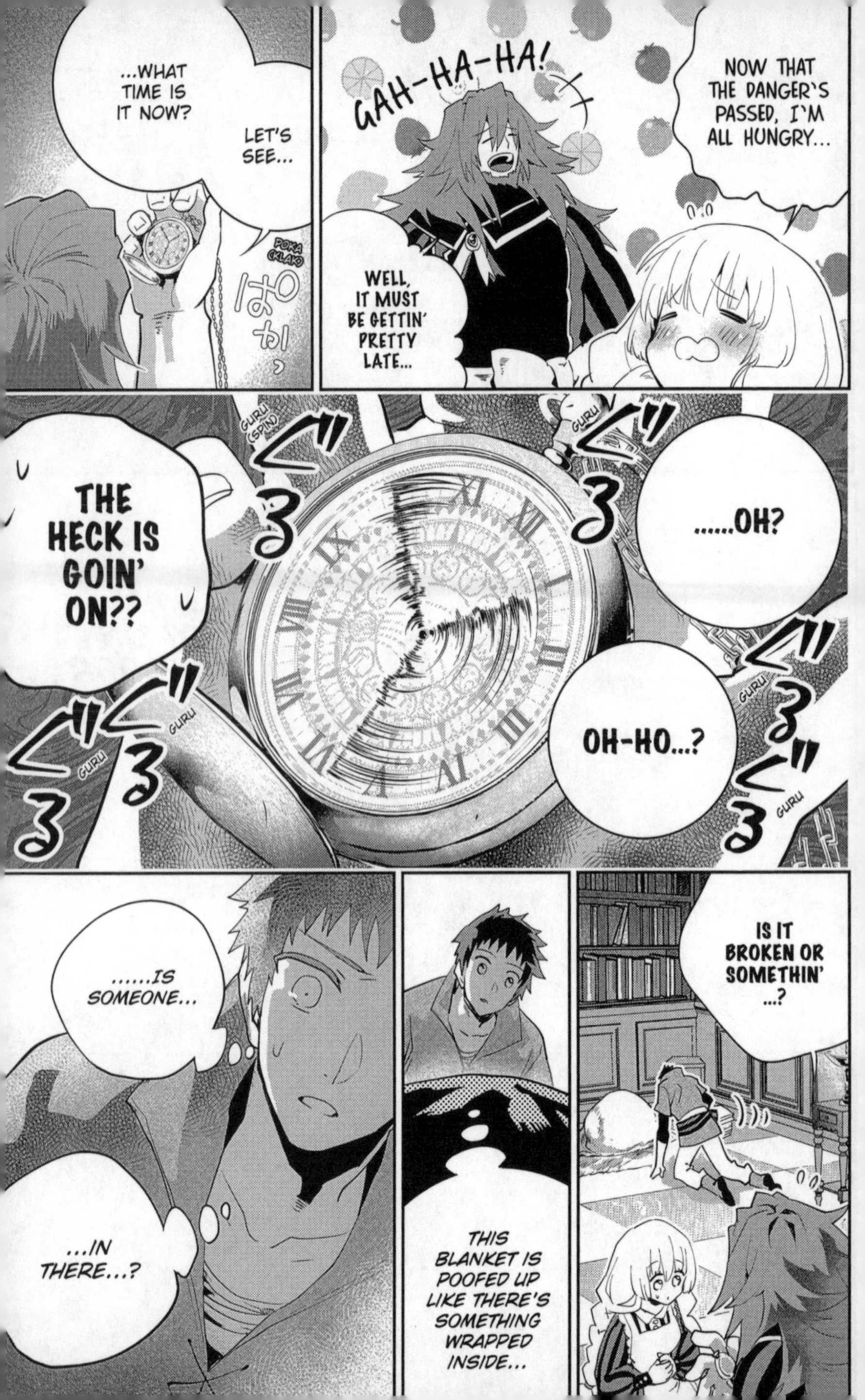
NOW THAT THE DANGER'S PASSED, I'M ALL HUNGRY...
GAH-HA-HA!
WELL, IT MUST BE GETTIN' PRETTY LATE...
...WHAT TIME IS IT NOW?
LET'S SEE...
POKA (KLAK)
ぱか
GURU
ぐる
......OH?
GURU (SPIN)
ぐる
THE HECK IS GOIN' ON??
OH-HO...?
GURU
ぐる
GURU
ぐる
GURU
ぐる
GURU
ぐる
IS IT BROKEN OR SOMETHIN' ...?
THIS BLANKET IS POOFED UP LIKE THERE'S SOMETHING WRAPPED INSIDE...
......IS SOMEONE...
...IN THERE...?

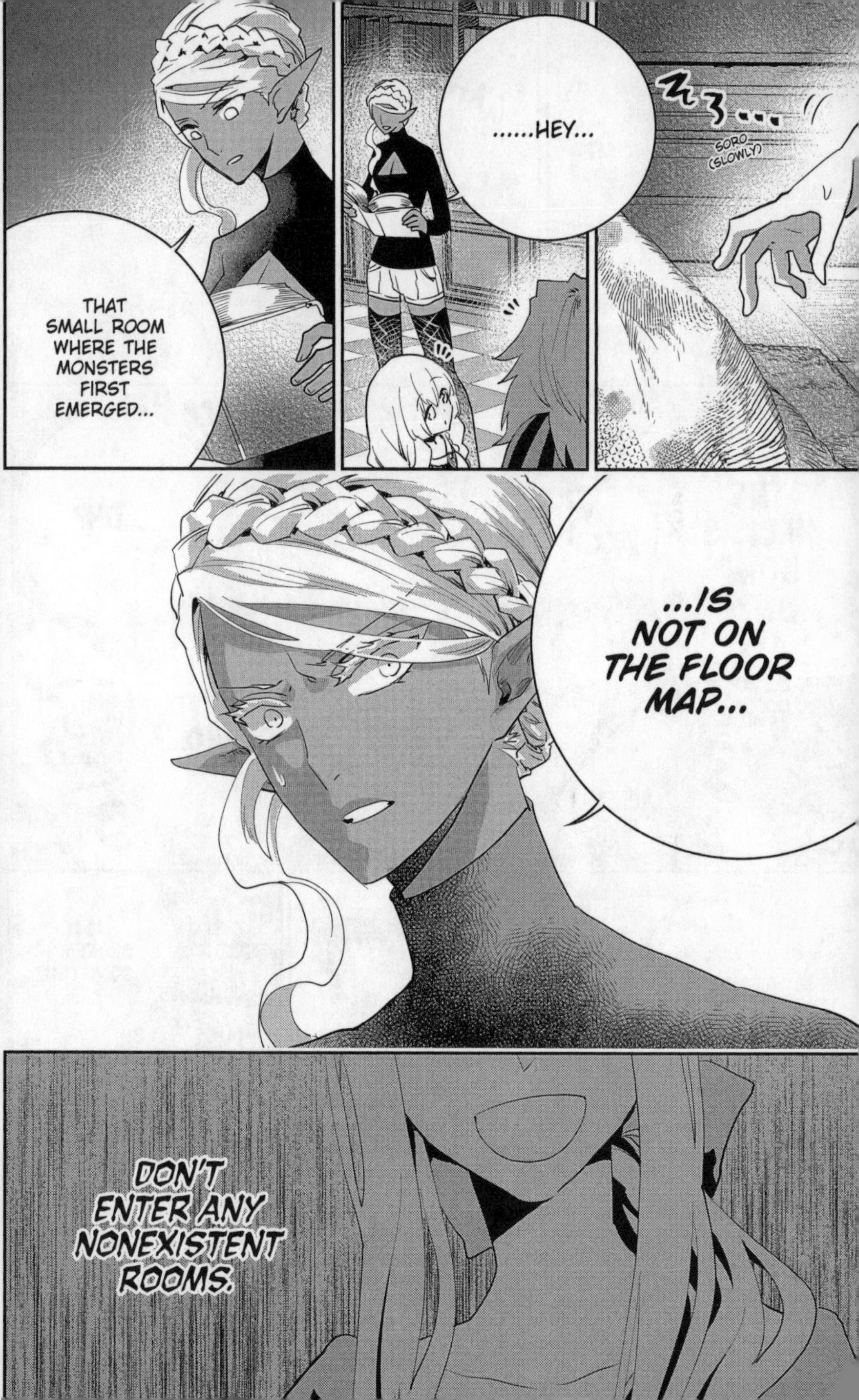
SORO (SLOWLY)
......HEY...
THAT SMALL ROOM WHERE THE MONSTERS FIRST EMERGED...
...IS NOT ON THE FLOOR MAP...
DON'T ENTER ANY NONEXISTENT ROOMS.

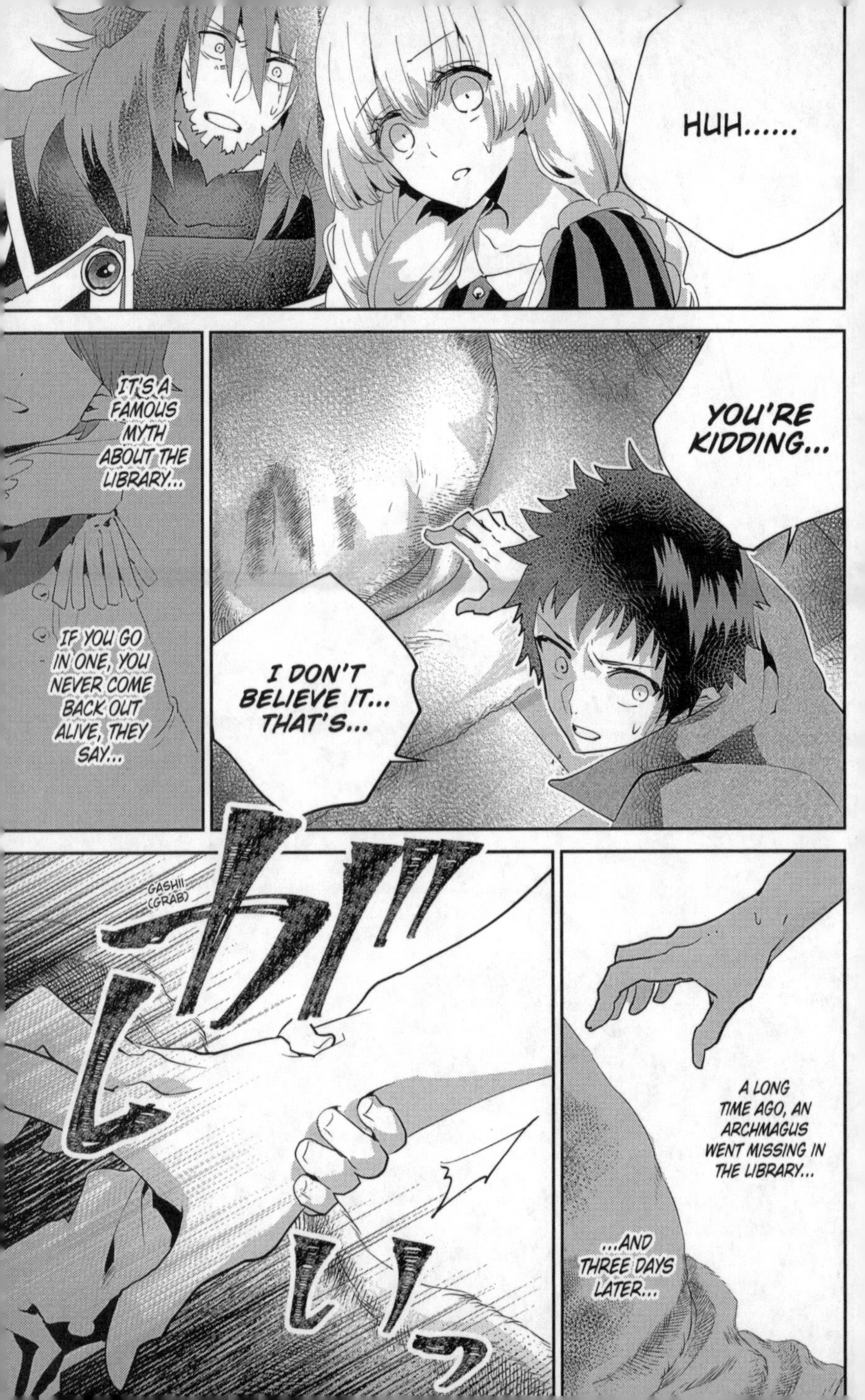
HUH......
YOU'RE KIDDING...
I DON'T BELIEVE IT... THAT'S...
IT'S A FAMOUS MYTH ABOUT THE LIBRARY...
IF YOU GO IN ONE, YOU NEVER COME BACK OUT ALIVE, THEY SAY...
A LONG TIME AGO, AN ARCHMAGUS WENT MISSING IN THE LIBRARY...
...AND THREE DAYS LATER...
GASHII (GRAB)

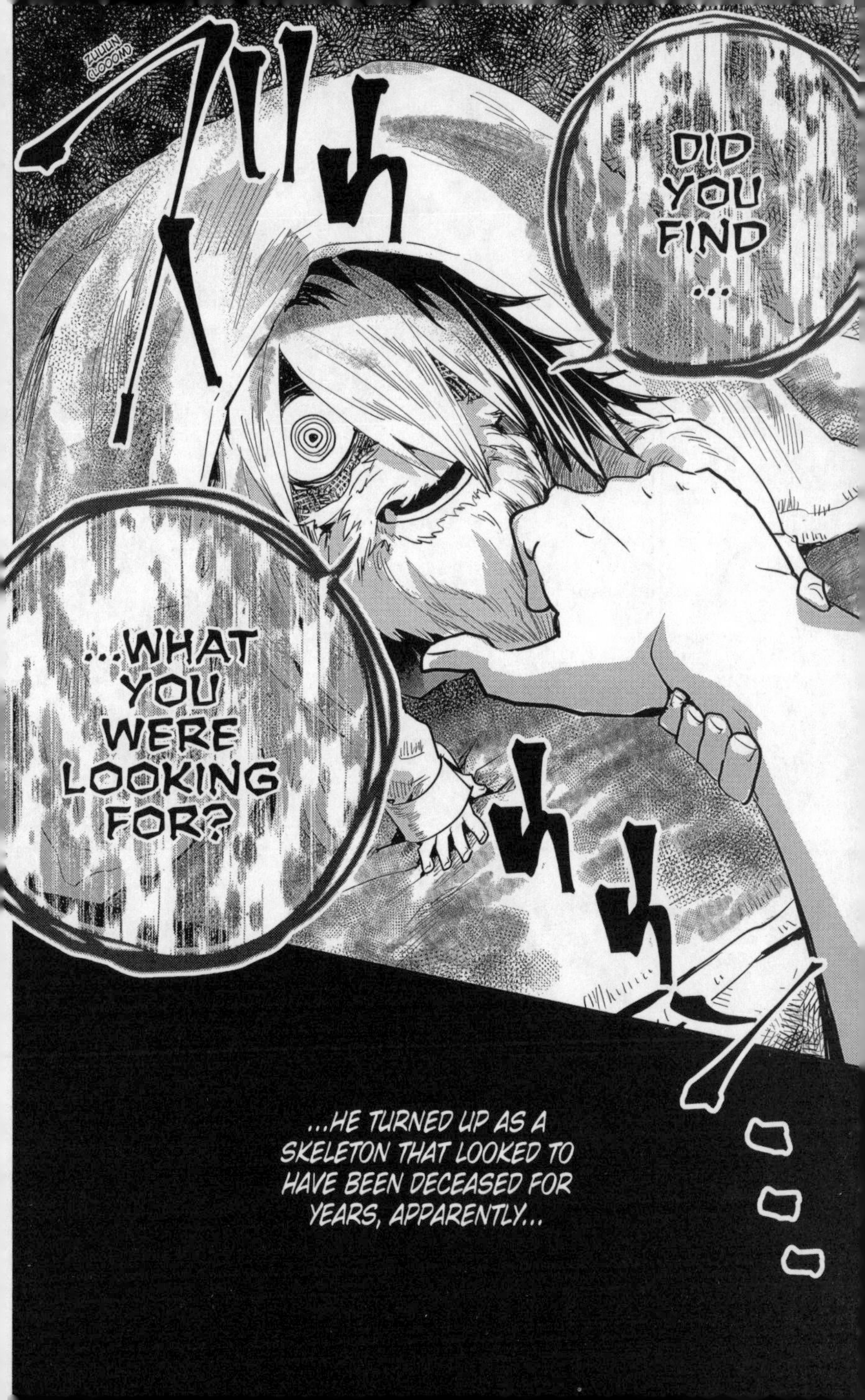
ZUIIIN (LOOOM)
DID YOU FIND...
...WHAT YOU WERE LOOKING FOR?
...HE TURNED UP AS A SKELETON THAT LOOKED TO HAVE BEEN DECEASED FOR YEARS, APPARENTLY...

FINAL FANTASY®
ファイナルファンタジー　ロスト・ストレンジャー
LOST STRANGER

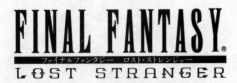

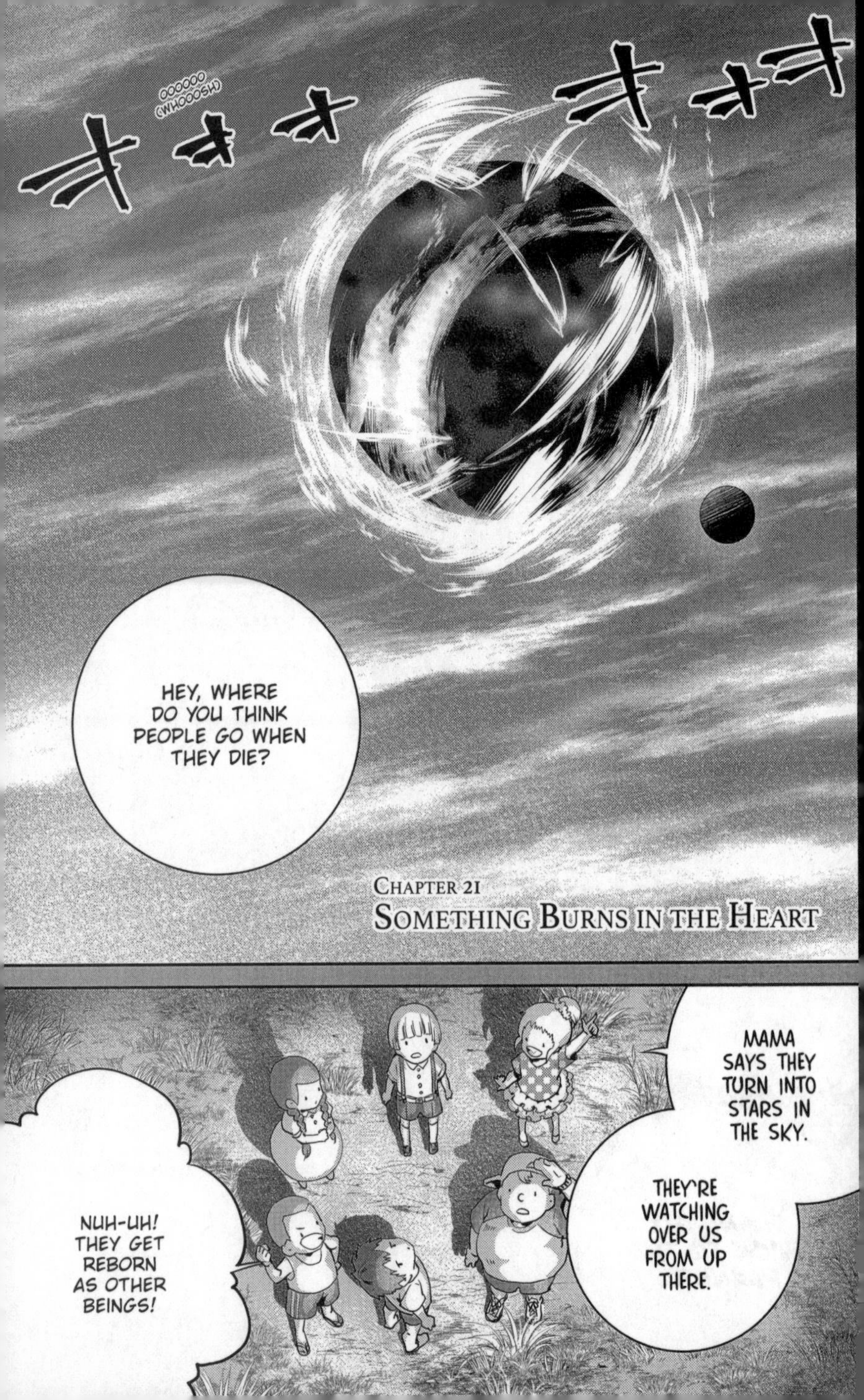
OOOOOO (WHOOOSH)
HEY, WHERE DO YOU THINK PEOPLE GO WHEN THEY DIE?
CHAPTER 21
SOMETHING BURNS IN THE HEART
MAMA SAYS THEY TURN INTO STARS IN THE SKY.
THEY'RE WATCHING OVER US FROM UP THERE.
NUH-UH! THEY GET REBORN AS OTHER BEINGS!

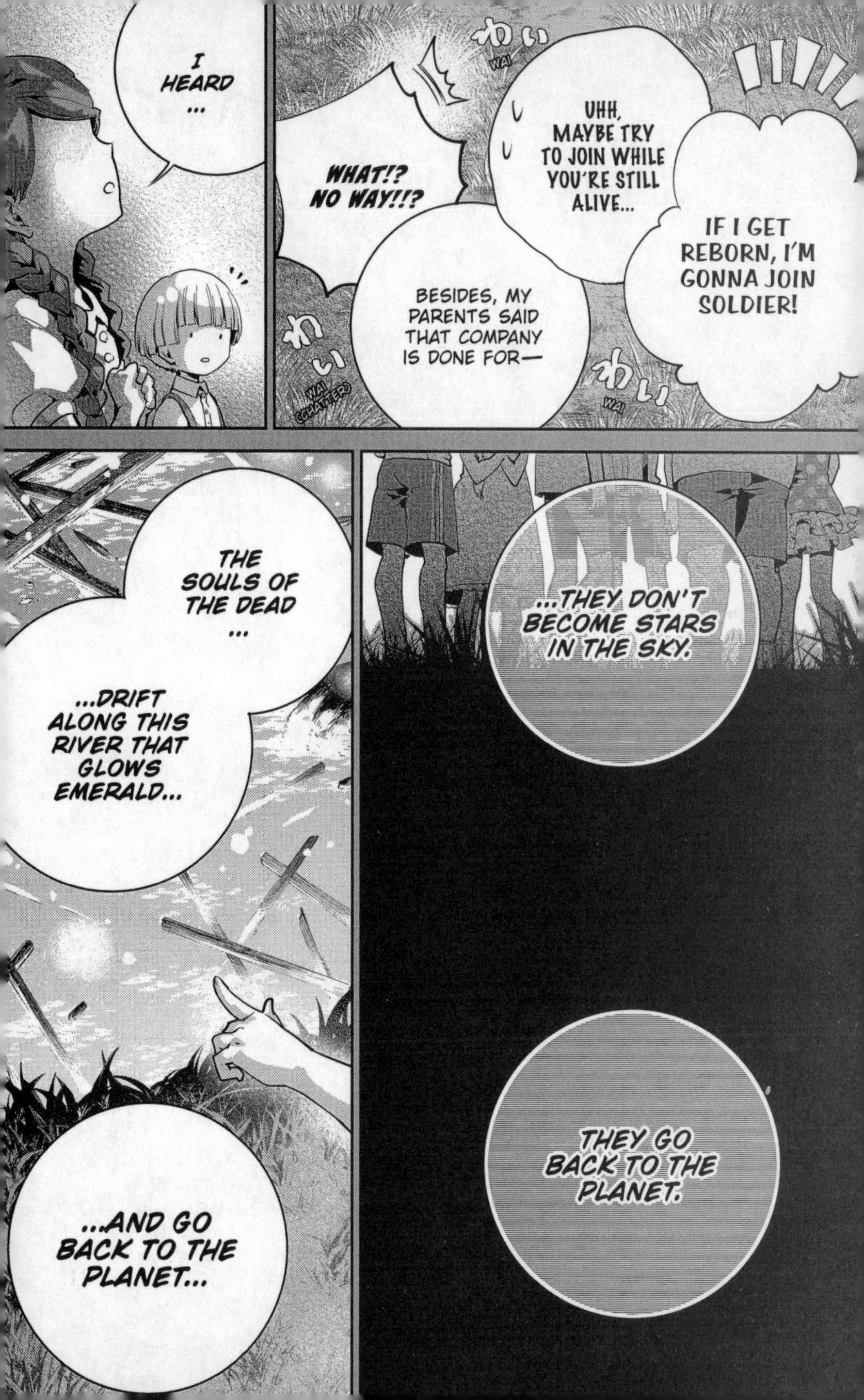
IF I GET REBORN, I'M GONNA JOIN SOLDIER!
UHH, MAYBE TRY TO JOIN WHILE YOU'RE STILL ALIVE...
わい
WAI
WHAT!? NO WAY!!?
BESIDES, MY PARENTS SAID THAT COMPANY IS DONE FOR—
わい
WAI
わい
WAI (CHATTERS)
I HEARD...
...THEY DON'T BECOME STARS IN THE SKY.
THEY GO BACK TO THE PLANET.
THE SOULS OF THE DEAD...
...DRIFT ALONG THIS RIVER THAT GLOWS EMERALD...
...AND GO BACK TO THE PLANET...

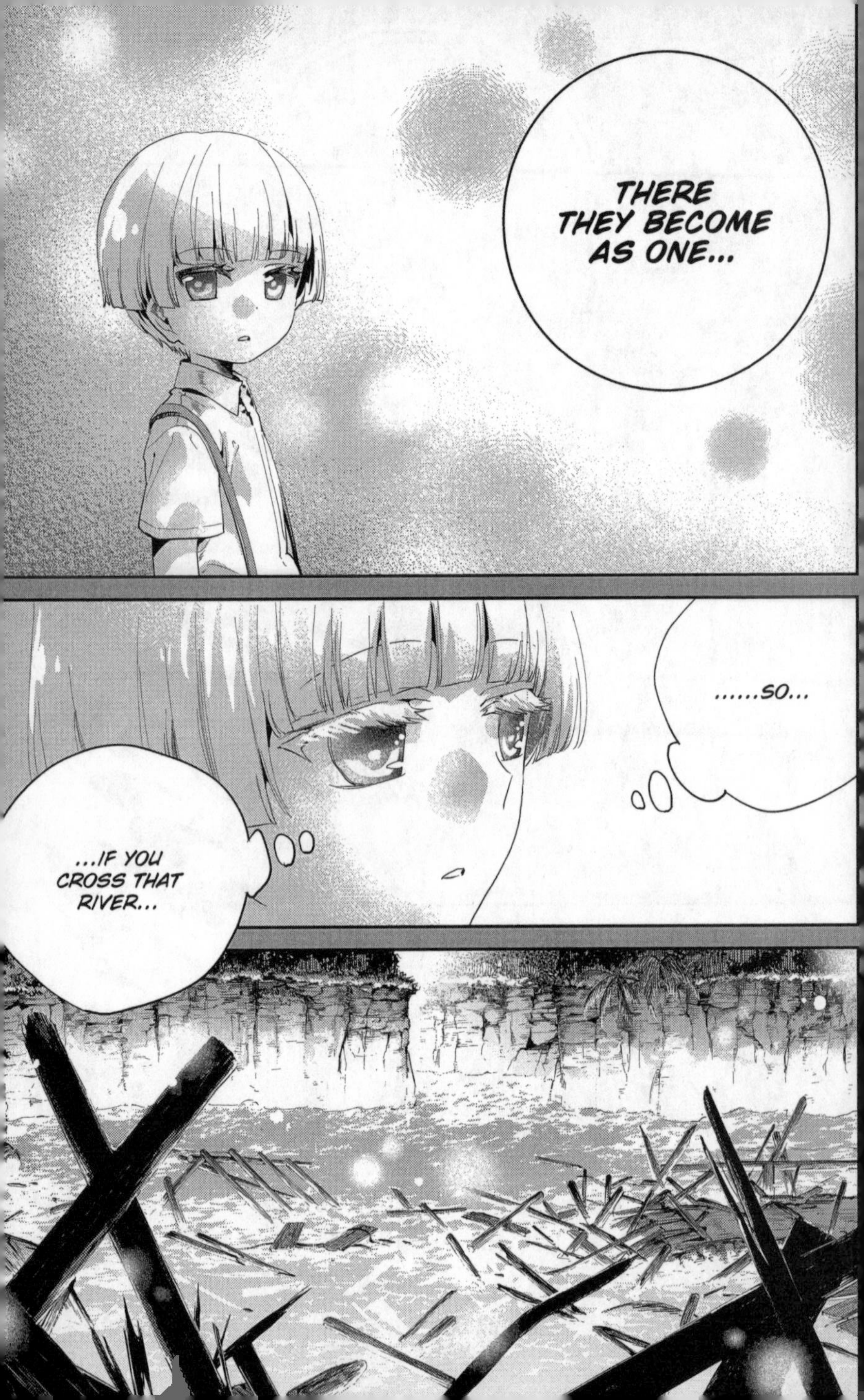
THERE THEY BECOME AS ONE...
......SO...
...IF YOU CROSS THAT RIVER...

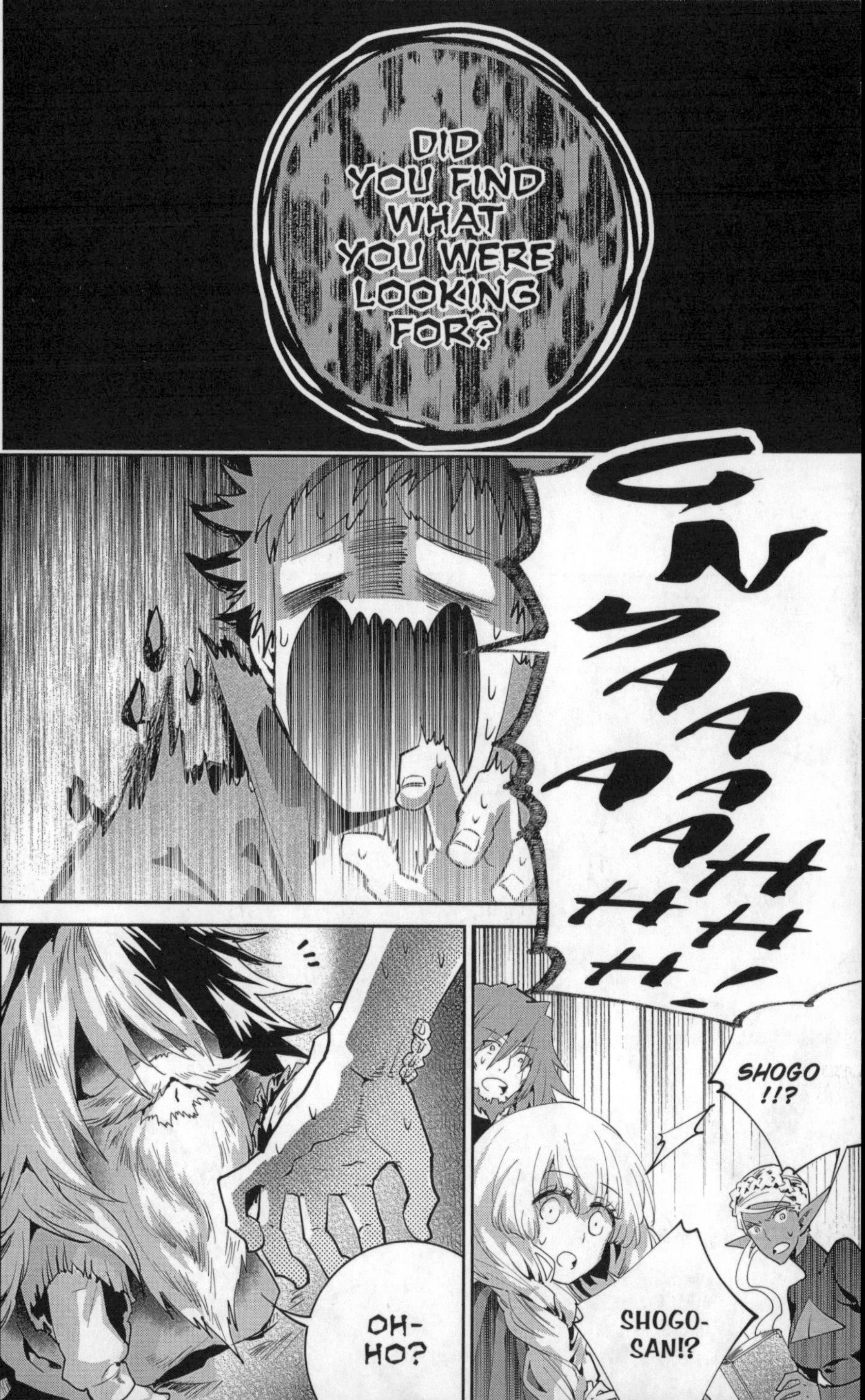

DID YOU FIND WHAT YOU WERE LOOKING FOR?
GNYAAAAAAHHHHH!
SHOGO!!?
SHOGO-SAN!?
OH-HO?

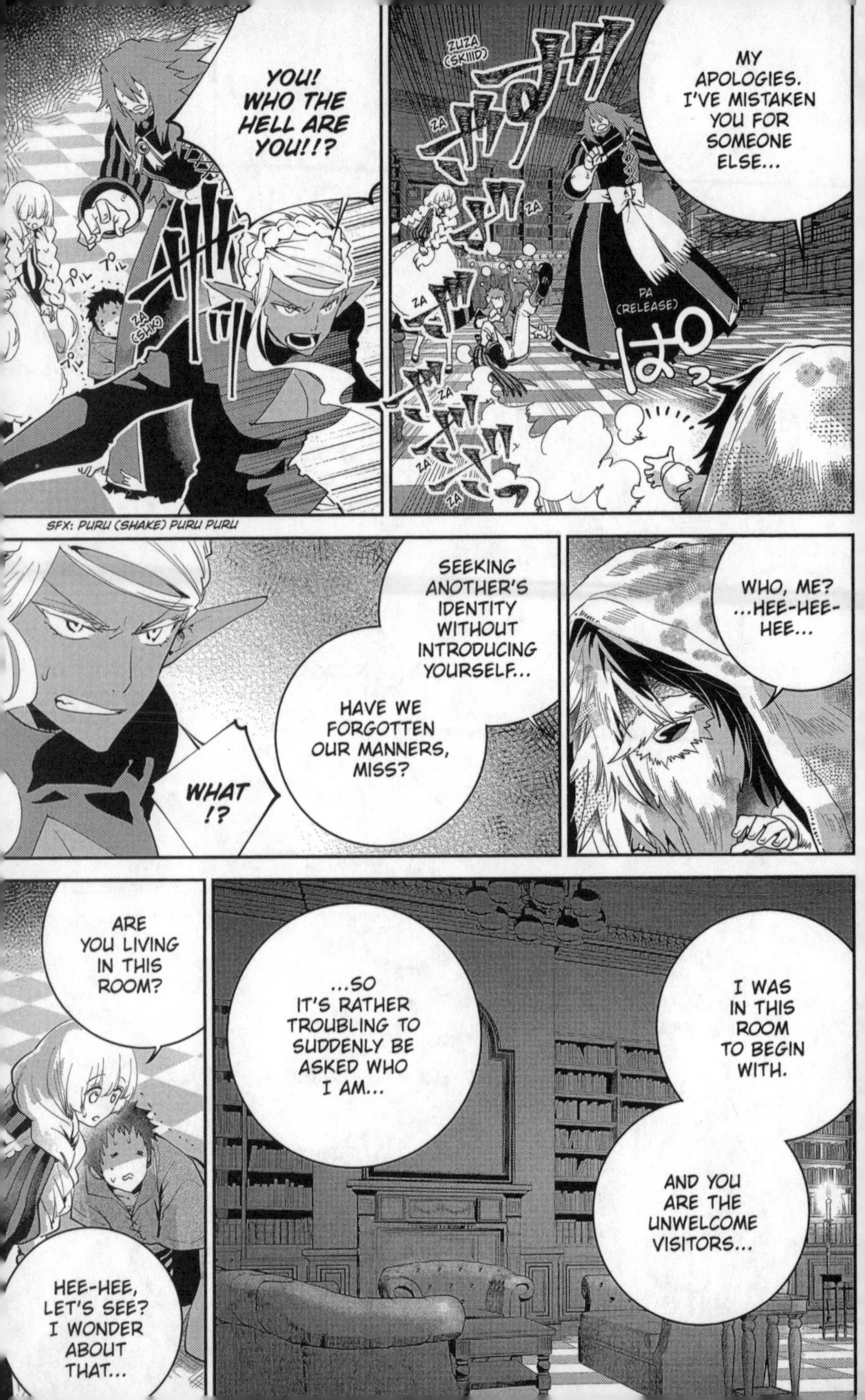

ZUZA (SKIIID)
ZA
MY APOLOGIES. I'VE MISTAKEN YOU FOR SOMEONE ELSE...
PA (RELEASE)
ぱっ
ZA
ZA
ZA
ZA
ZA
YOU! WHO THE HELL ARE YOU!!?
ZA (SHK)
SFX: PURU (SHAKE) PURU PURU
WHO, ME? ...HEE-HEE-HEE...
SEEKING ANOTHER'S IDENTITY WITHOUT INTRODUCING YOURSELF...
HAVE WE FORGOTTEN OUR MANNERS, MISS?
WHAT !?
I WAS IN THIS ROOM TO BEGIN WITH.
AND YOU ARE THE UNWELCOME VISITORS...
...SO IT'S RATHER TROUBLING TO SUDDENLY BE ASKED WHO I AM...
ARE YOU LIVING IN THIS ROOM?
HEE-HEE, LET'S SEE? I WONDER ABOUT THAT...

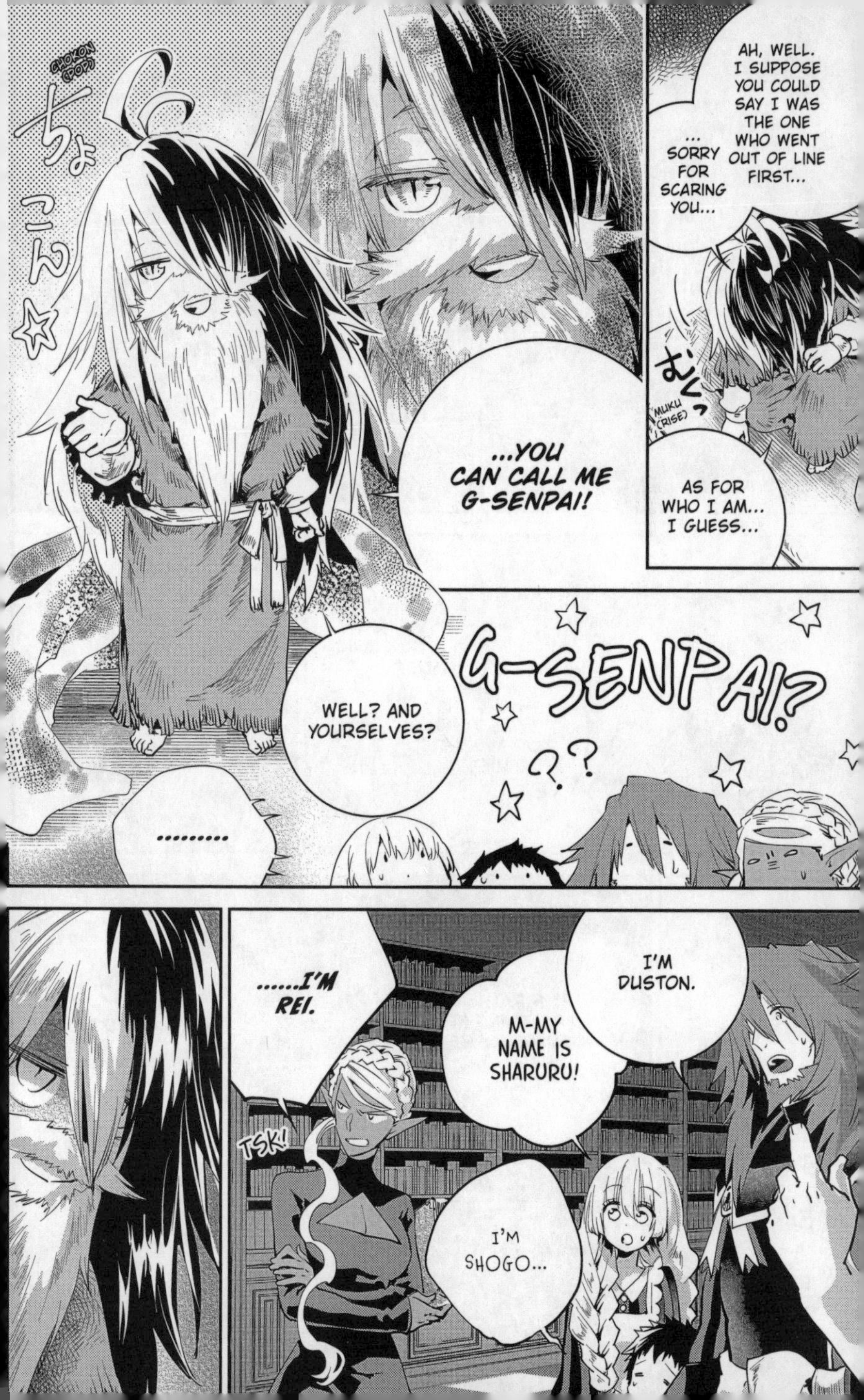
AH, WELL. I SUPPOSE YOU COULD SAY I WAS THE ONE WHO WENT OUT OF LINE FIRST...
...SORRY FOR SCARING YOU...
むくっ
MUKU (RISE)
AS FOR WHO I AM... I GUESS...
ちょこん☆
CHOKON (POP)
...YOU CAN CALL ME G-SENPAI!
G-SENPAI!?
??
WELL? AND YOURSELVES?
..........
I'M DUSTON.
M-MY NAME IS SHARURU!
......I'M REI.
TSK!
I'M SHOGO...

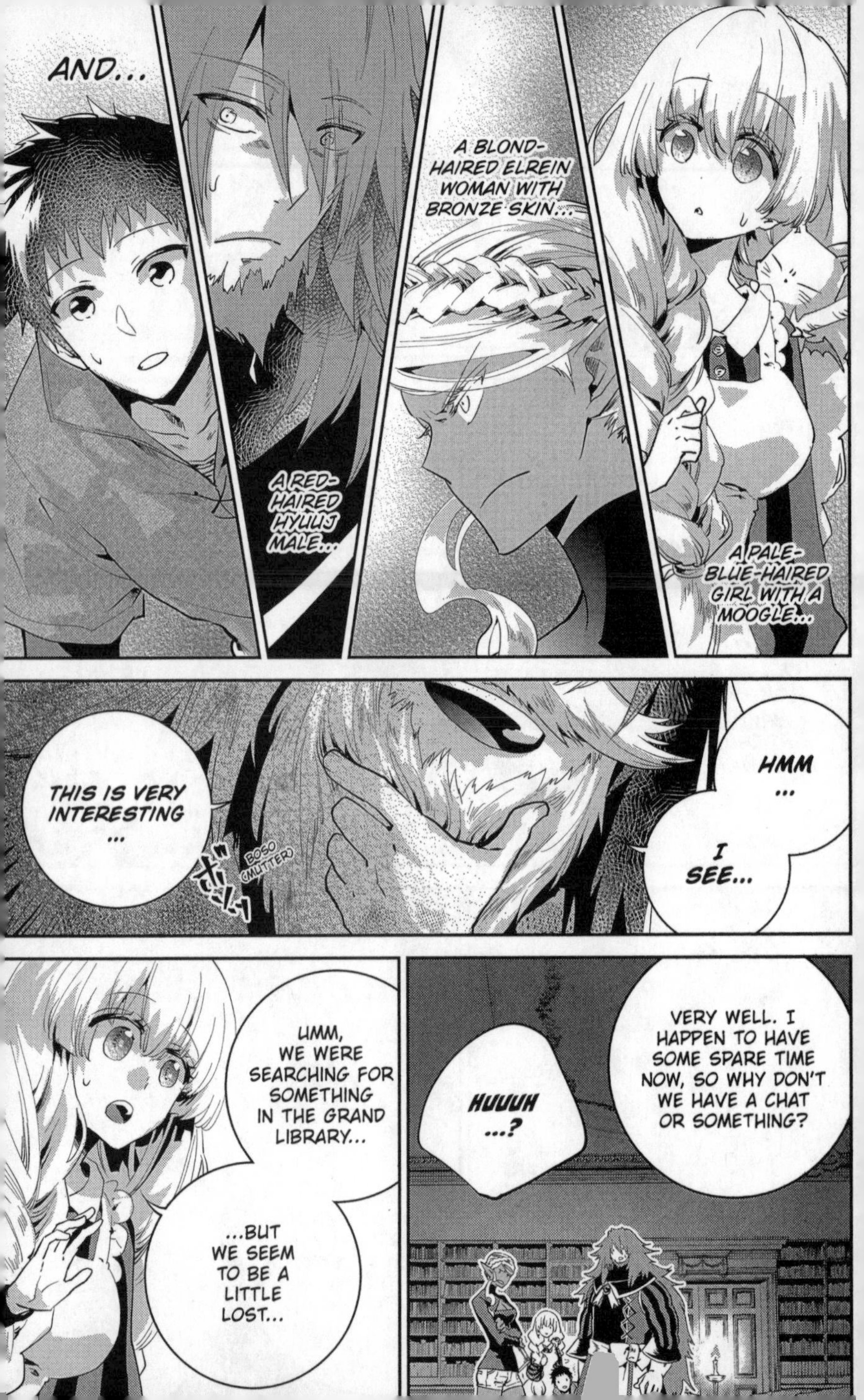

A PALE-BLUE-HAIRED GIRL WITH A MOOGLE...
A BLOND-HAIRED ELREIN WOMAN WITH BRONZE SKIN...
A RED-HAIRED HYUUJ MALE...
AND...
HMM ... I SEE...
THIS IS VERY INTERESTING ...
BOSO (MUTTER)
VERY WELL. I HAPPEN TO HAVE SOME SPARE TIME NOW, SO WHY DON'T WE HAVE A CHAT OR SOMETHING?
HUUUH ...?
UMM, WE WERE SEARCHING FOR SOMETHING IN THE GRAND LIBRARY...
...BUT WE SEEM TO BE A LITTLE LOST...

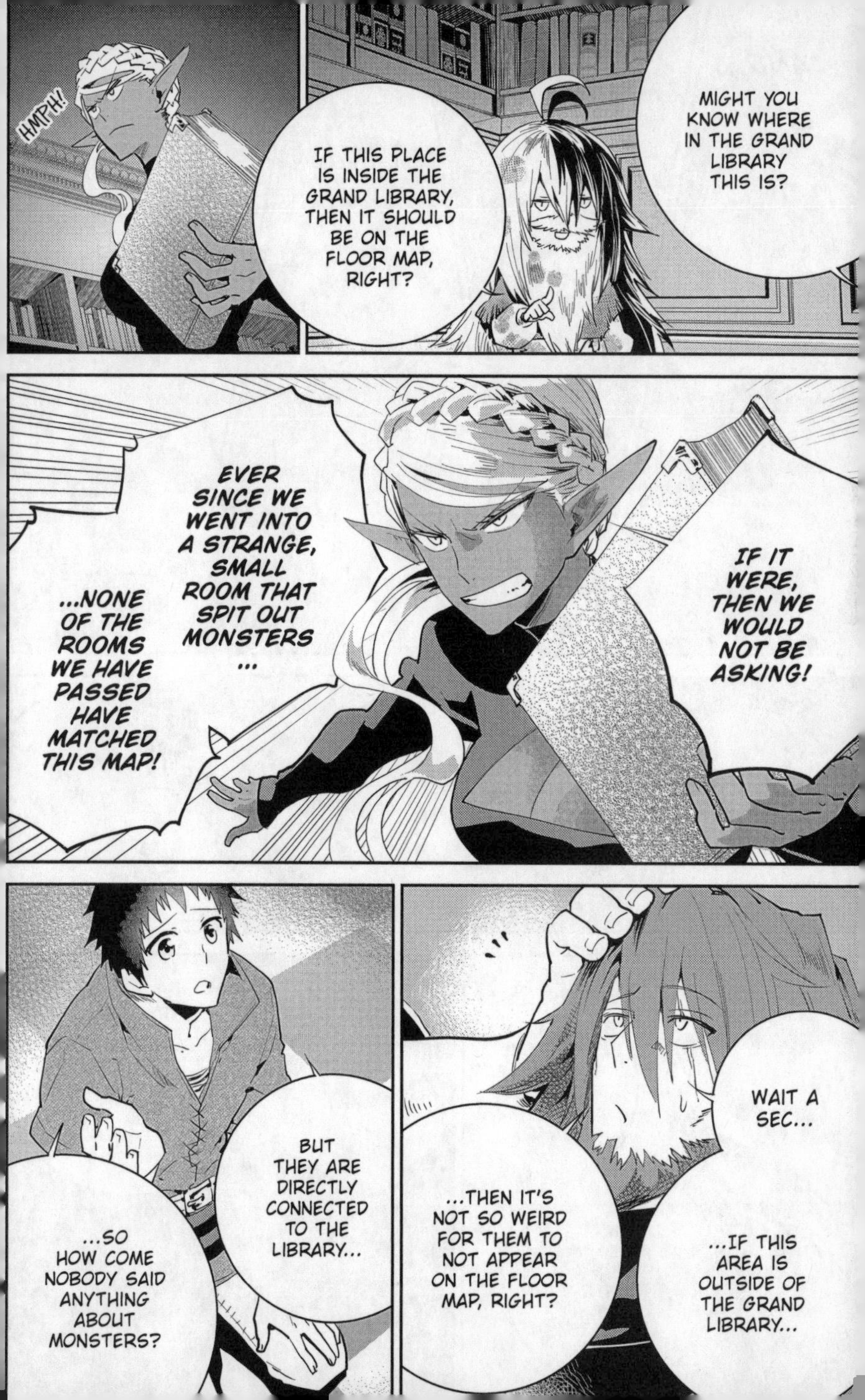
MIGHT YOU KNOW WHERE IN THE GRAND LIBRARY THIS IS?
IF THIS PLACE IS INSIDE THE GRAND LIBRARY, THEN IT SHOULD BE ON THE FLOOR MAP, RIGHT?
HMPH!
IF IT WERE, THEN WE WOULD NOT BE ASKING!
EVER SINCE WE WENT INTO A STRANGE, SMALL ROOM THAT SPIT OUT MONSTERS...
...NONE OF THE ROOMS WE HAVE PASSED HAVE MATCHED THIS MAP!
WAIT A SEC...
...IF THIS AREA IS OUTSIDE OF THE GRAND LIBRARY...
...THEN IT'S NOT SO WEIRD FOR THEM TO NOT APPEAR ON THE FLOOR MAP, RIGHT?
BUT THEY ARE DIRECTLY CONNECTED TO THE LIBRARY...
...SO HOW COME NOBODY SAID ANYTHING ABOUT MONSTERS?

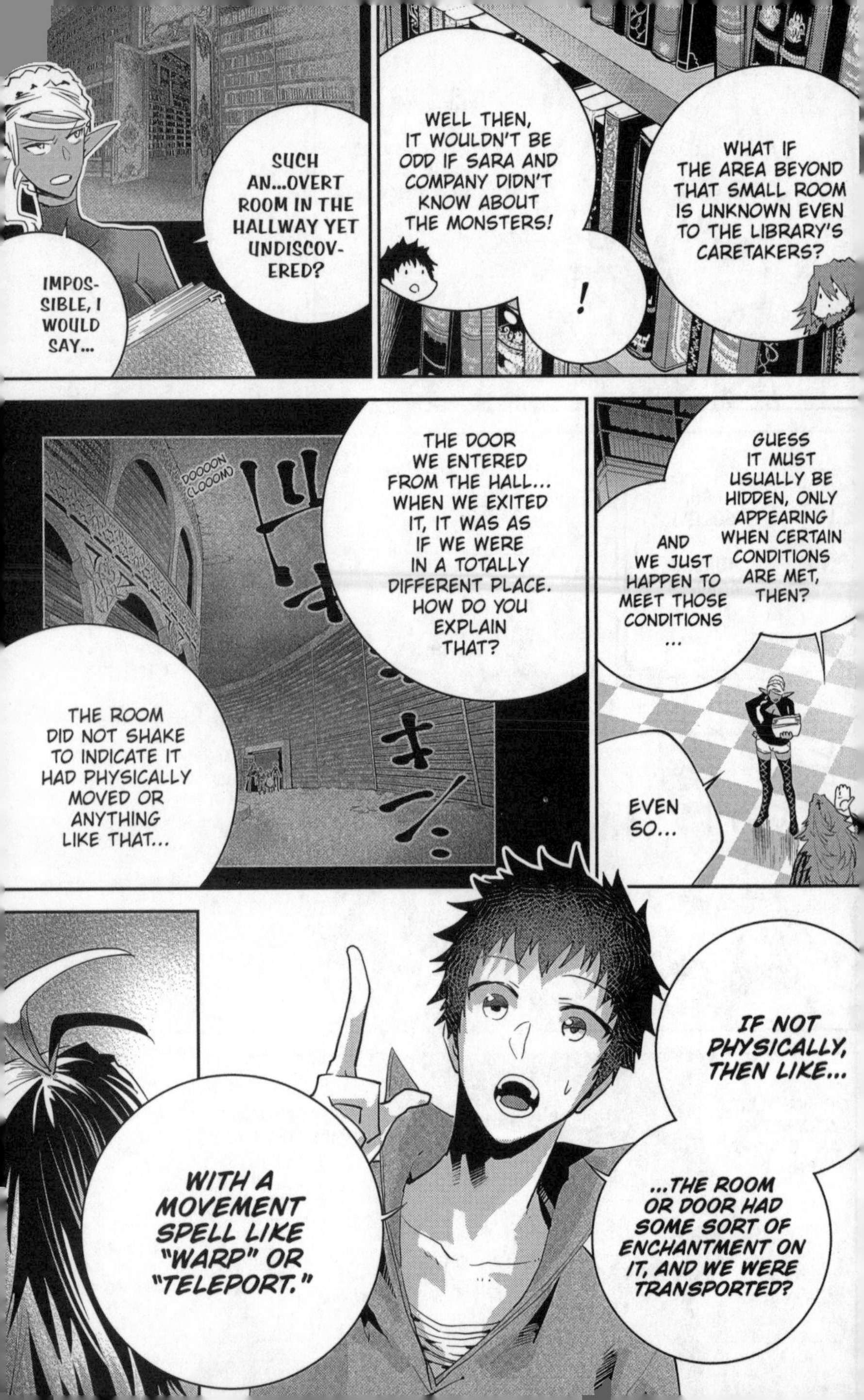
WHAT IF THE AREA BEYOND THAT SMALL ROOM IS UNKNOWN EVEN TO THE LIBRARY'S CARETAKERS?
WELL THEN, IT WOULDN'T BE ODD IF SARA AND COMPANY DIDN'T KNOW ABOUT THE MONSTERS!
!
SUCH AN...OVERT ROOM IN THE HALLWAY YET UNDISCOVERED?
IMPOSSIBLE, I WOULD SAY...
GUESS IT MUST USUALLY BE HIDDEN, ONLY APPEARING WHEN CERTAIN CONDITIONS ARE MET, THEN?
AND WE JUST HAPPEN TO MEET THOSE CONDITIONS...
EVEN SO...
THE DOOR WE ENTERED FROM THE HALL... WHEN WE EXITED IT, IT WAS AS IF WE WERE IN A TOTALLY DIFFERENT PLACE. HOW DO YOU EXPLAIN THAT?
DOOOON (LOOOM)
THE ROOM DID NOT SHAKE TO INDICATE IT HAD PHYSICALLY MOVED OR ANYTHING LIKE THAT...
IF NOT PHYSICALLY, THEN LIKE...
...THE ROOM OR DOOR HAD SOME SORT OF ENCHANTMENT ON IT, AND WE WERE TRANSPORTED?
WITH A MOVEMENT SPELL LIKE "WARP" OR "TELEPORT."

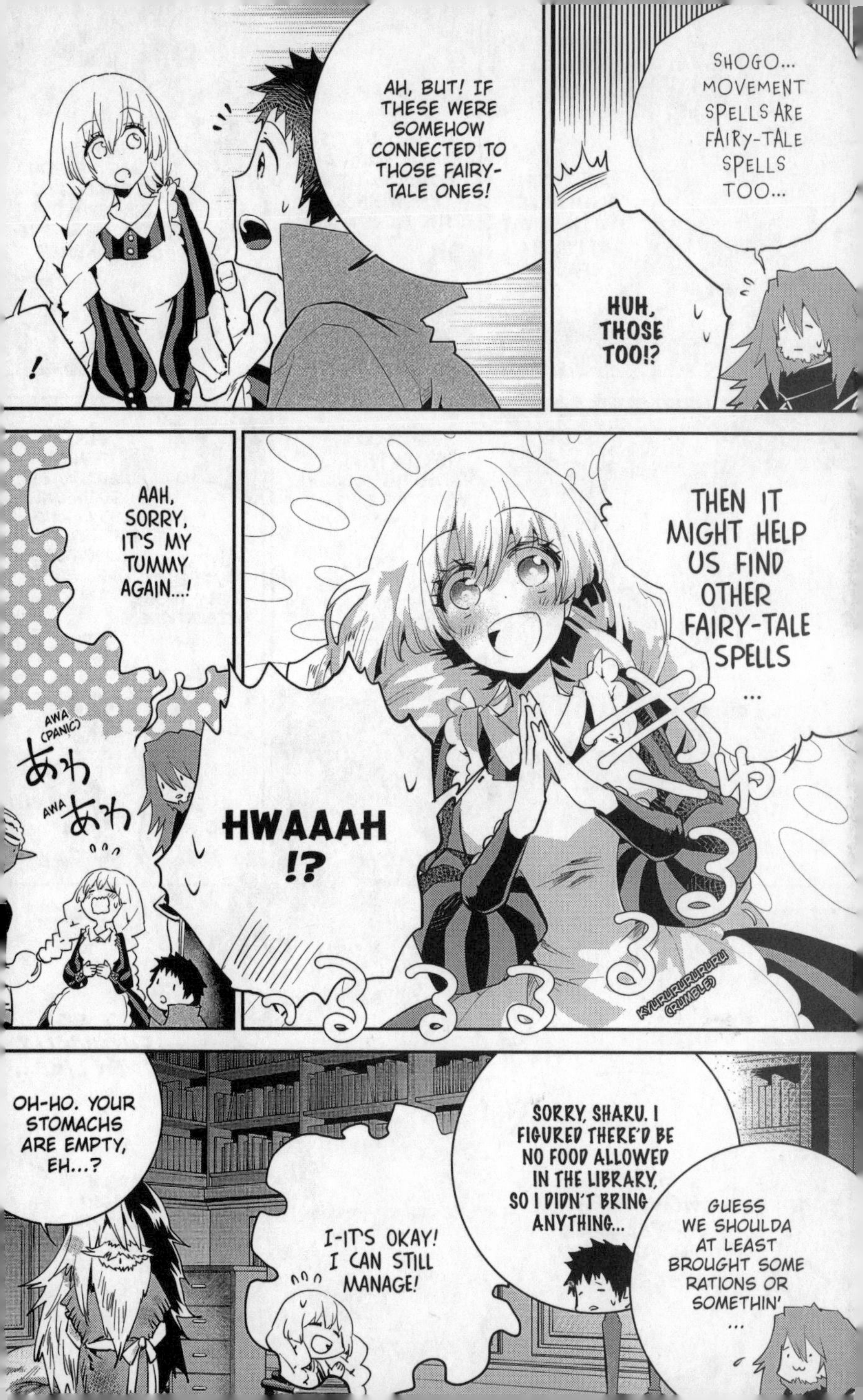
SHOGO... MOVEMENT SPELLS ARE FAIRY-TALE SPELLS TOO...
HUH, THOSE TOO!?
AH, BUT! IF THESE WERE SOMEHOW CONNECTED TO THOSE FAIRY-TALE ONES!
THEN IT MIGHT HELP US FIND OTHER FAIRY-TALE SPELLS ...
HWAAAH !?
KYURURURURURU (RUMBLE)
AAH, SORRY, IT'S MY TUMMY AGAIN...!
AWA (PANIC) あわ
AWA あわ
SORRY, SHARU. I FIGURED THERE'D BE NO FOOD ALLOWED IN THE LIBRARY, SO I DIDN'T BRING ANYTHING...
GUESS WE SHOULDA AT LEAST BROUGHT SOME RATIONS OR SOMETHIN' ...
I-IT'S OKAY! I CAN STILL MANAGE!
OH-HO. YOUR STOMACHS ARE EMPTY, EH...?

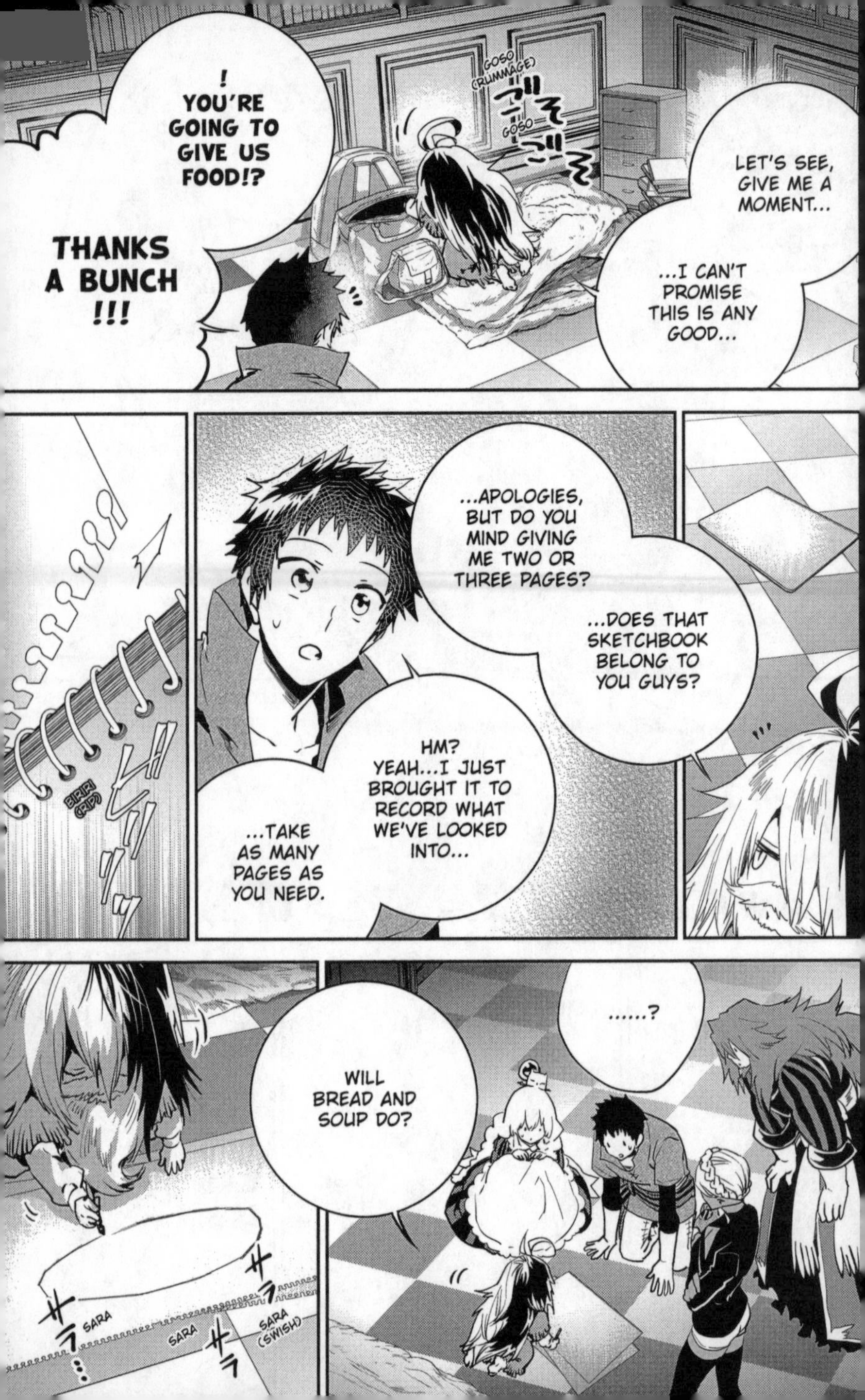
LET'S SEE, GIVE ME A MOMENT...
...I CAN'T PROMISE THIS IS ANY GOOD...
GOSO (RUMMAGE)
GOSO
! YOU'RE GOING TO GIVE US FOOD!?
THANKS A BUNCH!!!
...DOES THAT SKETCHBOOK BELONG TO YOU GUYS?
HM? YEAH...I JUST BROUGHT IT TO RECORD WHAT WE'VE LOOKED INTO...
...APOLOGIES, BUT DO YOU MIND GIVING ME TWO OR THREE PAGES?
...TAKE AS MANY PAGES AS YOU NEED.
BIRI (RIP)
......?
WILL BREAD AND SOUP DO?
SARA (SWISH)
SARA
SARA

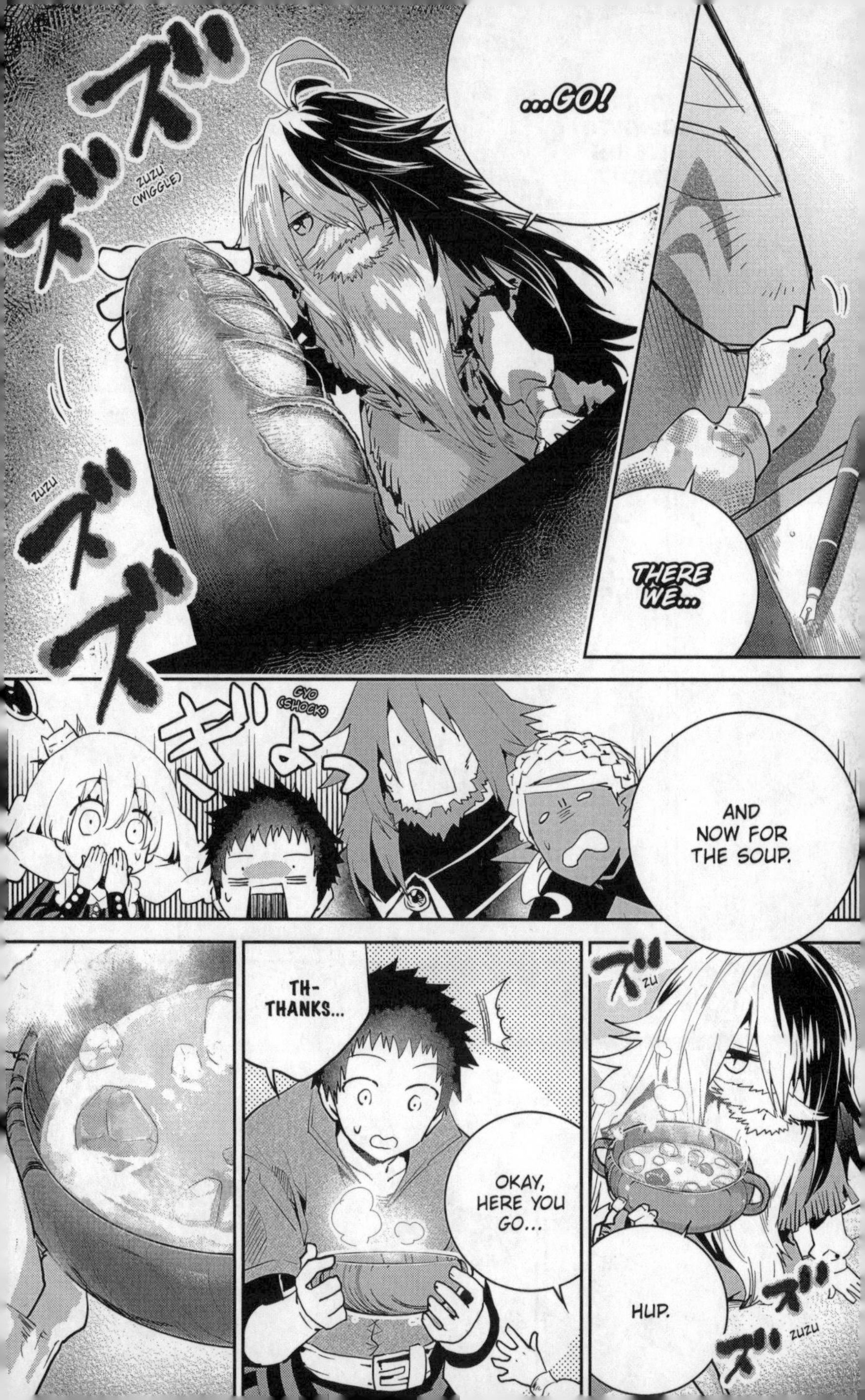
THERE WE...
...GO!
ZUZU (WIGGLE)
ZUZU
AND NOW FOR THE SOUP.
GYO (SHOCK)
ZU
HUP.
ZUZU
OKAY, HERE YOU GO...
TH- THANKS...

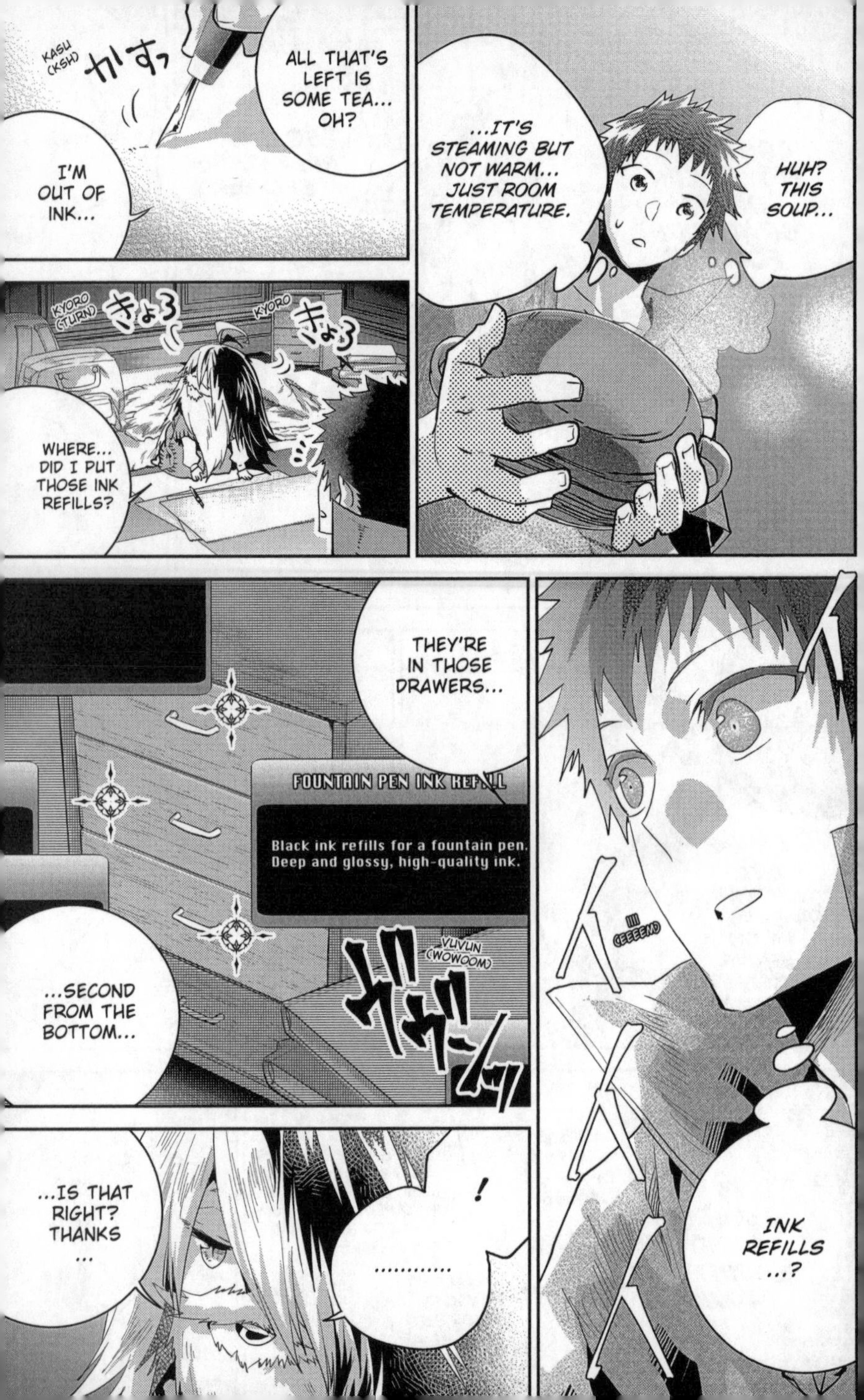
HUH? THIS SOUP...
...IT'S STEAMING BUT NOT WARM... JUST ROOM TEMPERATURE.
ALL THAT'S LEFT IS SOME TEA... OH?
KASU (KSH)
かすっ
I'M OUT OF INK...
KYORO
きょろ
KYORO (TURN)
きょろ
WHERE... DID I PUT THOSE INK REFILLS?
IIII (EEEEEM)
INK REFILLS ...?
THEY'RE IN THOSE DRAWERS...
FOUNTAIN PEN INK REFILL
Black ink refills for a fountain pen. Deep and glossy, high-quality ink.
VUVUN (WOWOOM)
...SECOND FROM THE BOTTOM...
!
...........
...IS THAT RIGHT? THANKS ...

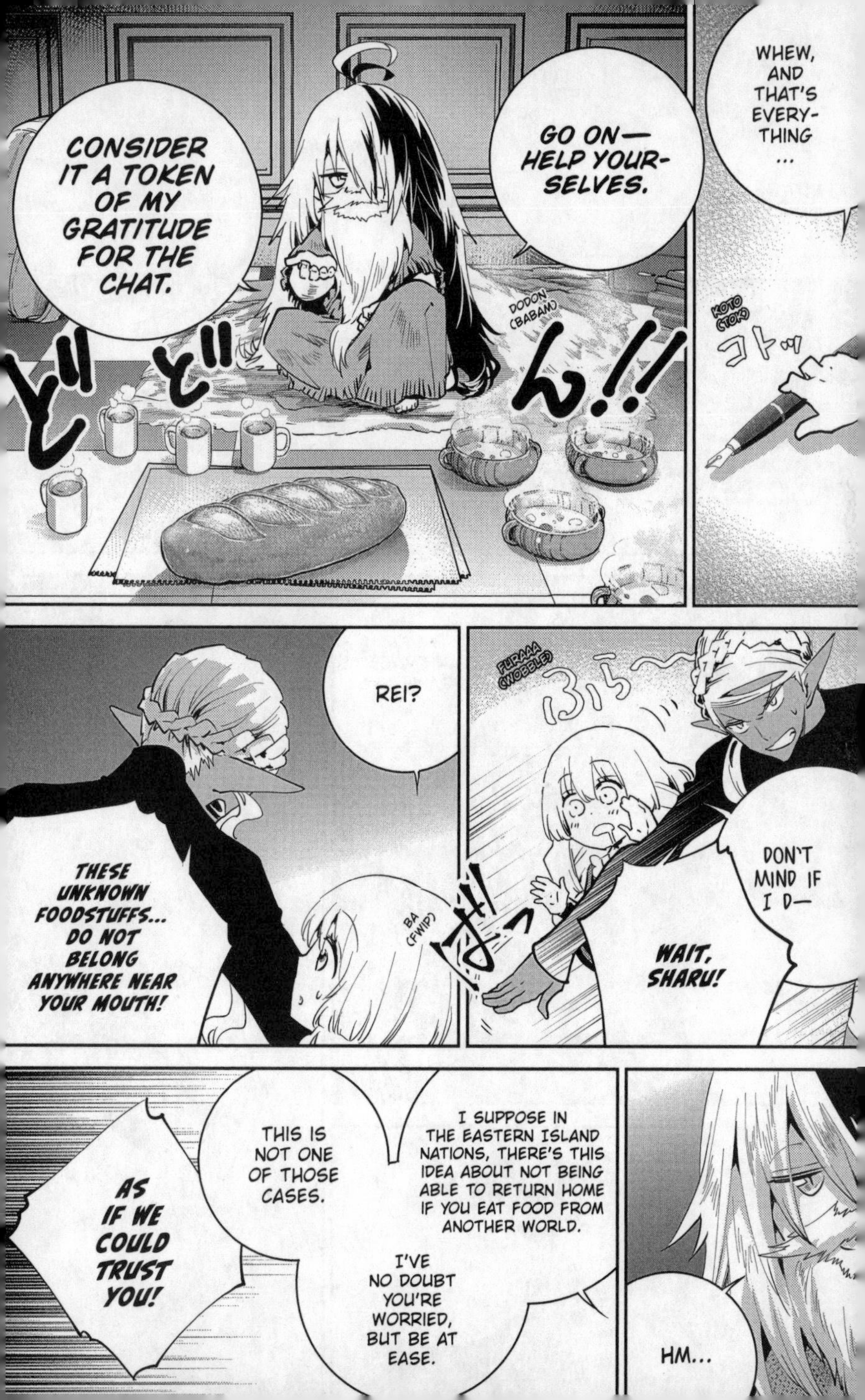
WHEW, AND THAT'S EVERYTHING...
KOTO (TOK)
コトッ
GO ON— HELP YOURSELVES.
CONSIDER IT A TOKEN OF MY GRATITUDE FOR THE CHAT.
DODON (BABAM)
どどん!!
FURAAA (WOBBLE)
ふら〜
DON'T MIND IF I D—
WAIT, SHARU!
BA (FWIP)
ばっ
REI?
THESE UNKNOWN FOODSTUFFS... DO NOT BELONG ANYWHERE NEAR YOUR MOUTH!
HM...
I SUPPOSE IN THE EASTERN ISLAND NATIONS, THERE'S THIS IDEA ABOUT NOT BEING ABLE TO RETURN HOME IF YOU EAT FOOD FROM ANOTHER WORLD.
I'VE NO DOUBT YOU'RE WORRIED, BUT BE AT EASE.
THIS IS NOT ONE OF THOSE CASES.
AS IF WE COULD TRUST YOU!

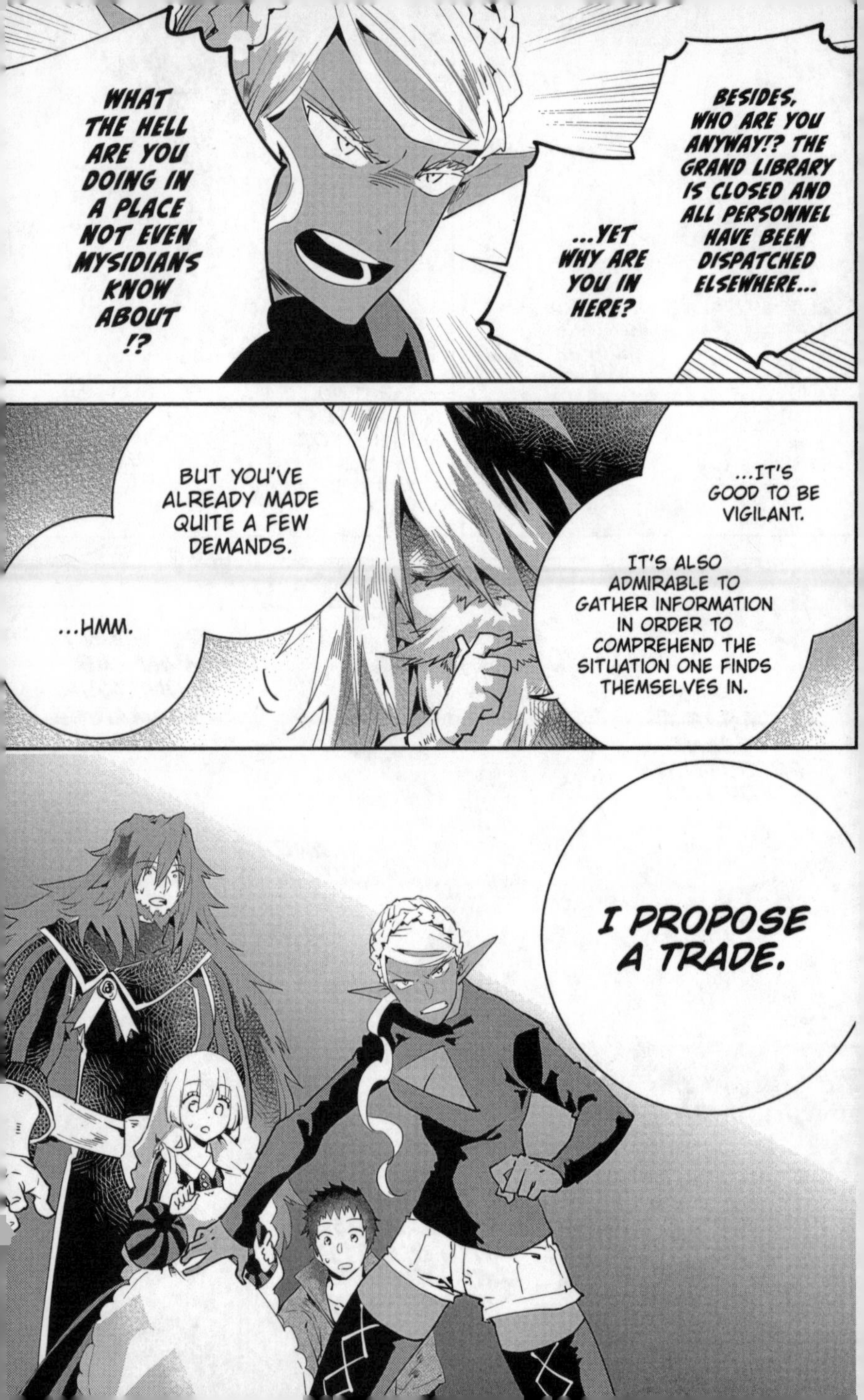
BESIDES, WHO ARE YOU ANYWAY!? THE GRAND LIBRARY IS CLOSED AND ALL PERSONNEL HAVE BEEN DISPATCHED ELSEWHERE...
...YET WHY ARE YOU IN HERE?
WHAT THE HELL ARE YOU DOING IN A PLACE NOT EVEN MYSIDIANS KNOW ABOUT!?
...IT'S GOOD TO BE VIGILANT.
IT'S ALSO ADMIRABLE TO GATHER INFORMATION IN ORDER TO COMPREHEND THE SITUATION ONE FINDS THEMSELVES IN.
BUT YOU'VE ALREADY MADE QUITE A FEW DEMANDS.
...HMM.
I PROPOSE A TRADE.

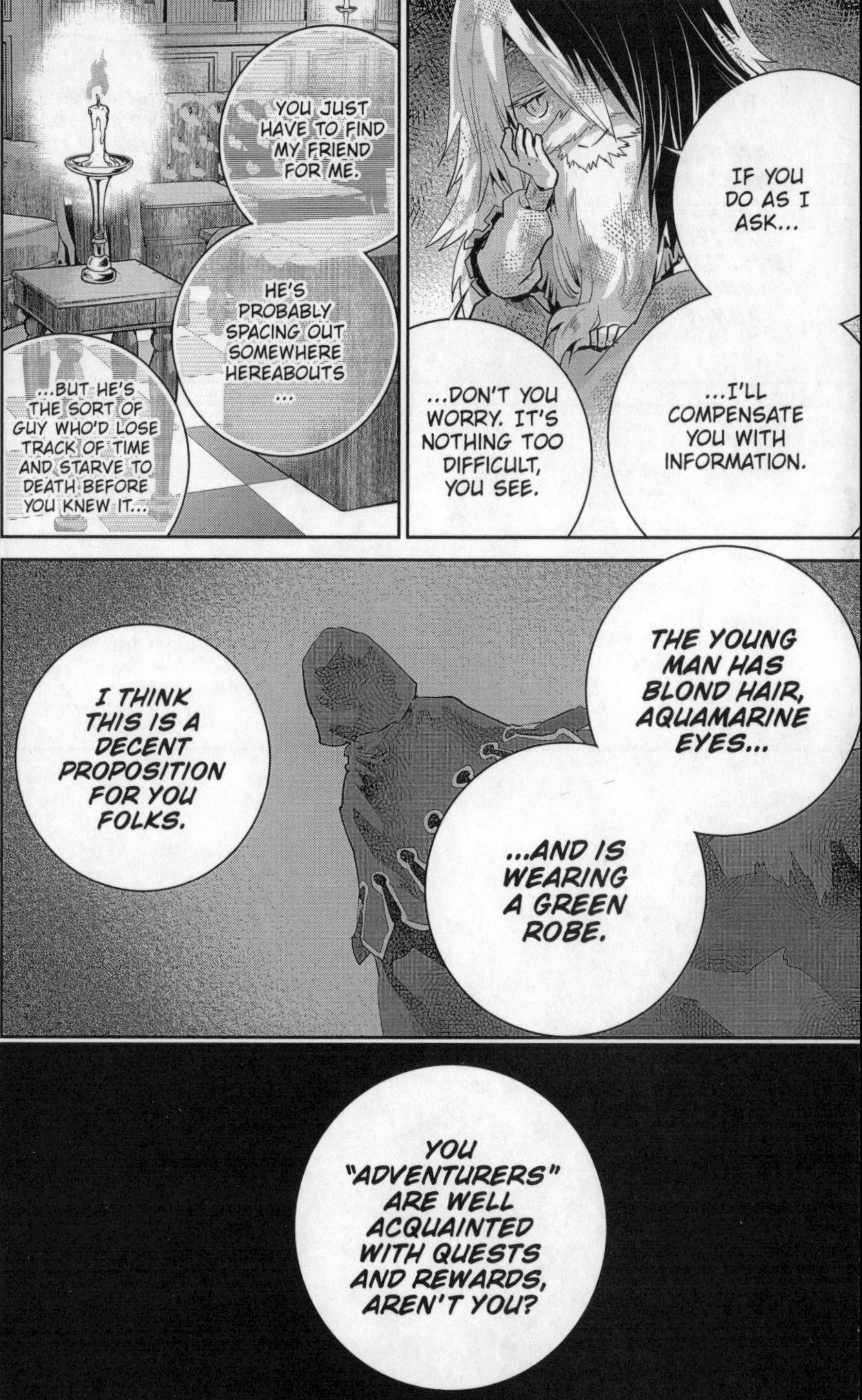
IF YOU DO AS I ASK...
...I'LL COMPENSATE YOU WITH INFORMATION.
...DON'T YOU WORRY. IT'S NOTHING TOO DIFFICULT, YOU SEE.
YOU JUST HAVE TO FIND MY FRIEND FOR ME.
HE'S PROBABLY SPACING OUT SOMEWHERE HEREABOUTS...
...BUT HE'S THE SORT OF GUY WHO'D LOSE TRACK OF TIME AND STARVE TO DEATH BEFORE YOU KNEW IT...
THE YOUNG MAN HAS BLOND HAIR, AQUAMARINE EYES...
...AND IS WEARING A GREEN ROBE.
I THINK THIS IS A DECENT PROPOSITION FOR YOU FOLKS.
YOU "ADVENTURERS" ARE WELL ACQUAINTED WITH QUESTS AND REWARDS, AREN'T YOU?

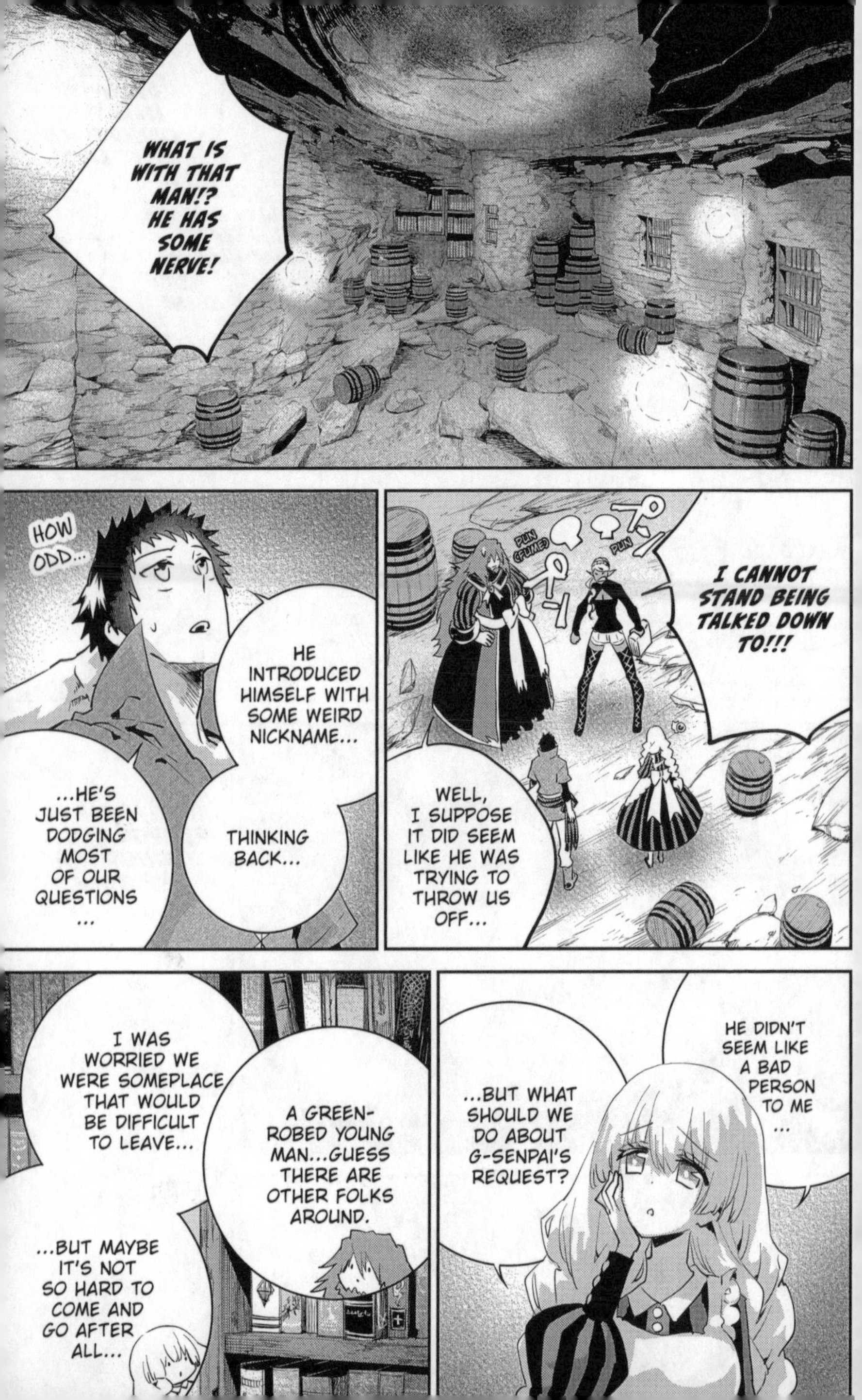
WHAT IS WITH THAT MAN!? HE HAS SOME NERVE!
PUN (FUME)
PUN
I CANNOT STAND BEING TALKED DOWN TO!!!
WELL, I SUPPOSE IT DID SEEM LIKE HE WAS TRYING TO THROW US OFF...
HOW ODD...
HE INTRODUCED HIMSELF WITH SOME WEIRD NICKNAME...
THINKING BACK...
...HE'S JUST BEEN DODGING MOST OF OUR QUESTIONS ...
HE DIDN'T SEEM LIKE A BAD PERSON TO ME ...
...BUT WHAT SHOULD WE DO ABOUT G-SENPAI'S REQUEST?
I WAS WORRIED WE WERE SOMEPLACE THAT WOULD BE DIFFICULT TO LEAVE...
A GREEN-ROBED YOUNG MAN...GUESS THERE ARE OTHER FOLKS AROUND.
...BUT MAYBE IT'S NOT SO HARD TO COME AND GO AFTER ALL...

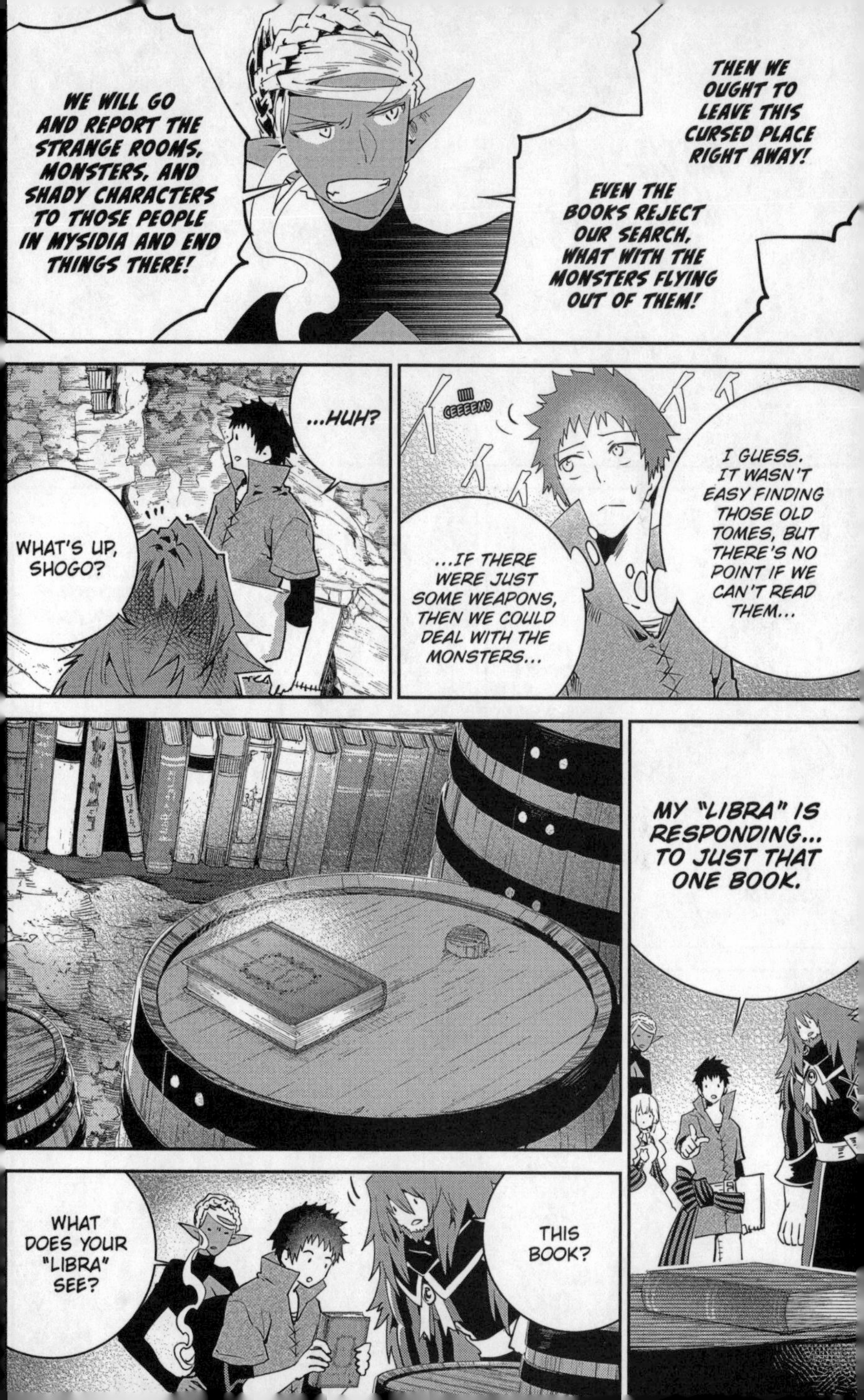
THEN WE OUGHT TO LEAVE THIS CURSED PLACE RIGHT AWAY!
EVEN THE BOOKS REJECT OUR SEARCH, WHAT WITH THE MONSTERS FLYING OUT OF THEM!
WE WILL GO AND REPORT THE STRANGE ROOMS, MONSTERS, AND SHADY CHARACTERS TO THOSE PEOPLE IN MYSIDIA AND END THINGS THERE!
I GUESS. IT WASN'T EASY FINDING THOSE OLD TOMES, BUT THERE'S NO POINT IF WE CAN'T READ THEM...
...IF THERE WERE JUST SOME WEAPONS, THEN WE COULD DEAL WITH THE MONSTERS...
...HUH?
WHAT'S UP, SHOGO?
MY "LIBRA" IS RESPONDING... TO JUST THAT ONE BOOK.
THIS BOOK?
WHAT DOES YOUR "LIBRA" SEE?

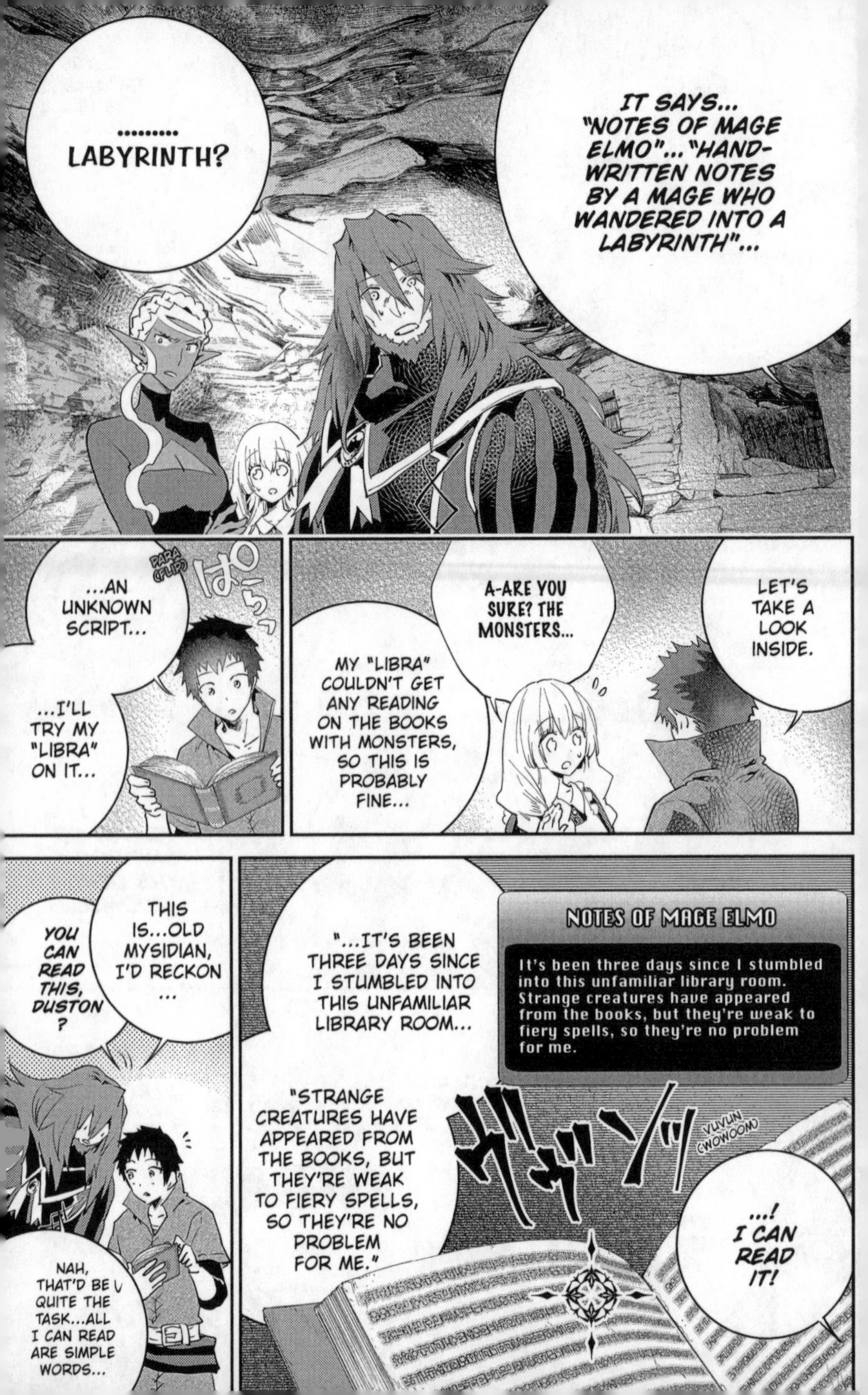
IT SAYS... "NOTES OF MAGE ELMO"... "HAND-WRITTEN NOTES BY A MAGE WHO WANDERED INTO A LABYRINTH"...
......... LABYRINTH?
LET'S TAKE A LOOK INSIDE.
A-ARE YOU SURE? THE MONSTERS...
MY "LIBRA" COULDN'T GET ANY READING ON THE BOOKS WITH MONSTERS, SO THIS IS PROBABLY FINE...
PARA (FLIP)
...AN UNKNOWN SCRIPT...
...I'LL TRY MY "LIBRA" ON IT...
NOTES OF MAGE ELMO
It's been three days since I stumbled into this unfamiliar library room. Strange creatures have appeared from the books, but they're weak to fiery spells, so they're no problem for me.
VUVUN (WOWOOM)
"...IT'S BEEN THREE DAYS SINCE I STUMBLED INTO THIS UNFAMILIAR LIBRARY ROOM...
"STRANGE CREATURES HAVE APPEARED FROM THE BOOKS, BUT THEY'RE WEAK TO FIERY SPELLS, SO THEY'RE NO PROBLEM FOR ME."
...! I CAN READ IT!
THIS IS...OLD MYSIDIAN, I'D RECKON...
YOU CAN READ THIS, DUSTON?
NAH, THAT'D BE QUITE THE TASK...ALL I CAN READ ARE SIMPLE WORDS...

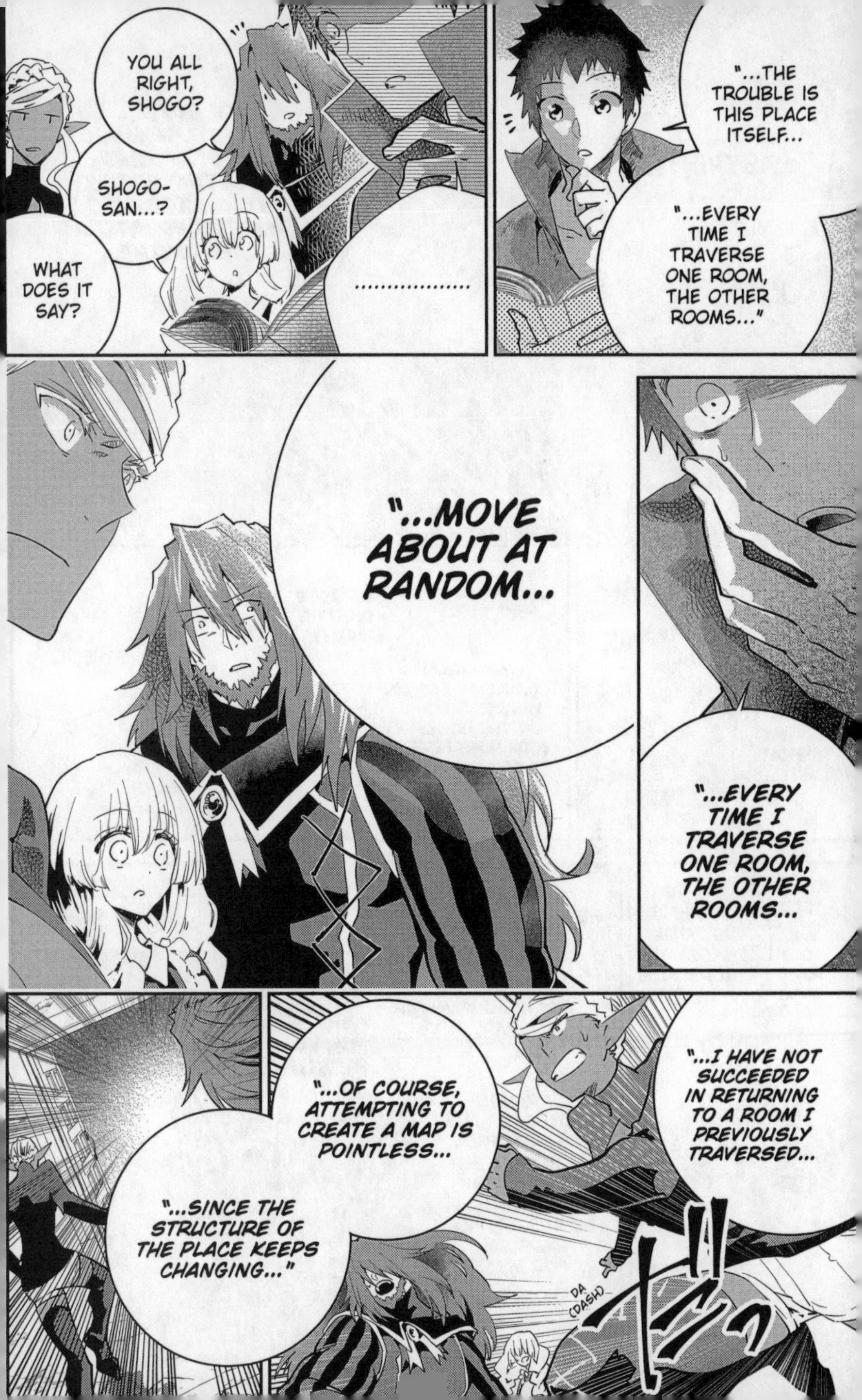
"...THE TROUBLE IS THIS PLACE ITSELF...
"...EVERY TIME I TRAVERSE ONE ROOM, THE OTHER ROOMS..."
YOU ALL RIGHT, SHOGO?
SHOGO-SAN...?
..................
WHAT DOES IT SAY?
"...EVERY TIME I TRAVERSE ONE ROOM, THE OTHER ROOMS...
"...MOVE ABOUT AT RANDOM...
"...I HAVE NOT SUCCEEDED IN RETURNING TO A ROOM I PREVIOUSLY TRAVERSED...
"...OF COURSE, ATTEMPTING TO CREATE A MAP IS POINTLESS...
"...SINCE THE STRUCTURE OF THE PLACE KEEPS CHANGING..."
DA (DASH)

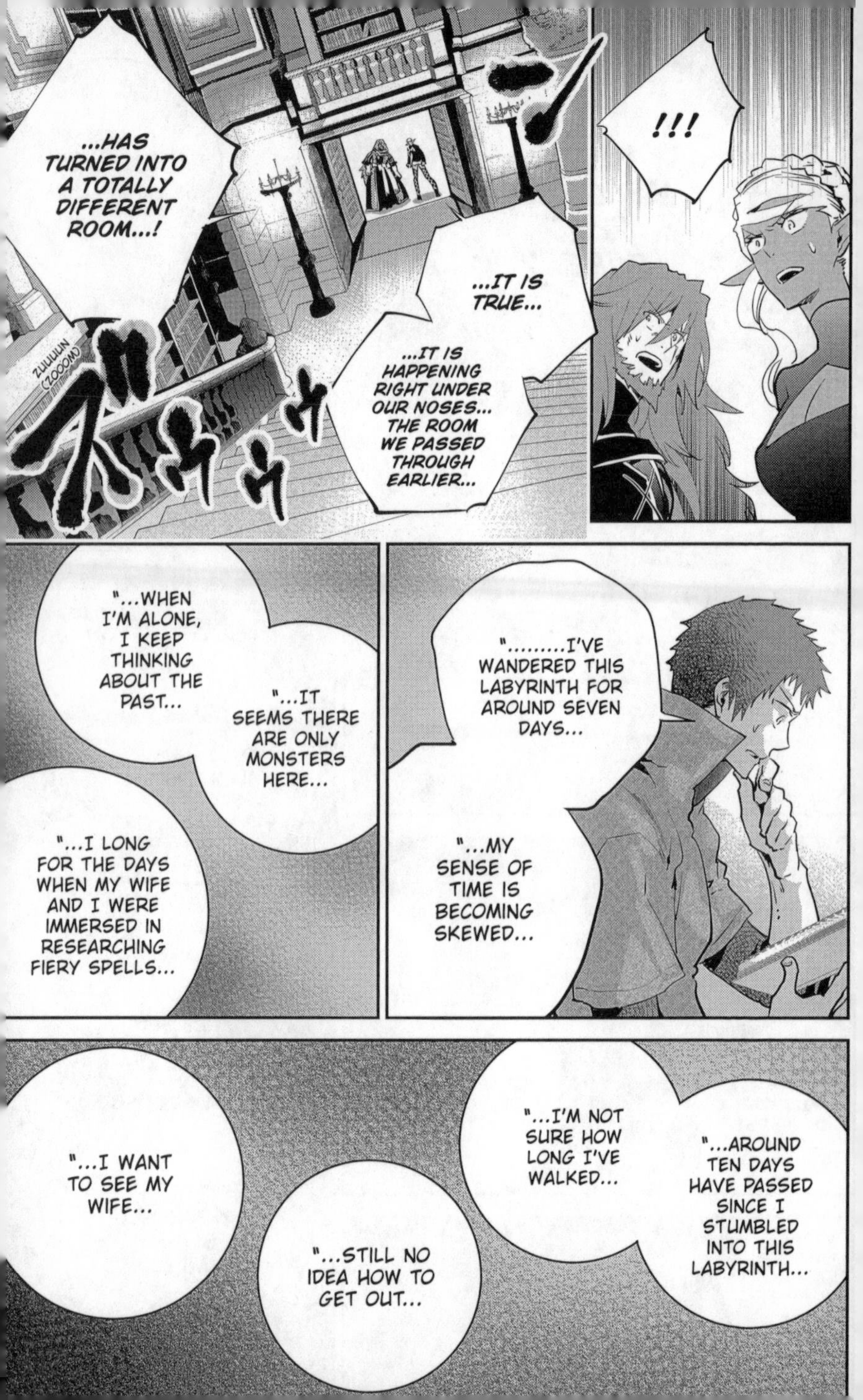
!!!
...IT IS TRUE...
...IT IS HAPPENING RIGHT UNDER OUR NOSES... THE ROOM WE PASSED THROUGH EARLIER...
...HAS TURNED INTO A TOTALLY DIFFERENT ROOM...!
ZUUUUN (ZOOOM)
"........I'VE WANDERED THIS LABYRINTH FOR AROUND SEVEN DAYS...
"...MY SENSE OF TIME IS BECOMING SKEWED...
"...IT SEEMS THERE ARE ONLY MONSTERS HERE...
"...WHEN I'M ALONE, I KEEP THINKING ABOUT THE PAST...
"...I LONG FOR THE DAYS WHEN MY WIFE AND I WERE IMMERSED IN RESEARCHING FIERY SPELLS...
"...AROUND TEN DAYS HAVE PASSED SINCE I STUMBLED INTO THIS LABYRINTH...
"...I'M NOT SURE HOW LONG I'VE WALKED...
"...STILL NO IDEA HOW TO GET OUT...
"...I WANT TO SEE MY WIFE...

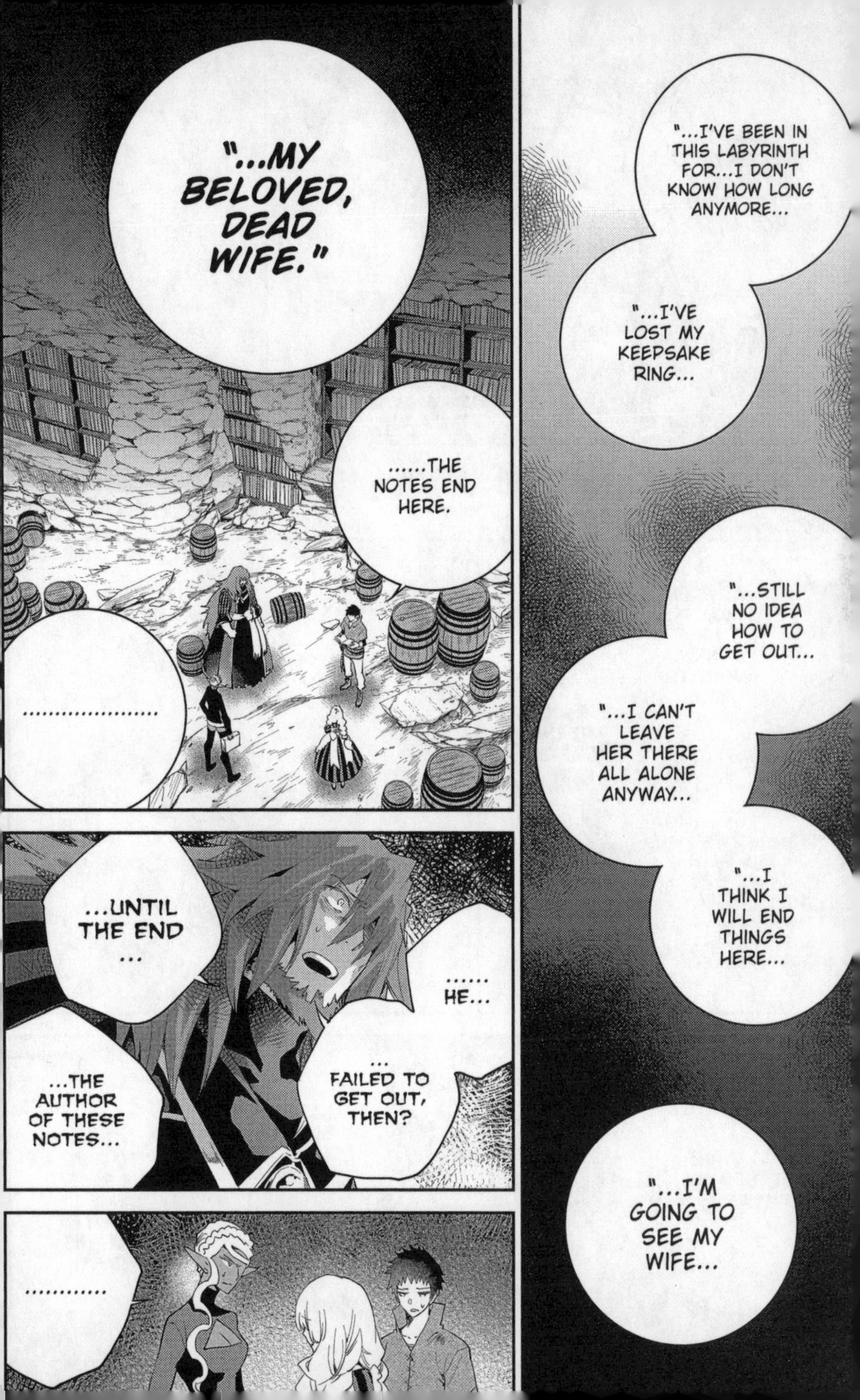
"...I'VE BEEN IN THIS LABYRINTH FOR...I DON'T KNOW HOW LONG ANYMORE...
"...I'VE LOST MY KEEPSAKE RING...
"...STILL NO IDEA HOW TO GET OUT...
"...I CAN'T LEAVE HER THERE ALL ALONE ANYWAY...
"...I THINK I WILL END THINGS HERE...
"...I'M GOING TO SEE MY WIFE...
"...MY BELOVED, DEAD WIFE."
......THE NOTES END HERE.
....................
...UNTIL THE END ...
...... HE...
...THE AUTHOR OF THESE NOTES...
... FAILED TO GET OUT, THEN?
............

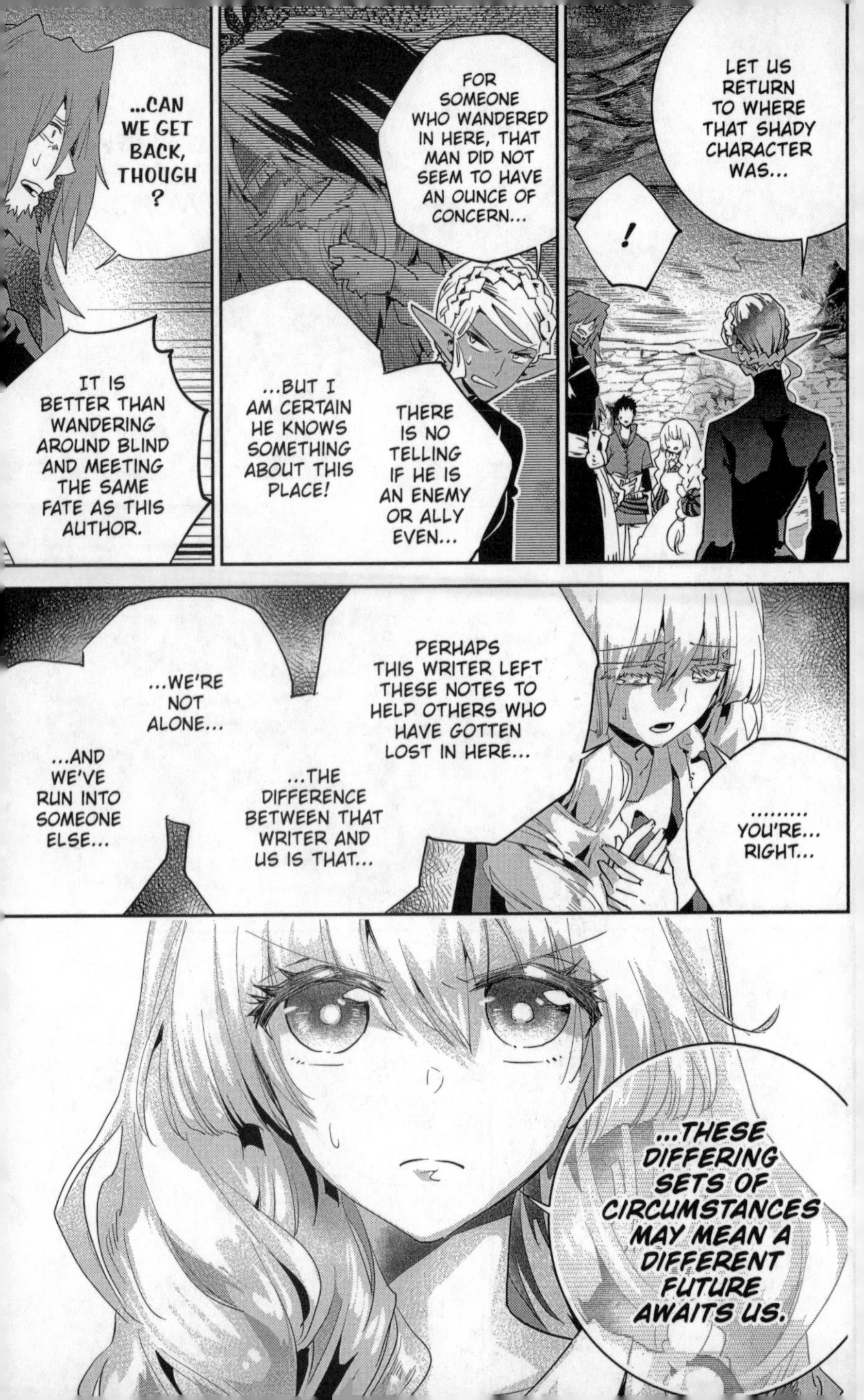
LET US RETURN TO WHERE THAT SHADY CHARACTER WAS...
!
FOR SOMEONE WHO WANDERED IN HERE, THAT MAN DID NOT SEEM TO HAVE AN OUNCE OF CONCERN...
THERE IS NO TELLING IF HE IS AN ENEMY OR ALLY EVEN...
...BUT I AM CERTAIN HE KNOWS SOMETHING ABOUT THIS PLACE!
...CAN WE GET BACK, THOUGH?
IT IS BETTER THAN WANDERING AROUND BLIND AND MEETING THE SAME FATE AS THIS AUTHOR.
........ YOU'RE... RIGHT...
PERHAPS THIS WRITER LEFT THESE NOTES TO HELP OTHERS WHO HAVE GOTTEN LOST IN HERE...
...THE DIFFERENCE BETWEEN THAT WRITER AND US IS THAT...
...WE'RE NOT ALONE...
...AND WE'VE RUN INTO SOMEONE ELSE...
...THESE DIFFERING SETS OF CIRCUMSTANCES MAY MEAN A DIFFERENT FUTURE AWAITS US.

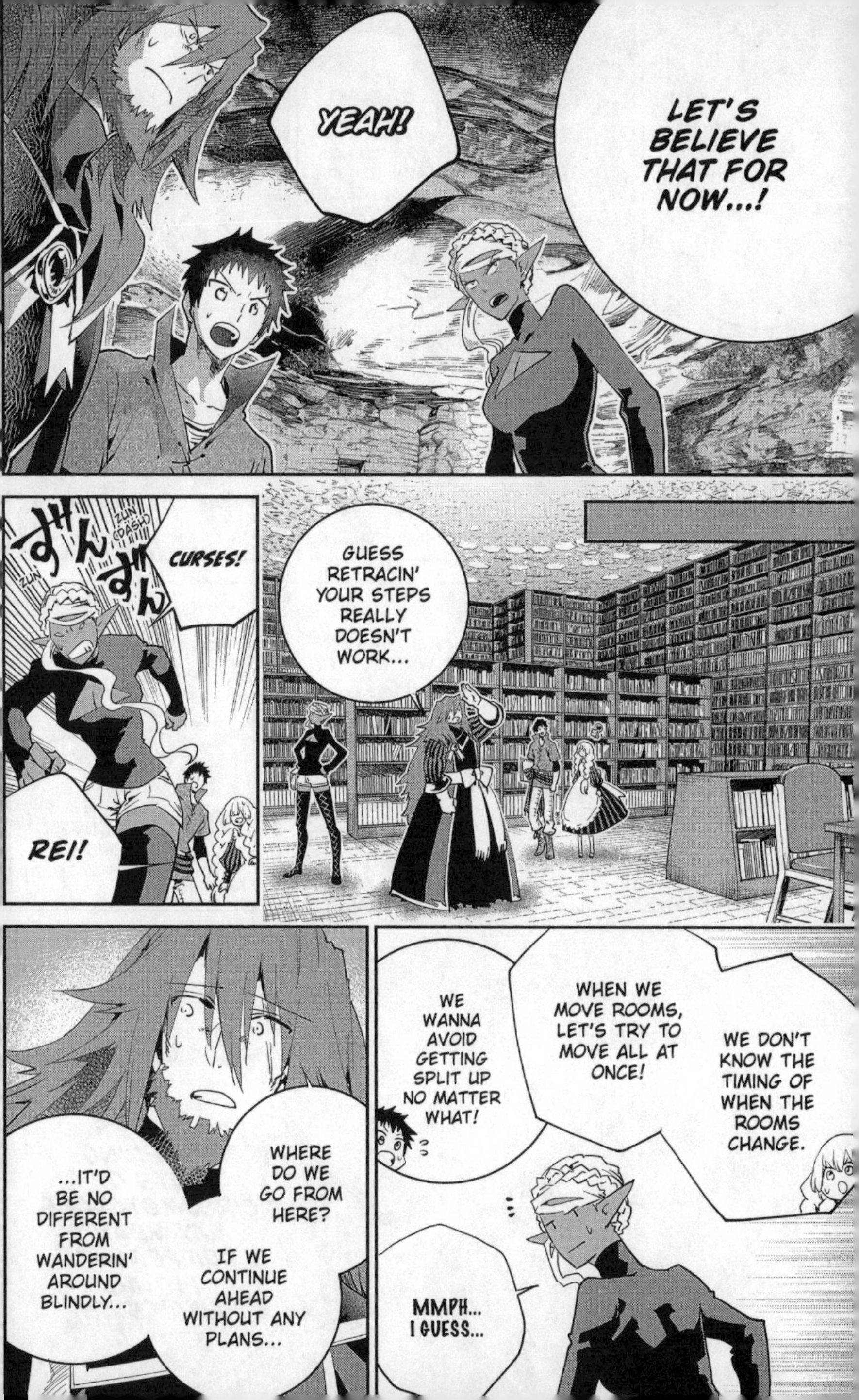
LET'S BELIEVE THAT FOR NOW...!
YEAH!
GUESS RETRACIN' YOUR STEPS REALLY DOESN'T WORK...
CURSES!
ずん ずん
ZUN (DASH)
ZUN
REI!
WE DON'T KNOW THE TIMING OF WHEN THE ROOMS CHANGE.
WHEN WE MOVE ROOMS, LET'S TRY TO MOVE ALL AT ONCE!
WE WANNA AVOID GETTING SPLIT UP NO MATTER WHAT!
MMPH... I GUESS...
WHERE DO WE GO FROM HERE?
IF WE CONTINUE AHEAD WITHOUT ANY PLANS...
...IT'D BE NO DIFFERENT FROM WANDERIN' AROUND BLINDLY...

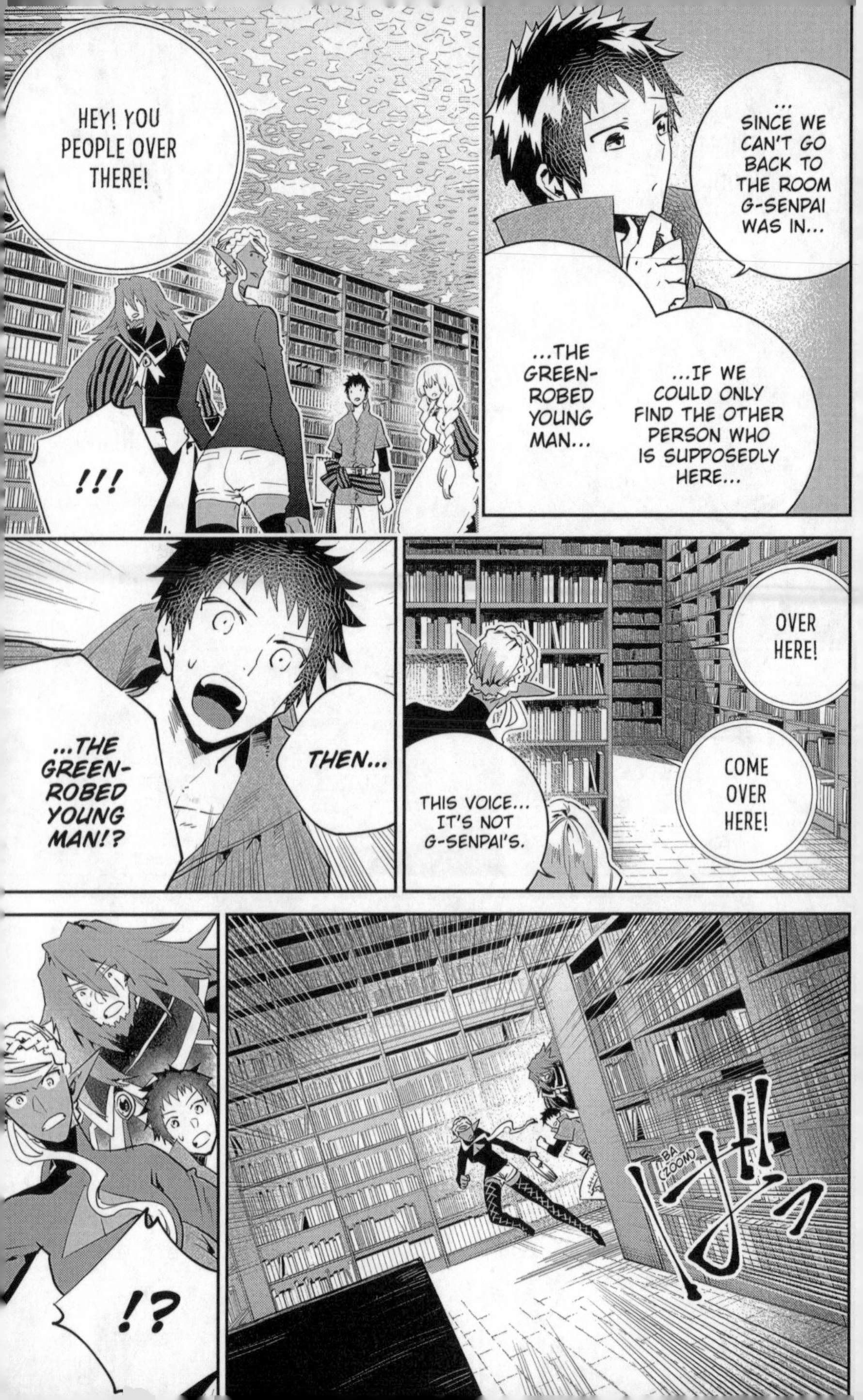
...
SINCE WE CAN'T GO BACK TO THE ROOM G-SENPAI WAS IN...
...IF WE COULD ONLY FIND THE OTHER PERSON WHO IS SUPPOSEDLY HERE...
...THE GREEN-ROBED YOUNG MAN...
HEY! YOU PEOPLE OVER THERE!
!!!
OVER HERE!
COME OVER HERE!
THIS VOICE... IT'S NOT G-SENPAI'S.
THEN...
...THE GREEN-ROBED YOUNG MAN!?
BA (ZOOM)
!?

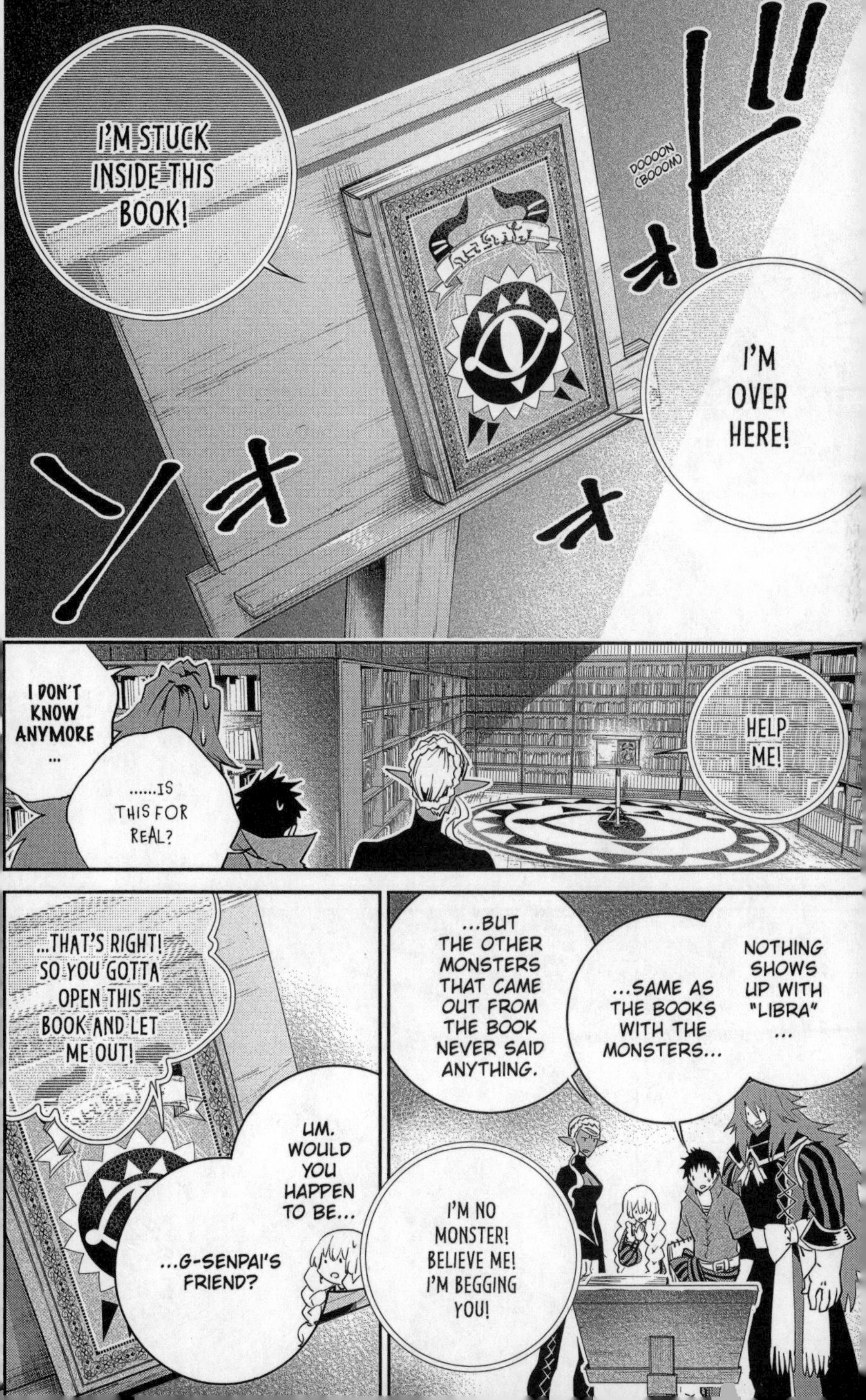
DOOOON (BOOOM)
I'M OVER HERE!
I'M STUCK INSIDE THIS BOOK!
HELP ME!
I DON'T KNOW ANYMORE ...
......IS THIS FOR REAL?
NOTHING SHOWS UP WITH "LIBRA" ...
...SAME AS THE BOOKS WITH THE MONSTERS...
...BUT THE OTHER MONSTERS THAT CAME OUT FROM THE BOOK NEVER SAID ANYTHING.
I'M NO MONSTER! BELIEVE ME! I'M BEGGING YOU!
UM. WOULD YOU HAPPEN TO BE...
...G-SENPAI'S FRIEND?
...THAT'S RIGHT! SO YOU GOTTA OPEN THIS BOOK AND LET ME OUT!

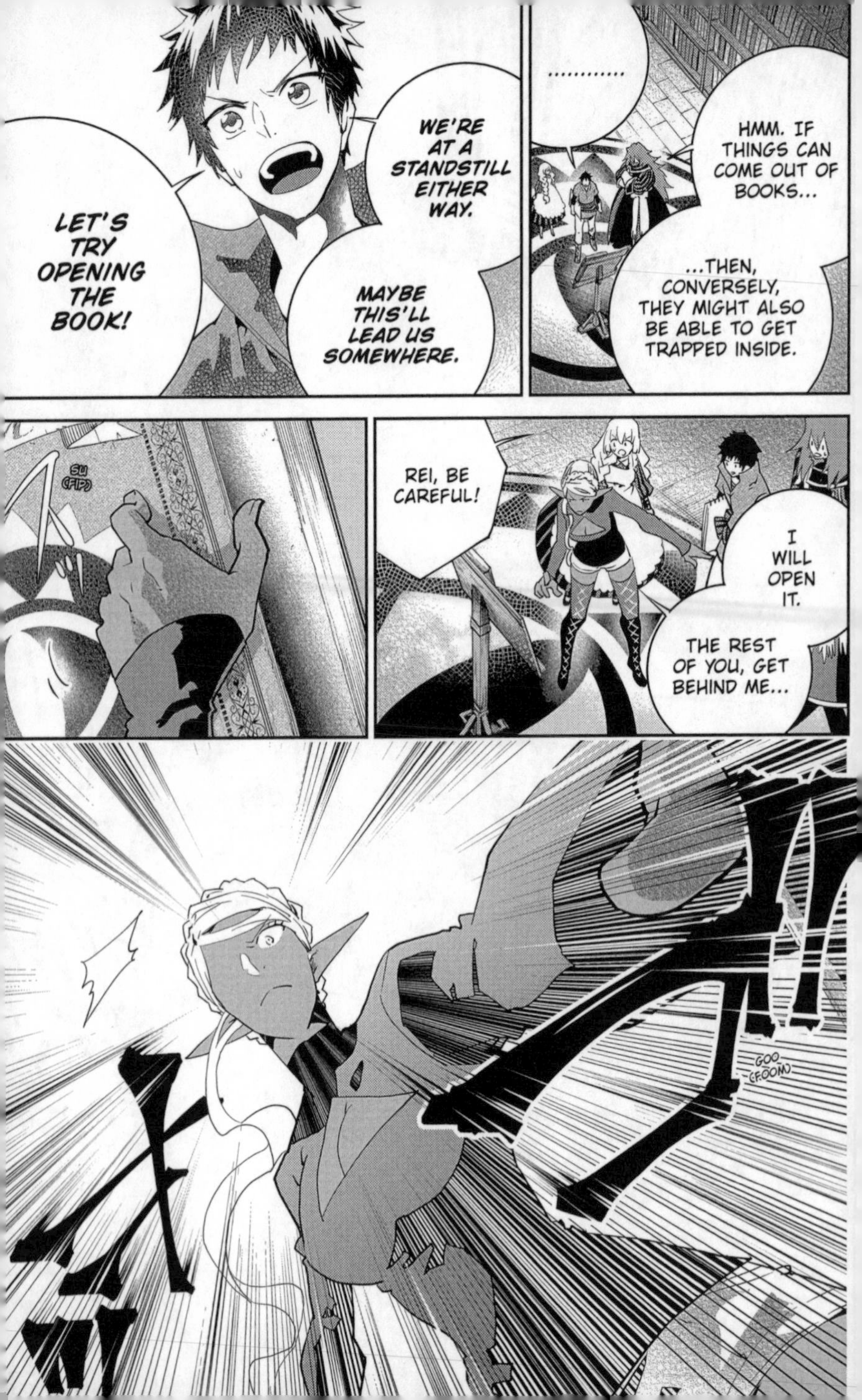
............
HMM. IF THINGS CAN COME OUT OF BOOKS...
...THEN, CONVERSELY, THEY MIGHT ALSO BE ABLE TO GET TRAPPED INSIDE.
WE'RE AT A STANDSTILL EITHER WAY.
LET'S TRY OPENING THE BOOK!
MAYBE THIS'LL LEAD US SOMEWHERE.
REI, BE CAREFUL!
I WILL OPEN IT.
THE REST OF YOU, GET BEHIND ME...
SU (FIP)
GOO (F-OOM)

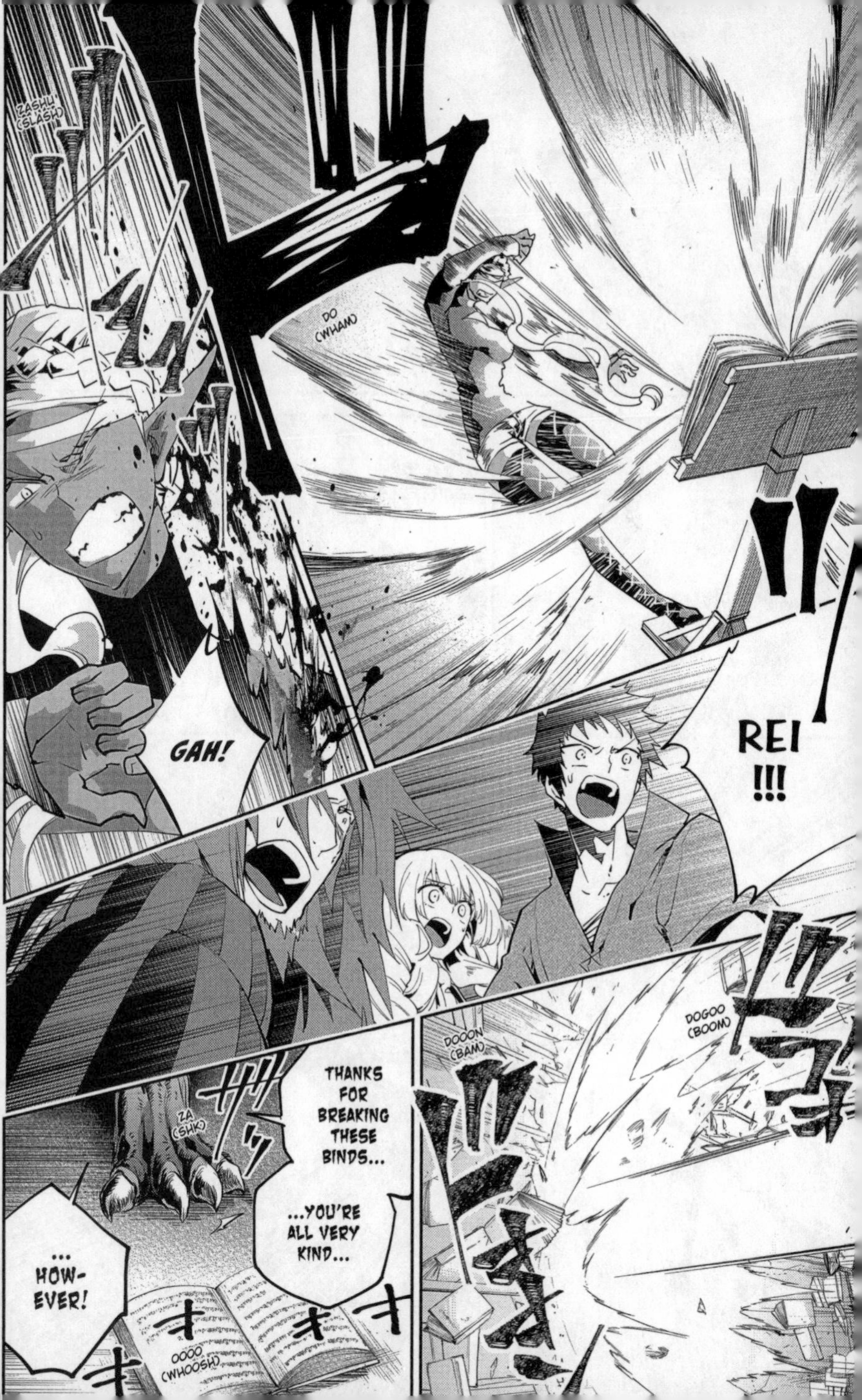
DO (WHAM)
ZASHU (SLASH)
GAH!
REI !!!
DOGOO (BOOM)
DOOON (BAM)
ZA (SHK)
THANKS FOR BREAKING THESE BINDS...
...YOU'RE ALL VERY KIND...
...HOW-EVER!
OOOO (WHOOSH)

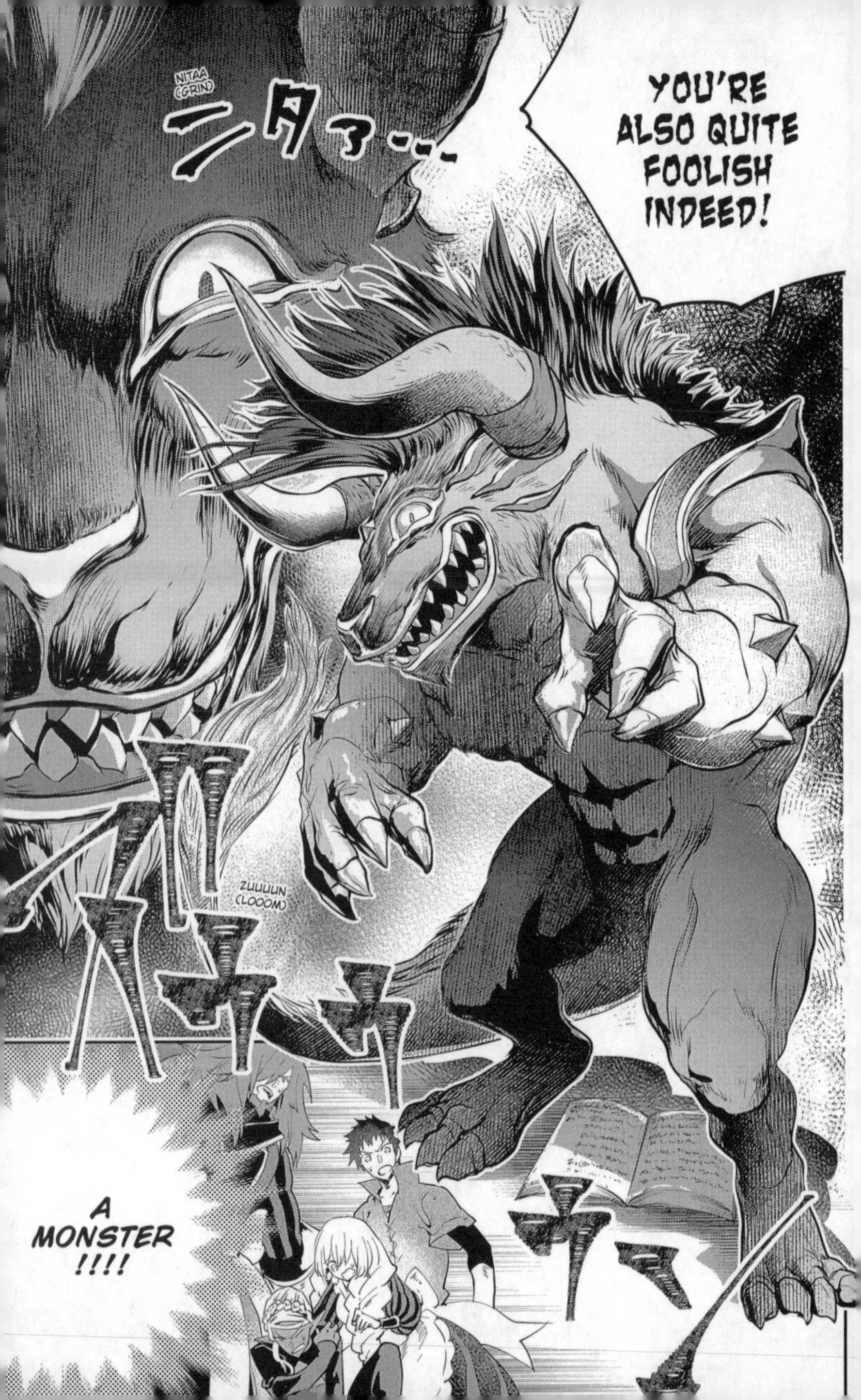
YOU'RE ALSO QUITE FOOLISH INDEED!
NITAA (GRIN)
ニタァ…
ZUUUUN (LOOOM)
A MONSTER !!!!

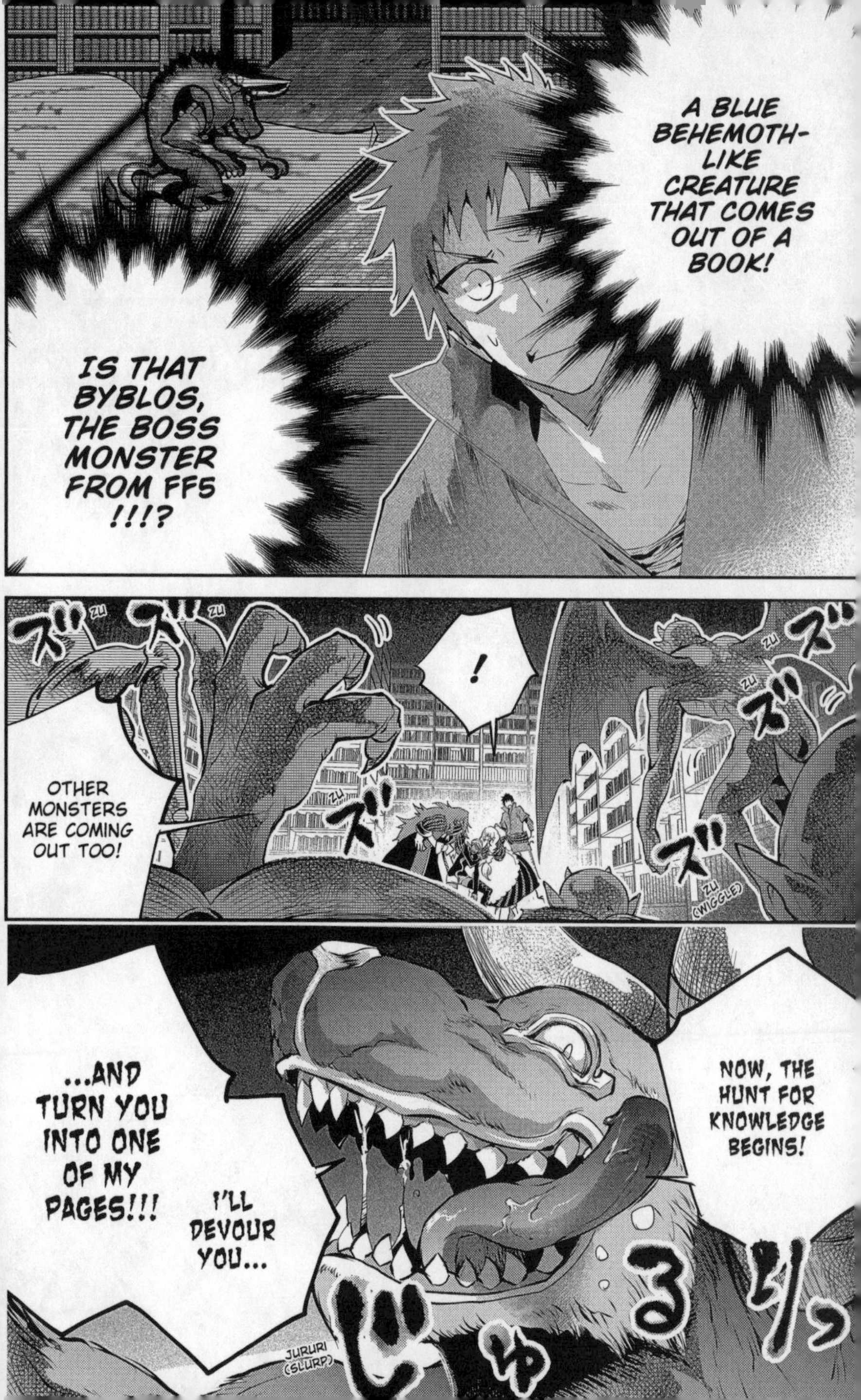
A BLUE BEHEMOTH-LIKE CREATURE THAT COMES OUT OF A BOOK!
IS THAT BYBLOS, THE BOSS MONSTER FROM FF5 !!!?
ZU
ZU
ZU
!
ZU
OTHER MONSTERS ARE COMING OUT TOO!
ZU (WIGGLE)
NOW, THE HUNT FOR KNOWLEDGE BEGINS!
I'LL DEVOUR YOU...
...AND TURN YOU INTO ONE OF MY PAGES!!!
JURURI (SLURP)

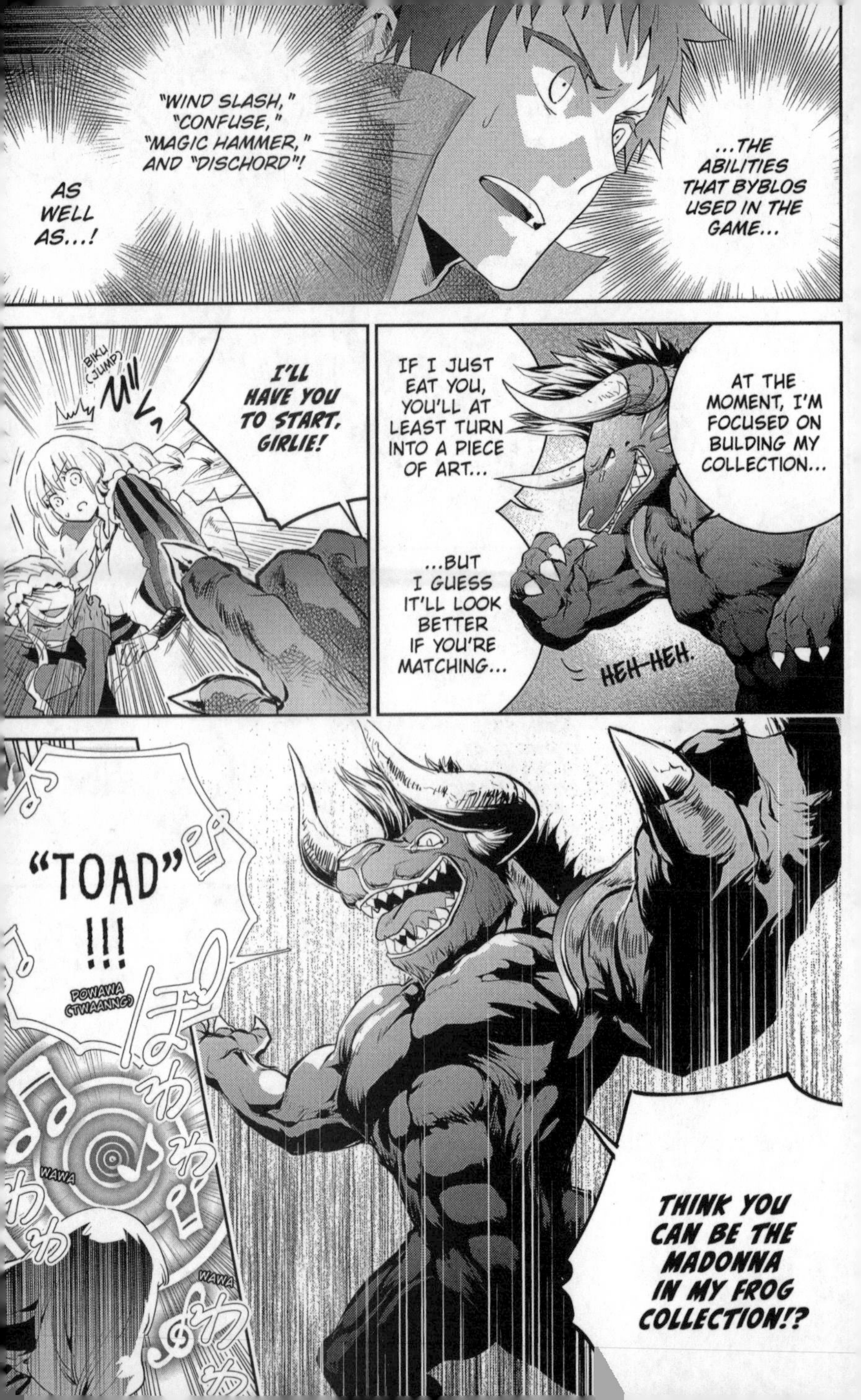
...THE ABILITIES THAT BYBLOS USED IN THE GAME...
"WIND SLASH," "CONFUSE," "MAGIC HAMMER," AND "DISCHORD"!
AS WELL AS...!
AT THE MOMENT, I'M FOCUSED ON BULDING MY COLLECTION...
IF I JUST EAT YOU, YOU'LL AT LEAST TURN INTO A PIECE OF ART...
...BUT I GUESS IT'LL LOOK BETTER IF YOU'RE MATCHING...
HEH-HEH.
I'LL HAVE YOU TO START, GIRLIE!
BIKU (JUMP)
THINK YOU CAN BE THE MADONNA IN MY FROG COLLECTION!?
"TOAD" !!!
POWAWA (TWAANNG)
WAWA
WAWA

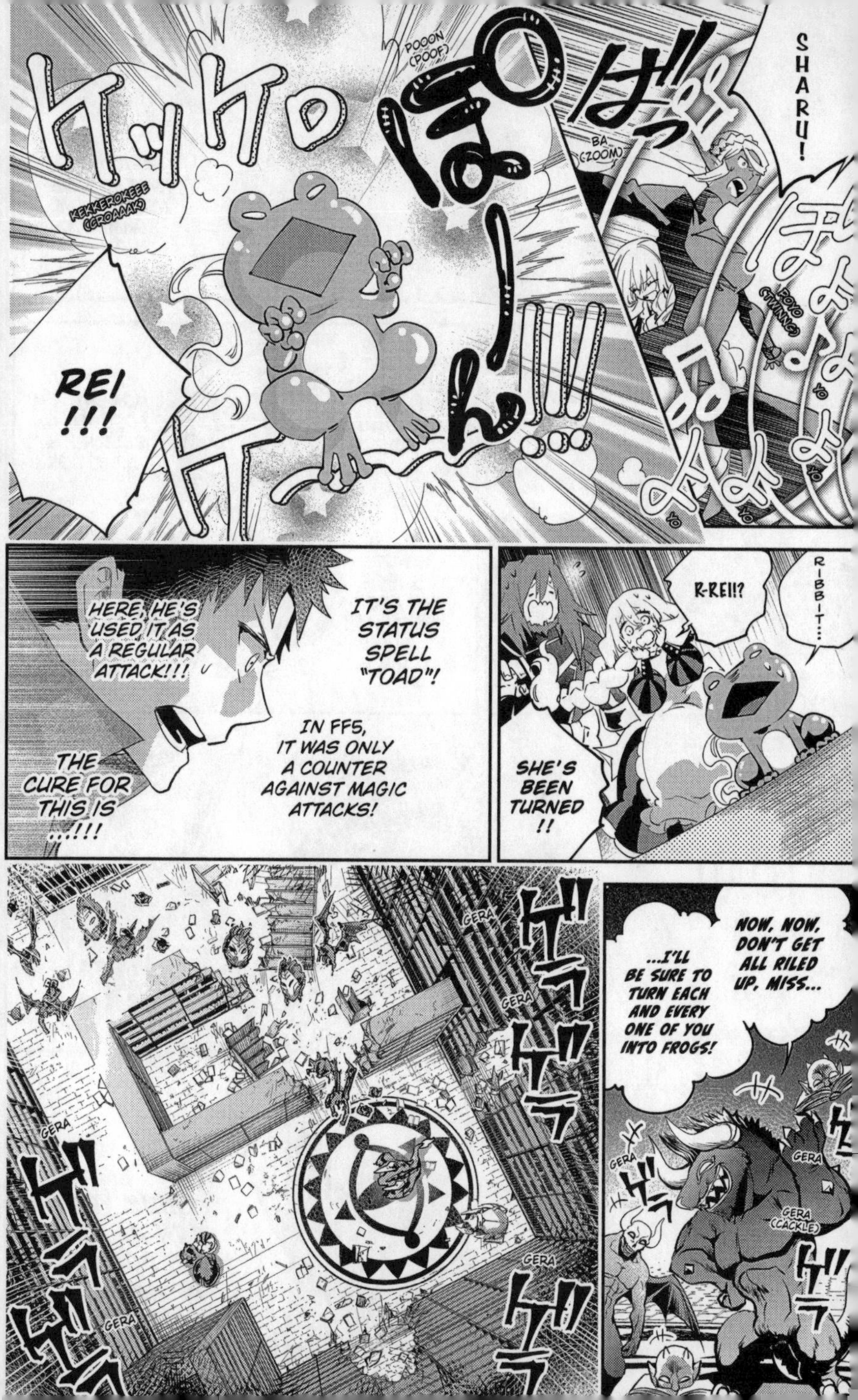

SHARU!
BA (ZOOM)
POYO (TWING)
YO
YO
YO
YO
POOON (POOF)
KEKKEROKEEE (CROAAAK)
REI !!!
RIBBIT...
R-REI!?
SHE'S BEEN TURNED !!
IT'S THE STATUS SPELL "TOAD"!
HERE, HE'S USED IT AS A REGULAR ATTACK!!!
IN FF5, IT WAS ONLY A COUNTER AGAINST MAGIC ATTACKS!
THE CURE FOR THIS IS ...!!!
NOW, NOW, DON'T GET ALL RILED UP, MISS...
...I'LL BE SURE TO TURN EACH AND EVERY ONE OF YOU INTO FROGS!
GERA
GERA
GERA (CACKLE)
GERA
GERA
GERA
GERA

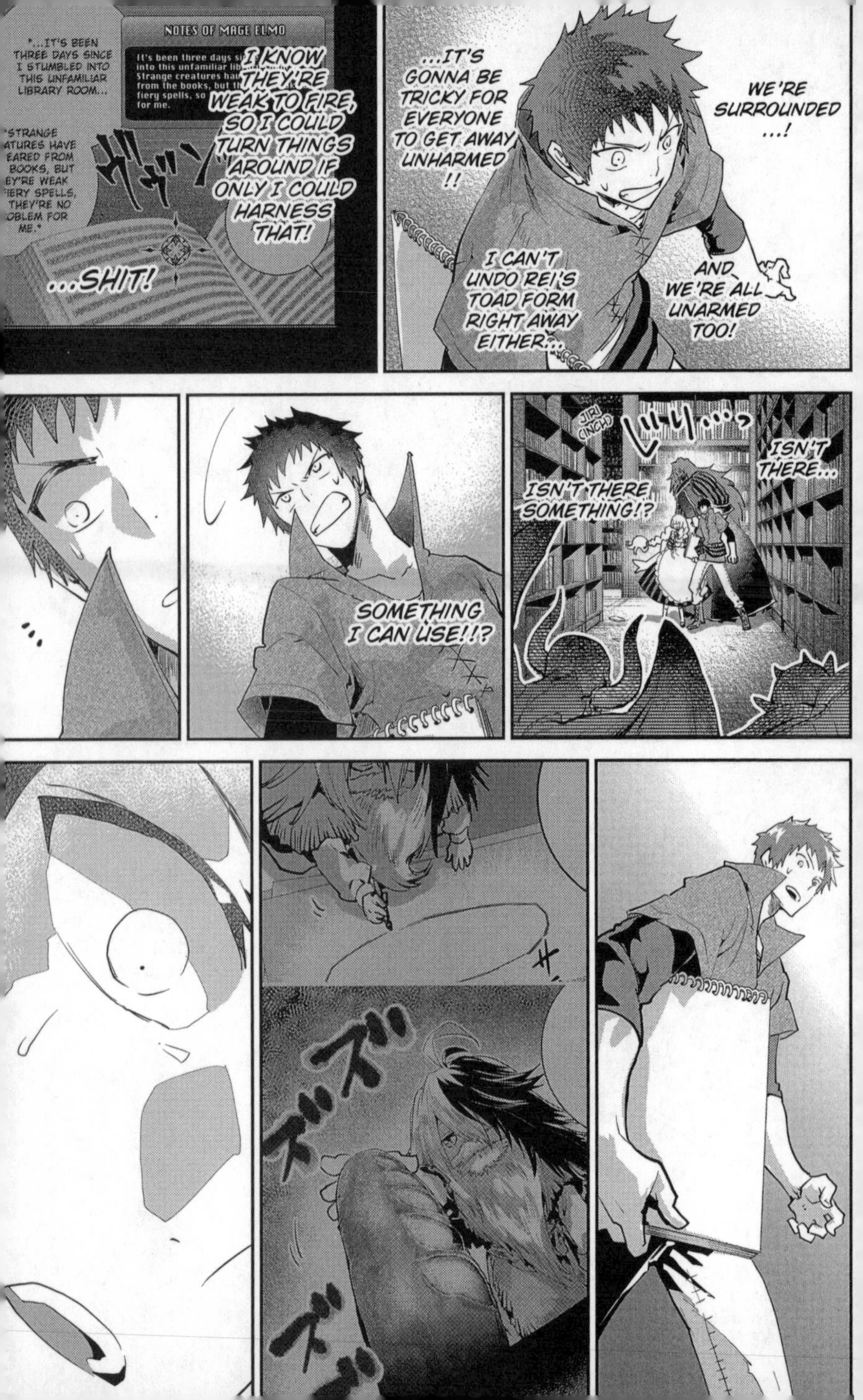
WE'RE SURROUNDED ...!
...IT'S GONNA BE TRICKY FOR EVERYONE TO GET AWAY UNHARMED!!
AND WE'RE ALL UNARMED TOO!
I CAN'T UNDO REI'S TOAD FORM RIGHT AWAY EITHER...
NOTES OF MAGE ELMO
"...IT'S BEEN THREE DAYS SINCE I STUMBLED INTO THIS UNFAMILIAR LIBRARY ROOM...
I KNOW THEY'RE WEAK TO FIRE, SO I COULD TURN THINGS AROUND IF ONLY I COULD HARNESS THAT!
...SHIT!
ISN'T THERE...
JIRI (INCH)
ISN'T THERE SOMETHING!?
SOMETHING I CAN USE!!?
...

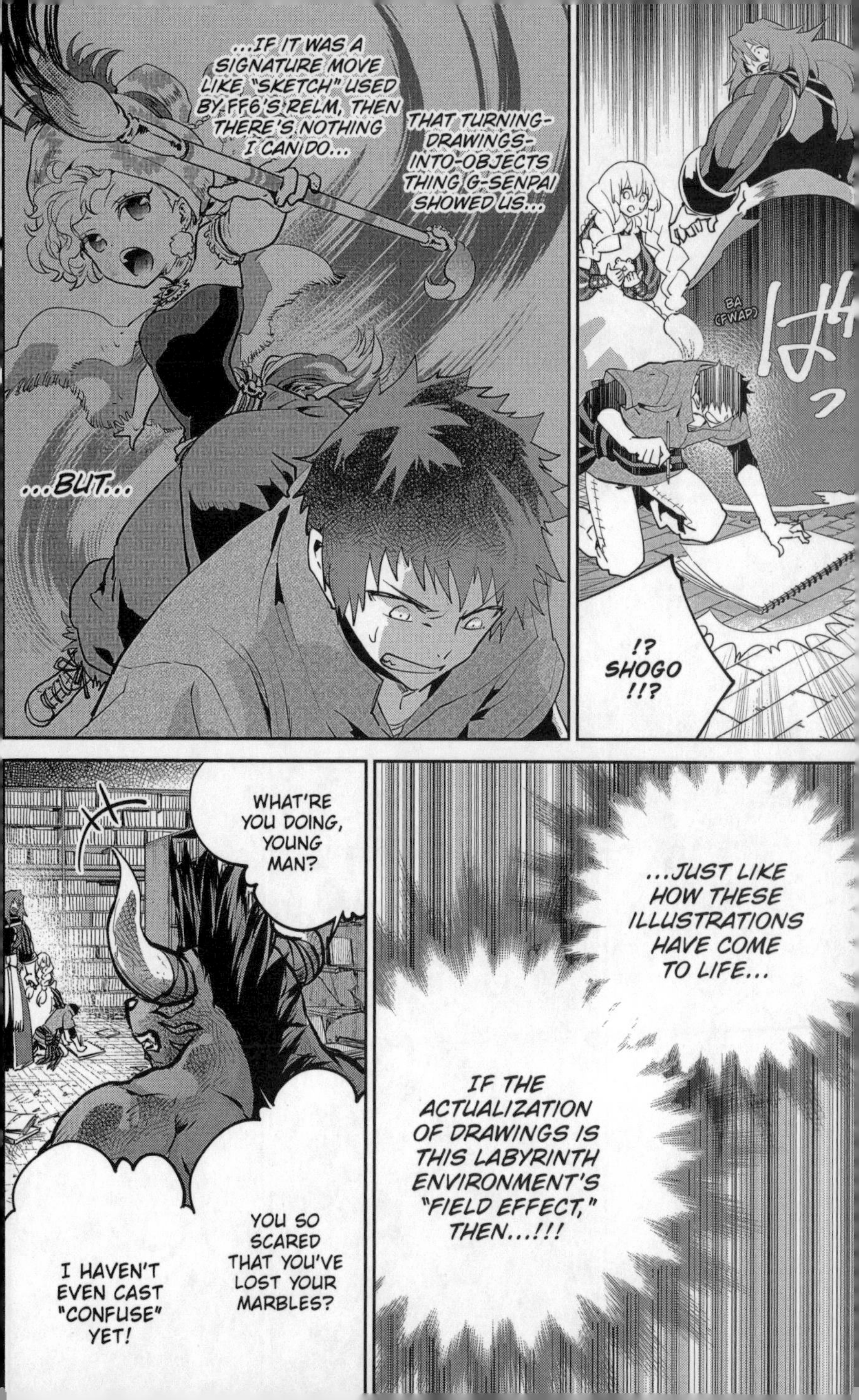
BA (FWAP)
はっ
!? SHOGO !!?
...IF IT WAS A SIGNATURE MOVE LIKE "SKETCH" USED BY FF6'S RELM, THEN THERE'S NOTHING I CAN DO...
THAT TURNING-DRAWINGS-INTO-OBJECTS THING G-SENPAI SHOWED US...
...BUT...
...JUST LIKE HOW THESE ILLUSTRATIONS HAVE COME TO LIFE...
IF THE ACTUALIZATION OF DRAWINGS IS THIS LABYRINTH ENVIRONMENT'S "FIELD EFFECT," THEN...!!!
WHAT'RE YOU DOING, YOUNG MAN?
YOU SO SCARED THAT YOU'VE LOST YOUR MARBLES?
I HAVEN'T EVEN CAST "CONFUSE" YET!

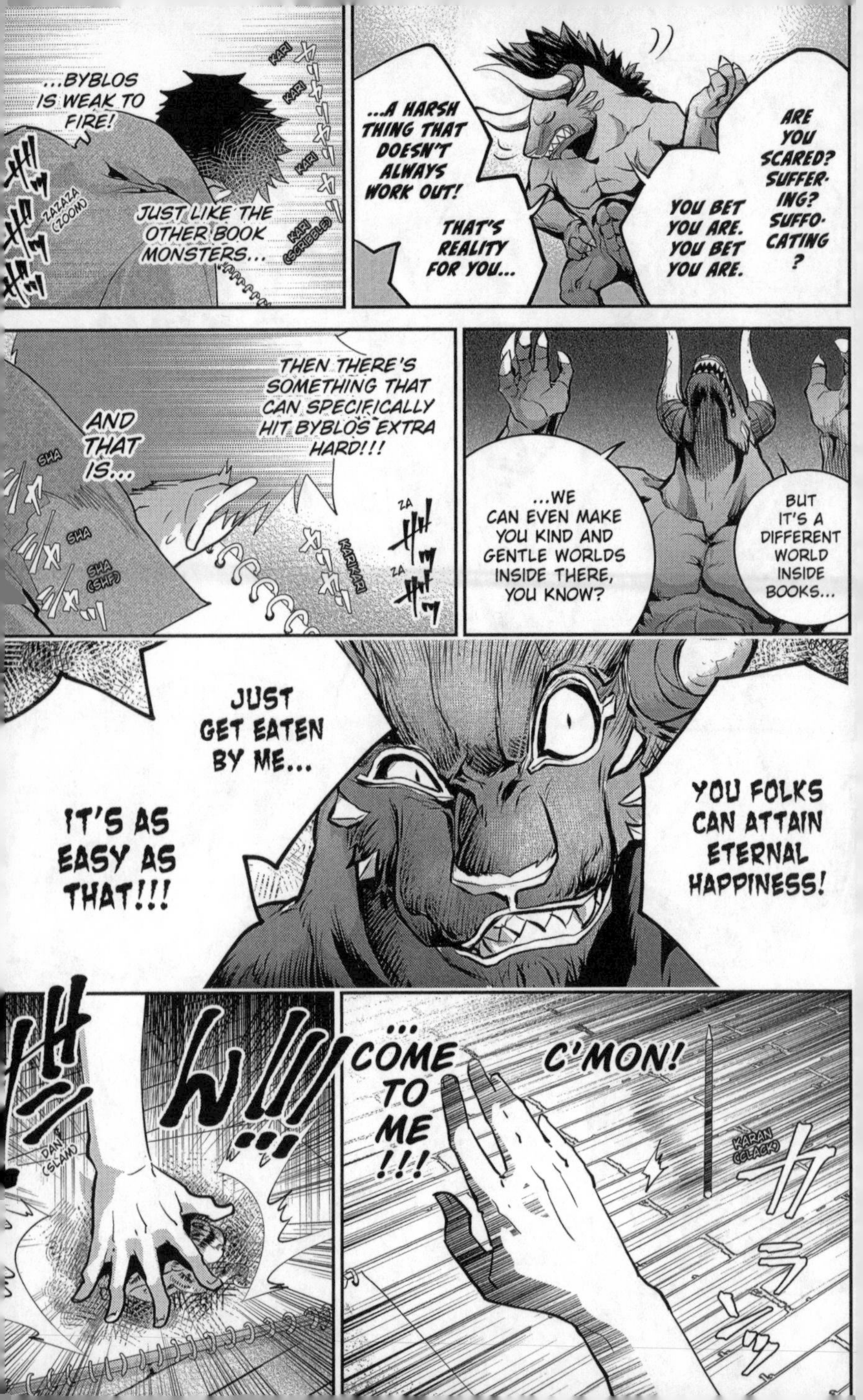
ARE YOU SCARED? SUFFERING? SUFFOCATING?
YOU BET YOU ARE. YOU BET YOU ARE.
...A HARSH THING THAT DOESN'T ALWAYS WORK OUT!
THAT'S REALITY FOR YOU...
KARI KARI KARI KARI (SCRIBBLE)
...BYBLOS IS WEAK TO FIRE!
JUST LIKE THE OTHER BOOK MONSTERS...
ZAZAZA (ZOOM)
BUT IT'S A DIFFERENT WORLD INSIDE BOOKS...
...WE CAN EVEN MAKE YOU KIND AND GENTLE WORLDS INSIDE THERE, YOU KNOW?
ZA ZA
KARIKARI
THEN THERE'S SOMETHING THAT CAN SPECIFICALLY HIT BYBLOS EXTRA HARD!!!
AND THAT IS...
SHA SHA SHA (SHF)
YOU FOLKS CAN ATTAIN ETERNAL HAPPINESS!
JUST GET EATEN BY ME...
IT'S AS EASY AS THAT!!!
C'MON!
KARAN (CLACK)
...COME TO ME!!!
DAN (SLAM)

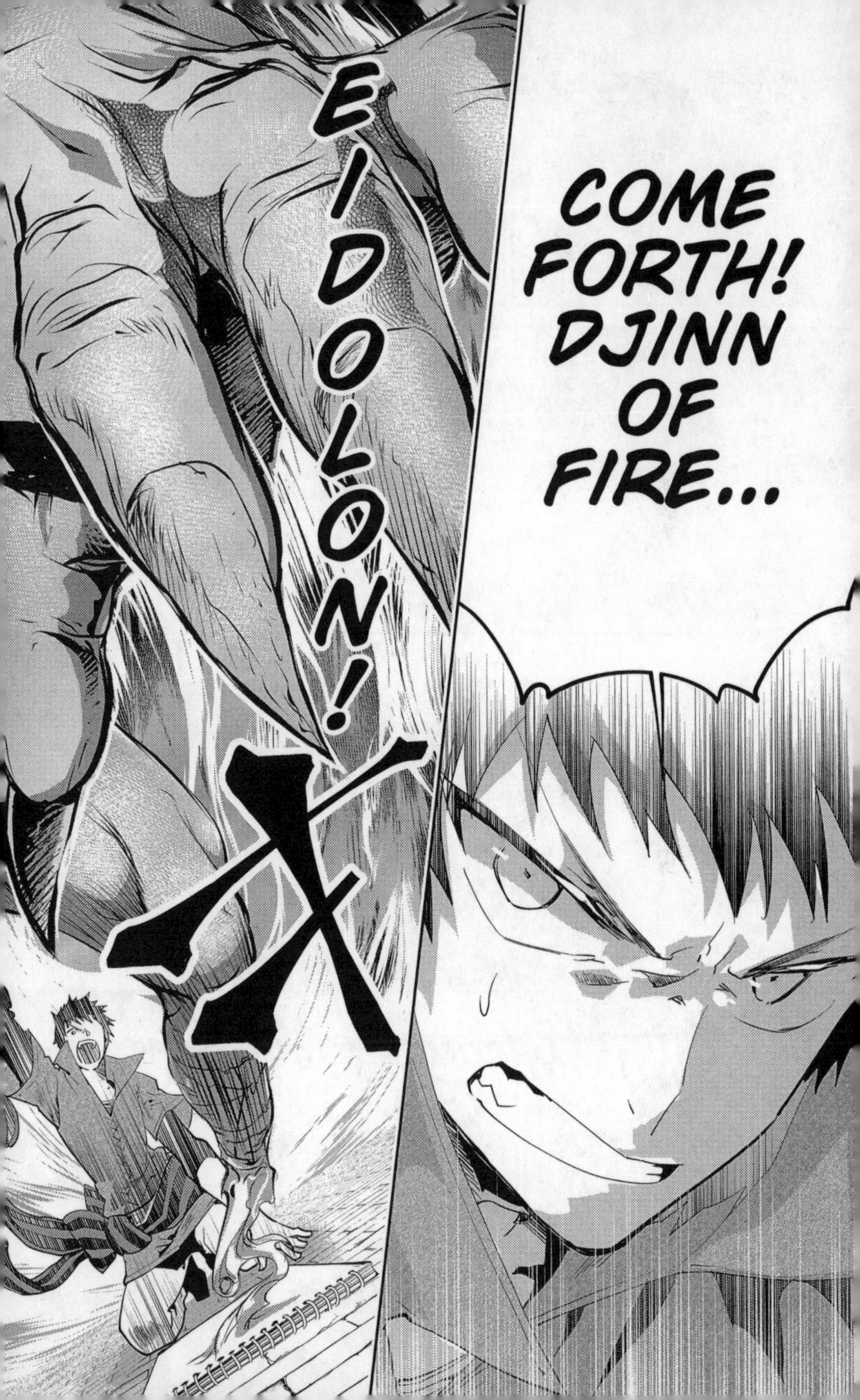
COME FORTH! DJINN OF FIRE...
EIDOLON!

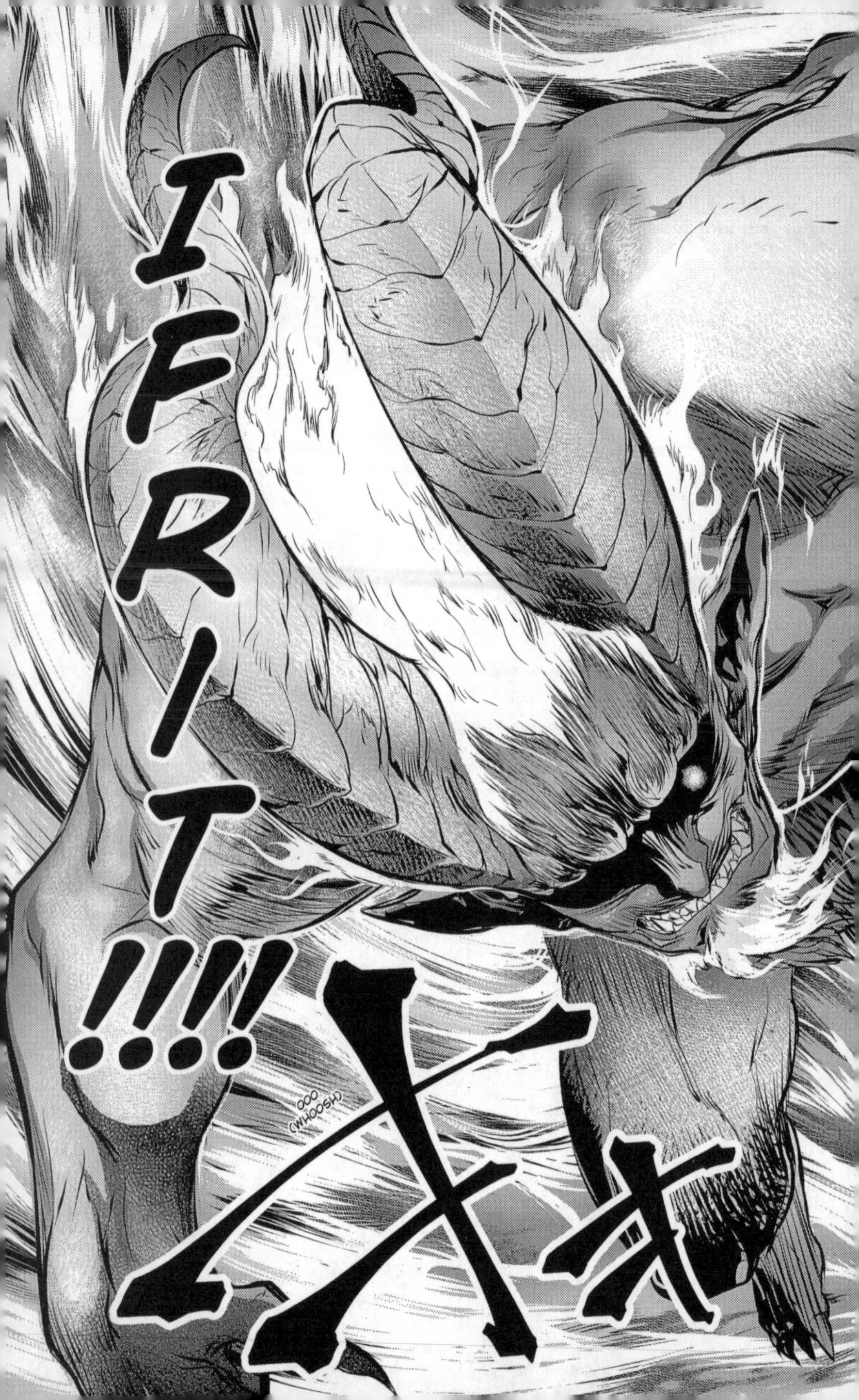
IFRIT!!!!
ズオ
OOO
(WHOOSH)

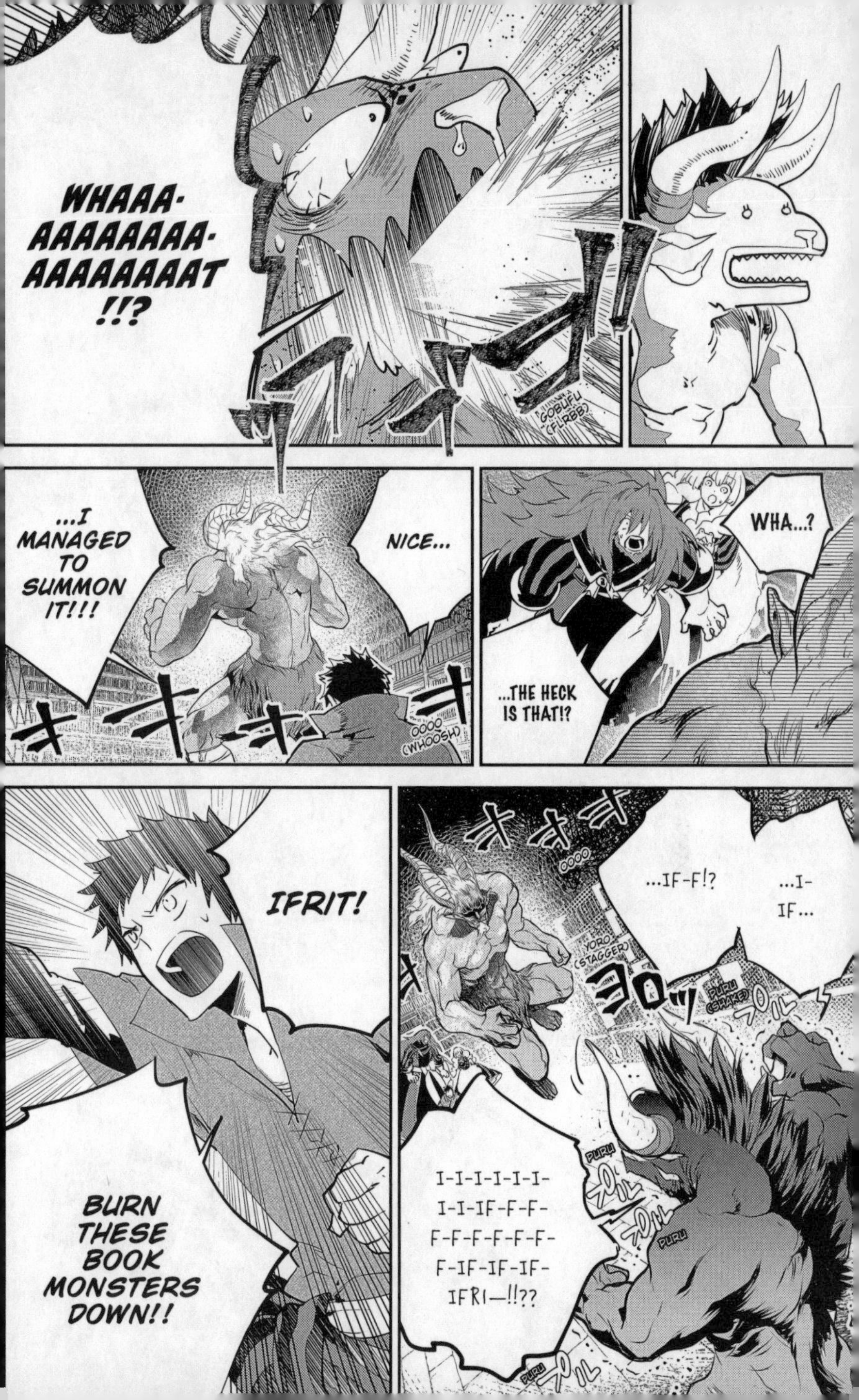
WHAAA-AAAAAAAA-AAAAAAAAT!!?
GOBUFU (FLRBB)
WHA...?
...THE HECK IS THAT!?
NICE...
...I MANAGED TO SUMMON IT!!!
OOOO (WHOOSH)
...I-IF...
...IF-F!?
OOOO
YORO (STAGGER)
PURU (SHAKE)
PURU
I-I-I-I-I-I-I-I-IF-F-F-F-F-F-F-F-F-F-IF-IF-IF-IFRI—!!??
PURU
PURU
IFRIT!
BURN THESE BOOK MONSTERS DOWN!!

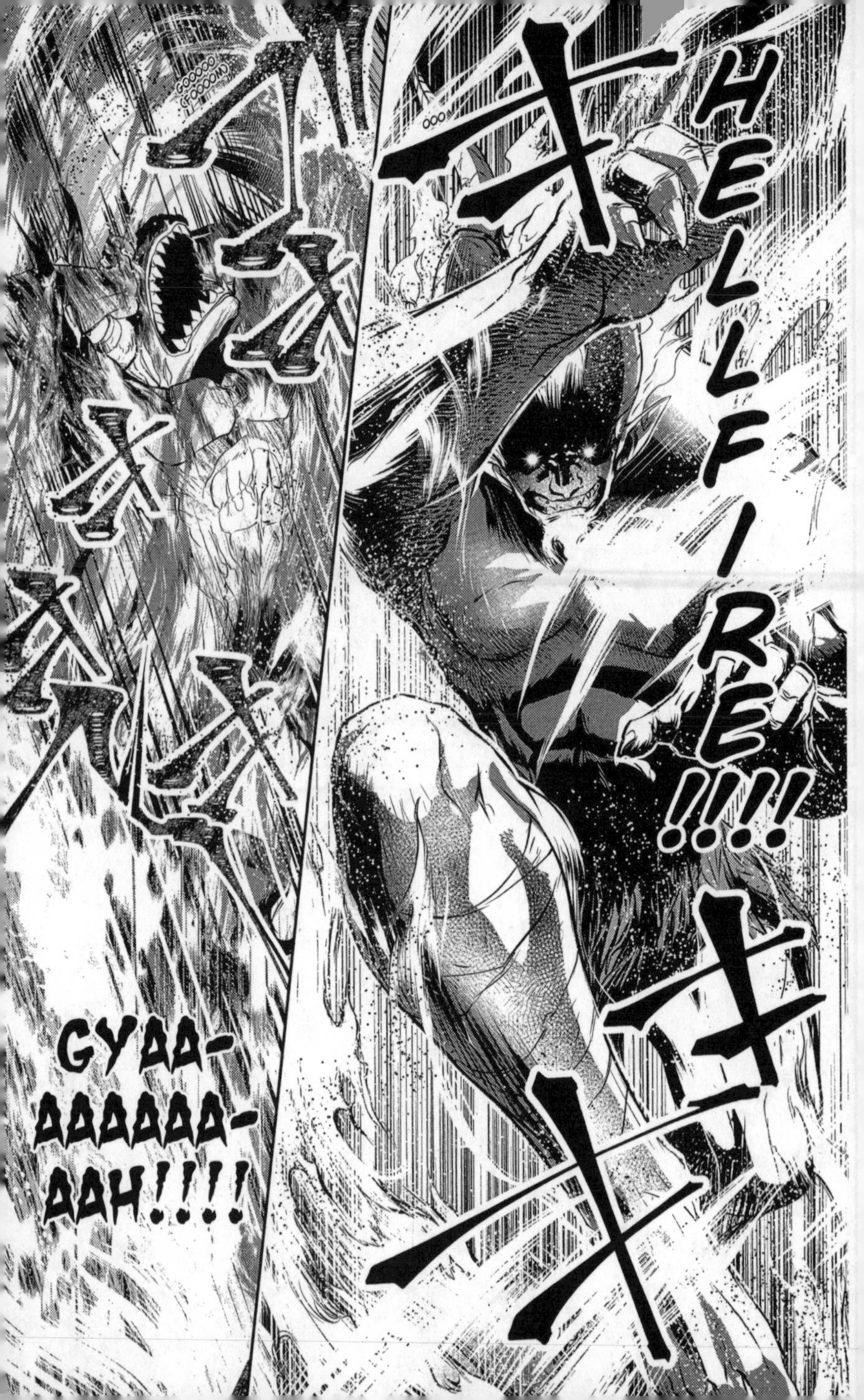
HELLFIRE!!!!
GOOOOO (FOOOOM)
GYAA-AAAAAA-AAH!!!!

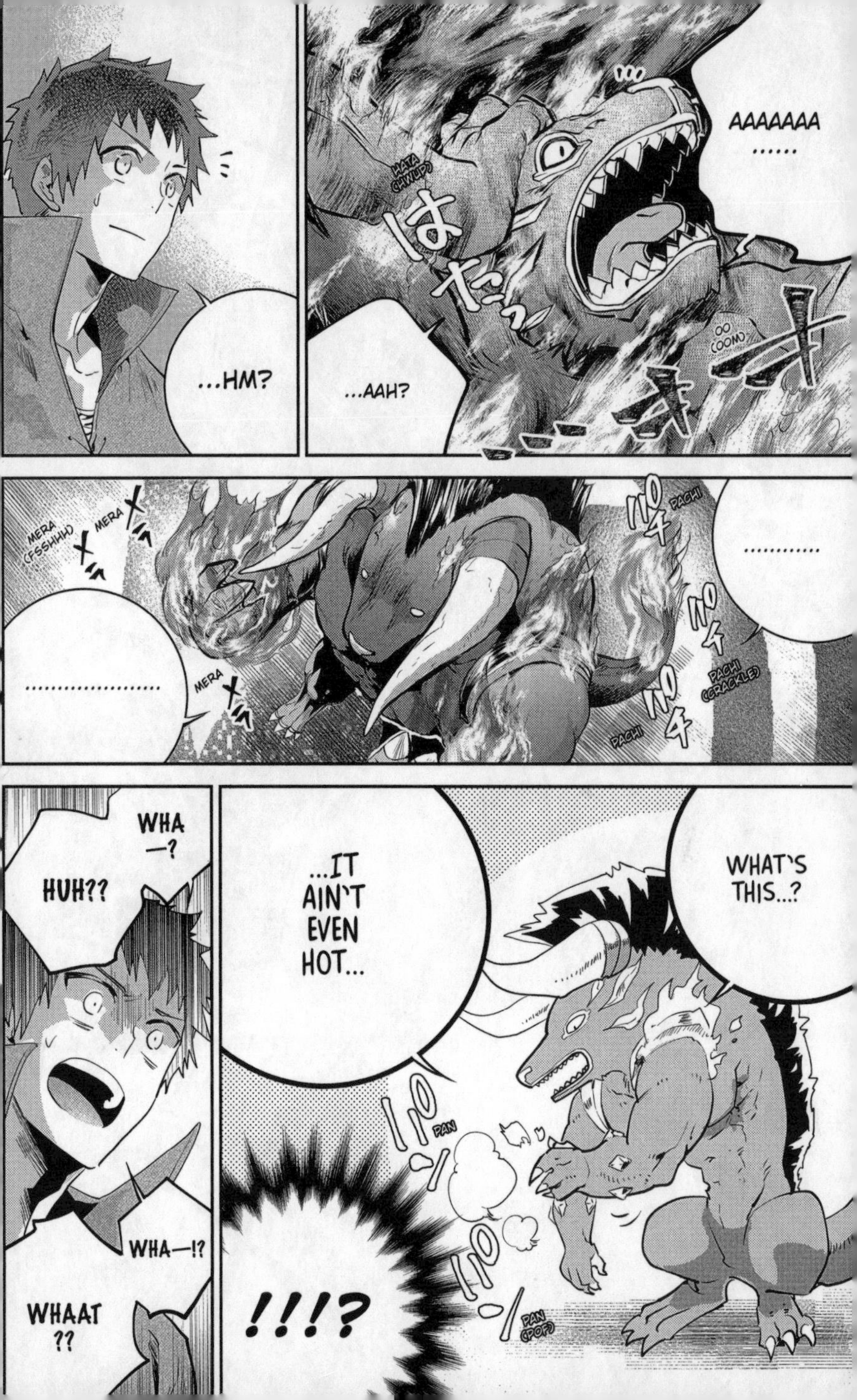
AAAAAAA ......
HATA (HWUP)
OO (OOM)
...AAH?
...HM?
...........
PACHI
PACHI (CRACKLE)
PACHI
MERA (FSSHHH)
MERA
.....................
MERA
WHAT'S THIS...?
...IT AIN'T EVEN HOT...
PAN
!!!?
PAN (POP)
WHA—?
HUH??
WHA—!?
WHAAT ??

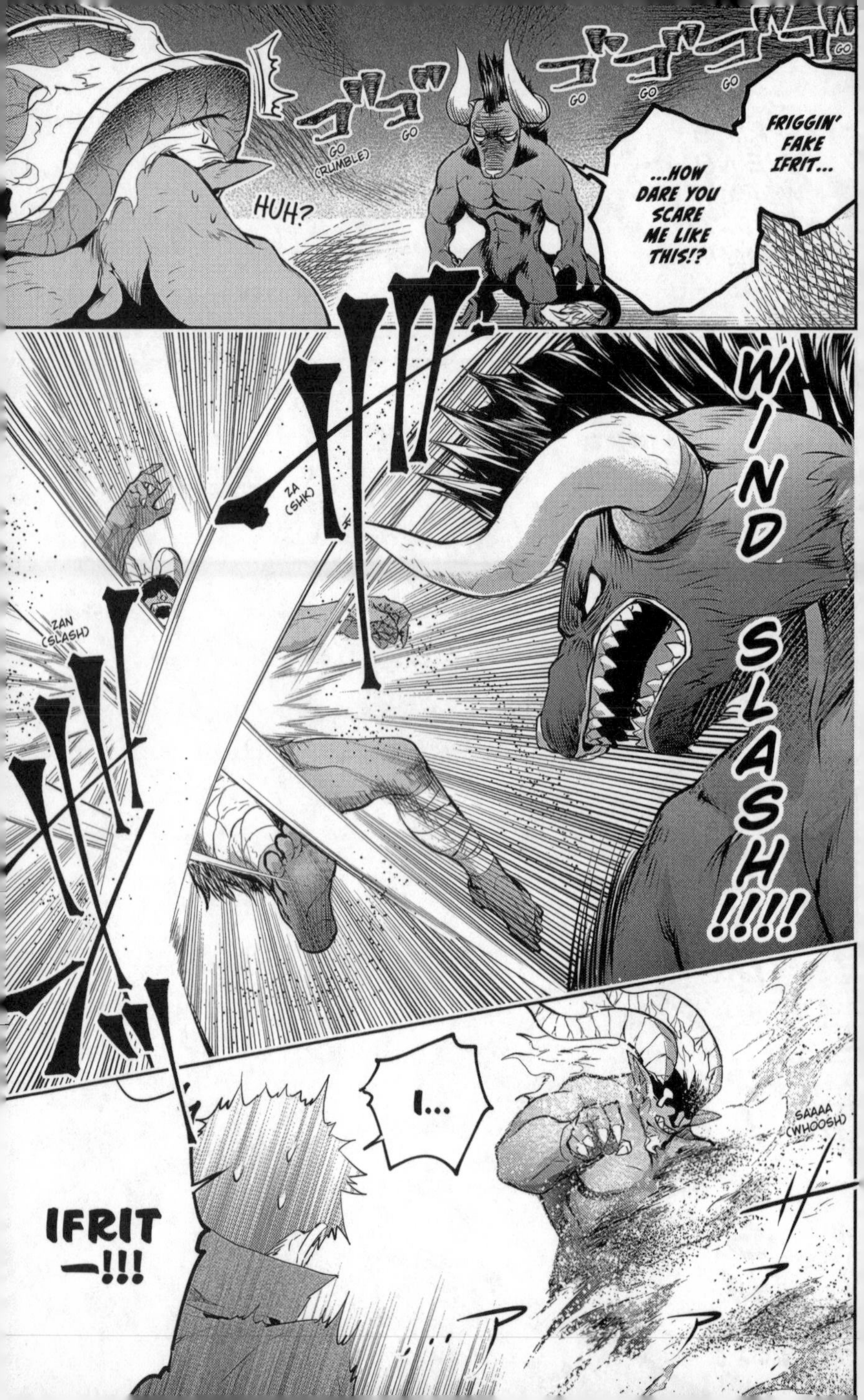
GO GO GO GO
FRIGGIN' FAKE IFRIT...
...HOW DARE YOU SCARE ME LIKE THIS!?
GO GO (RUMBLE)
HUH?
WIND SLASH!!!!
ZA (SHK)
ZAN (SLASH)
SAAAA (WHOOSH)
I...
IFRIT—!!!

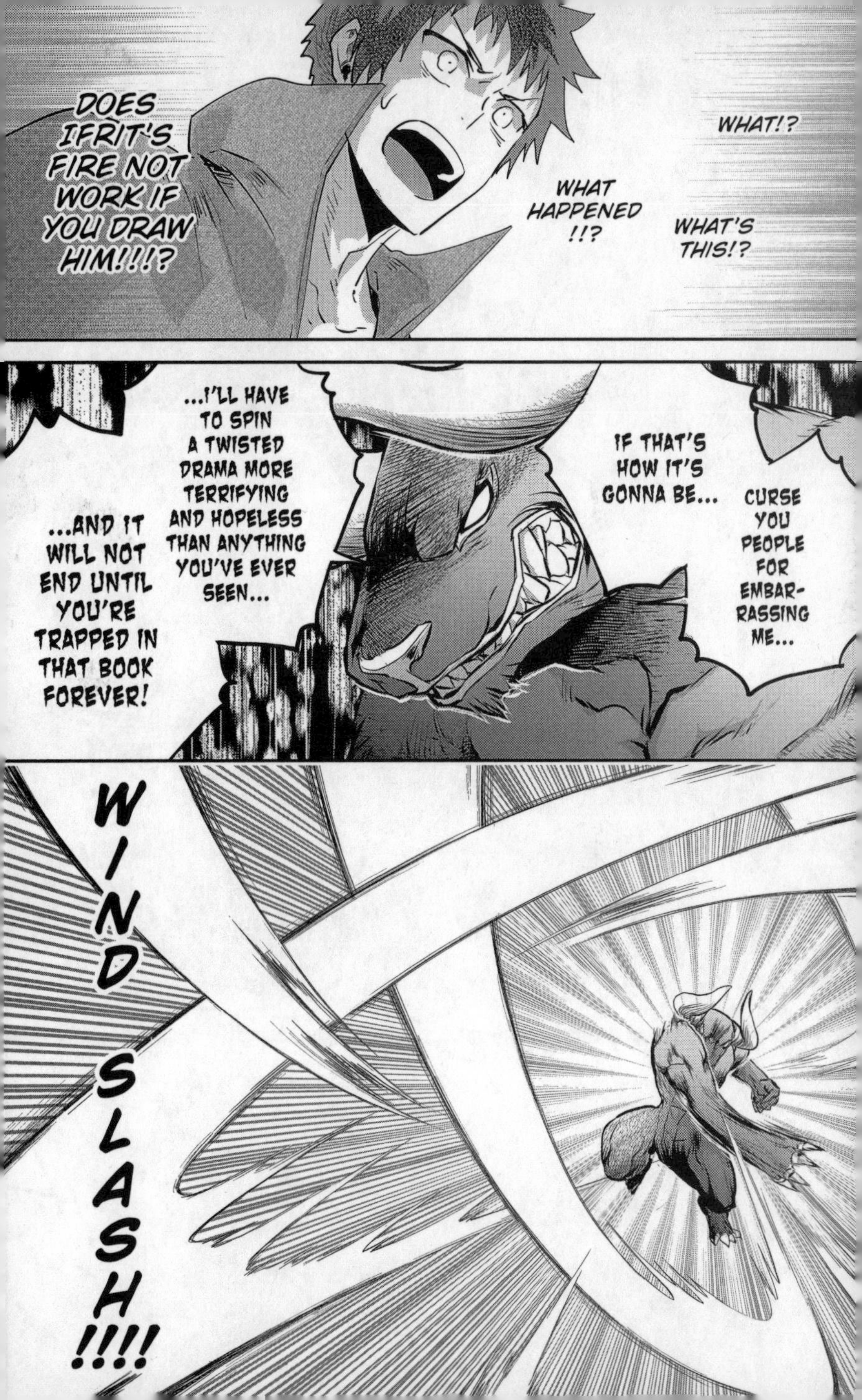
WHAT!?
WHAT'S THIS!?
WHAT HAPPENED!!?
DOES IFRIT'S FIRE NOT WORK IF YOU DRAW HIM!!!?
CURSE YOU PEOPLE FOR EMBARRASSING ME...
IF THAT'S HOW IT'S GONNA BE...
...I'LL HAVE TO SPIN A TWISTED DRAMA MORE TERRIFYING AND HOPELESS THAN ANYTHING YOU'VE EVER SEEN...
...AND IT WILL NOT END UNTIL YOU'RE TRAPPED IN THAT BOOK FOREVER!
WIND SLASH!!!!

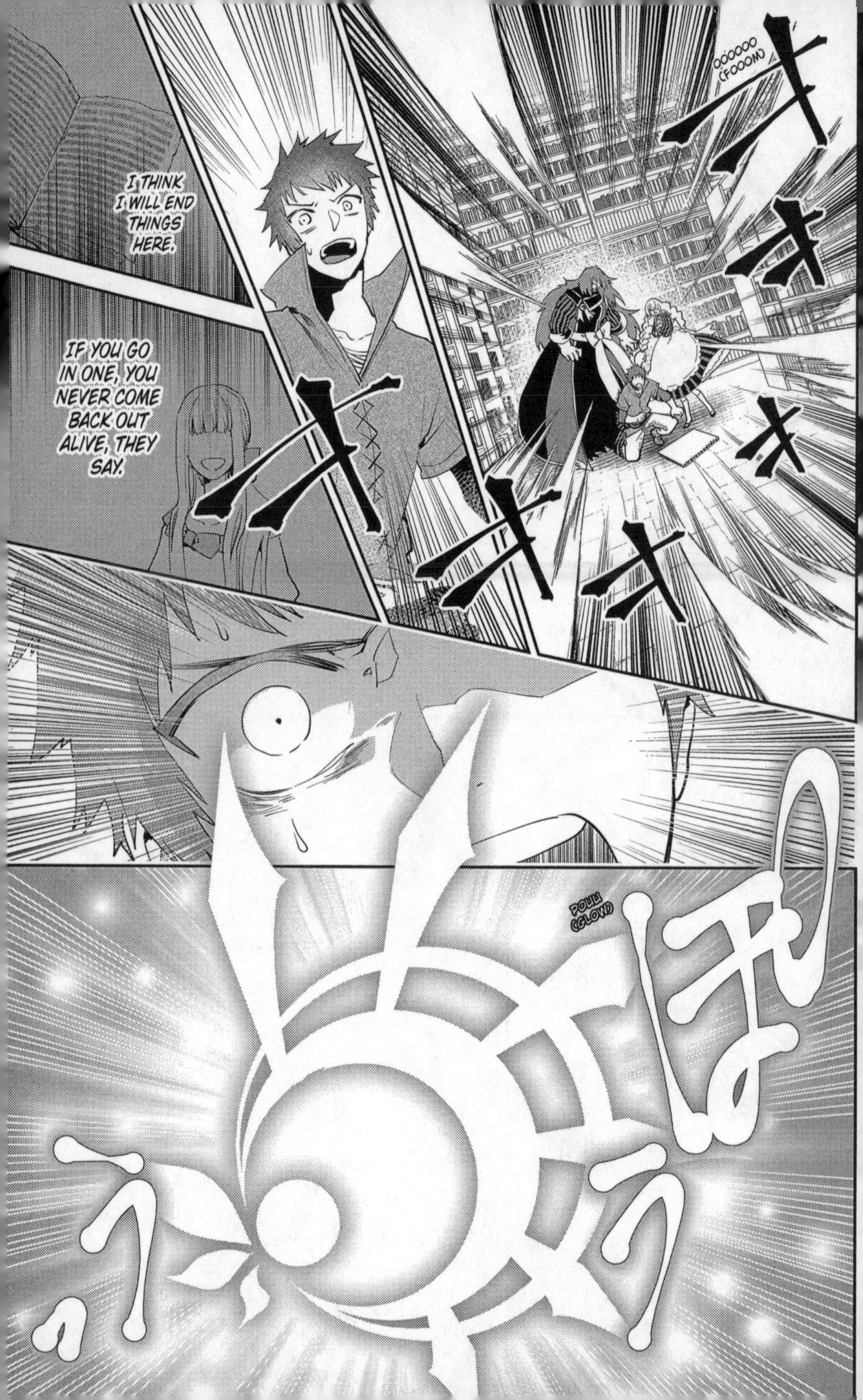
OOOOOO (FOOOM)
I THINK I WILL END THINGS HERE.
IF YOU GO IN ONE, YOU NEVER COME BACK OUT ALIVE, THEY SAY.
POUU (GLOW)

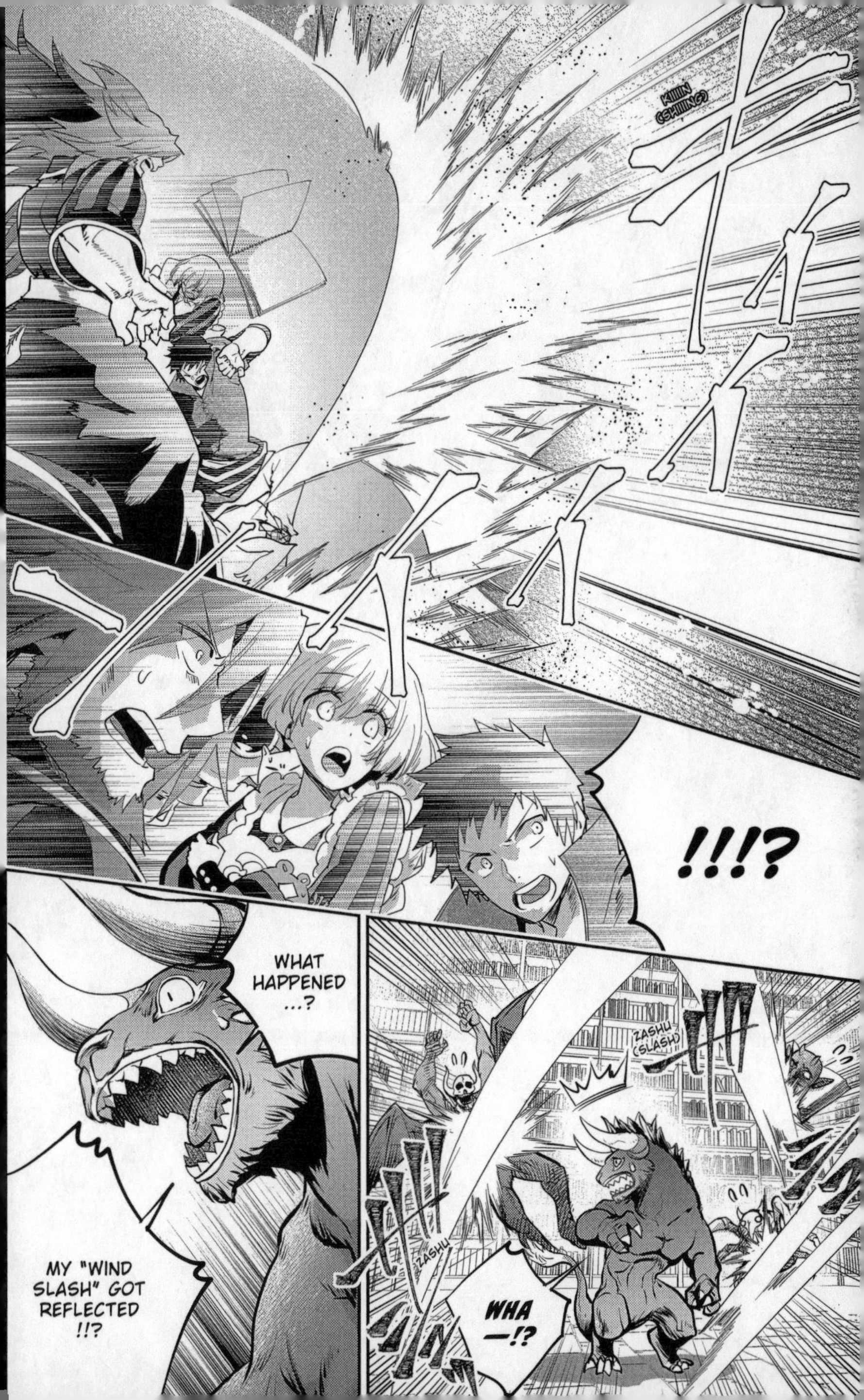
KIIIN (SHIIING)
!!!?
ZASHU (SLASH)
ZASHU
WHA—!?
WHAT HAPPENED ...?
MY "WIND SLASH" GOT REFLECTED !!?

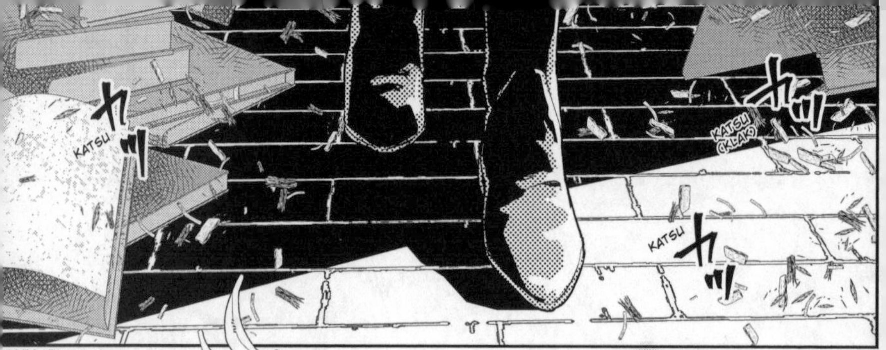
KATSU (KLAK)
KATSU
KATSU

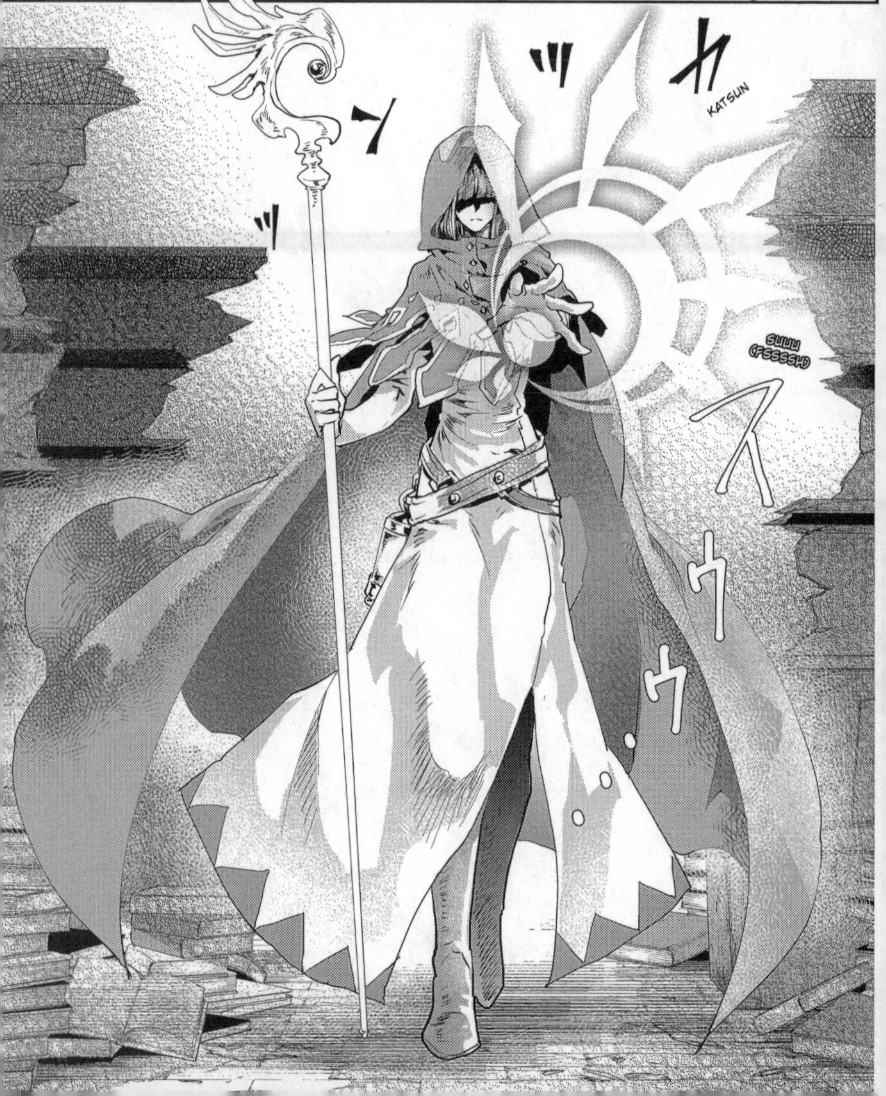
KATSUN
SUUU (FSSSSH)

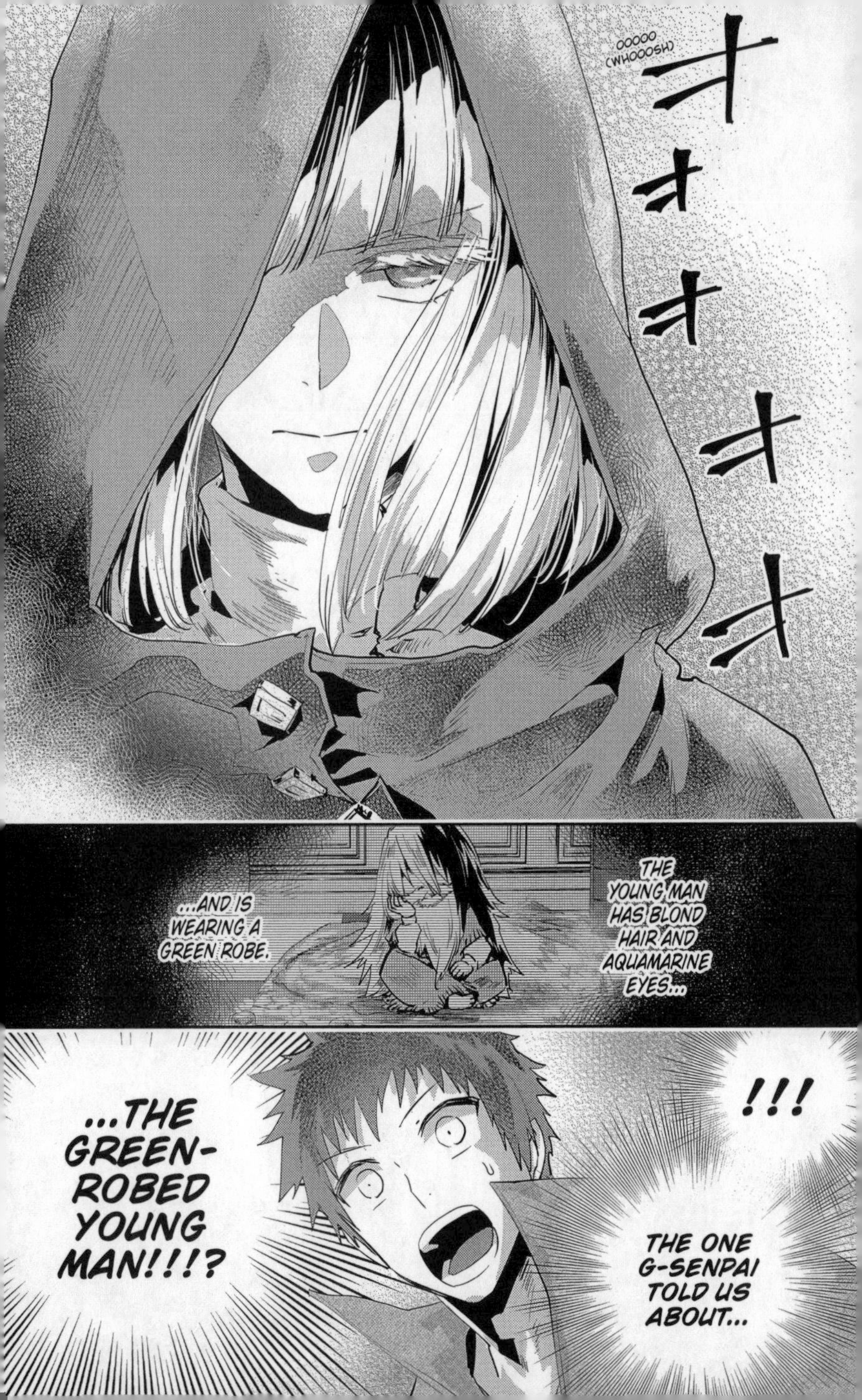
オォォォォォ
OOOOO (WHOOOSH)
THE YOUNG MAN HAS BLOND HAIR AND AQUAMARINE EYES...
...AND IS WEARING A GREEN ROBE.
!!!
THE ONE G-SENPAI TOLD US ABOUT...
...THE GREEN-ROBED YOUNG MAN!!!?

FINAL FANTASY®
ファイナルファンタジー　ロスト・ストレンジャー
LOST STRANGER

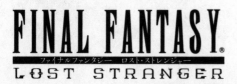

# Chapter 22 A Place to Call Home

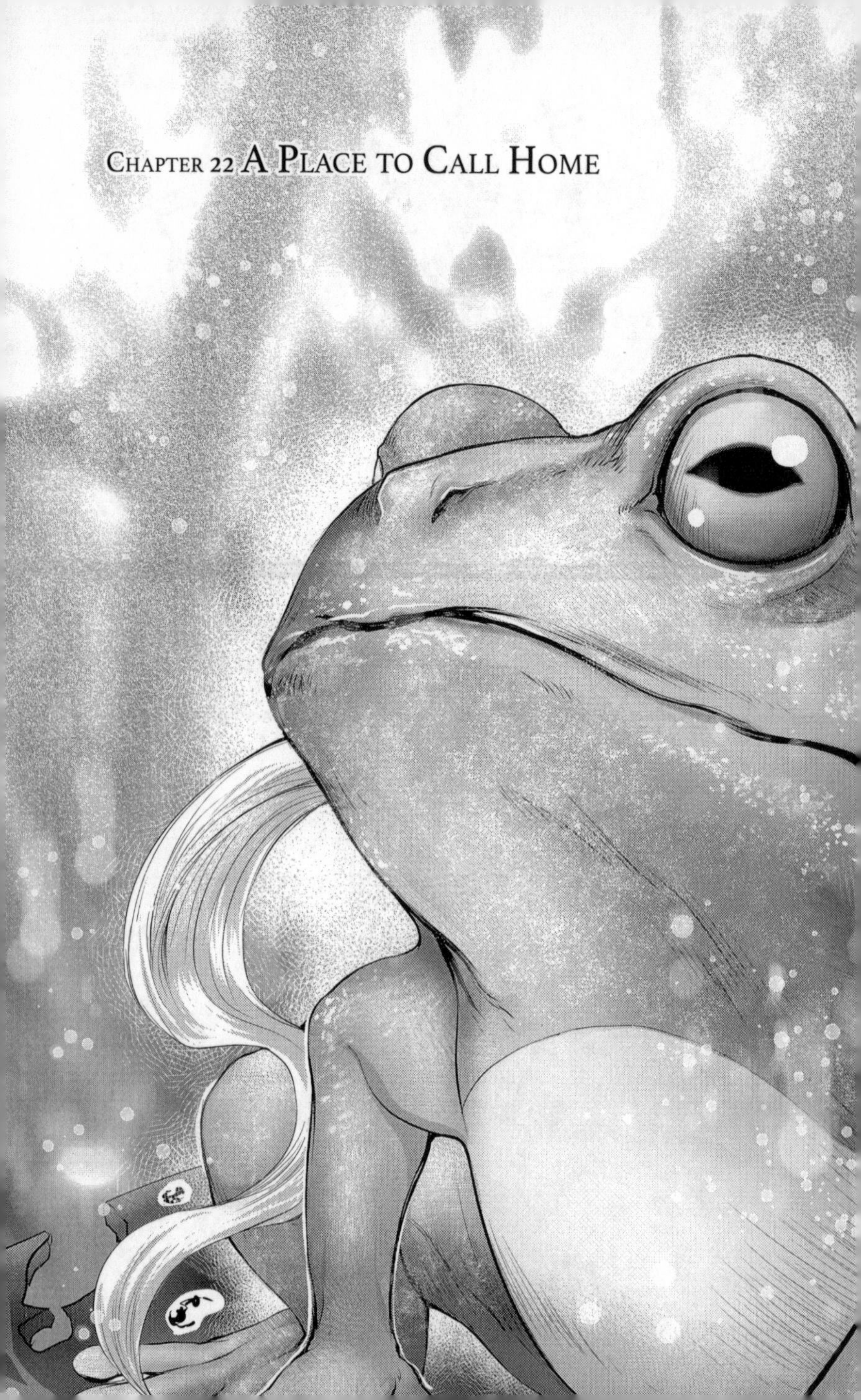

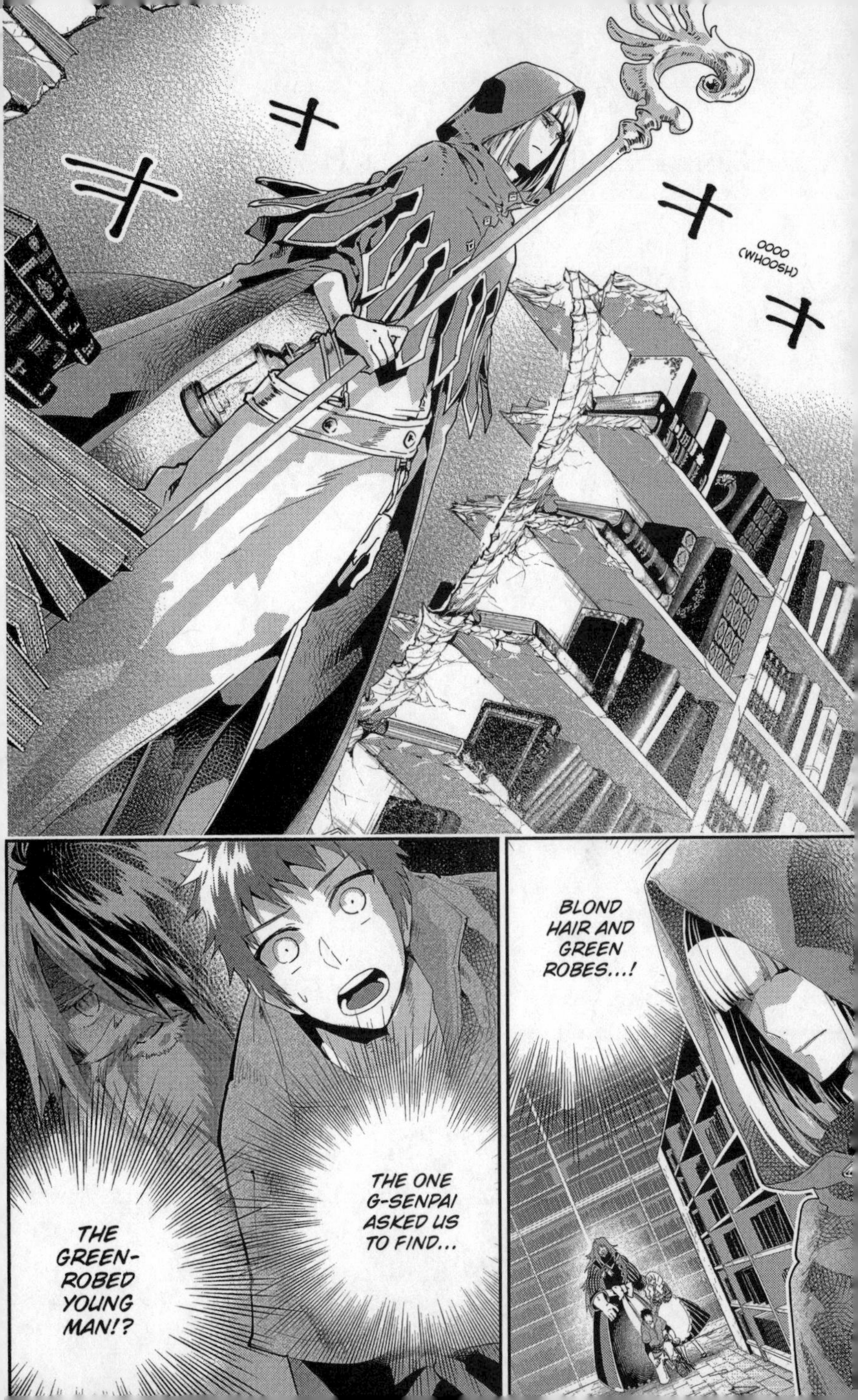
OOOO
(WHOOSH)
BLOND HAIR AND GREEN ROBES...!
THE ONE G-SENPAI ASKED US TO FIND...
THE GREEN-ROBED YOUNG MAN!?

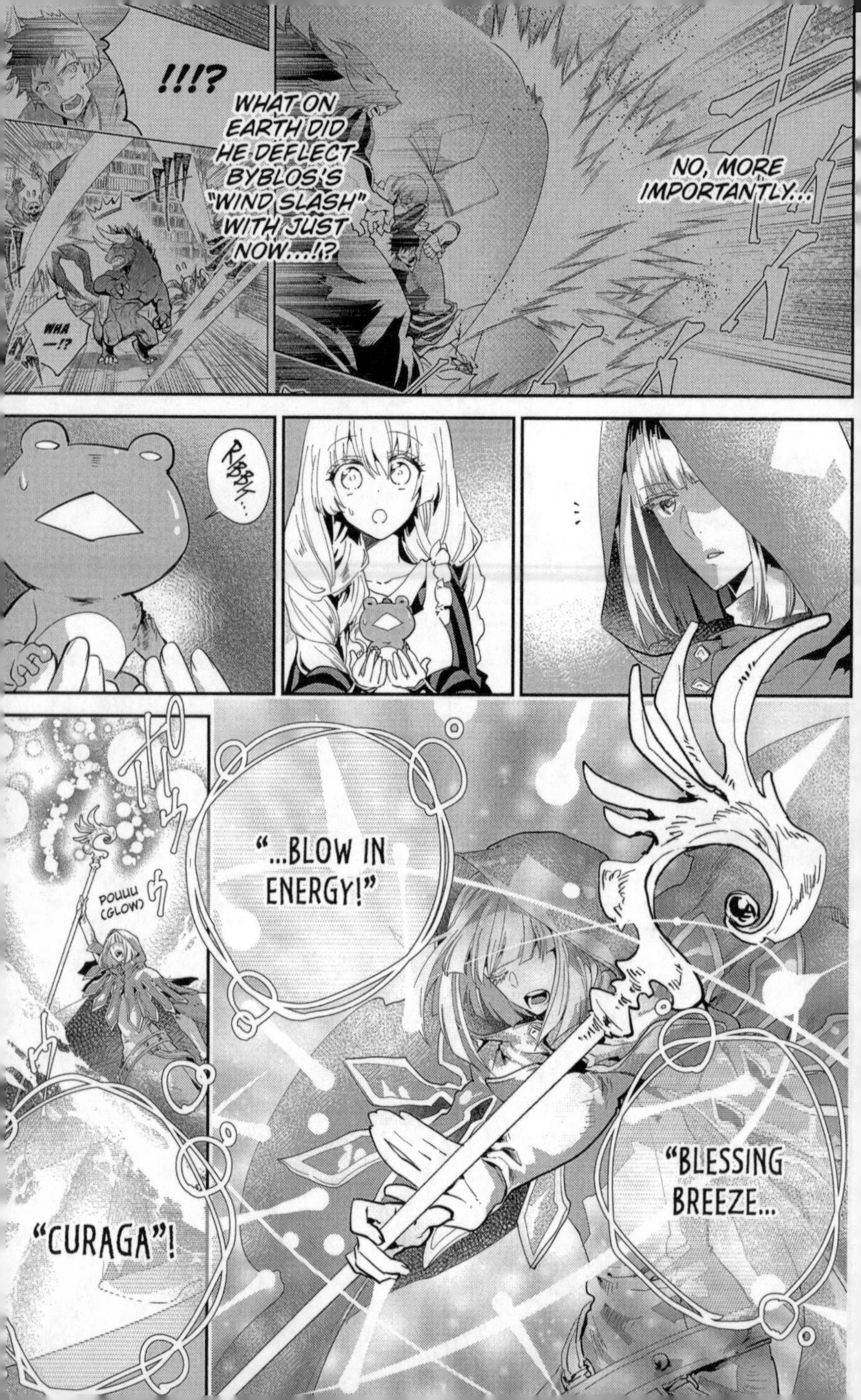
!!!?
WHAT ON EARTH DID HE DEFLECT BYBLOS'S "WIND SLASH" WITH JUST NOW...!?
NO, MORE IMPORTANTLY...
WHA —!?
RIBBIT...
"BLESSING BREEZE...
"...BLOW IN ENERGY!"
POUUU (GLOW)
"CURAGA"!

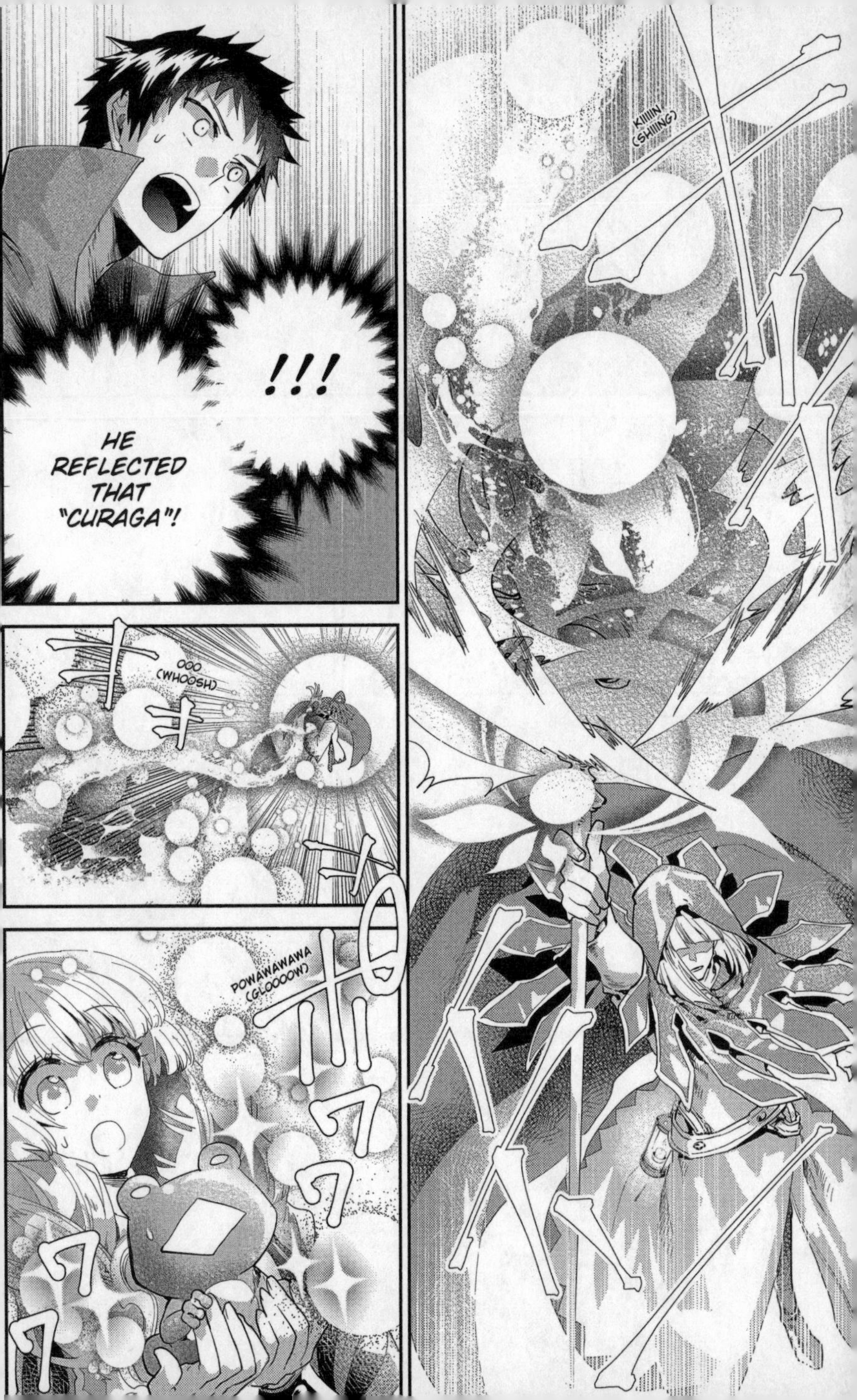
KIIIIN (SHIIING)
!!!
HE REFLECTED THAT "CURAGA"!
OOO (WHOOSH)
POWAWAWAWA (GLOOOOW)

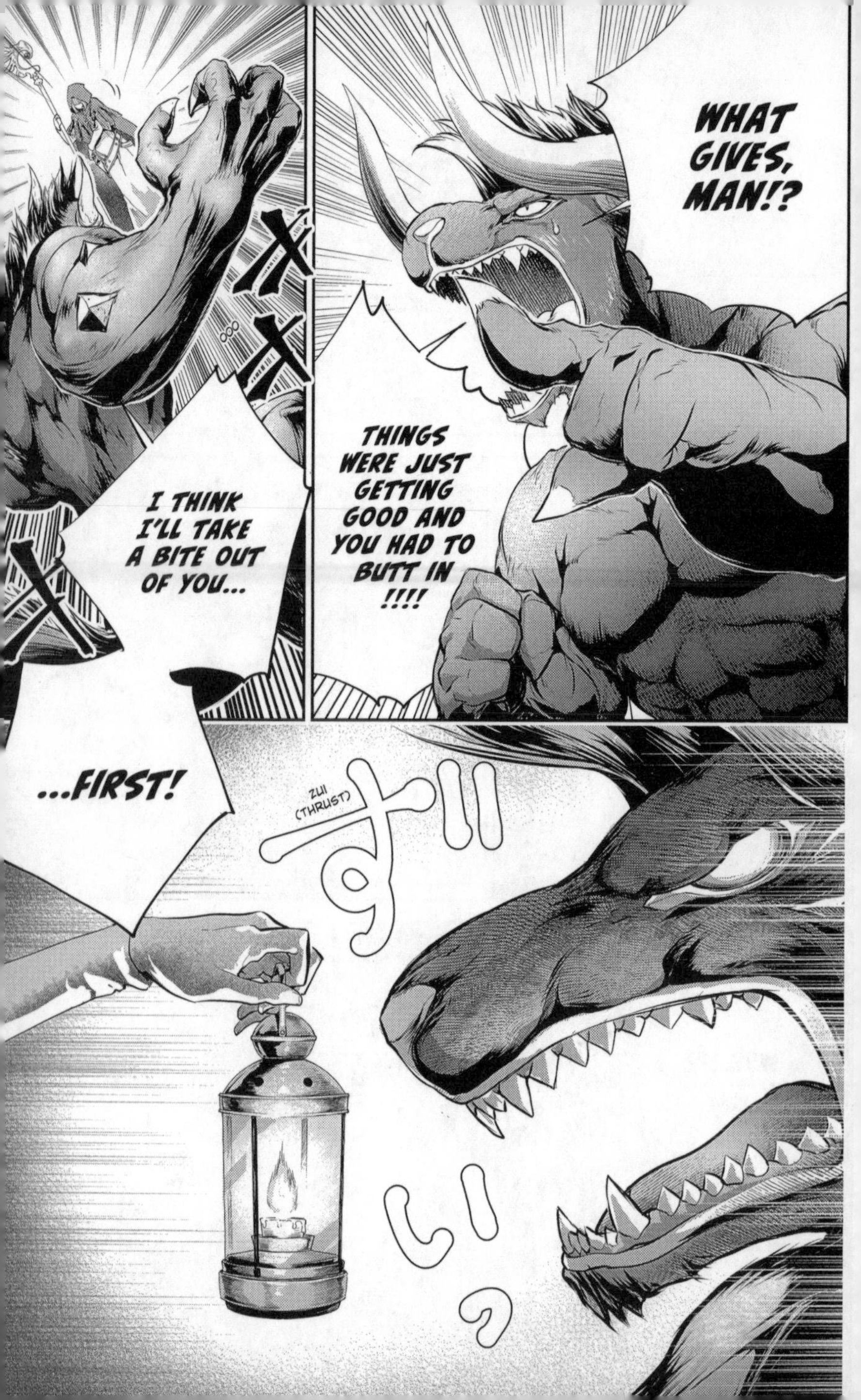
WHAT GIVES, MAN!?
THINGS WERE JUST GETTING GOOD AND YOU HAD TO BUTT IN !!!!
I THINK I'LL TAKE A BITE OUT OF YOU...
...FIRST!
ZUI (THRUST)

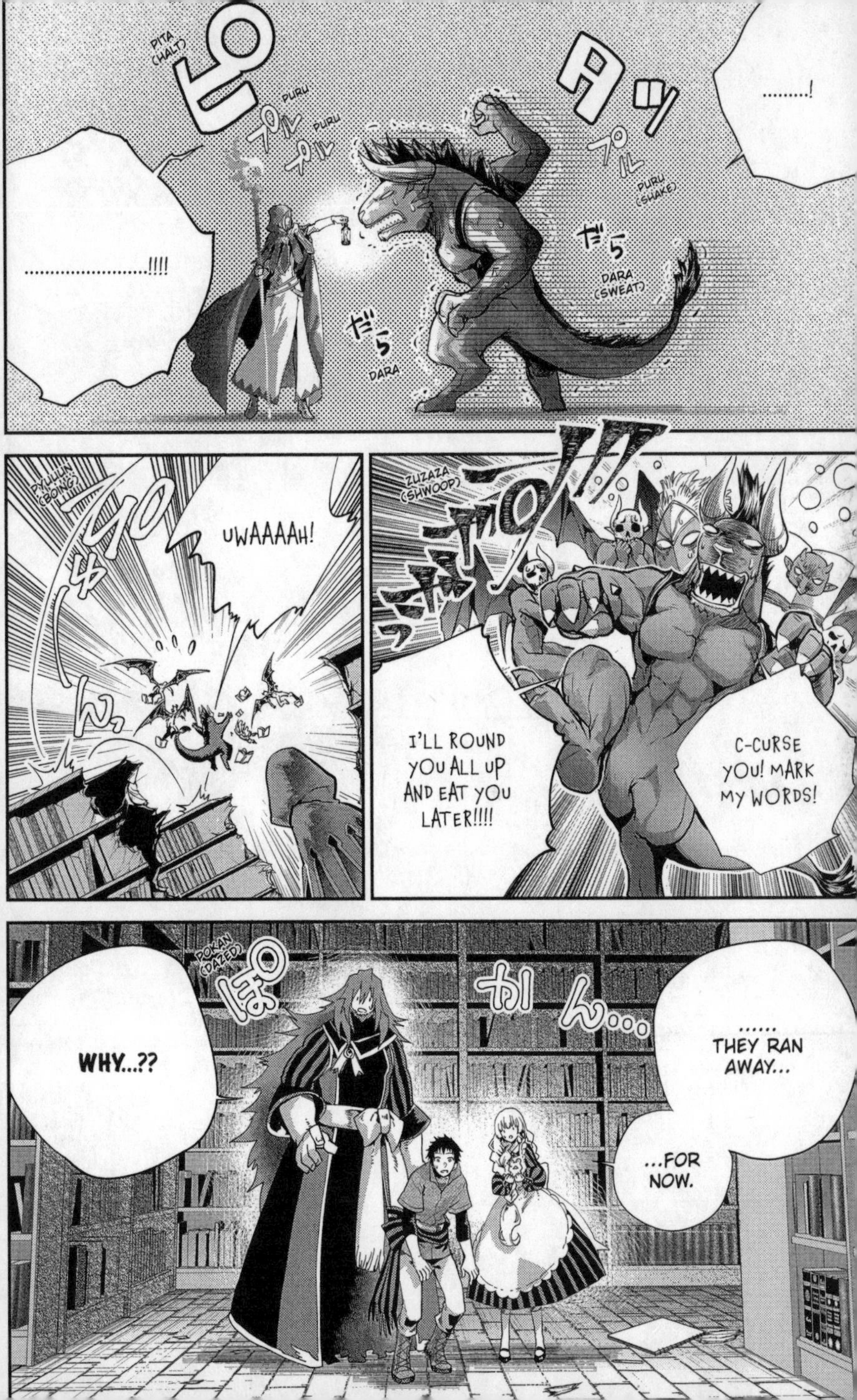
.........!
PURU (SHAKE)
DARA (SWEAT)
PITA (HALT)
PURU
PURU
.........................!!!!
DARA
ZUZAZA (SHWOOP)
C-CURSE YOU! MARK MY WORDS!
I'LL ROUND YOU ALL UP AND EAT YOU LATER!!!!
PYUUUN (BOING)
UWAAAAH!
...... THEY RAN AWAY...
POKAN (DAZED)
WHY...??
...FOR NOW.

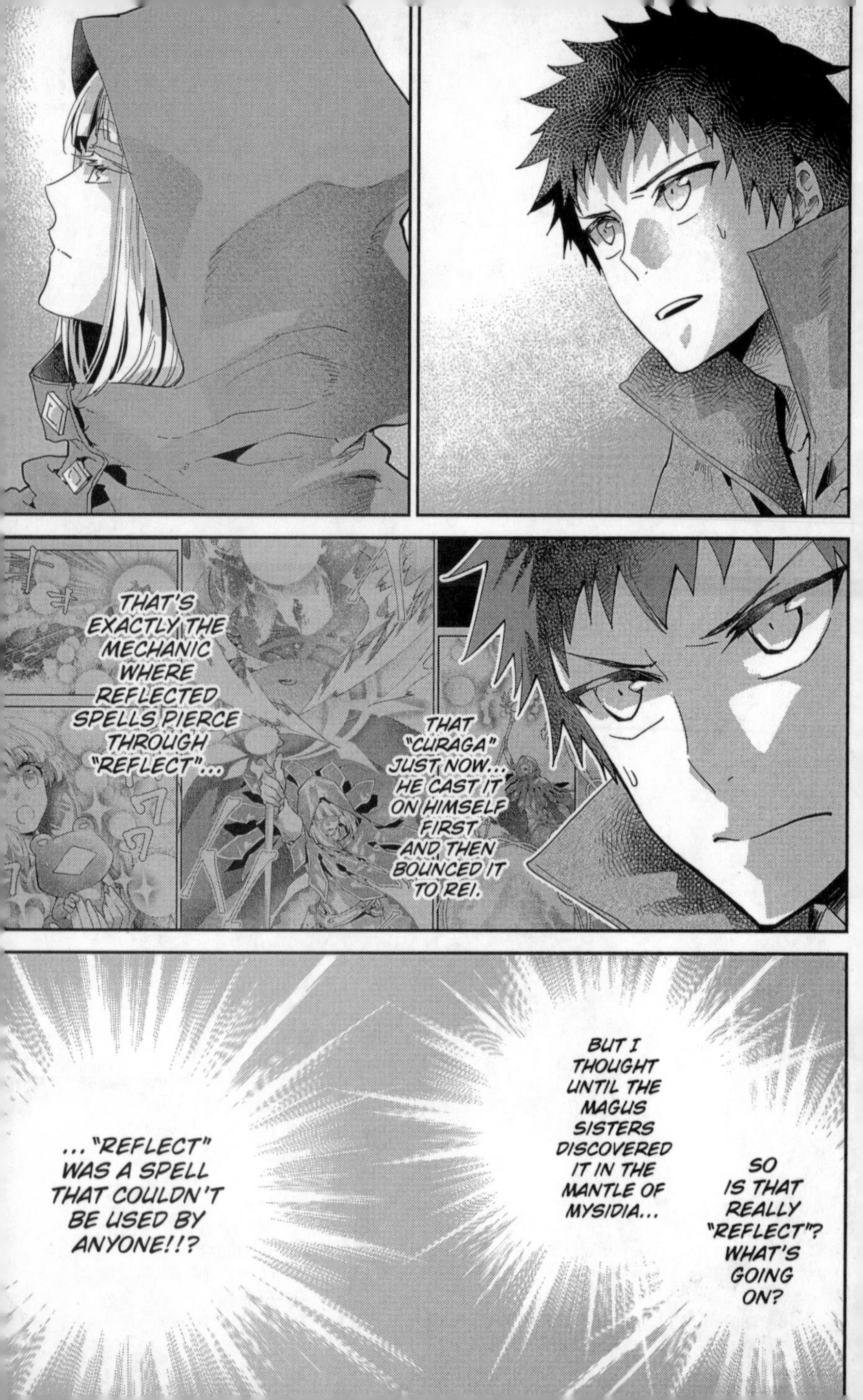
THAT "CURAGA" JUST NOW... HE CAST IT ON HIMSELF FIRST AND THEN BOUNCED IT TO REI.
THAT'S EXACTLY THE MECHANIC WHERE REFLECTED SPELLS PIERCE THROUGH "REFLECT"...
SO IS THAT REALLY "REFLECT"? WHAT'S GOING ON?
BUT I THOUGHT UNTIL THE MAGUS SISTERS DISCOVERED IT IN THE MANTLE OF MYSIDIA...
... "REFLECT" WAS A SPELL THAT COULDN'T BE USED BY ANYONE!!?

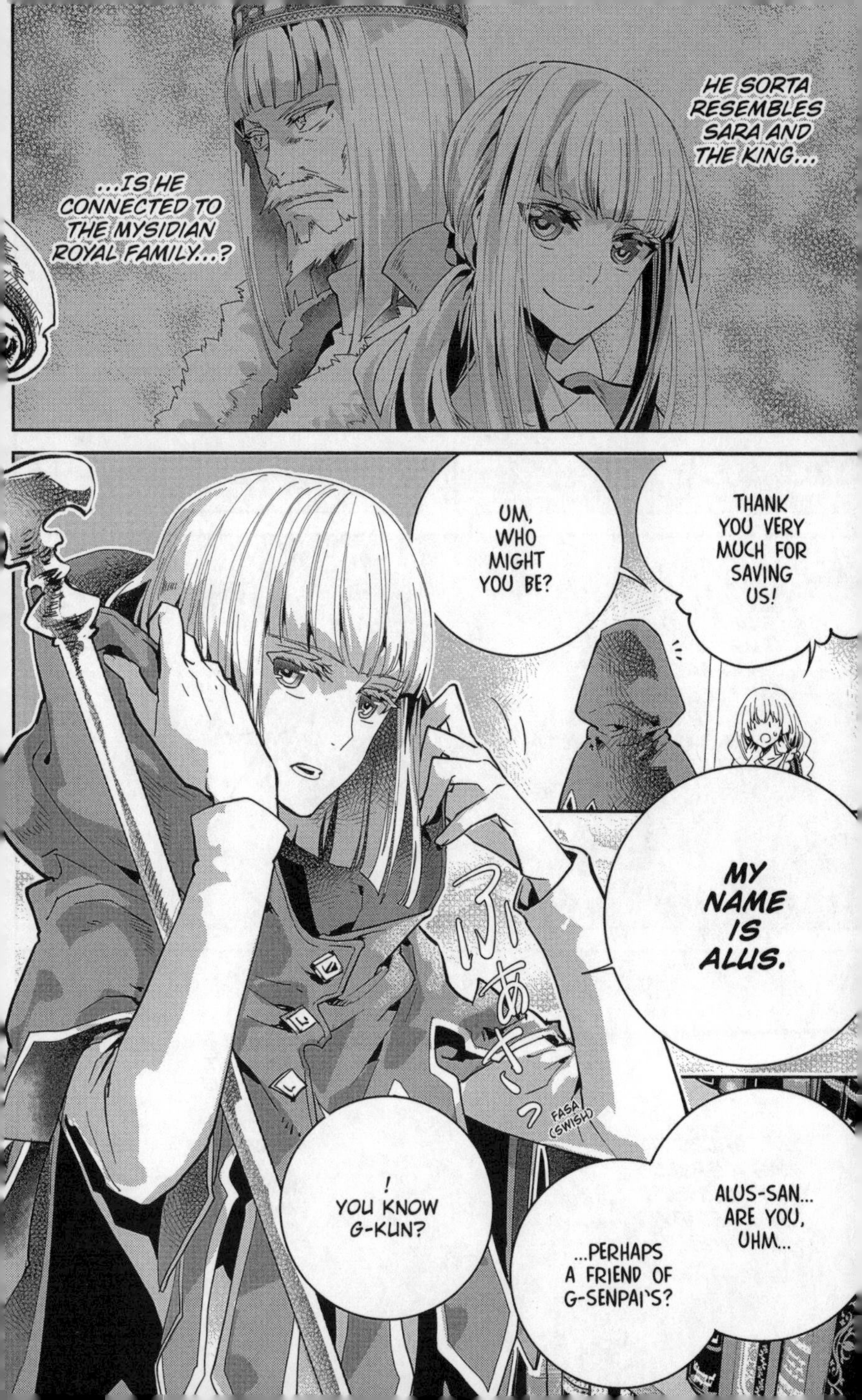
HE SORTA RESEMBLES SARA AND THE KING...
...IS HE CONNECTED TO THE MYSIDIAN ROYAL FAMILY...?
THANK YOU VERY MUCH FOR SAVING US!
UM, WHO MIGHT YOU BE?
MY NAME IS ALUS.
ふあさっ
FASA (SWISH)
ALUS-SAN... ARE YOU, UHM...
...PERHAPS A FRIEND OF G-SENPAI'S?
! YOU KNOW G-KUN?

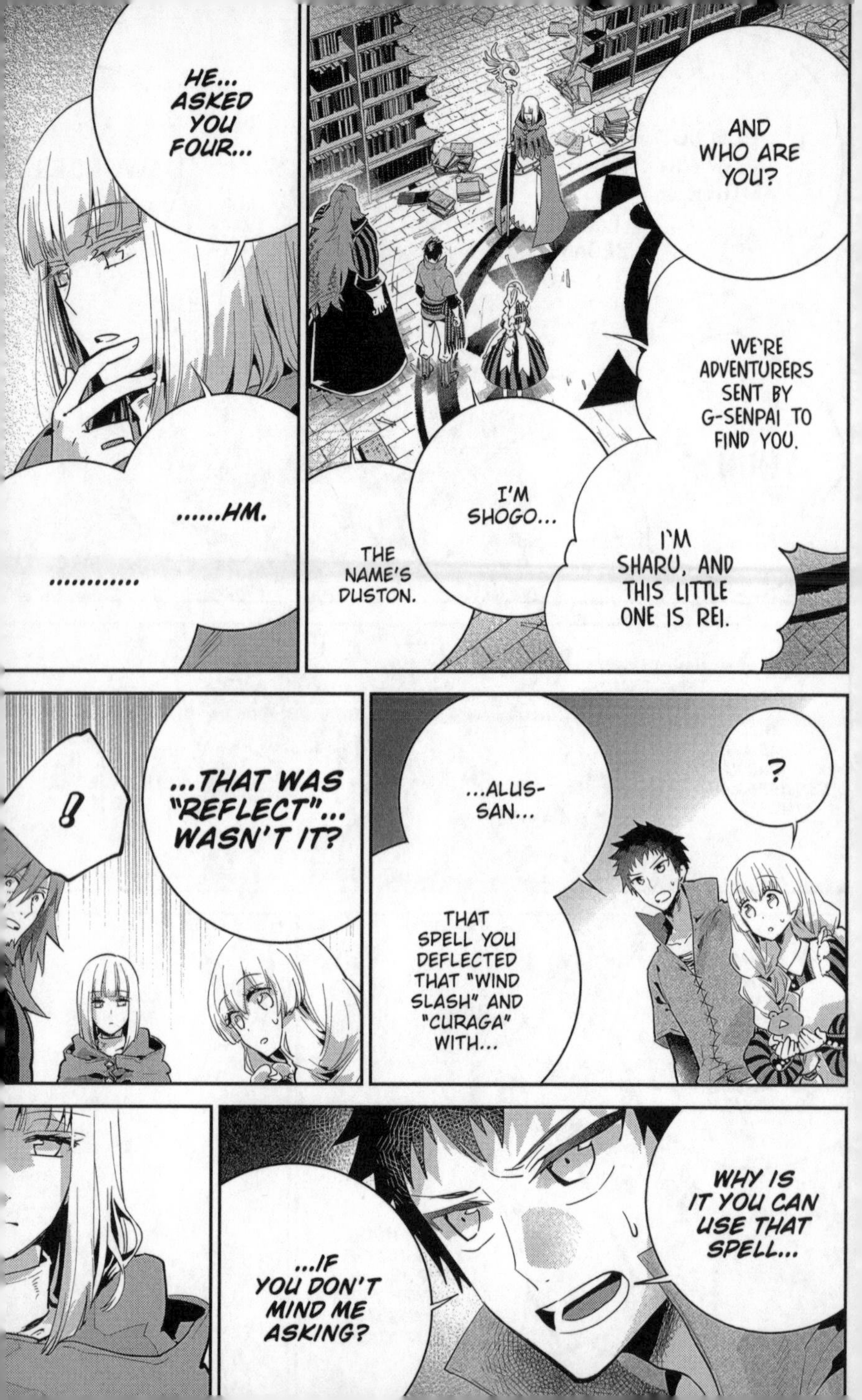
AND WHO ARE YOU?
WE'RE ADVENTURERS SENT BY G-SENPAI TO FIND YOU.
I'M SHARU, AND THIS LITTLE ONE IS REI.
I'M SHOGO...
THE NAME'S DUSTON.
HE... ASKED YOU FOUR...
......HM.
............
?
...ALUS-SAN...
THAT SPELL YOU DEFLECTED THAT "WIND SLASH" AND "CURAGA" WITH...
...THAT WAS "REFLECT"... WASN'T IT?
!
WHY IS IT YOU CAN USE THAT SPELL...
...IF YOU DON'T MIND ME ASKING?

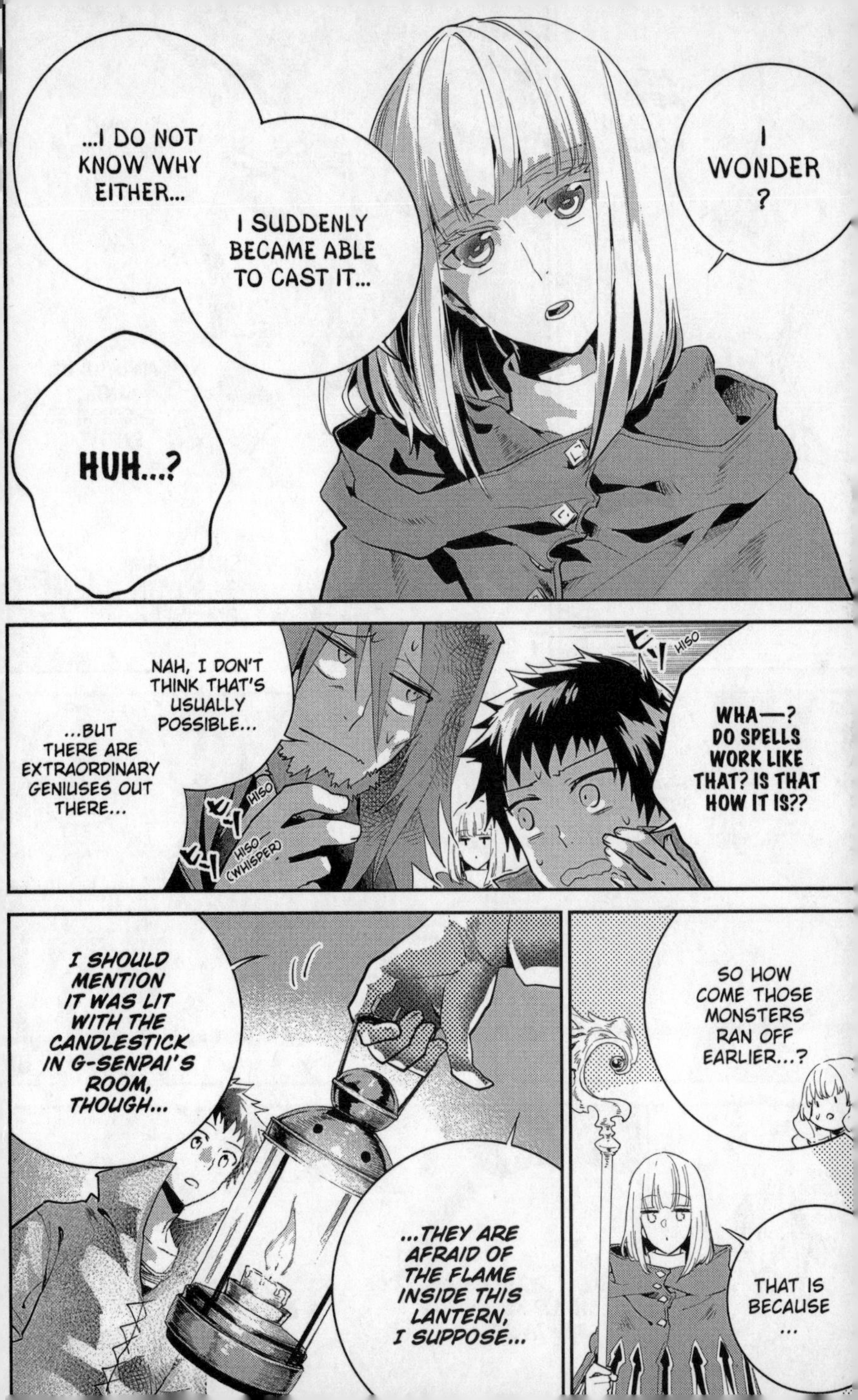
I WONDER ?
...I DO NOT KNOW WHY EITHER...
I SUDDENLY BECAME ABLE TO CAST IT...
HUH...?
HISO
WHA—? DO SPELLS WORK LIKE THAT? IS THAT HOW IT IS??
NAH, I DON'T THINK THAT'S USUALLY POSSIBLE...
...BUT THERE ARE EXTRAORDINARY GENIUSES OUT THERE...
HISO
HISO— (WHISPER)
SO HOW COME THOSE MONSTERS RAN OFF EARLIER...?
THAT IS BECAUSE ...
...THEY ARE AFRAID OF THE FLAME INSIDE THIS LANTERN, I SUPPOSE...
I SHOULD MENTION IT WAS LIT WITH THE CANDLESTICK IN G-SENPAI'S ROOM, THOUGH...

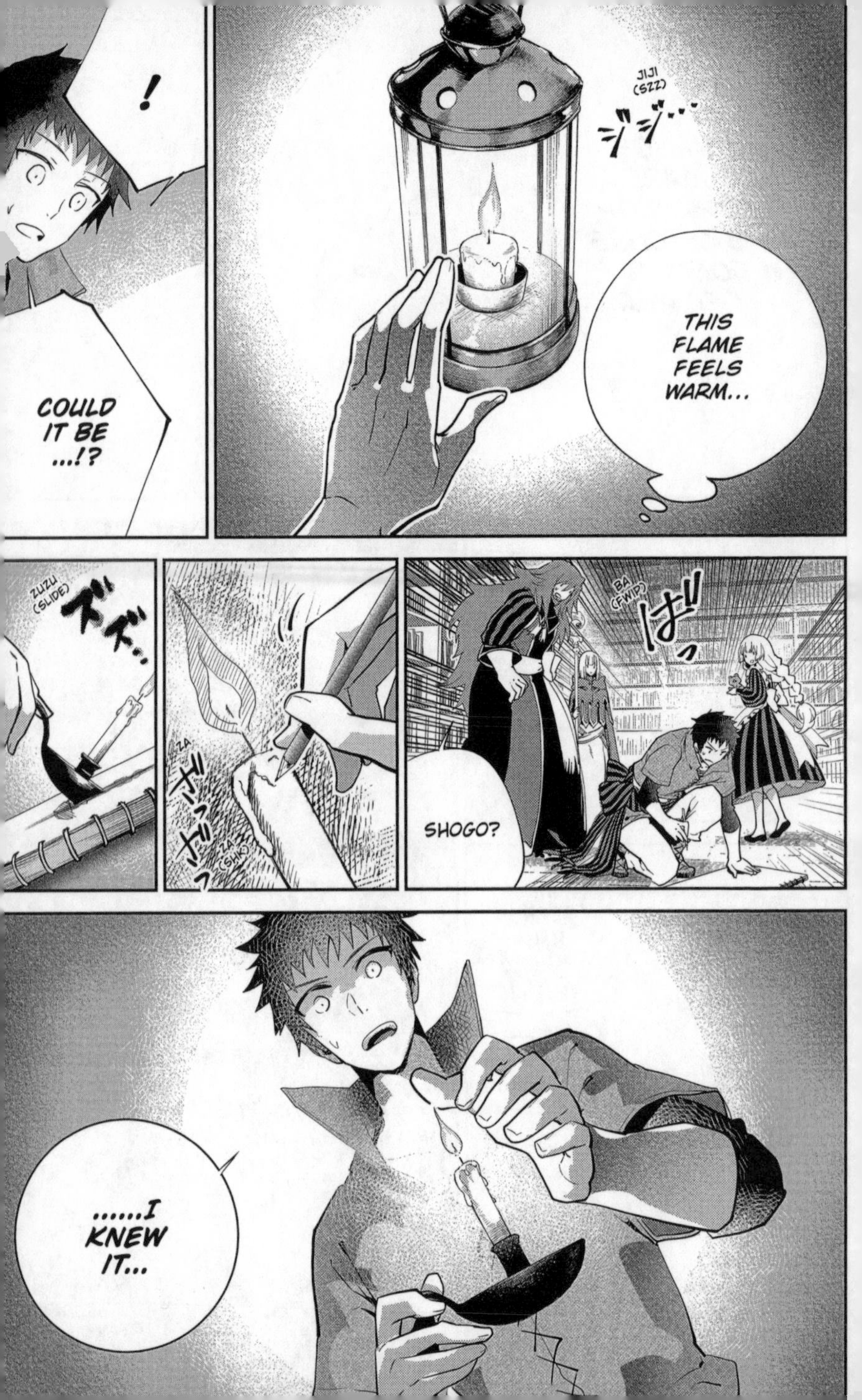
JIJI (SZZ)
THIS FLAME FEELS WARM...
!
COULD IT BE ...!?
BA (FWIP)
SHOGO?
ZA ZA (SHK)
ZUZU (SLIDE)
......I KNEW IT...

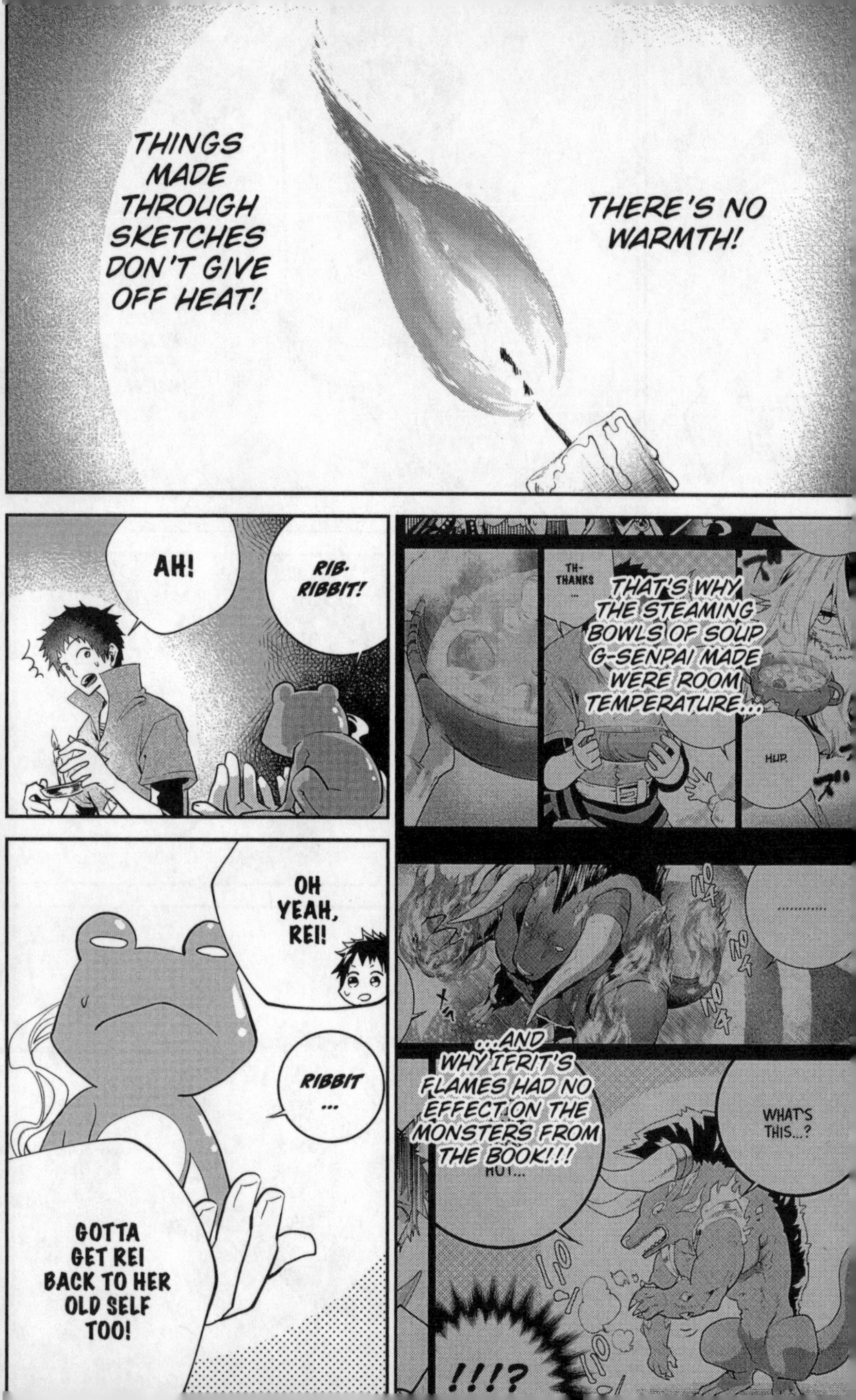
THERE'S NO WARMTH!
THINGS MADE THROUGH SKETCHES DON'T GIVE OFF HEAT!
HUP.
TH-THANKS...
THAT'S WHY THE STEAMING BOWLS OF SOUP G-SENPAI MADE WERE ROOM TEMPERATURE...
............
WHAT'S THIS...?
...AND WHY IFRIT'S FLAMES HAD NO EFFECT ON THE MONSTERS FROM THE BOOK!!!
!!!?
RIB-RIBBIT!
AH!
OH YEAH, REI!
RIBBIT...
GOTTA GET REI BACK TO HER OLD SELF TOO!

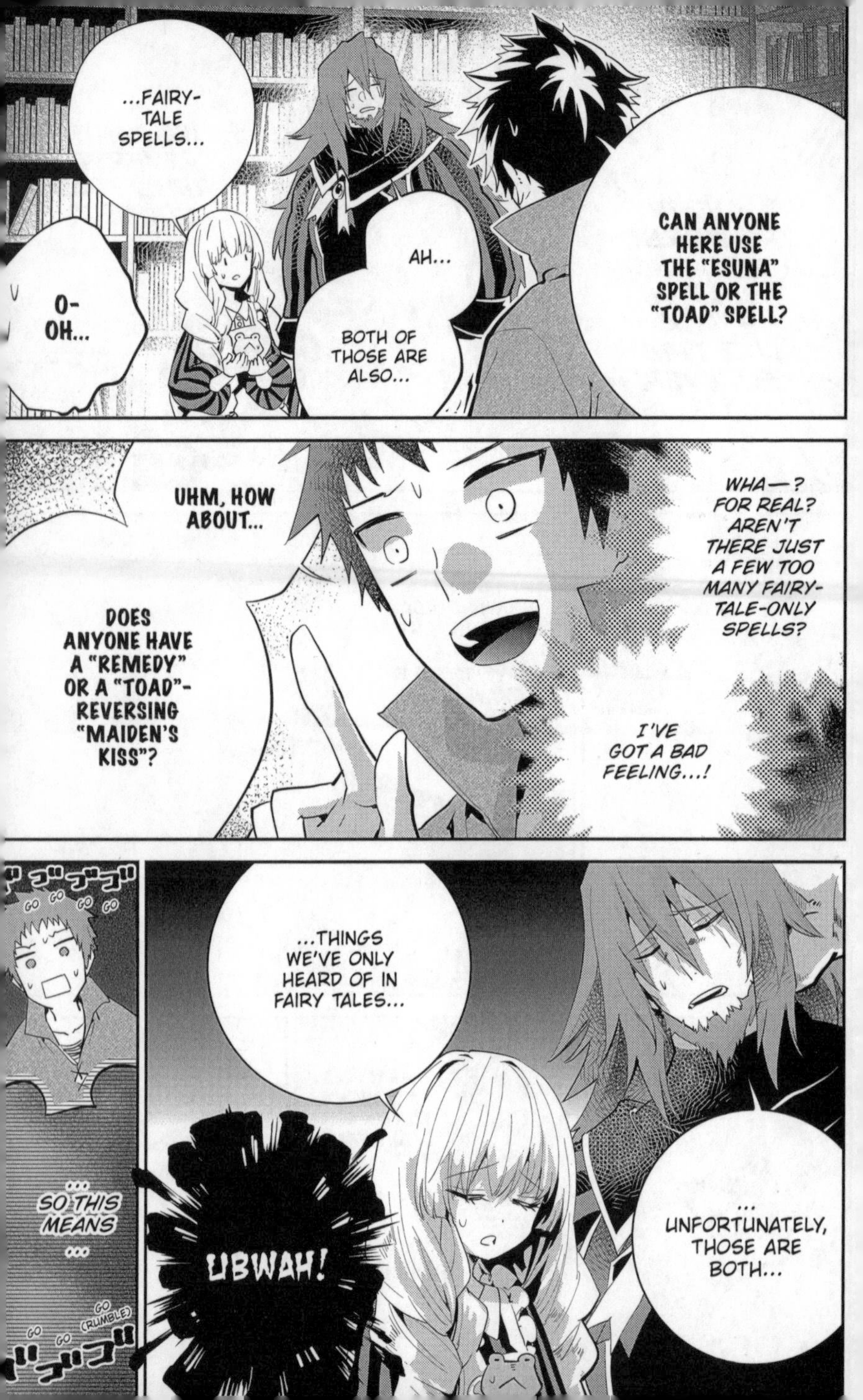
CAN ANYONE HERE USE THE "ESUNA" SPELL OR THE "TOAD" SPELL?
AH...
BOTH OF THOSE ARE ALSO...
...FAIRY-TALE SPELLS...
O-OH...
WHA—? FOR REAL? AREN'T THERE JUST A FEW TOO MANY FAIRY-TALE-ONLY SPELLS?
I'VE GOT A BAD FEELING...!
UHM, HOW ABOUT...
DOES ANYONE HAVE A "REMEDY" OR A "TOAD"-REVERSING "MAIDEN'S KISS"?
...UNFORTUNATELY, THOSE ARE BOTH...
...THINGS WE'VE ONLY HEARD OF IN FAIRY TALES...
UBWAH!
GO GO GO GO
...SO THIS MEANS...
GO GO GO (RUMBLE)

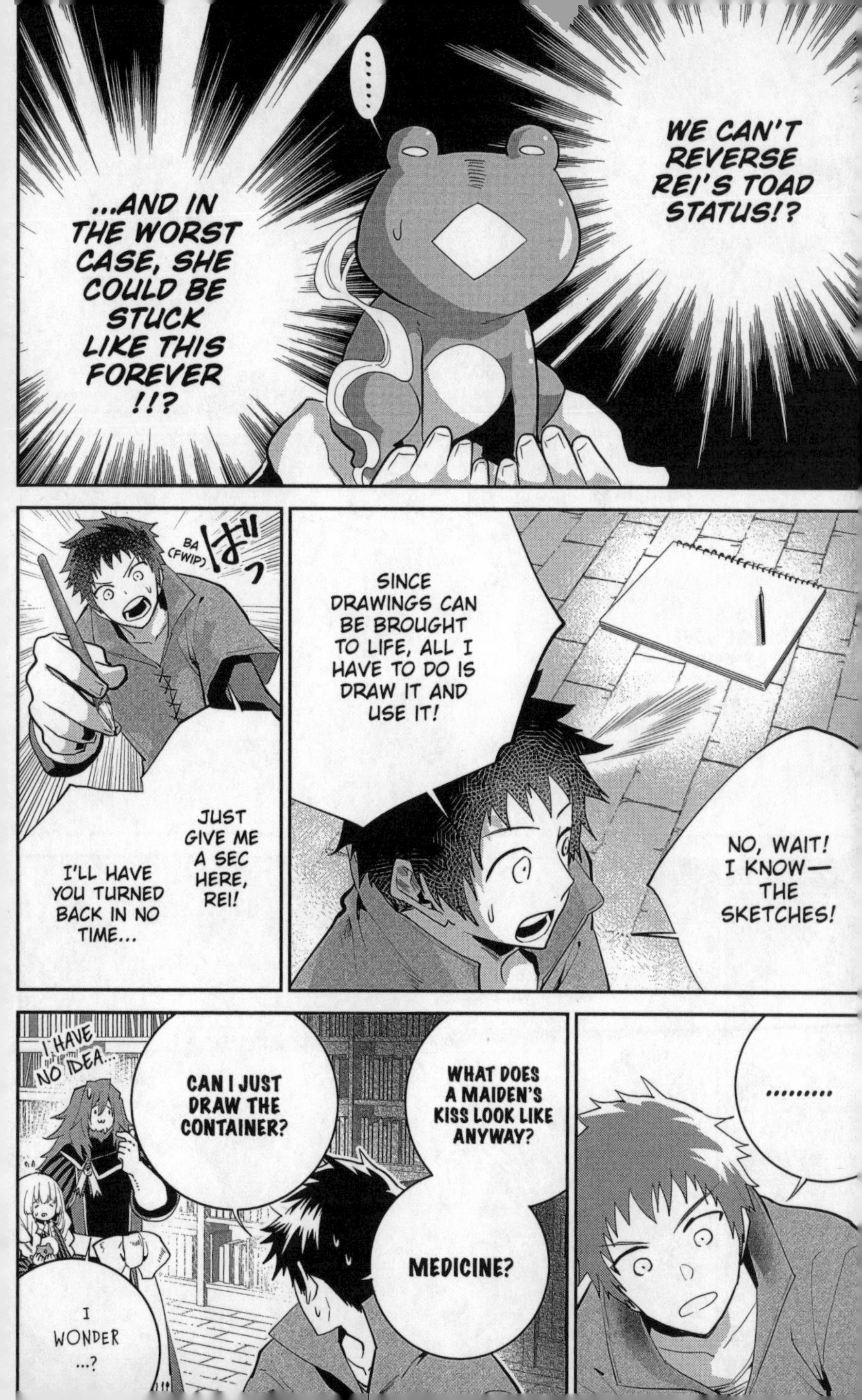
WE CAN'T REVERSE REI'S TOAD STATUS!?
...AND IN THE WORST CASE, SHE COULD BE STUCK LIKE THIS FOREVER!!?
......
NO, WAIT! I KNOW—THE SKETCHES!
SINCE DRAWINGS CAN BE BROUGHT TO LIFE, ALL I HAVE TO DO IS DRAW IT AND USE IT!
BA (FWIP)
JUST GIVE ME A SEC HERE, REI!
I'LL HAVE YOU TURNED BACK IN NO TIME...
.........
WHAT DOES A MAIDEN'S KISS LOOK LIKE ANYWAY?
CAN I JUST DRAW THE CONTAINER?
I HAVE NO IDEA...
MEDICINE?
I WONDER ...?

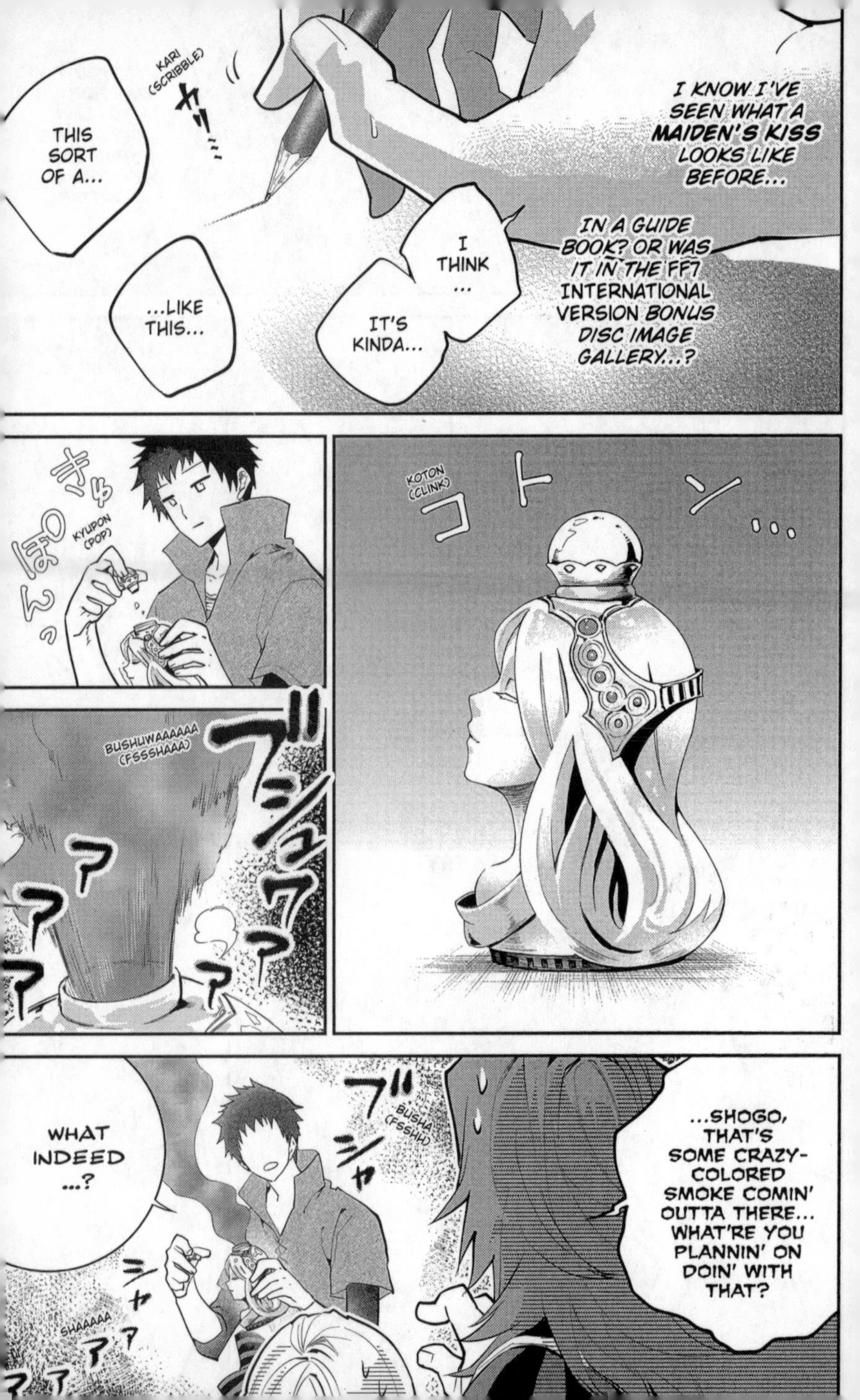
I KNOW I'VE SEEN WHAT A **MAIDEN'S KISS** LOOKS LIKE BEFORE...
IN A GUIDE BOOK? OR WAS IT IN THE FF7 INTERNATIONAL VERSION BONUS DISC IMAGE GALLERY...?
I THINK...
IT'S KINDA...
KARI (SCRIBBLE)
THIS SORT OF A...
...LIKE THIS...
KOTON (CLINK)
KYUPON (POP)
BUSHUWAAAAAA (FSSSHAAA)
...SHOGO, THAT'S SOME CRAZY-COLORED SMOKE COMIN' OUTTA THERE... WHAT'RE YOU PLANNIN' ON DOIN' WITH THAT?
BUSHA (FSSHH)
WHAT INDEED...?
SHAAAAA

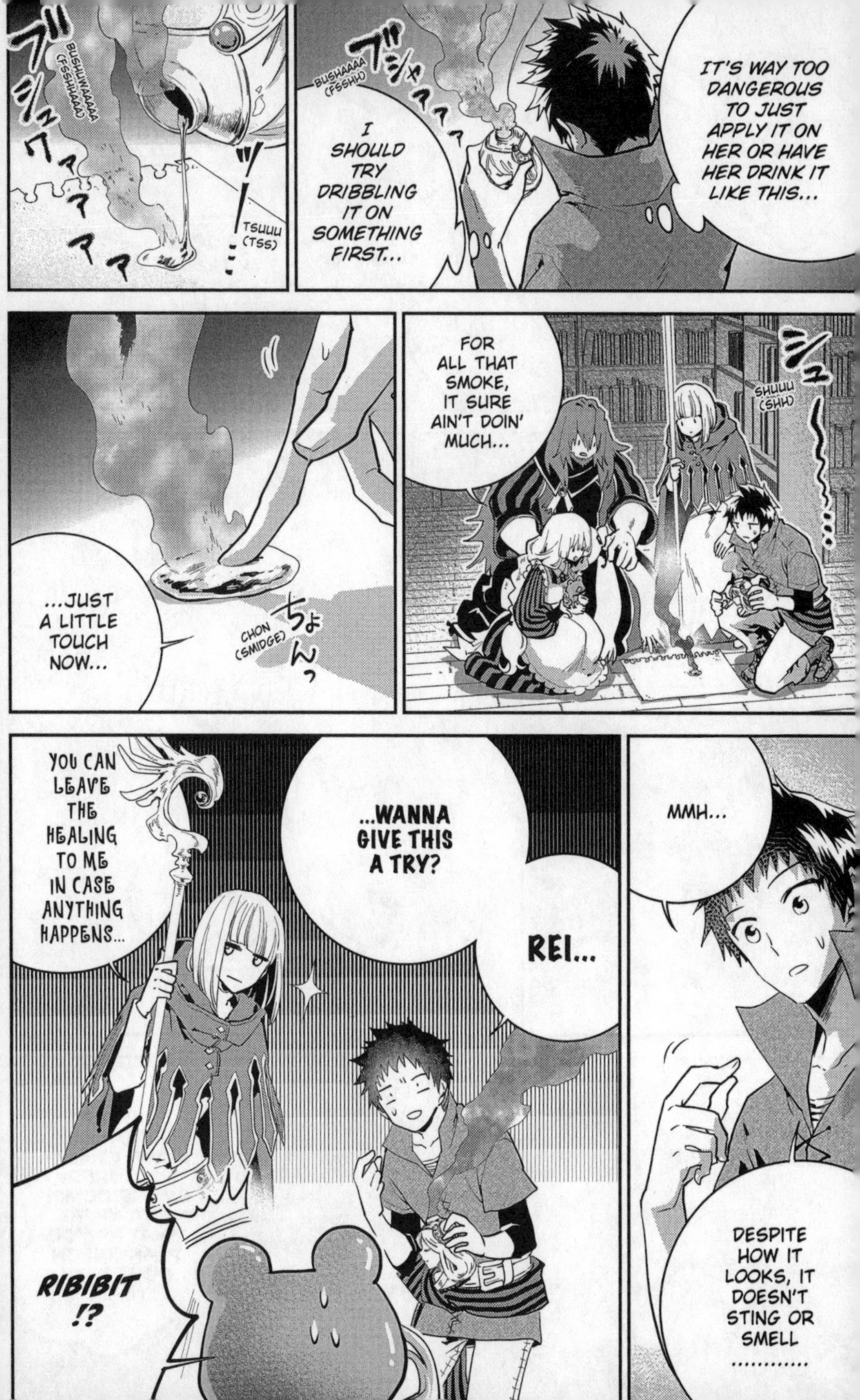
IT'S WAY TOO DANGEROUS TO JUST APPLY IT ON HER OR HAVE HER DRINK IT LIKE THIS...
BUSHAAAA (FSSHH)
I SHOULD TRY DRIBBLING IT ON SOMETHING FIRST...
BUSHUWAAAAA (FSSHAAA)
TSUUU (TSS)
SHUUU (SHH)
FOR ALL THAT SMOKE, IT SURE AIN'T DOIN' MUCH...
...JUST A LITTLE TOUCH NOW...
CHON (SMIDGE)
MMH...
DESPITE HOW IT LOOKS, IT DOESN'T STING OR SMELL ............
REI...
...WANNA GIVE THIS A TRY?
YOU CAN LEAVE THE HEALING TO ME IN CASE ANYTHING HAPPENS...
RIBIBIT !?

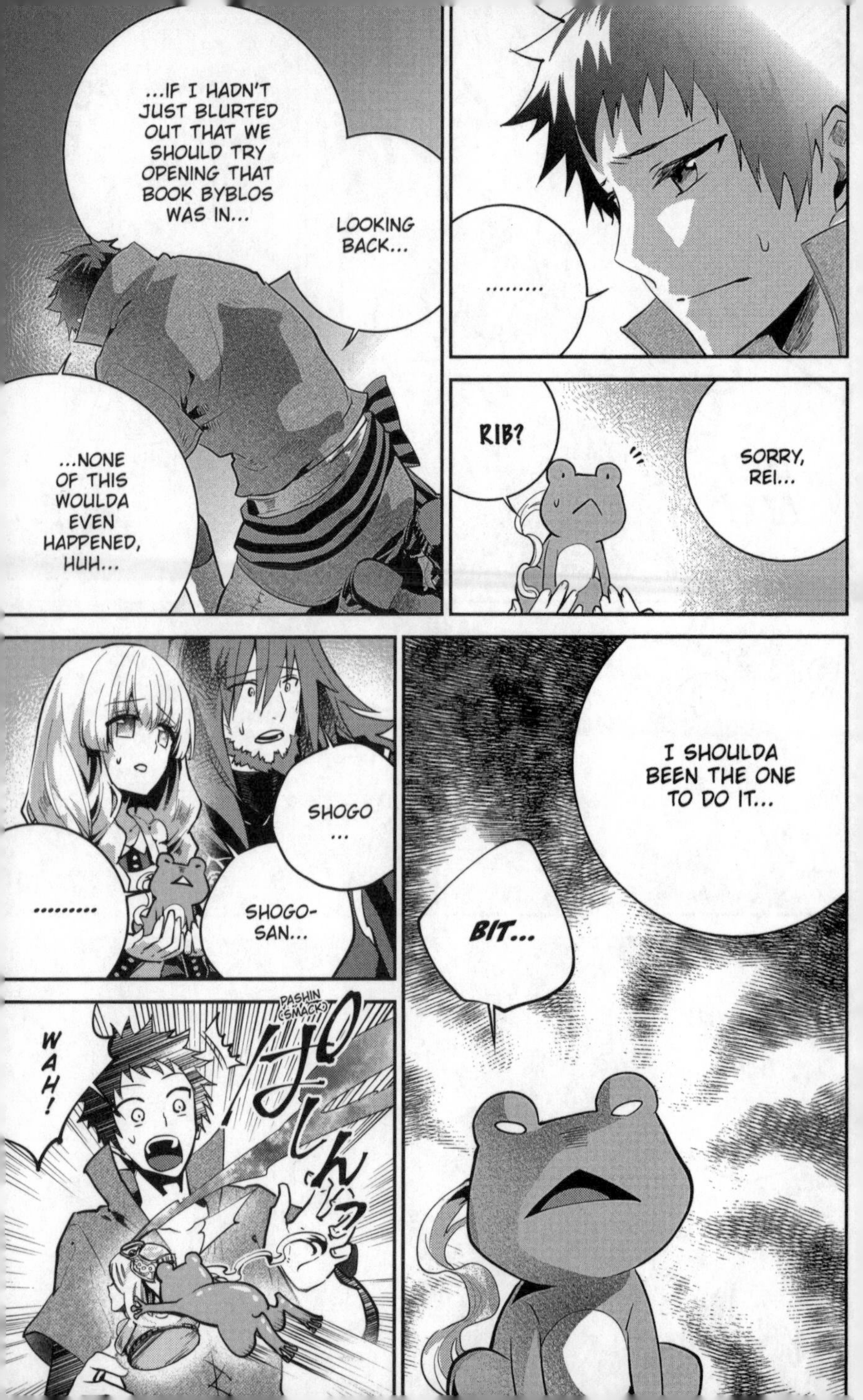
.........
SORRY, REI...
RIB?
LOOKING BACK...
...IF I HADN'T JUST BLURTED OUT THAT WE SHOULD TRY OPENING THAT BOOK BYBLOS WAS IN...
...NONE OF THIS WOULDA EVEN HAPPENED, HUH...
I SHOULDA BEEN THE ONE TO DO IT...
BIT...
SHOGO...
SHOGO-SAN...
.........
PASHIN (SMACK)
WAH!

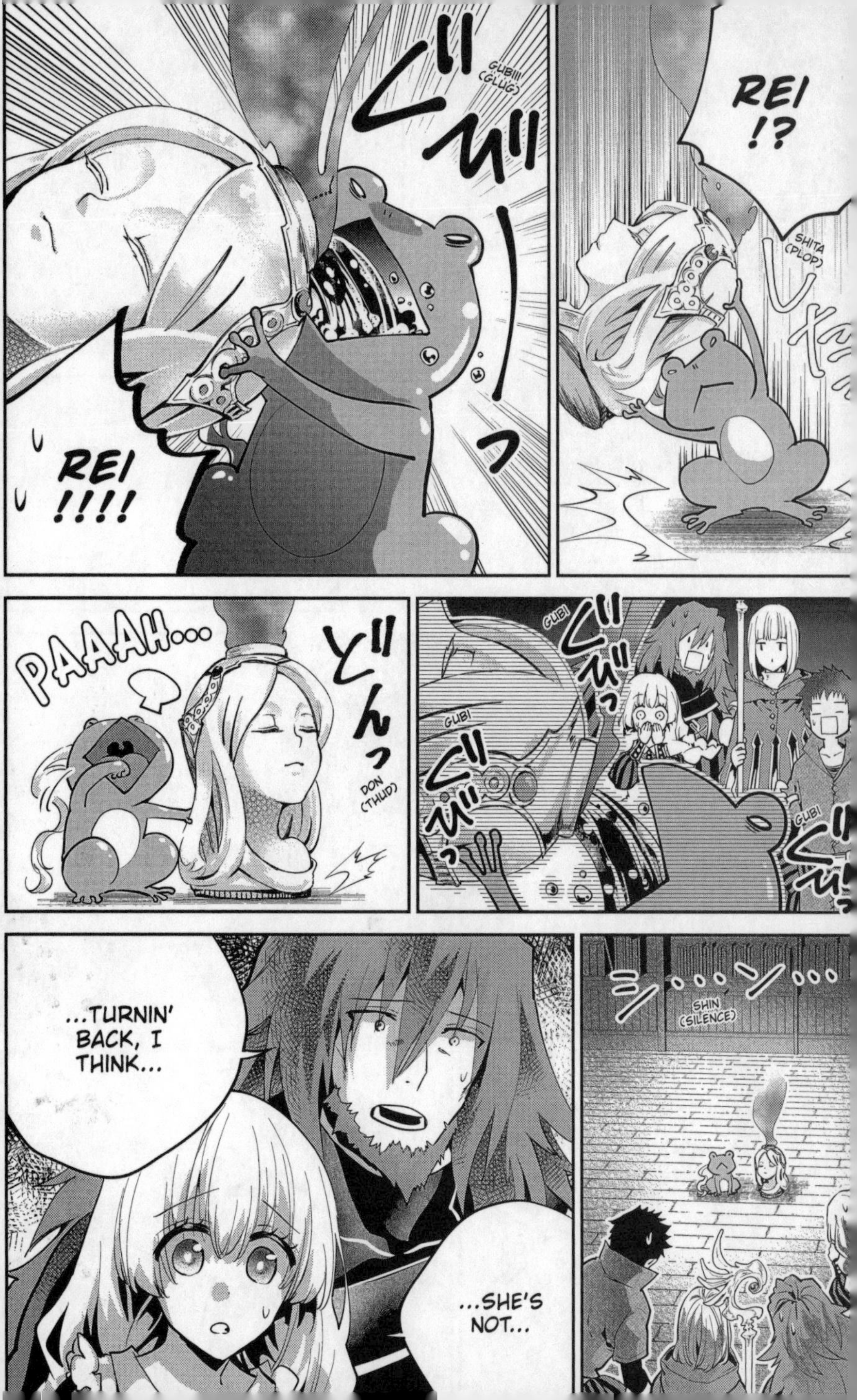
REI !?
SHITA (PLOP)
GUBIII (GLUG)
REI !!!!
GUBI
GUBI
GUBI
PAAAH...
DON (THUD)
SHIN (SILENCE)
...SHE'S NOT...
...TURNIN' BACK, I THINK...

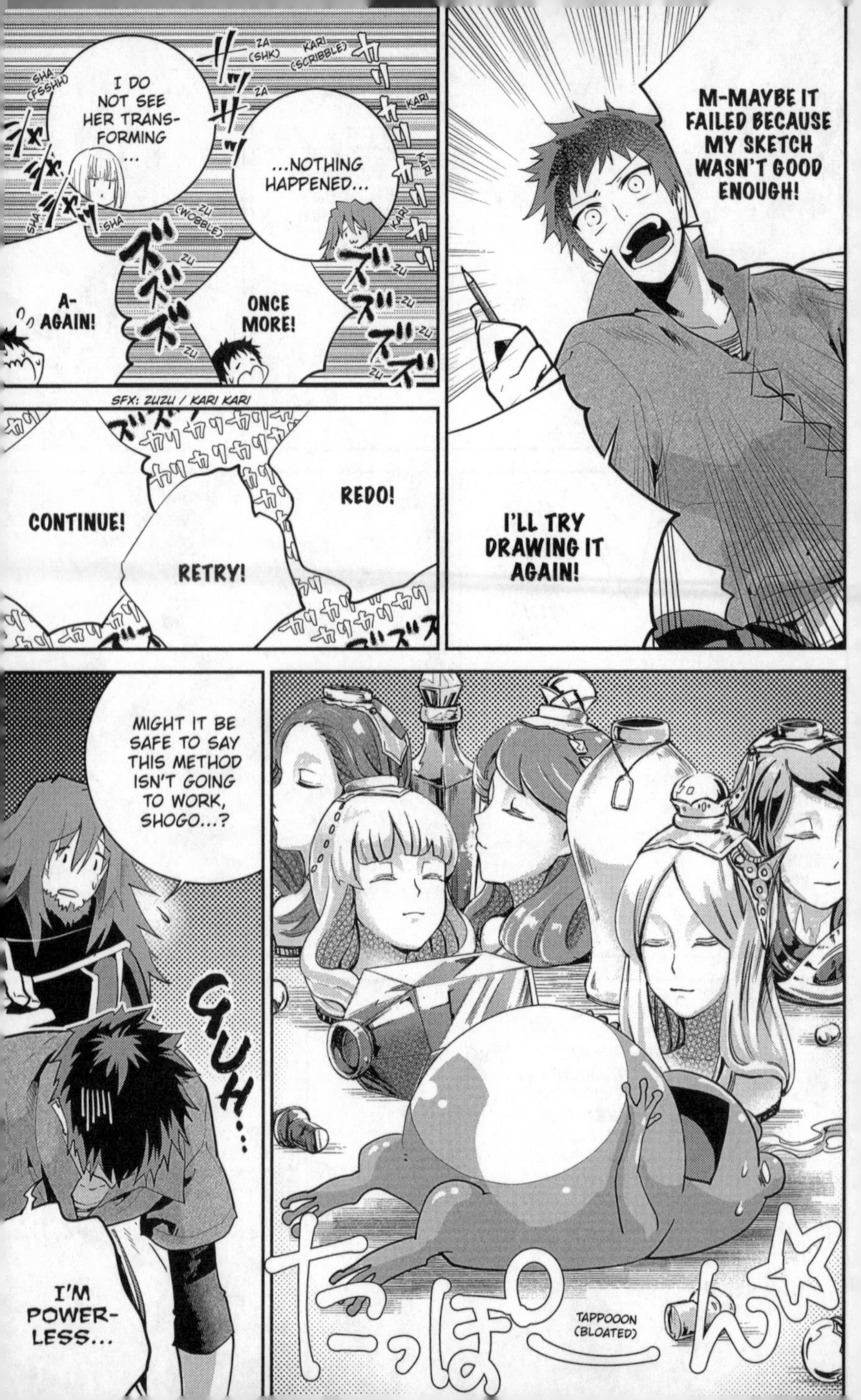
M-MAYBE IT FAILED BECAUSE MY SKETCH WASN'T GOOD ENOUGH!
I'LL TRY DRAWING IT AGAIN!
KARI (SCRIBBLE)
ZA (SHK)
...NOTHING HAPPENED...
I DO NOT SEE HER TRANS-FORMING ...
SHA (FSSHH)
ZU (WOBBLE)
ONCE MORE!
A-AGAIN!
SFX: ZUZU / KARI KARI
REDO!
CONTINUE!
RETRY!
TAPPOOON (BLOATED)
MIGHT IT BE SAFE TO SAY THIS METHOD ISN'T GOING TO WORK, SHOGO...?
GUH...
I'M POWER-LESS...

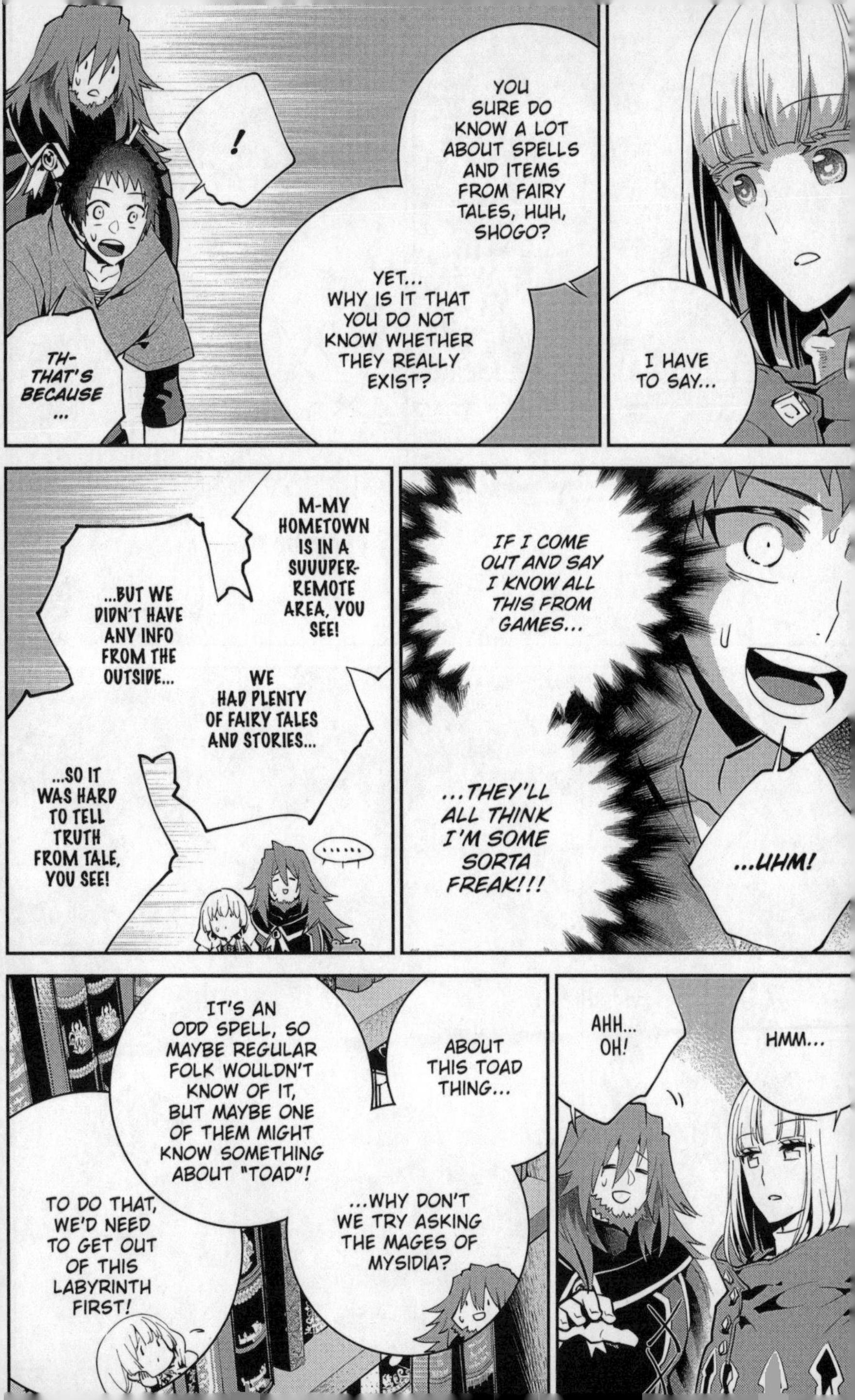
I HAVE TO SAY...
YOU SURE DO KNOW A LOT ABOUT SPELLS AND ITEMS FROM FAIRY TALES, HUH, SHOGO?
YET... WHY IS IT THAT YOU DO NOT KNOW WHETHER THEY REALLY EXIST?
!
TH- THAT'S BECAUSE ...
IF I COME OUT AND SAY I KNOW ALL THIS FROM GAMES...
...UHM!
...THEY'LL ALL THINK I'M SOME SORTA FREAK!!!
M-MY HOMETOWN IS IN A SUUUPER-REMOTE AREA, YOU SEE!
...BUT WE DIDN'T HAVE ANY INFO FROM THE OUTSIDE...
WE HAD PLENTY OF FAIRY TALES AND STORIES...
...SO IT WAS HARD TO TELL TRUTH FROM TALE, YOU SEE!
......
HMM...
AHH... OH!
ABOUT THIS TOAD THING...
IT'S AN ODD SPELL, SO MAYBE REGULAR FOLK WOULDN'T KNOW OF IT, BUT MAYBE ONE OF THEM MIGHT KNOW SOMETHING ABOUT "TOAD"!
...WHY DON'T WE TRY ASKING THE MAGES OF MYSIDIA?
TO DO THAT, WE'D NEED TO GET OUT OF THIS LABYRINTH FIRST!

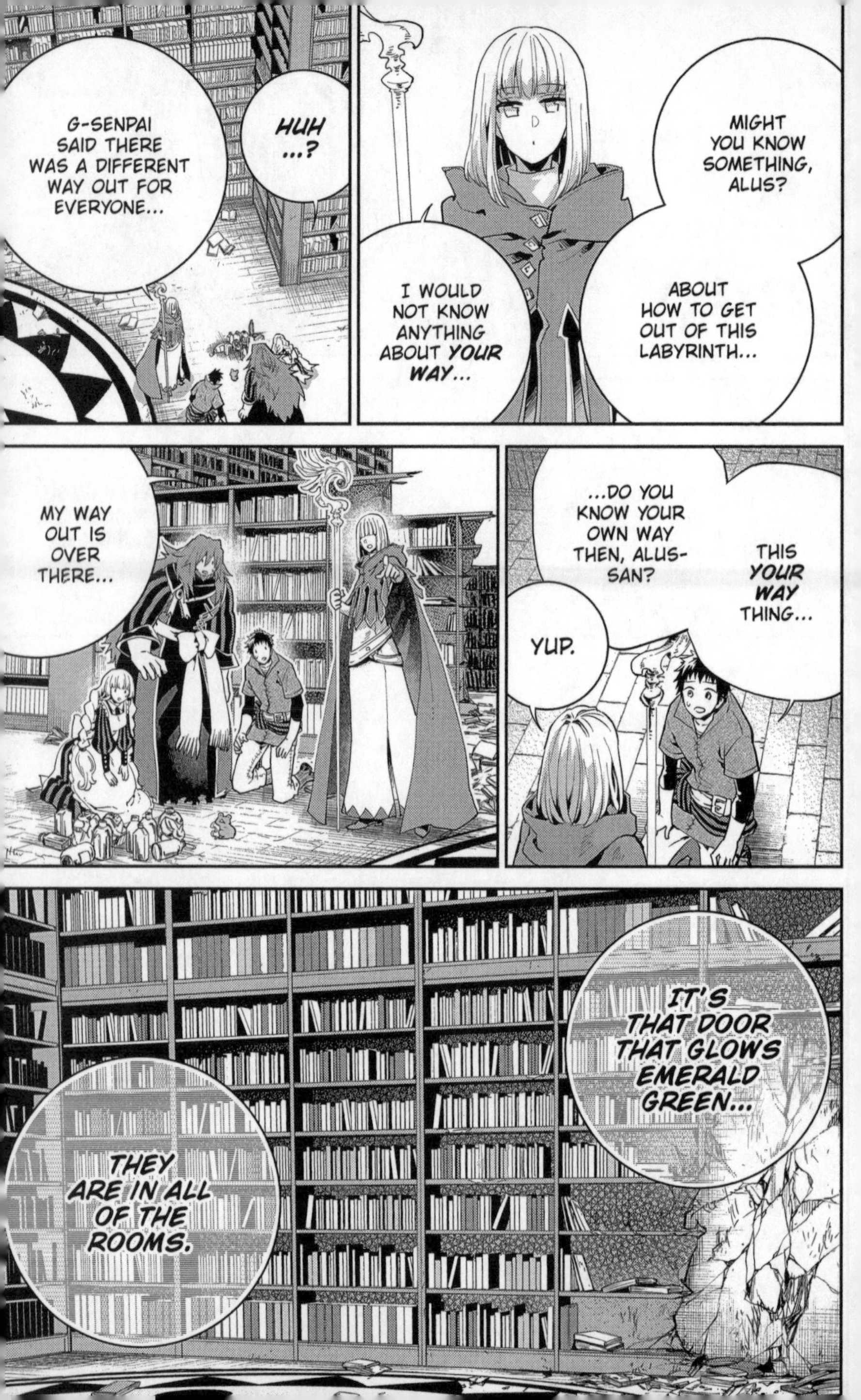
MIGHT YOU KNOW SOMETHING, ALUS?
ABOUT HOW TO GET OUT OF THIS LABYRINTH...
I WOULD NOT KNOW ANYTHING ABOUT YOUR WAY...
HUH ...?
G-SENPAI SAID THERE WAS A DIFFERENT WAY OUT FOR EVERYONE...
THIS YOUR WAY THING...
...DO YOU KNOW YOUR OWN WAY THEN, ALUS-SAN?
YUP.
MY WAY OUT IS OVER THERE...
IT'S THAT DOOR THAT GLOWS EMERALD GREEN...
THEY ARE IN ALL OF THE ROOMS.

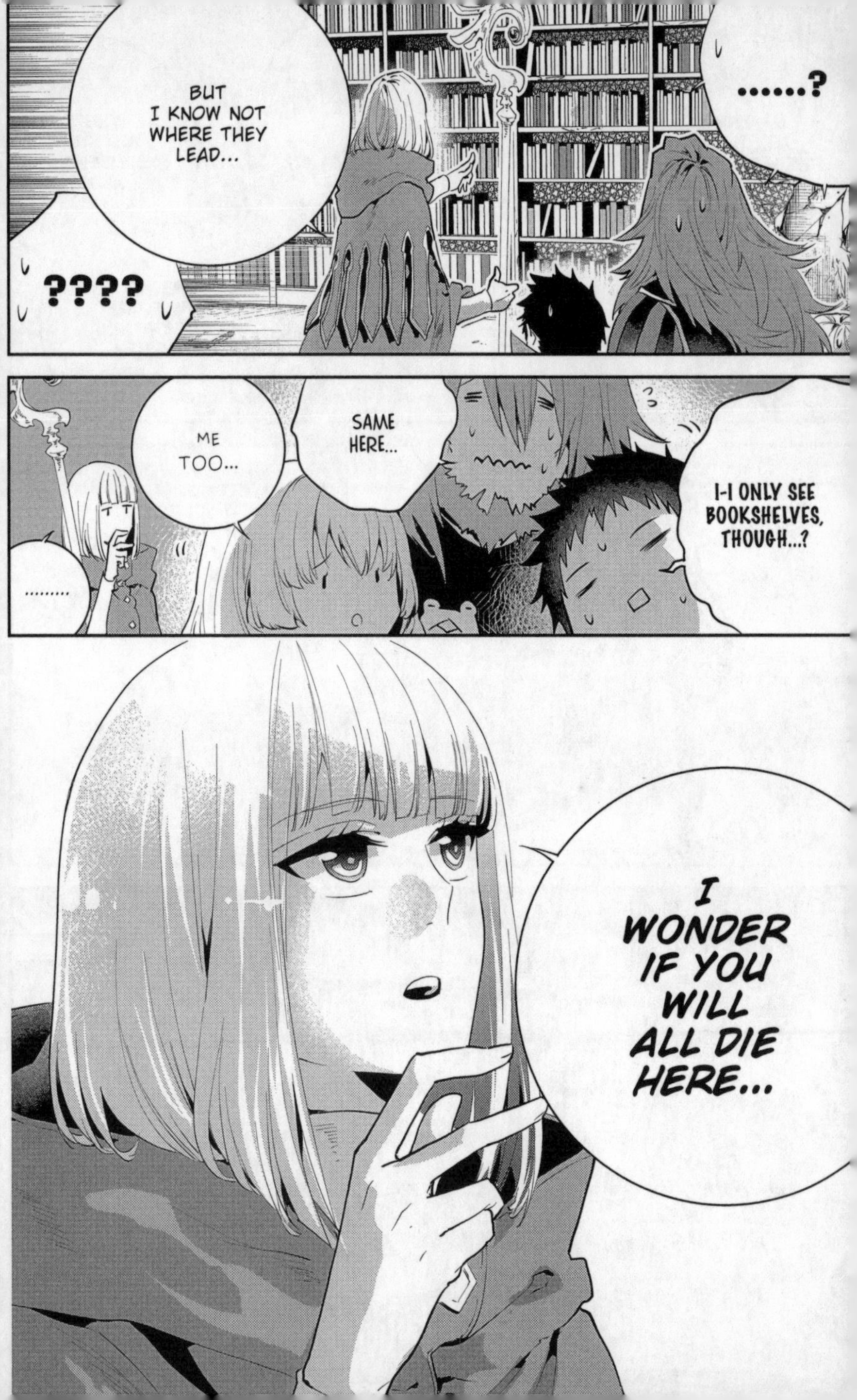
......?
BUT I KNOW NOT WHERE THEY LEAD...
????
I-I ONLY SEE BOOKSHELVES, THOUGH...?
SAME HERE...
ME TOO...
.........
I WONDER IF YOU WILL ALL DIE HERE...

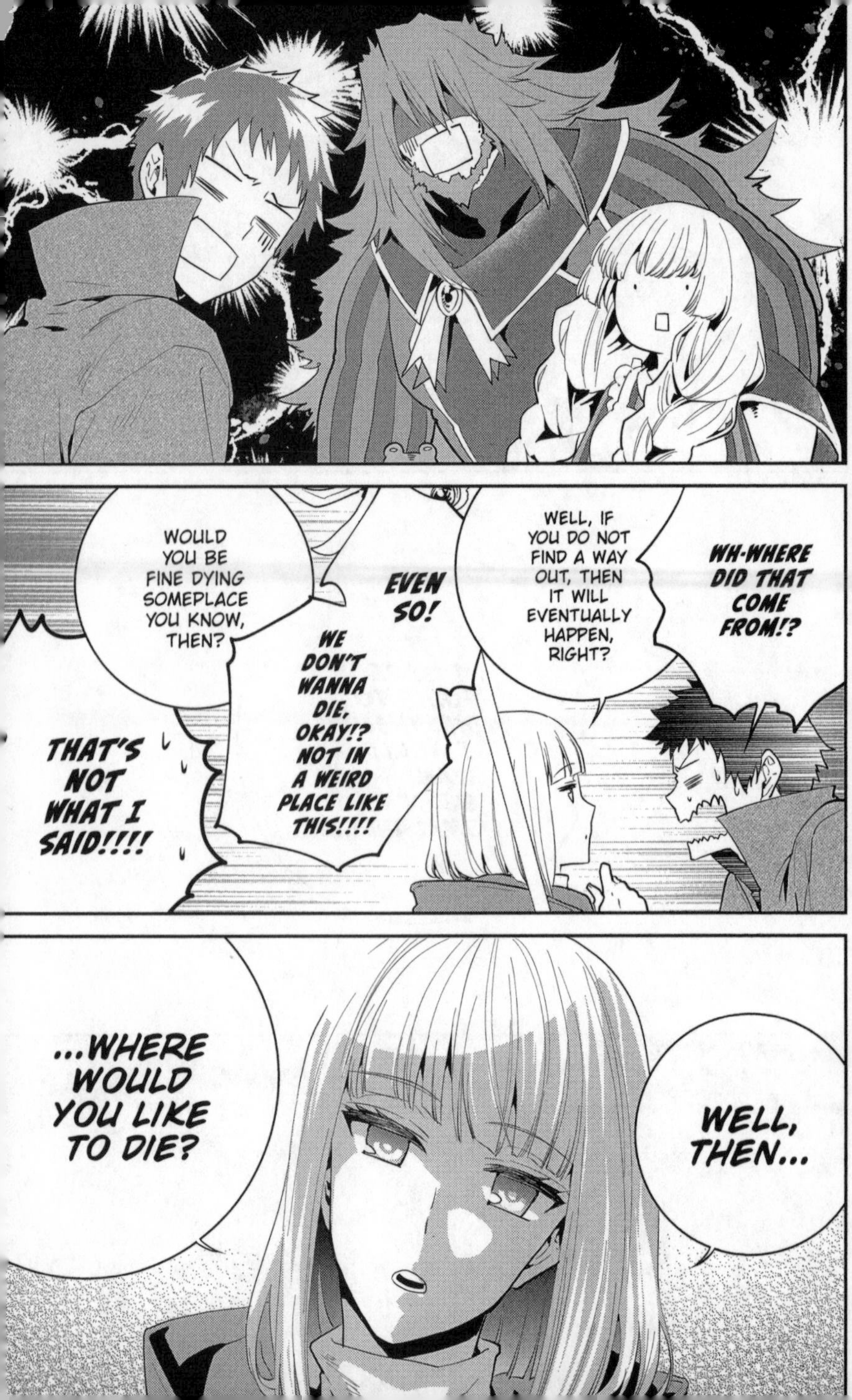
WH-WHERE DID THAT COME FROM!?
WELL, IF YOU DO NOT FIND A WAY OUT, THEN IT WILL EVENTUALLY HAPPEN, RIGHT?
EVEN SO!
WE DON'T WANNA DIE, OKAY!? NOT IN A WEIRD PLACE LIKE THIS!!!!
WOULD YOU BE FINE DYING SOMEPLACE YOU KNOW, THEN?
THAT'S NOT WHAT I SAID!!!!
WELL, THEN...
...WHERE WOULD YOU LIKE TO DIE?

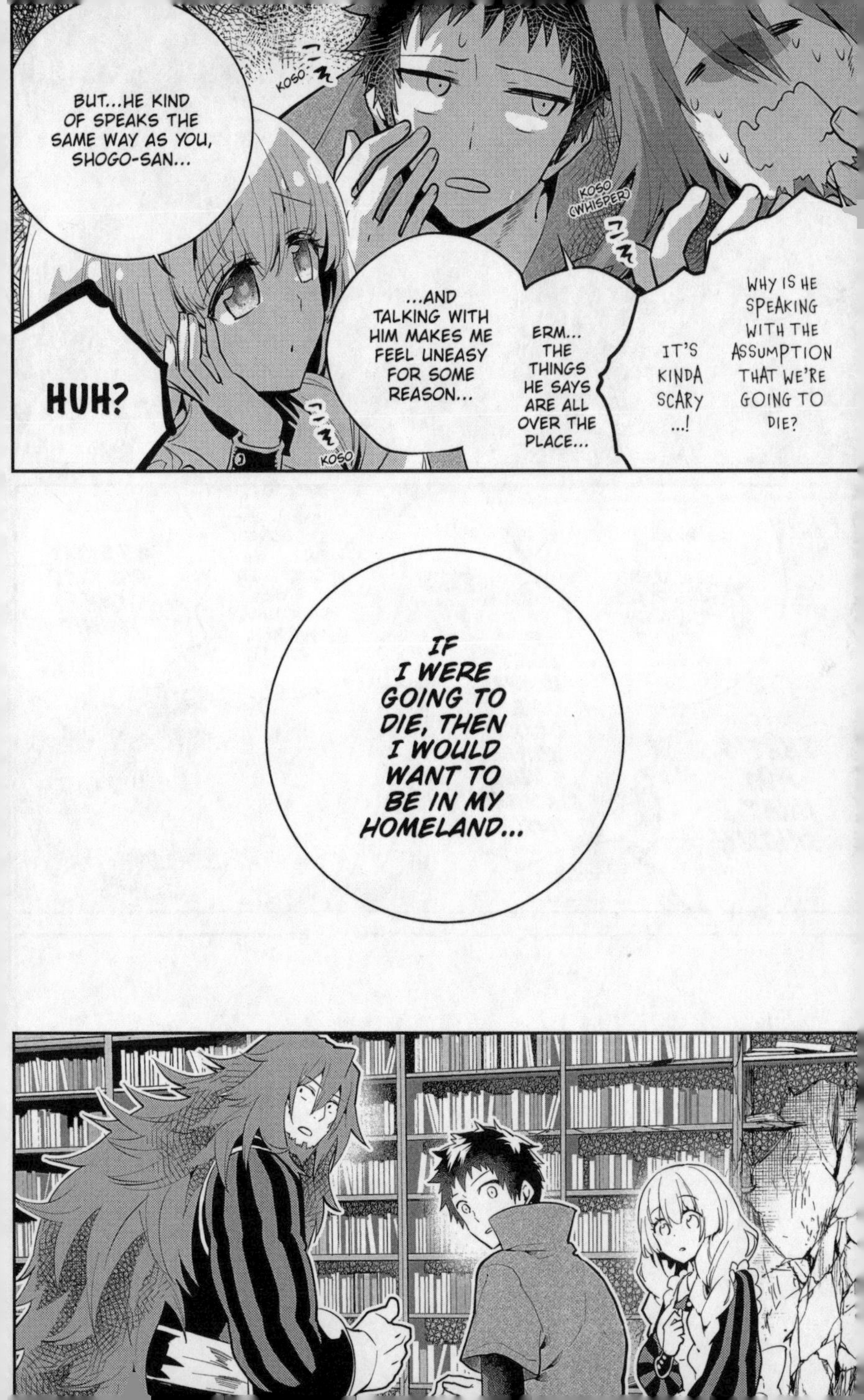

WHY IS HE SPEAKING WITH THE ASSUMPTION THAT WE'RE GOING TO DIE?
IT'S KINDA SCARY ...!
KOSO (WHISPER)
ERM... THE THINGS HE SAYS ARE ALL OVER THE PLACE...
...AND TALKING WITH HIM MAKES ME FEEL UNEASY FOR SOME REASON...
KOSO
KOSO
BUT...HE KIND OF SPEAKS THE SAME WAY AS YOU, SHOGO-SAN...
HUH?
IF I WERE GOING TO DIE, THEN I WOULD WANT TO BE IN MY HOMELAND...

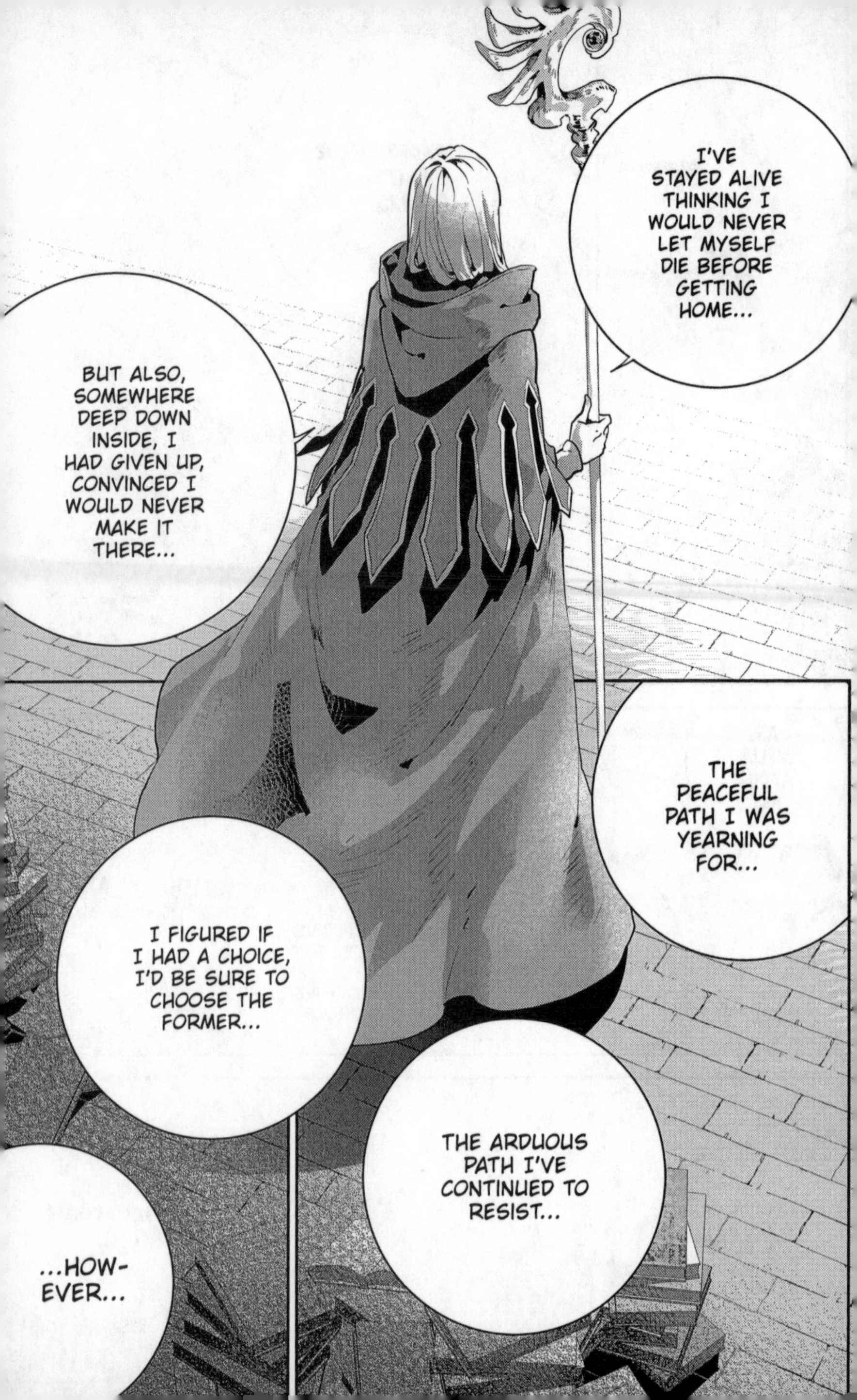
I'VE STAYED ALIVE THINKING I WOULD NEVER LET MYSELF DIE BEFORE GETTING HOME...
BUT ALSO, SOMEWHERE DEEP DOWN INSIDE, I HAD GIVEN UP, CONVINCED I WOULD NEVER MAKE IT THERE...
THE PEACEFUL PATH I WAS YEARNING FOR...
THE ARDUOUS PATH I'VE CONTINUED TO RESIST...
I FIGURED IF I HAD A CHOICE, I'D BE SURE TO CHOOSE THE FORMER...
...HOW-EVER...

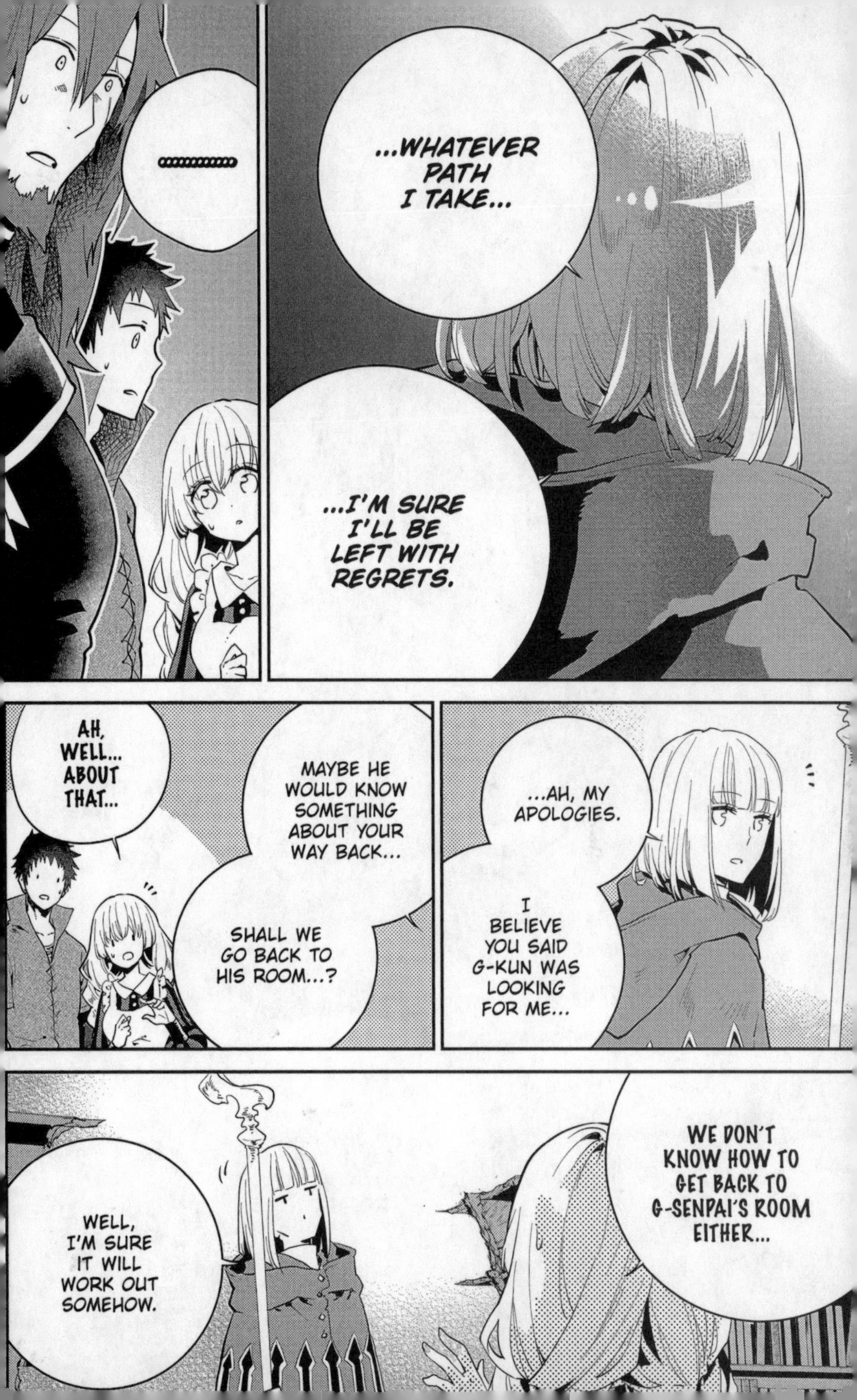
...WHATEVER PATH I TAKE...
...I'M SURE I'LL BE LEFT WITH REGRETS.
............
...AH, MY APOLOGIES.
I BELIEVE YOU SAID G-KUN WAS LOOKING FOR ME...
MAYBE HE WOULD KNOW SOMETHING ABOUT YOUR WAY BACK...
SHALL WE GO BACK TO HIS ROOM...?
AH, WELL... ABOUT THAT...
WE DON'T KNOW HOW TO GET BACK TO G-SENPAI'S ROOM EITHER...
WELL, I'M SURE IT WILL WORK OUT SOMEHOW.

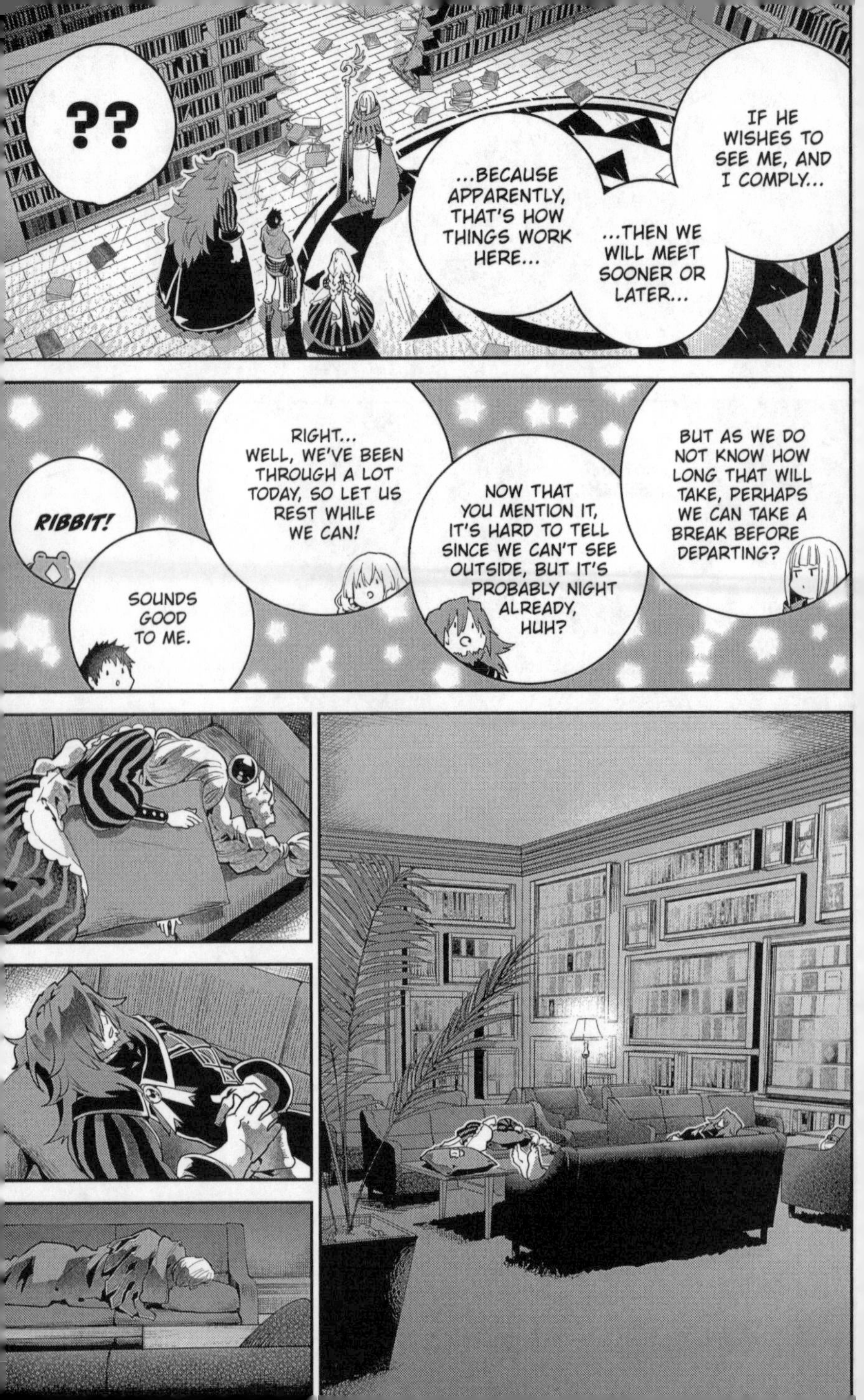
IF HE WISHES TO SEE ME, AND I COMPLY...
...THEN WE WILL MEET SOONER OR LATER...
...BECAUSE APPARENTLY, THAT'S HOW THINGS WORK HERE...
??
BUT AS WE DO NOT KNOW HOW LONG THAT WILL TAKE, PERHAPS WE CAN TAKE A BREAK BEFORE DEPARTING?
NOW THAT YOU MENTION IT, IT'S HARD TO TELL SINCE WE CAN'T SEE OUTSIDE, BUT IT'S PROBABLY NIGHT ALREADY, HUH?
RIGHT... WELL, WE'VE BEEN THROUGH A LOT TODAY, SO LET US REST WHILE WE CAN!
RIBBIT!
SOUNDS GOOD TO ME.

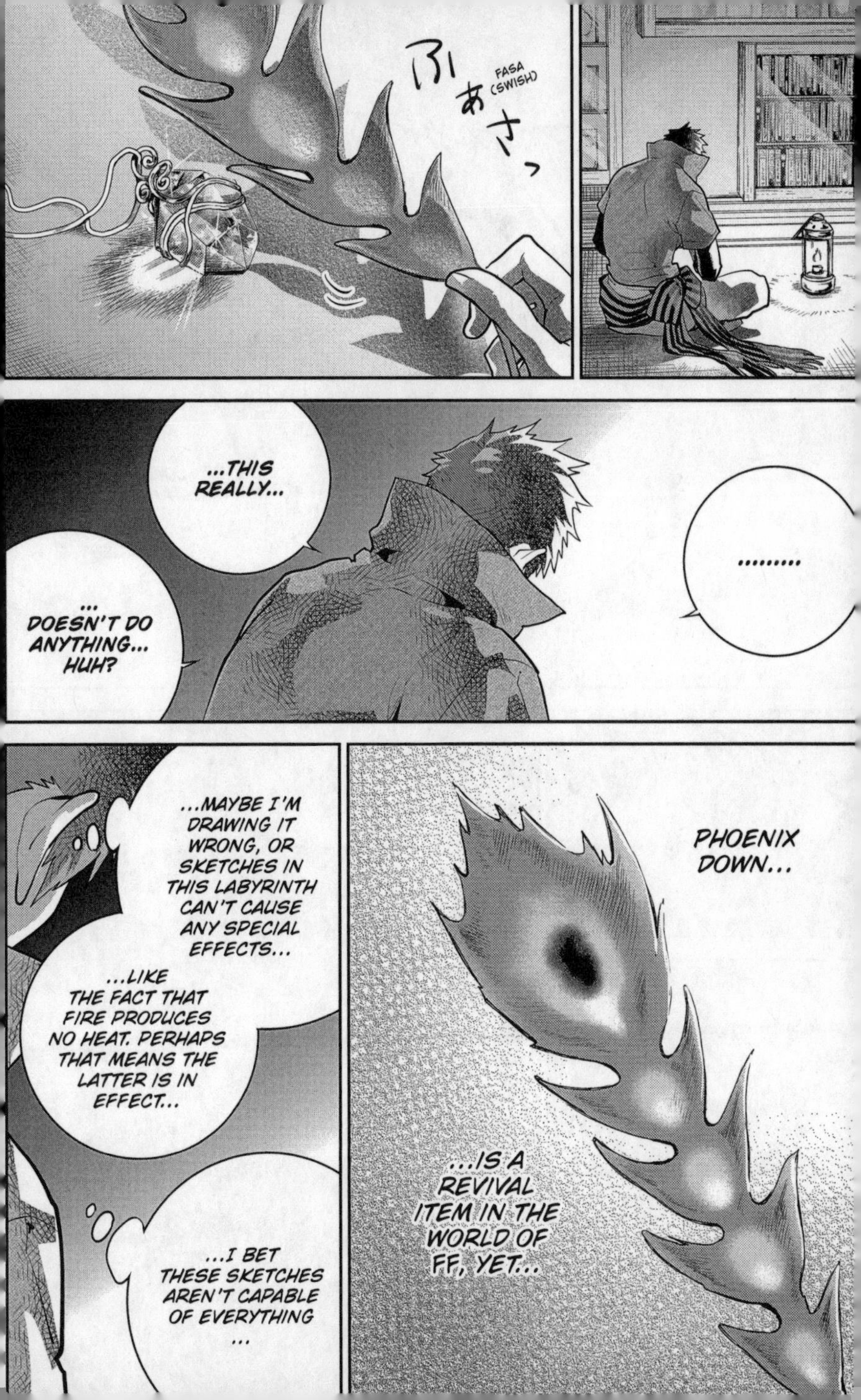
ふあさっ
FASA (SWISH)
.........
...THIS REALLY...
...DOESN'T DO ANYTHING... HUH?
PHOENIX DOWN...
...IS A REVIVAL ITEM IN THE WORLD OF FF, YET...
...MAYBE I'M DRAWING IT WRONG, OR SKETCHES IN THIS LABYRINTH CAN'T CAUSE ANY SPECIAL EFFECTS...
...LIKE THE FACT THAT FIRE PRODUCES NO HEAT. PERHAPS THAT MEANS THE LATTER IS IN EFFECT...
...I BET THESE SKETCHES AREN'T CAPABLE OF EVERYTHING...

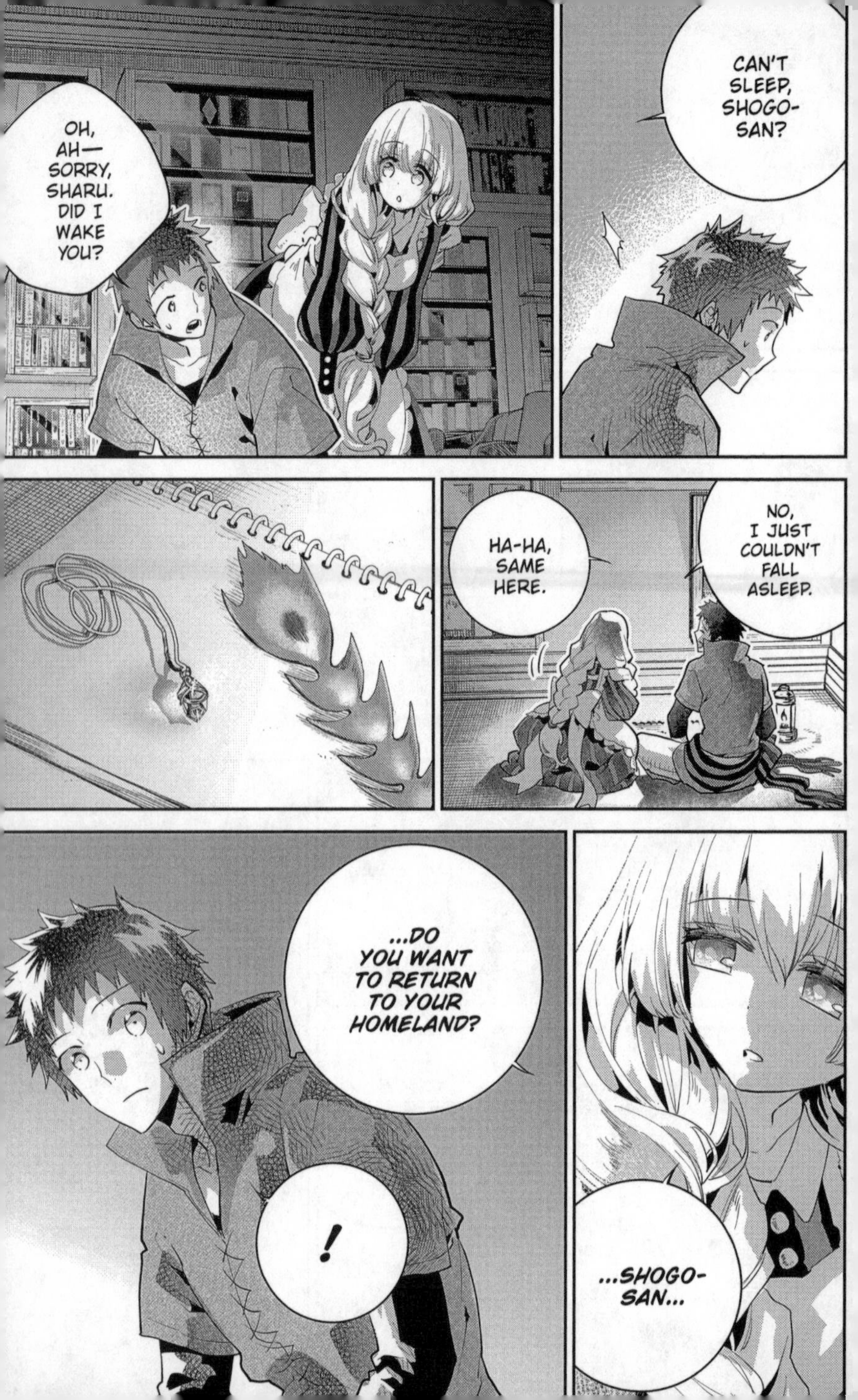
CAN'T SLEEP, SHOGO-SAN?
OH, AH— SORRY, SHARU. DID I WAKE YOU?
NO, I JUST COULDN'T FALL ASLEEP.
HA-HA, SAME HERE.
...SHOGO-SAN...
...DO YOU WANT TO RETURN TO YOUR HOMELAND?
!

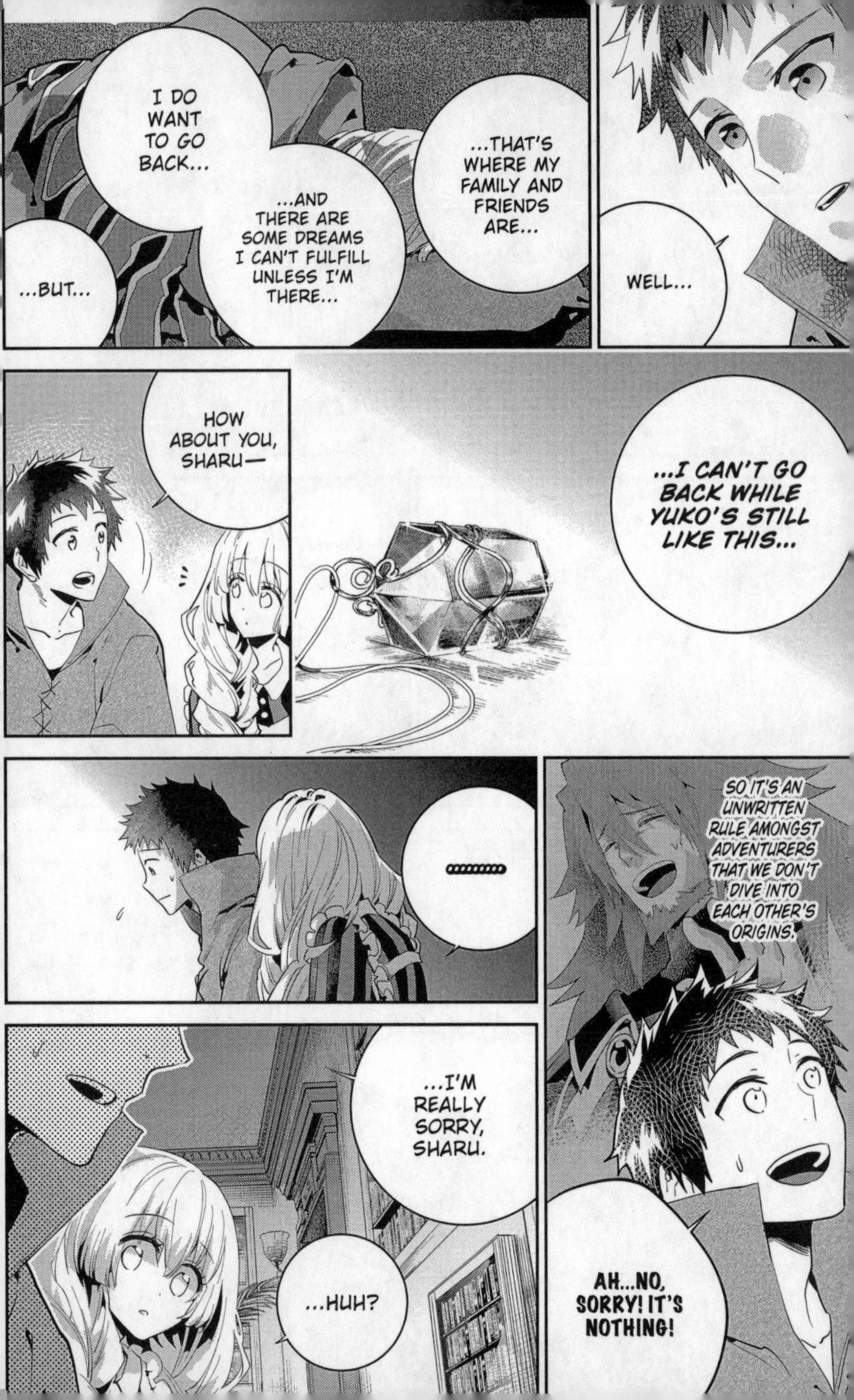
WELL...
...THAT'S WHERE MY FAMILY AND FRIENDS ARE...
...AND THERE ARE SOME DREAMS I CAN'T FULFILL UNLESS I'M THERE...
I DO WANT TO GO BACK...
...BUT...
...I CAN'T GO BACK WHILE YUKO'S STILL LIKE THIS...
HOW ABOUT YOU, SHARU—
SO IT'S AN UNWRITTEN RULE AMONGST ADVENTURERS THAT WE DON'T DIVE INTO EACH OTHER'S ORIGINS.
AH...NO, SORRY! IT'S NOTHING!
.........
...I'M REALLY SORRY, SHARU.
...HUH?

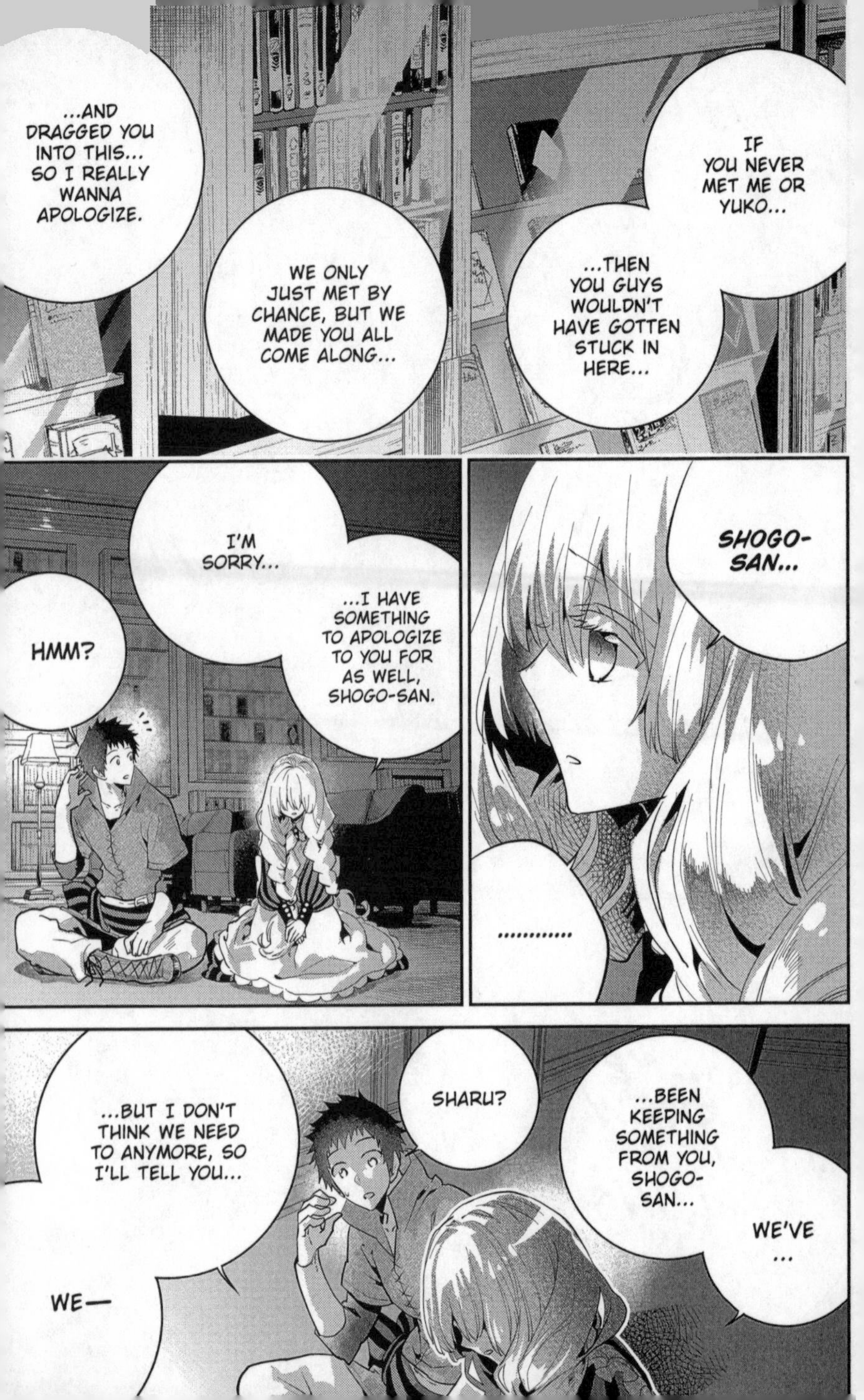
IF YOU NEVER MET ME OR YUKO...
...THEN YOU GUYS WOULDN'T HAVE GOTTEN STUCK IN HERE...
WE ONLY JUST MET BY CHANCE, BUT WE MADE YOU ALL COME ALONG...
...AND DRAGGED YOU INTO THIS... SO I REALLY WANNA APOLOGIZE.
SHOGO-SAN...
............
I'M SORRY...
...I HAVE SOMETHING TO APOLOGIZE TO YOU FOR AS WELL, SHOGO-SAN.
HMM?
WE'VE ...
...BEEN KEEPING SOMETHING FROM YOU, SHOGO-SAN...
SHARU?
...BUT I DON'T THINK WE NEED TO ANYMORE, SO I'LL TELL YOU...
WE—

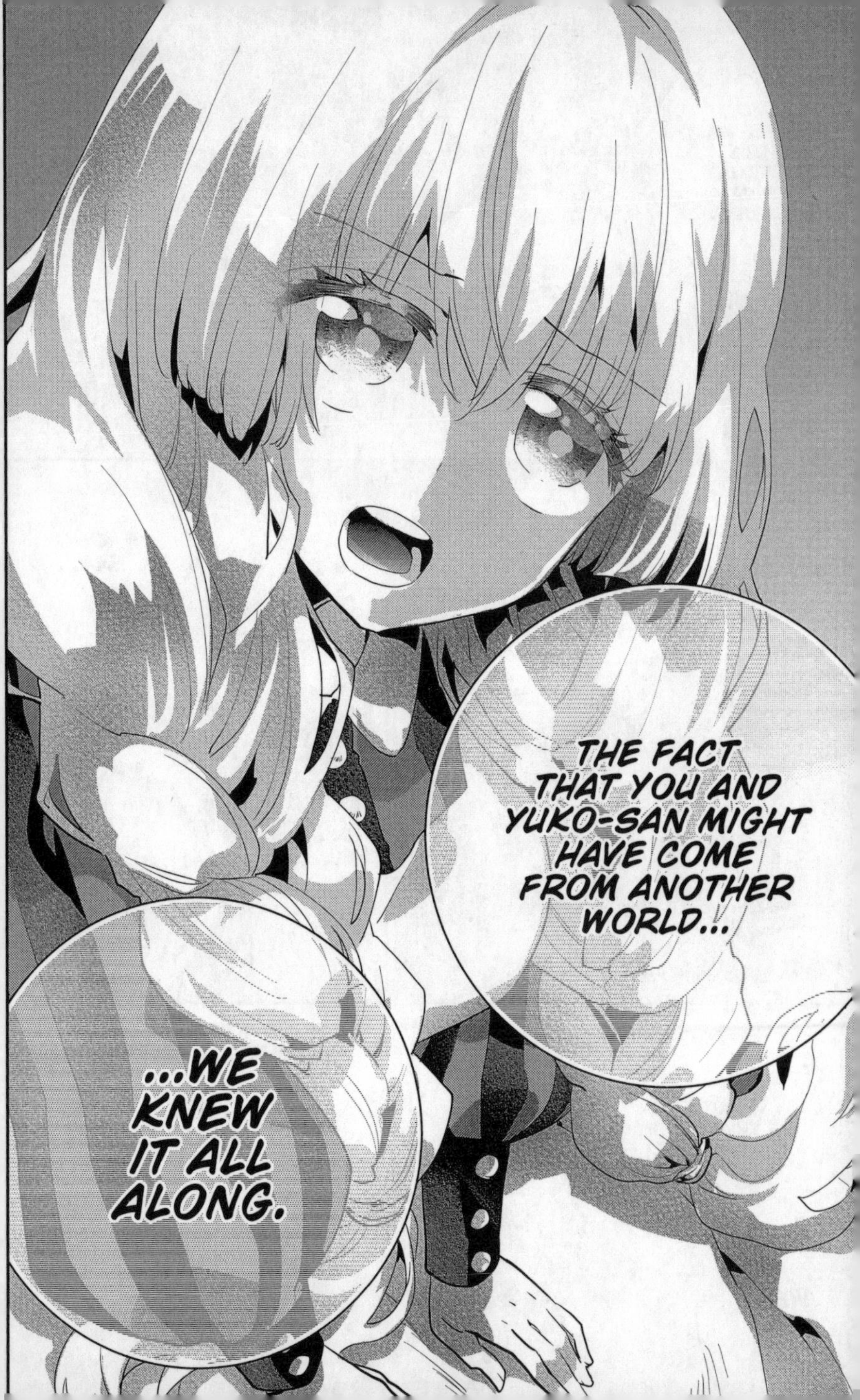
THE FACT THAT YOU AND YUKO-SAN MIGHT HAVE COME FROM ANOTHER WORLD...
...WE KNEW IT ALL ALONG.

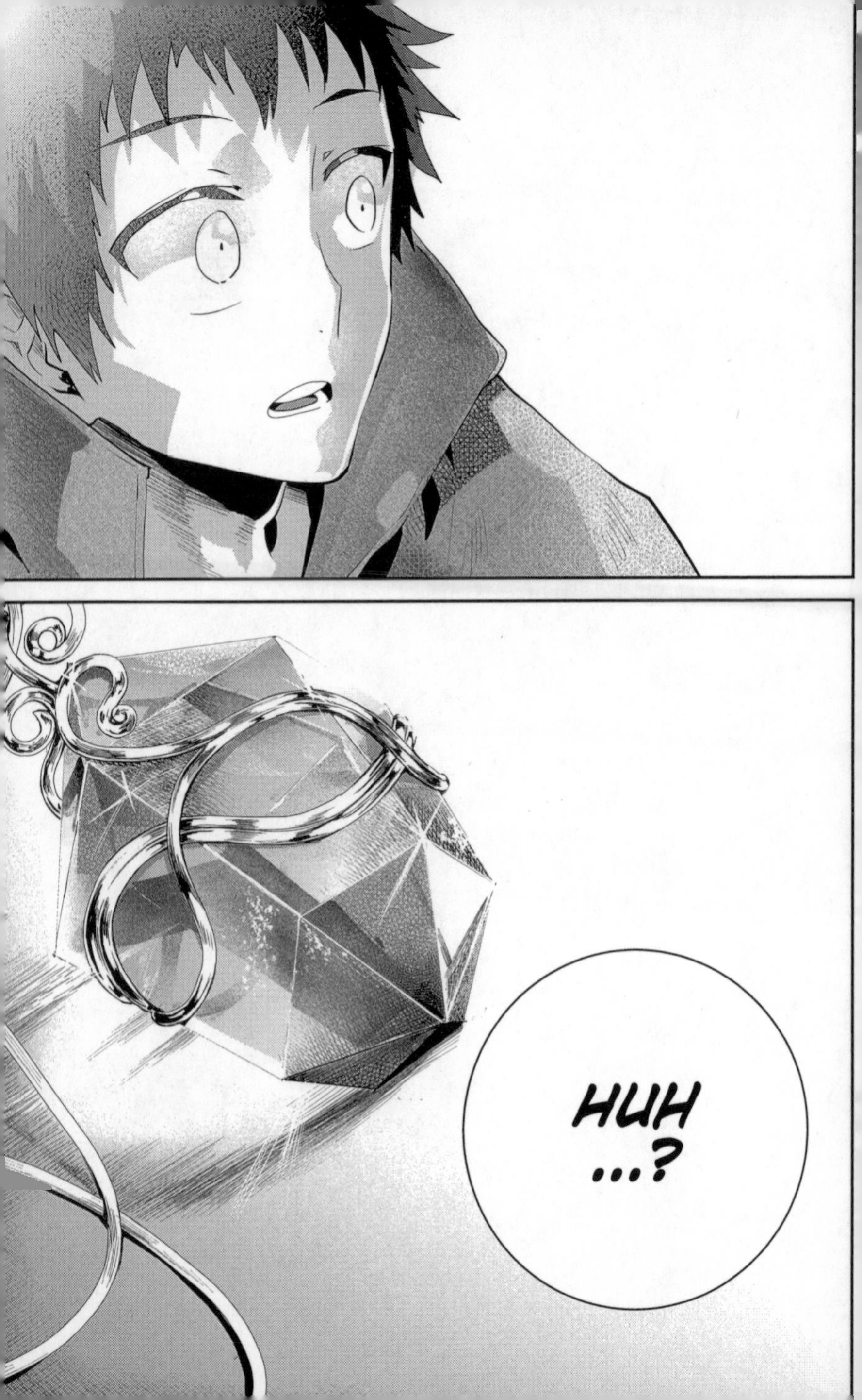
HUH ...?

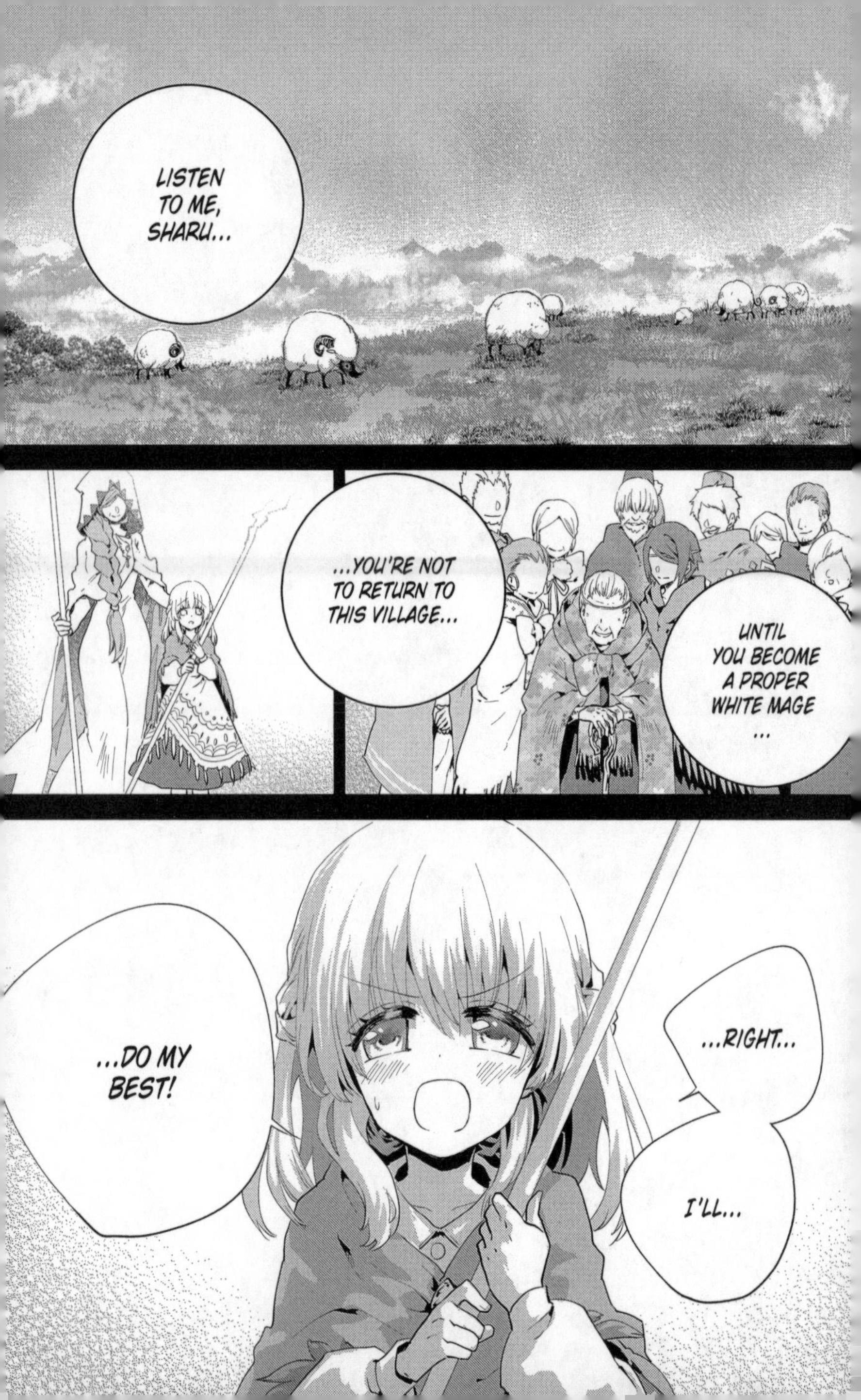
LISTEN TO ME, SHARU...
...YOU'RE NOT TO RETURN TO THIS VILLAGE...
UNTIL YOU BECOME A PROPER WHITE MAGE ...
...RIGHT...
I'LL...
...DO MY BEST!

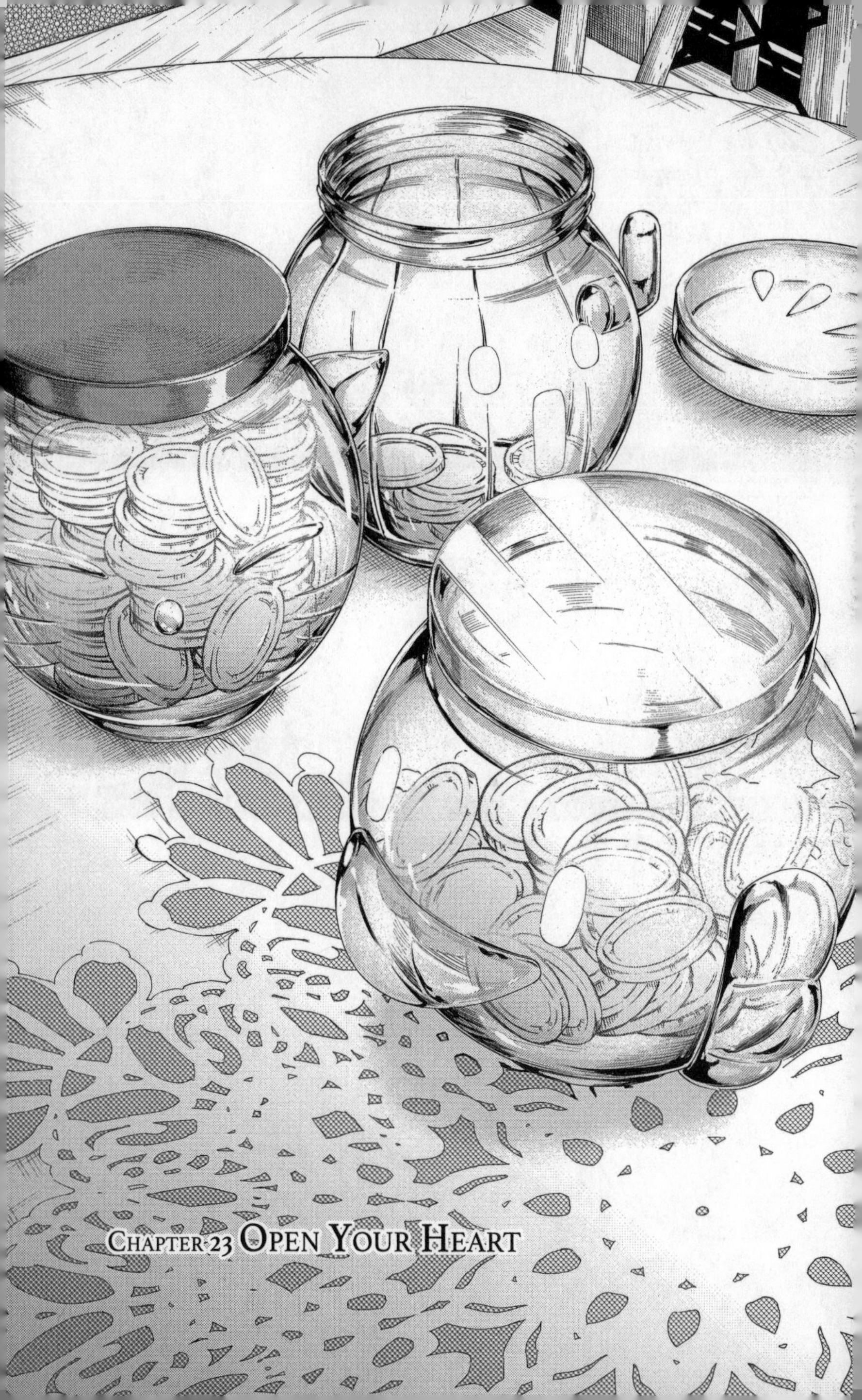

# Chapter 23 Open Your Heart

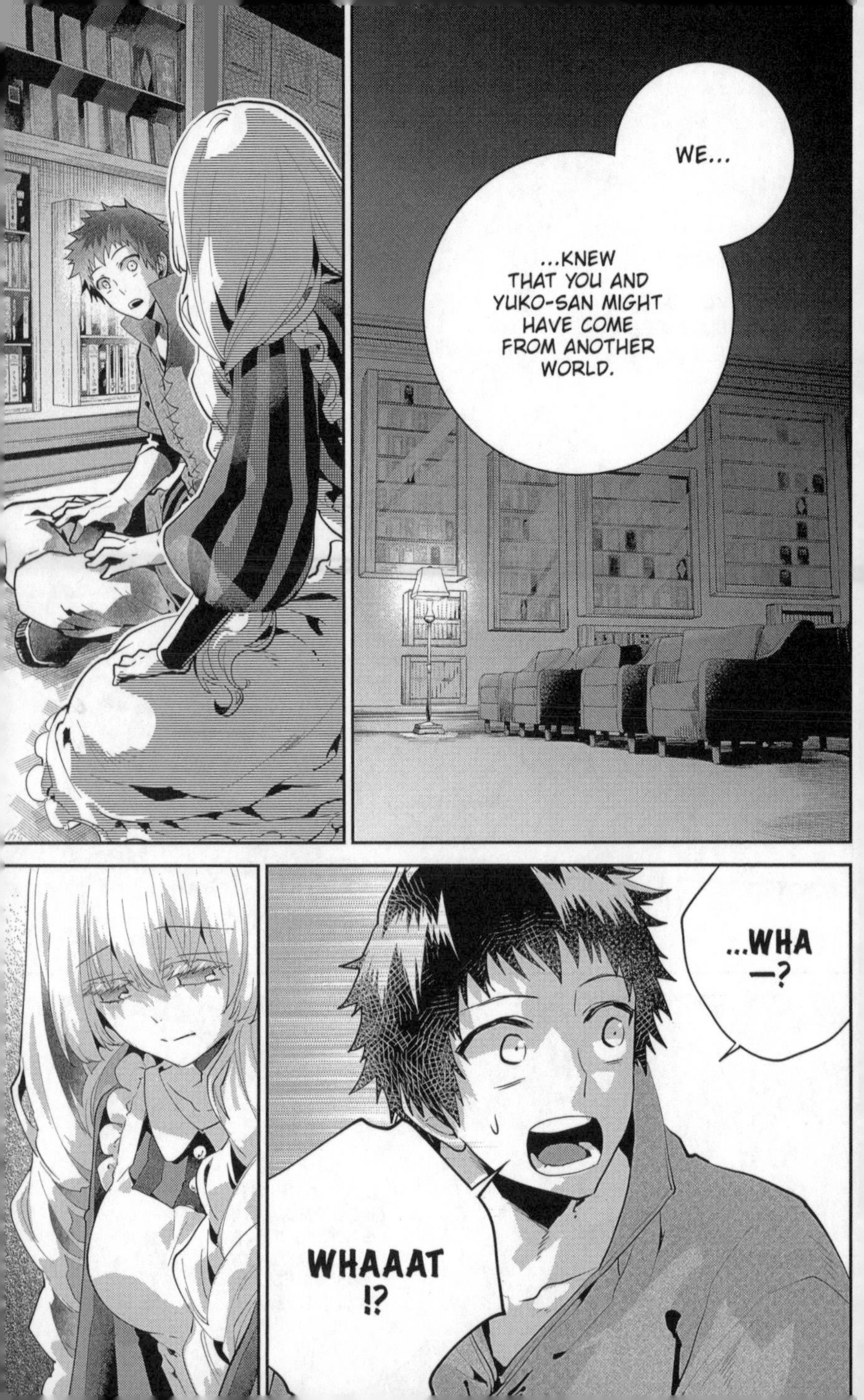
WE...
...KNEW THAT YOU AND YUKO-SAN MIGHT HAVE COME FROM ANOTHER WORLD.
...WHA—?
WHAAAT!?

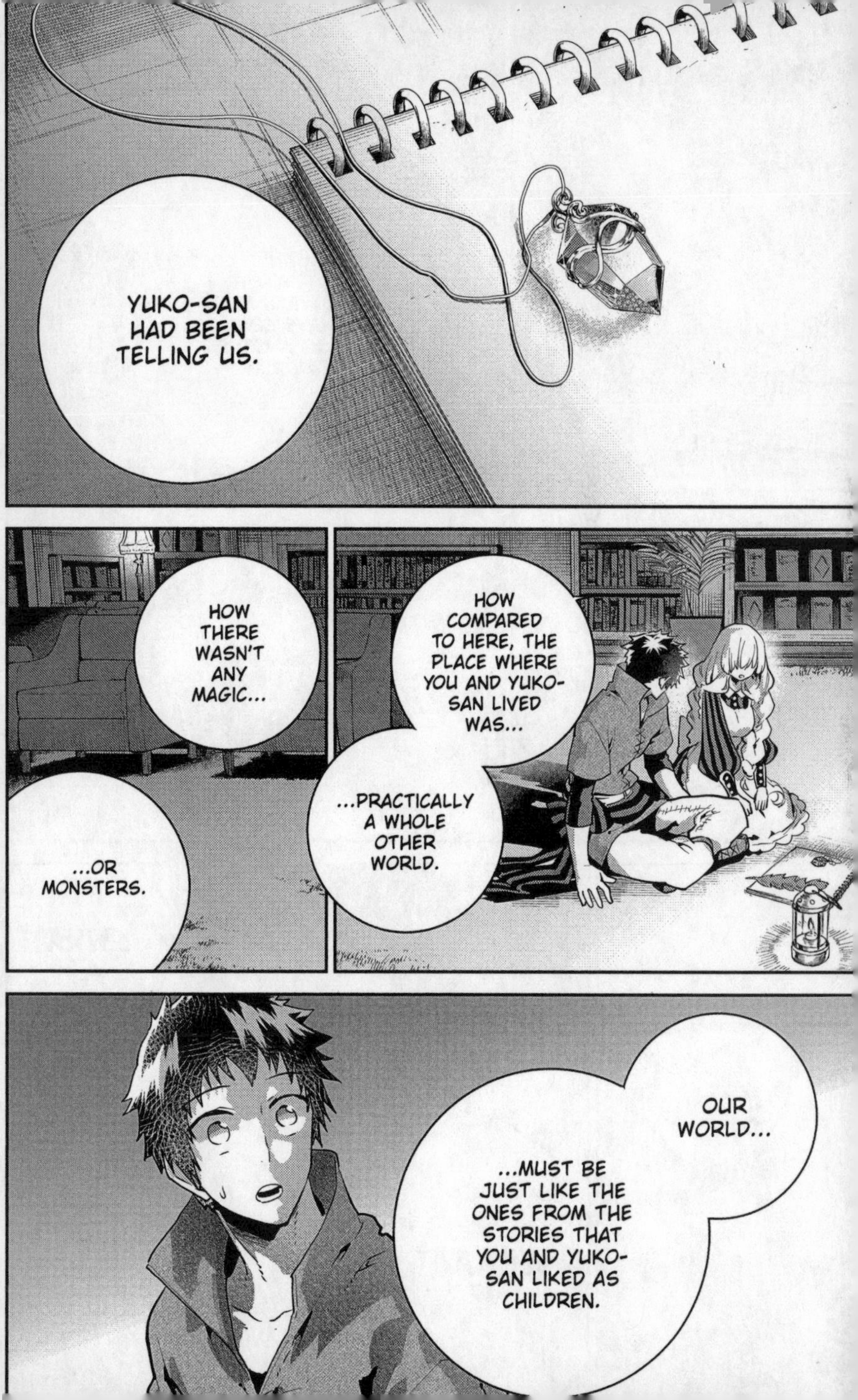
YUKO-SAN HAD BEEN TELLING US.
HOW COMPARED TO HERE, THE PLACE WHERE YOU AND YUKO-SAN LIVED WAS...
...PRACTICALLY A WHOLE OTHER WORLD.
HOW THERE WASN'T ANY MAGIC...
...OR MONSTERS.
OUR WORLD...
...MUST BE JUST LIKE THE ONES FROM THE STORIES THAT YOU AND YUKO-SAN LIKED AS CHILDREN.

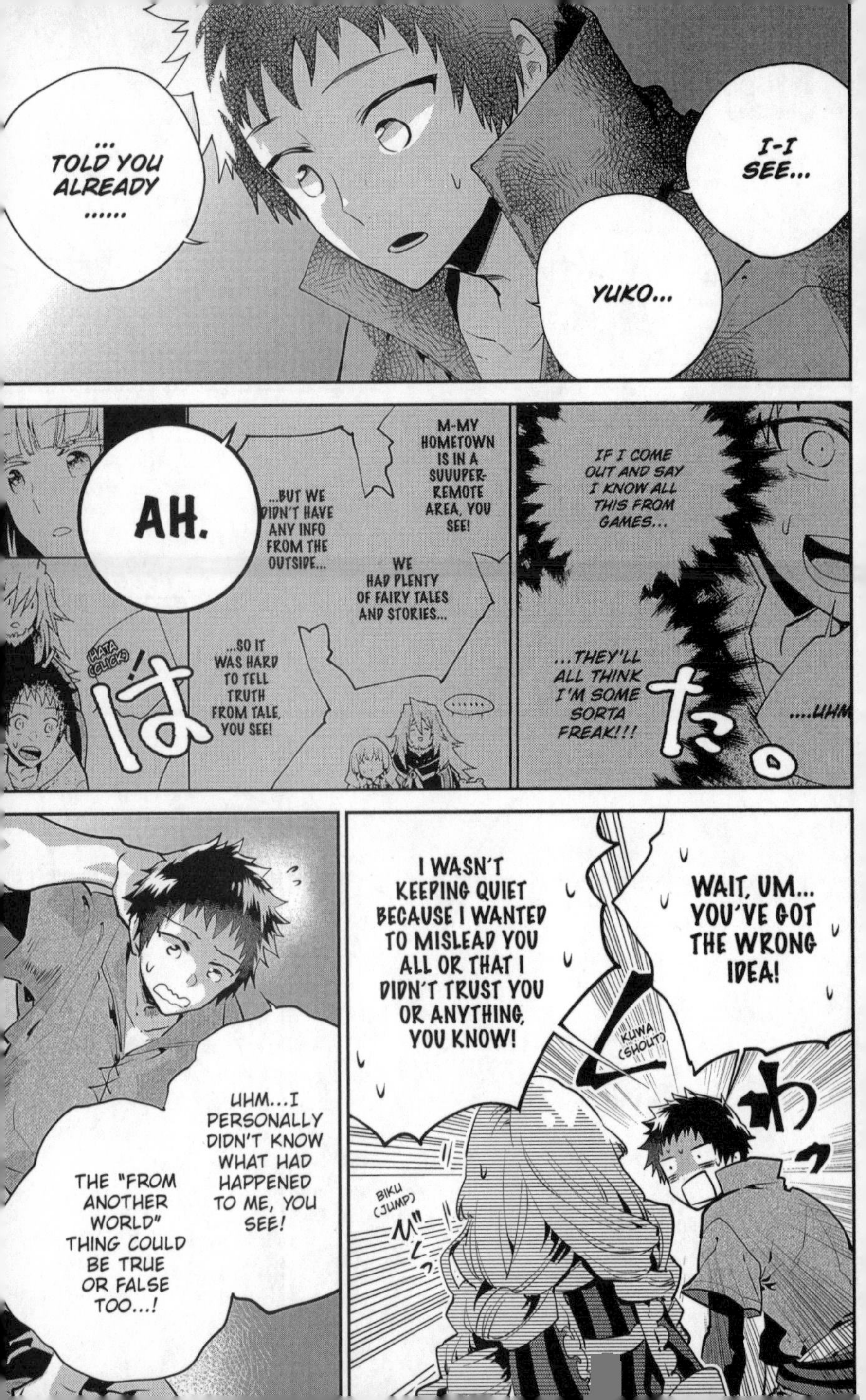
I-I SEE...
YUKO...
... TOLD YOU ALREADY ......
....UHM
IF I COME OUT AND SAY I KNOW ALL THIS FROM GAMES...
...THEY'LL ALL THINK I'M SOME SORTA FREAK!!!
た。
M-MY HOMETOWN IS IN A SUUUPER-REMOTE AREA, YOU SEE!
...BUT WE DIDN'T HAVE ANY INFO FROM THE OUTSIDE...
WE HAD PLENTY OF FAIRY TALES AND STORIES...
...SO IT WAS HARD TO TELL TRUTH FROM TALE, YOU SEE!
......
AH.
HATA (CLICK)
は!
WAIT, UM... YOU'VE GOT THE WRONG IDEA!
I WASN'T KEEPING QUIET BECAUSE I WANTED TO MISLEAD YOU ALL OR THAT I DIDN'T TRUST YOU OR ANYTHING, YOU KNOW!
KUWA (SHOUT)
わっ
BIKU (JUMP)
びくっ
UHM...I PERSONALLY DIDN'T KNOW WHAT HAD HAPPENED TO ME, YOU SEE!
THE "FROM ANOTHER WORLD" THING COULD BE TRUE OR FALSE TOO...!

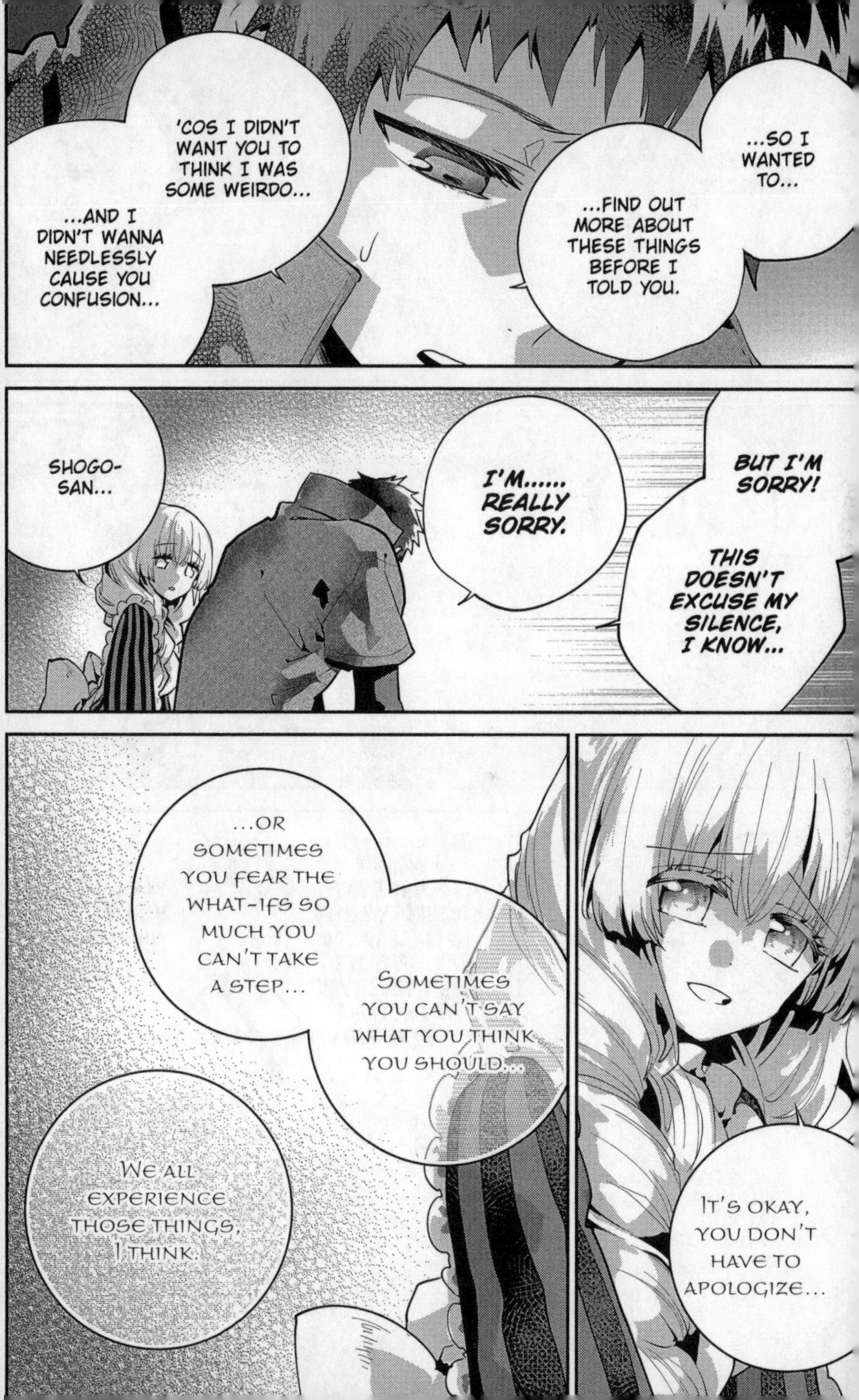
...SO I WANTED TO...
...FIND OUT MORE ABOUT THESE THINGS BEFORE I TOLD YOU.
'COS I DIDN'T WANT YOU TO THINK I WAS SOME WEIRDO...
...AND I DIDN'T WANNA NEEDLESSLY CAUSE YOU CONFUSION...
BUT I'M SORRY!
THIS DOESN'T EXCUSE MY SILENCE, I KNOW...
I'M...... REALLY SORRY.
SHOGO-SAN...
IT'S OKAY, YOU DON'T HAVE TO APOLOGIZE...
SOMETIMES YOU CAN'T SAY WHAT YOU THINK YOU SHOULD...
...OR SOMETIMES YOU FEAR THE WHAT-IFS SO MUCH YOU CAN'T TAKE A STEP...
WE ALL EXPERIENCE THOSE THINGS, I THINK.

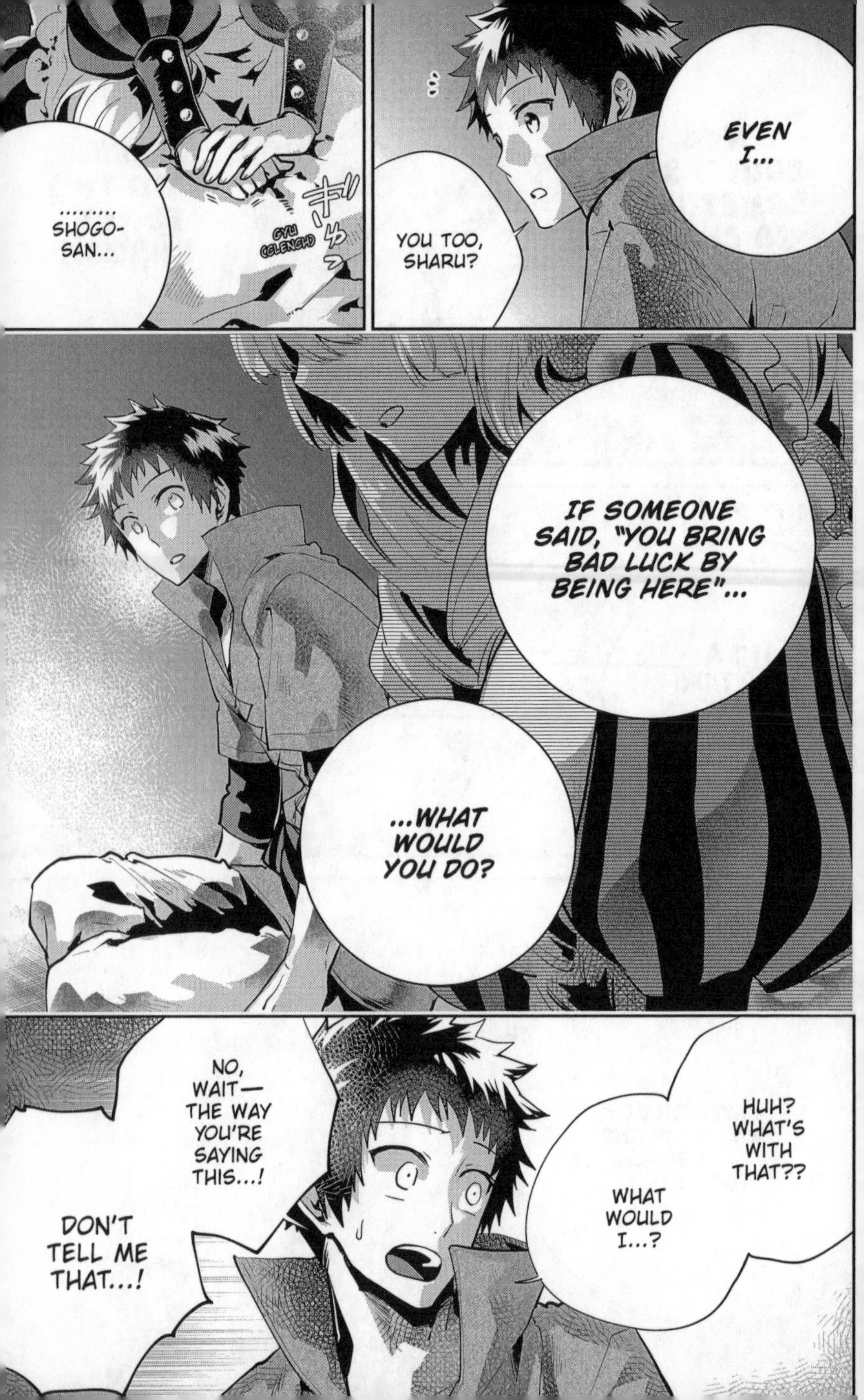
EVEN I...
YOU TOO, SHARU?
........ SHOGO-SAN...
GYU (CLENCH)
IF SOMEONE SAID, "YOU BRING BAD LUCK BY BEING HERE"...
...WHAT WOULD YOU DO?
HUH? WHAT'S WITH THAT??
WHAT WOULD I...?
NO, WAIT— THE WAY YOU'RE SAYING THIS...!
DON'T TELL ME THAT...!

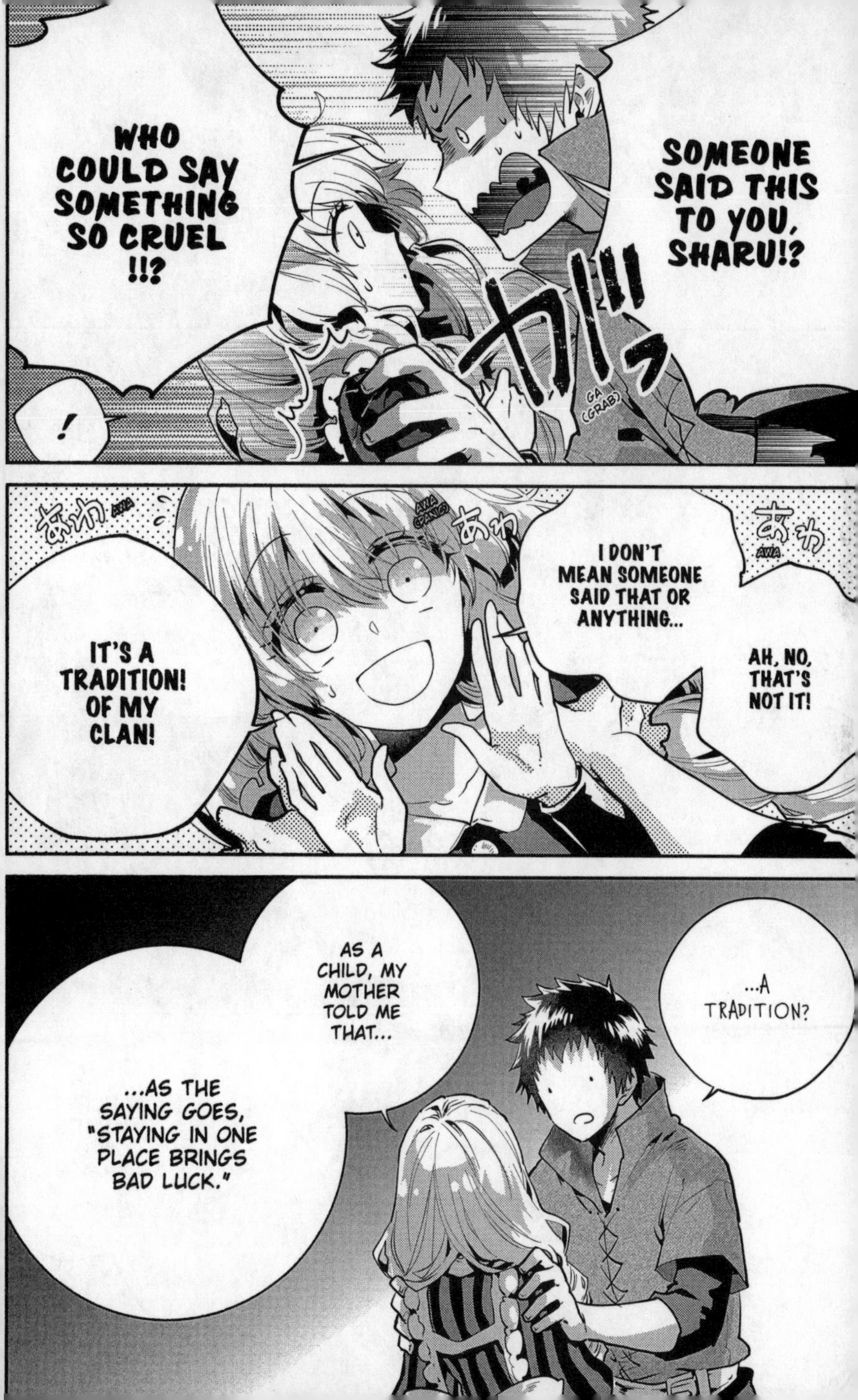
SOMEONE SAID THIS TO YOU, SHARU!?
WHO COULD SAY SOMETHING SO CRUEL !!?
GA (GRAB)
!
AWA
AH, NO, THAT'S NOT IT!
I DON'T MEAN SOMEONE SAID THAT OR ANYTHING...
AWA (PANIC)
IT'S A TRADITION! OF MY CLAN!
AWA
...A TRADITION?
AS A CHILD, MY MOTHER TOLD ME THAT...
...AS THE SAYING GOES, "STAYING IN ONE PLACE BRINGS BAD LUCK."

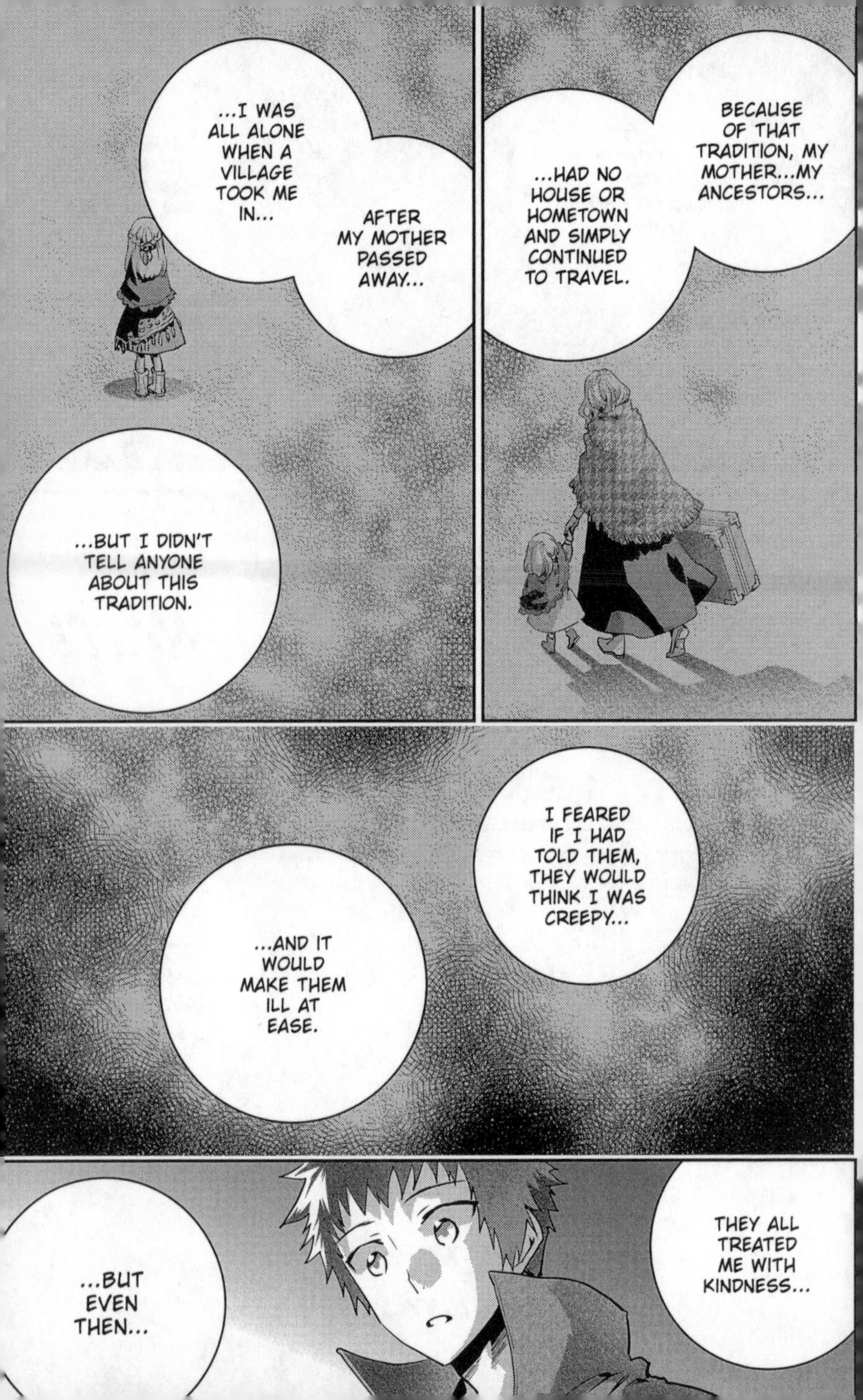
BECAUSE OF THAT TRADITION, MY MOTHER...MY ANCESTORS...
...HAD NO HOUSE OR HOMETOWN AND SIMPLY CONTINUED TO TRAVEL.
AFTER MY MOTHER PASSED AWAY...
...I WAS ALL ALONE WHEN A VILLAGE TOOK ME IN...
...BUT I DIDN'T TELL ANYONE ABOUT THIS TRADITION.
I FEARED IF I HAD TOLD THEM, THEY WOULD THINK I WAS CREEPY...
...AND IT WOULD MAKE THEM ILL AT EASE.
THEY ALL TREATED ME WITH KINDNESS...
...BUT EVEN THEN...

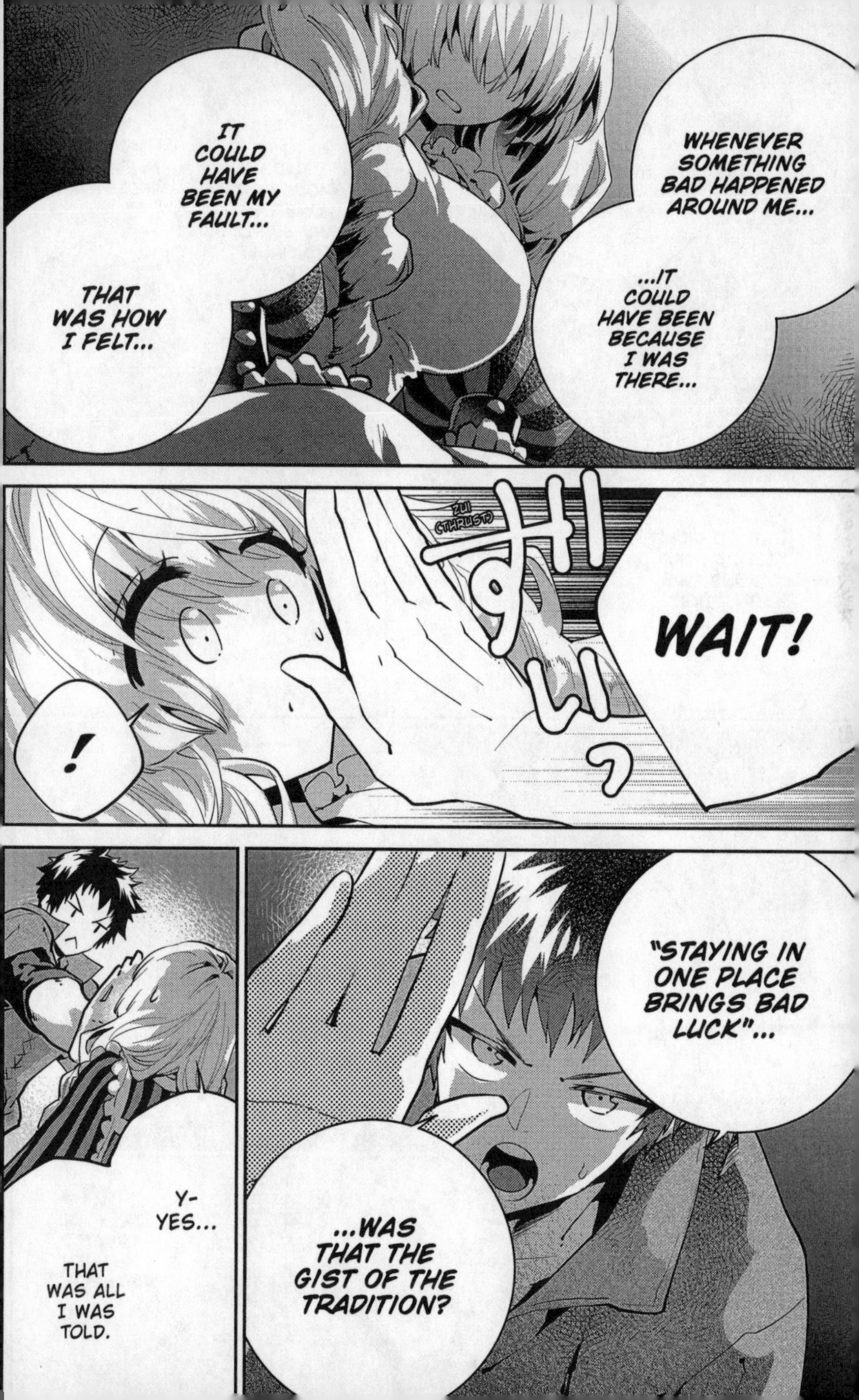
WHENEVER SOMETHING BAD HAPPENED AROUND ME...
...IT COULD HAVE BEEN BECAUSE I WAS THERE...
IT COULD HAVE BEEN MY FAULT...
THAT WAS HOW I FELT...
WAIT!
ずいっ
ZUI (THRUST)
!
"STAYING IN ONE PLACE BRINGS BAD LUCK"...
...WAS THAT THE GIST OF THE TRADITION?
Y- YES...
THAT WAS ALL I WAS TOLD.

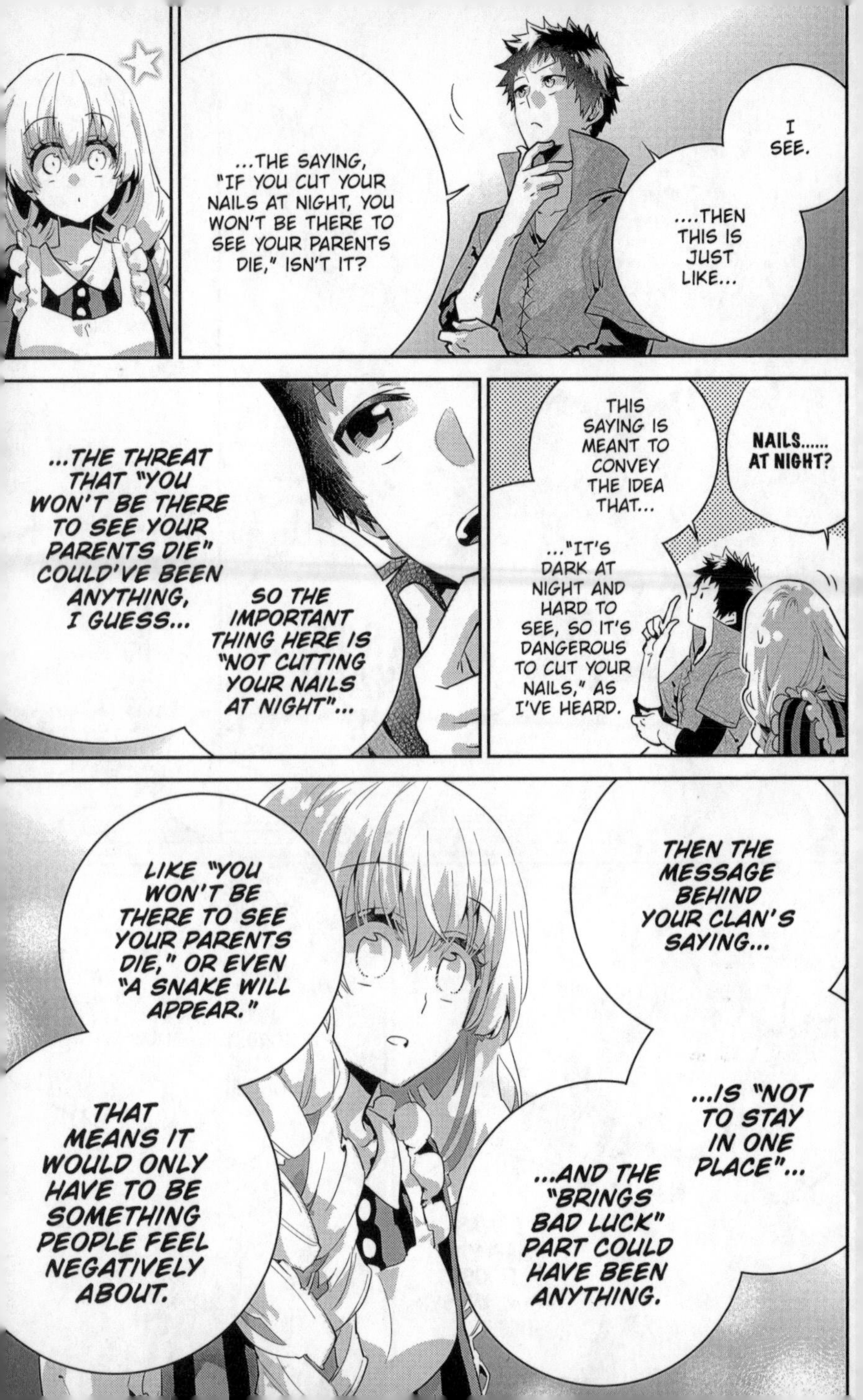
I SEE.
....THEN THIS IS JUST LIKE...
...THE SAYING, "IF YOU CUT YOUR NAILS AT NIGHT, YOU WON'T BE THERE TO SEE YOUR PARENTS DIE," ISN'T IT?
NAILS...... AT NIGHT?
THIS SAYING IS MEANT TO CONVEY THE IDEA THAT...
..."IT'S DARK AT NIGHT AND HARD TO SEE, SO IT'S DANGEROUS TO CUT YOUR NAILS," AS I'VE HEARD.
SO THE IMPORTANT THING HERE IS "NOT CUTTING YOUR NAILS AT NIGHT"...
...THE THREAT THAT "YOU WON'T BE THERE TO SEE YOUR PARENTS DIE" COULD'VE BEEN ANYTHING, I GUESS...
THEN THE MESSAGE BEHIND YOUR CLAN'S SAYING...
...IS "NOT TO STAY IN ONE PLACE"...
...AND THE "BRINGS BAD LUCK" PART COULD HAVE BEEN ANYTHING.
LIKE "YOU WON'T BE THERE TO SEE YOUR PARENTS DIE," OR EVEN "A SNAKE WILL APPEAR."
THAT MEANS IT WOULD ONLY HAVE TO BE SOMETHING PEOPLE FEEL NEGATIVELY ABOUT.

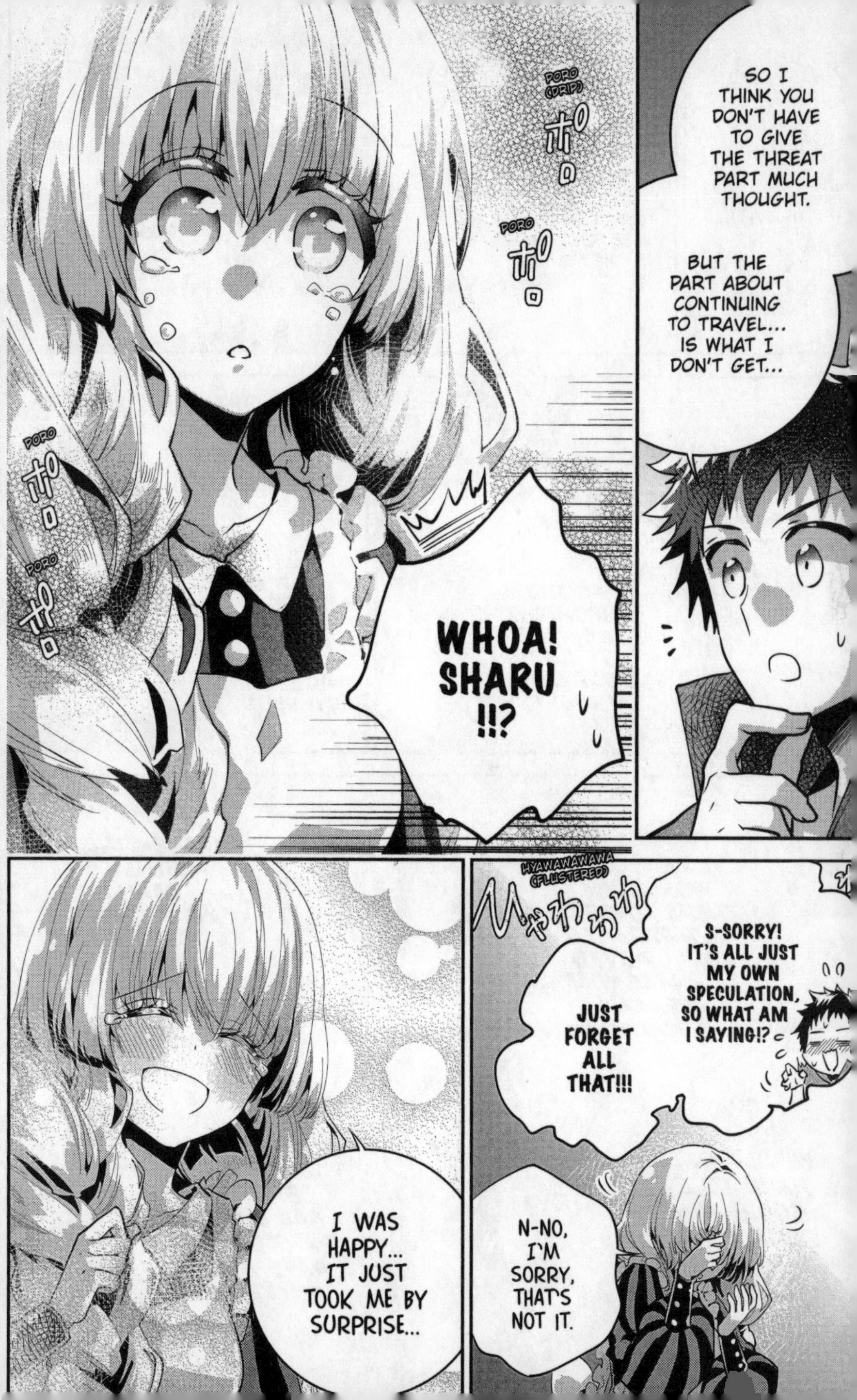
SO I THINK YOU DON'T HAVE TO GIVE THE THREAT PART MUCH THOUGHT.
BUT THE PART ABOUT CONTINUING TO TRAVEL... IS WHAT I DON'T GET...
PORO (DRIP)
PORO
WHOA! SHARU!!?
PORO
PORO
HYAWAWAWAWA (FLUSTERED)
S-SORRY! IT'S ALL JUST MY OWN SPECULATION, SO WHAT AM I SAYING!?
JUST FORGET ALL THAT!!!
N-NO, I'M SORRY, THAT'S NOT IT.
I WAS HAPPY... IT JUST TOOK ME BY SURPRISE...

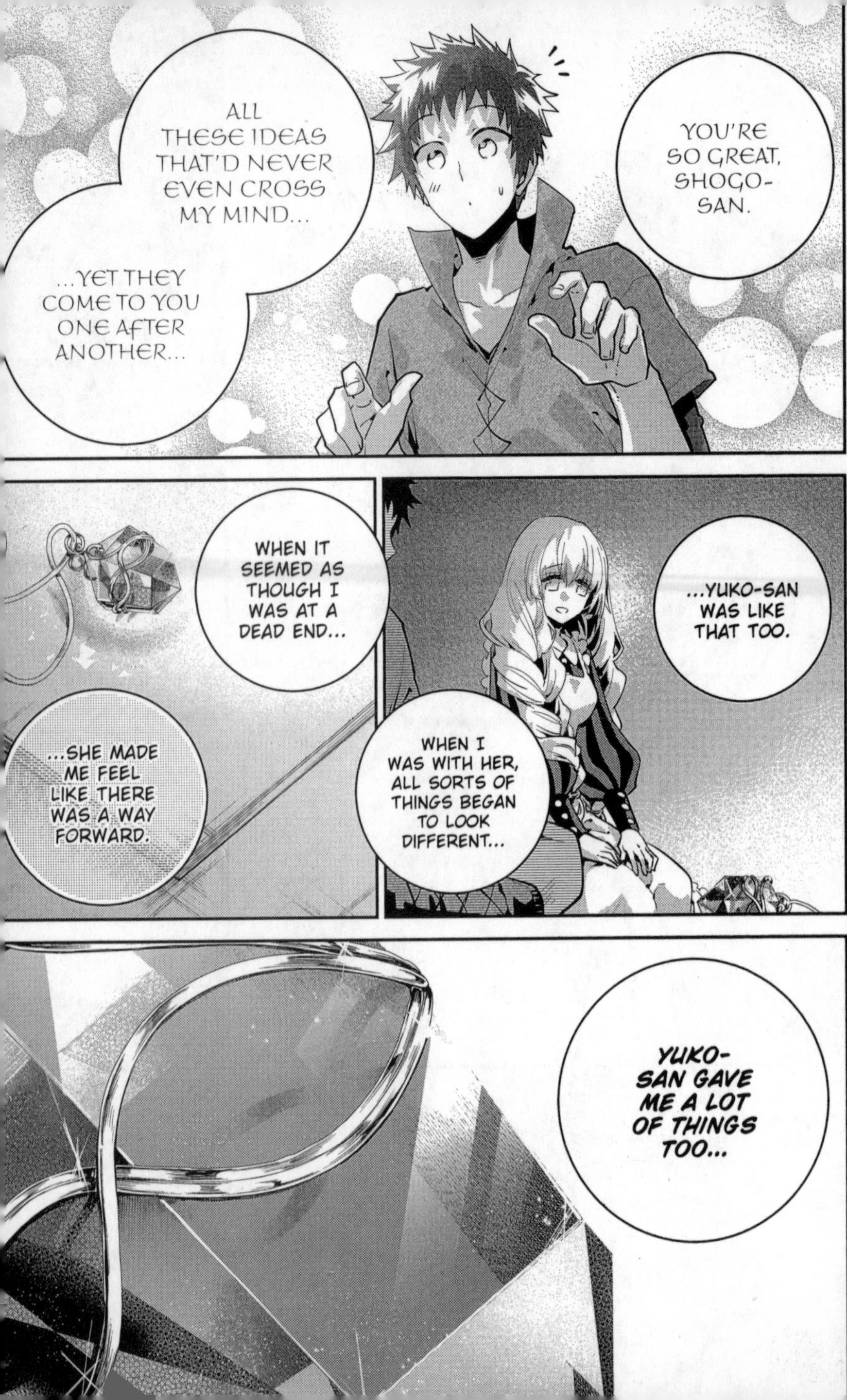
YOU'RE SO GREAT, SHOGO-SAN.
ALL THESE IDEAS THAT'D NEVER EVEN CROSS MY MIND...
...YET THEY COME TO YOU ONE AFTER ANOTHER...
...YUKO-SAN WAS LIKE THAT TOO.
WHEN I WAS WITH HER, ALL SORTS OF THINGS BEGAN TO LOOK DIFFERENT...
WHEN IT SEEMED AS THOUGH I WAS AT A DEAD END...
...SHE MADE ME FEEL LIKE THERE WAS A WAY FORWARD.
YUKO-SAN GAVE ME A LOT OF THINGS TOO...

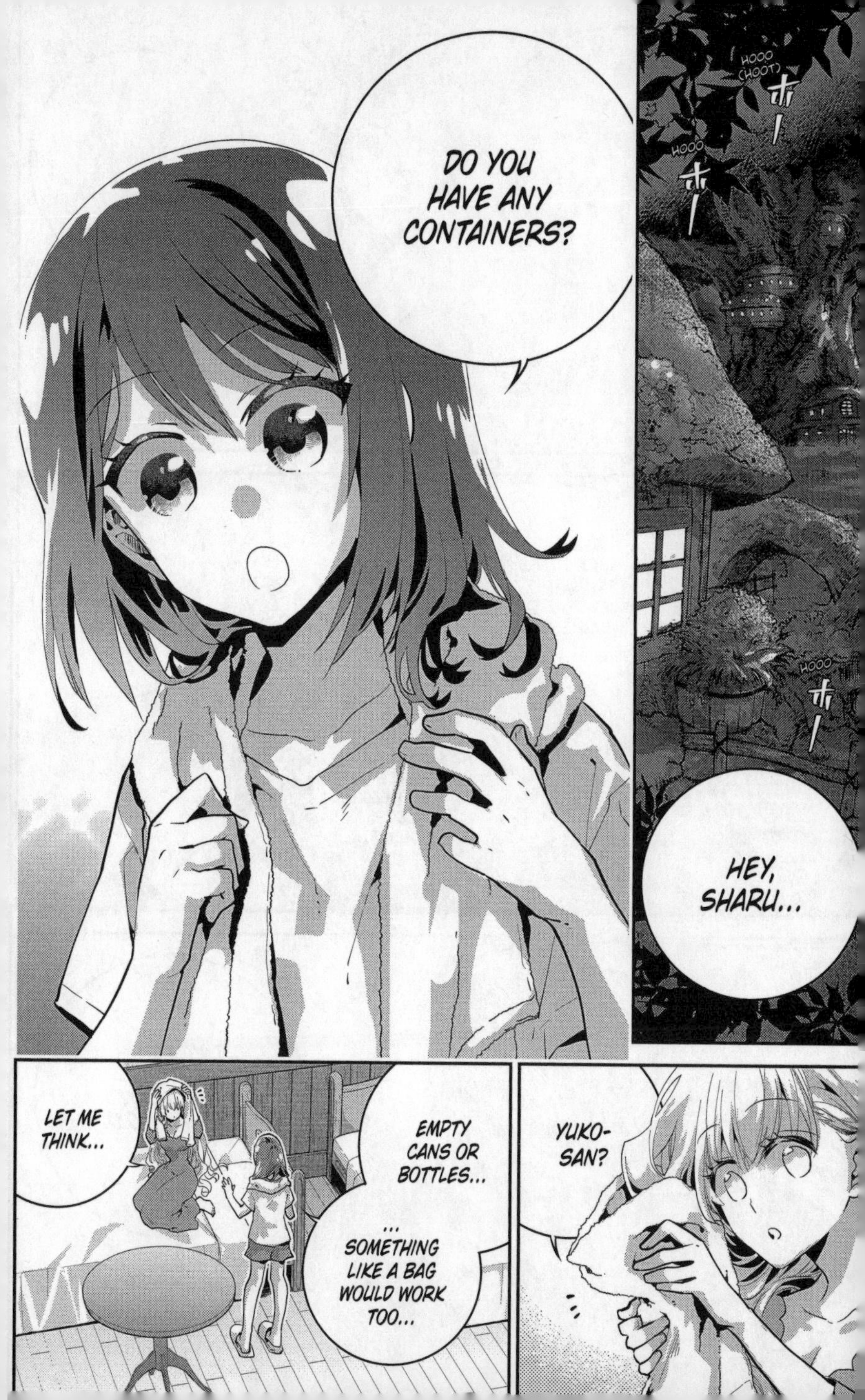
HOOO (HOOT)
HOOO
HOOO
HEY, SHARU...
DO YOU HAVE ANY CONTAINERS?
YUKO-SAN?
EMPTY CANS OR BOTTLES...
... SOMETHING LIKE A BAG WOULD WORK TOO...
LET ME THINK...

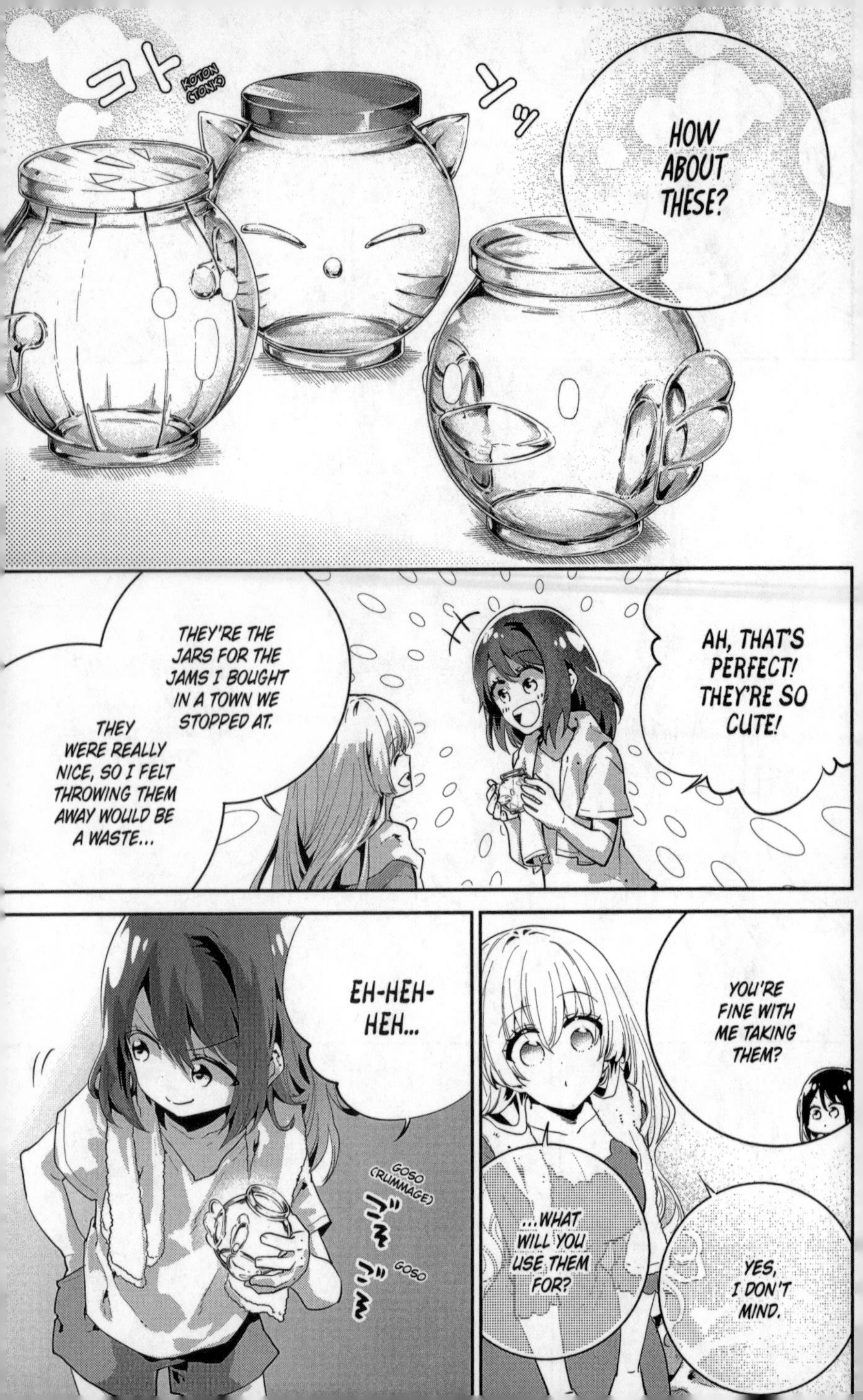
HOW ABOUT THESE?
ソッ
コト
KOTON (TONK)
AH, THAT'S PERFECT! THEY'RE SO CUTE!
THEY'RE THE JARS FOR THE JAMS I BOUGHT IN A TOWN WE STOPPED AT.
THEY WERE REALLY NICE, SO I FELT THROWING THEM AWAY WOULD BE A WASTE...
YOU'RE FINE WITH ME TAKING THEM?
YES, I DON'T MIND.
...WHAT WILL YOU USE THEM FOR?
EH-HEH-HEH...
GOSO (RUMMAGE)
ゴソ
GOSO
ゴソ

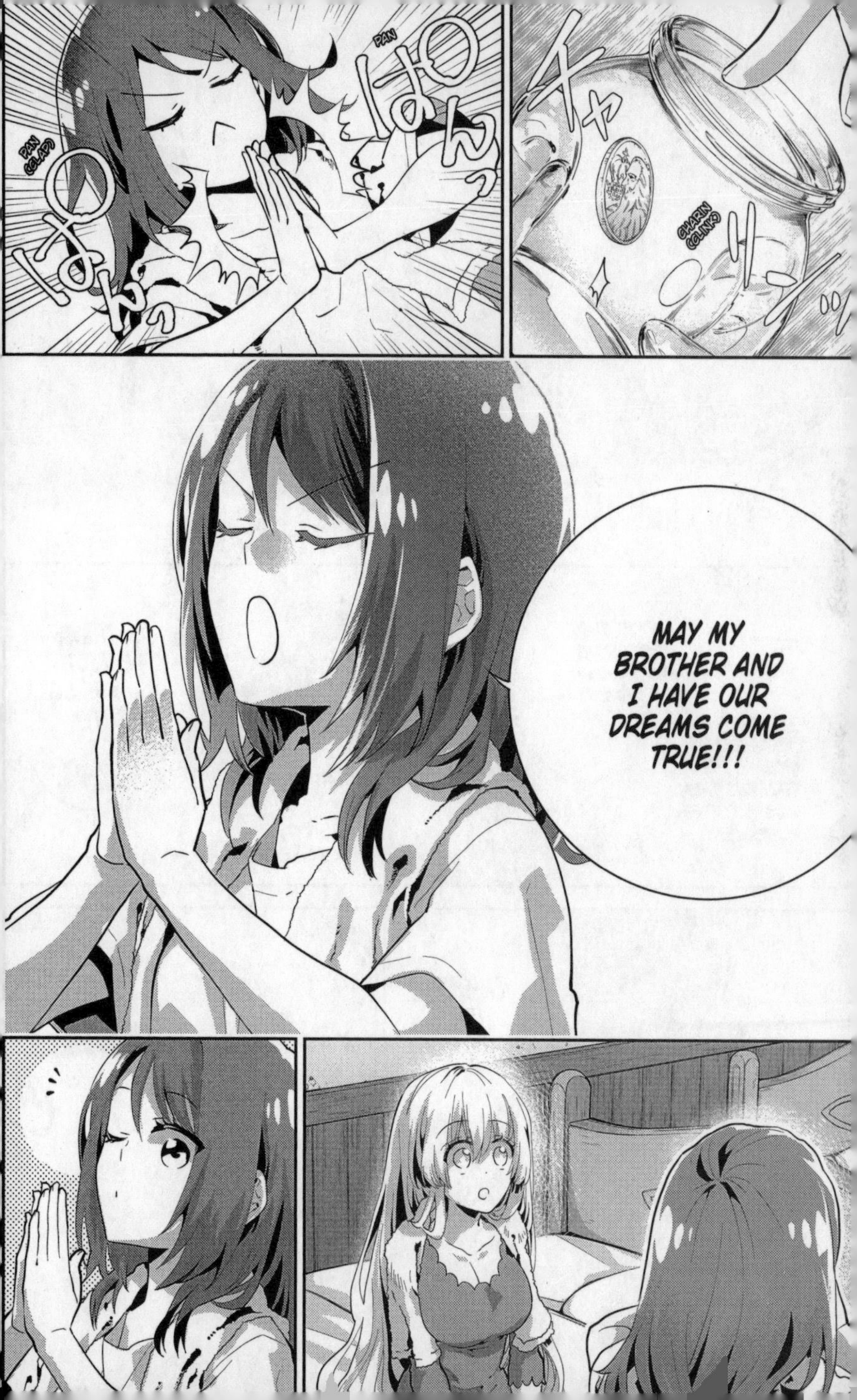
CHARIN (CLINK)
PAN
PAN (CLAP)
MAY MY BROTHER AND I HAVE OUR DREAMS COME TRUE!!!

IT'S A PIGGY BANK FOR WISHES!

YOU START BY DECIDING ON ONE WISH YOU WANT FULFILLED THE MOST...

...AND THEN PUT IN A COIN AT THE END OF EACH DAY.

WHEN THE CONTAINER BECOMES FULL, YOU PREPARE ANOTHER...

DO THIS ONE DAY AFTER ANOTHER, UNTIL YOUR WISH IS FULFILLED....

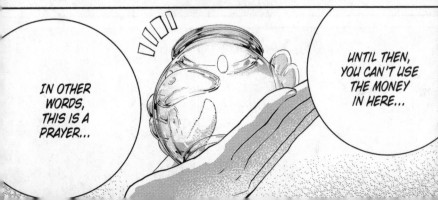

UNTIL THEN, YOU CAN'T USE THE MONEY IN HERE...

IN OTHER WORDS, THIS IS A PRAYER...

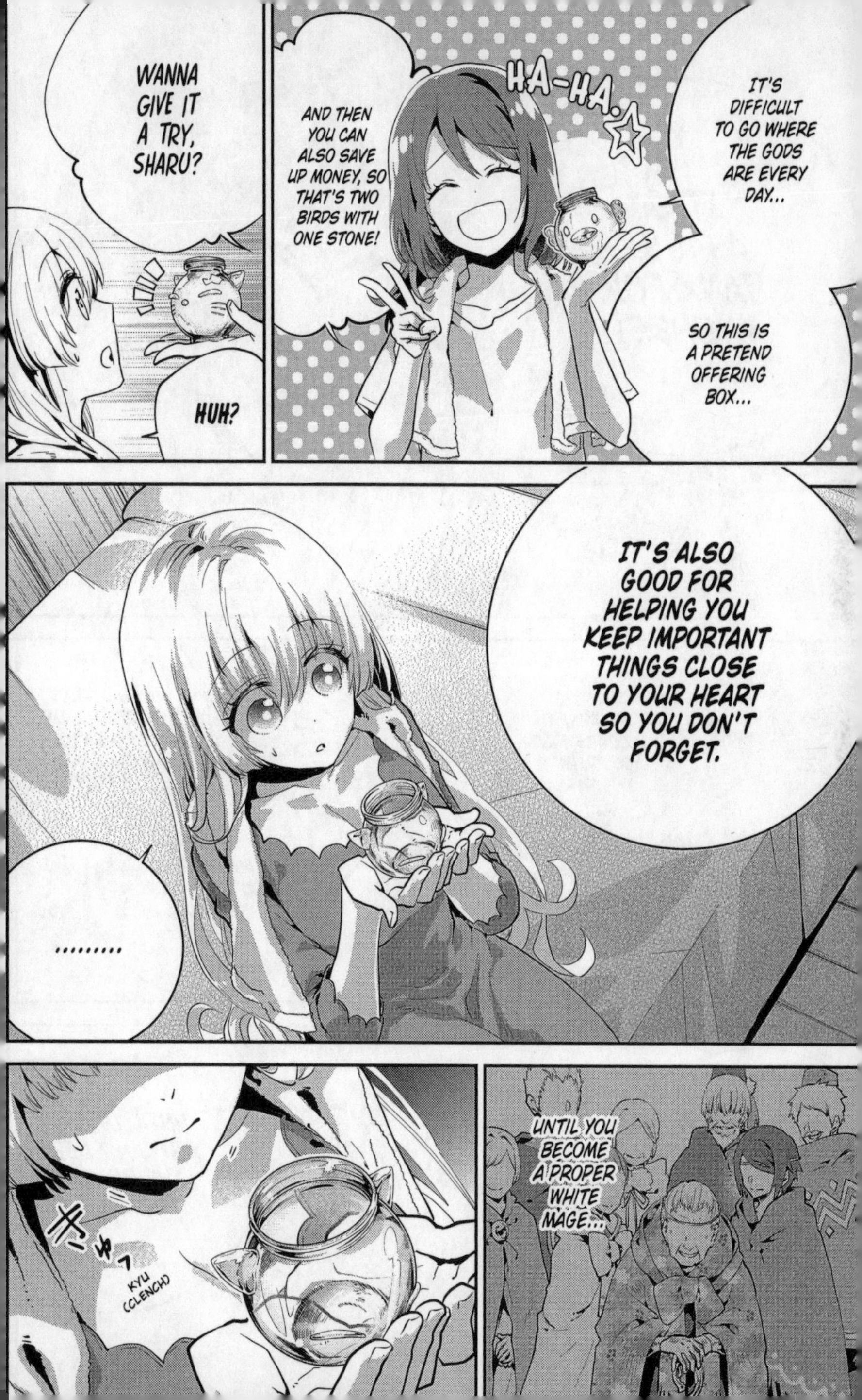
IT'S DIFFICULT TO GO WHERE THE GODS ARE EVERY DAY...
SO THIS IS A PRETEND OFFERING BOX...
HA-HA.☆
AND THEN YOU CAN ALSO SAVE UP MONEY, SO THAT'S TWO BIRDS WITH ONE STONE!
WANNA GIVE IT A TRY, SHARU?
HUH?
IT'S ALSO GOOD FOR HELPING YOU KEEP IMPORTANT THINGS CLOSE TO YOUR HEART SO YOU DON'T FORGET.
..........
UNTIL YOU BECOME A PROPER WHITE MAGE...
KYU (CLENCH)

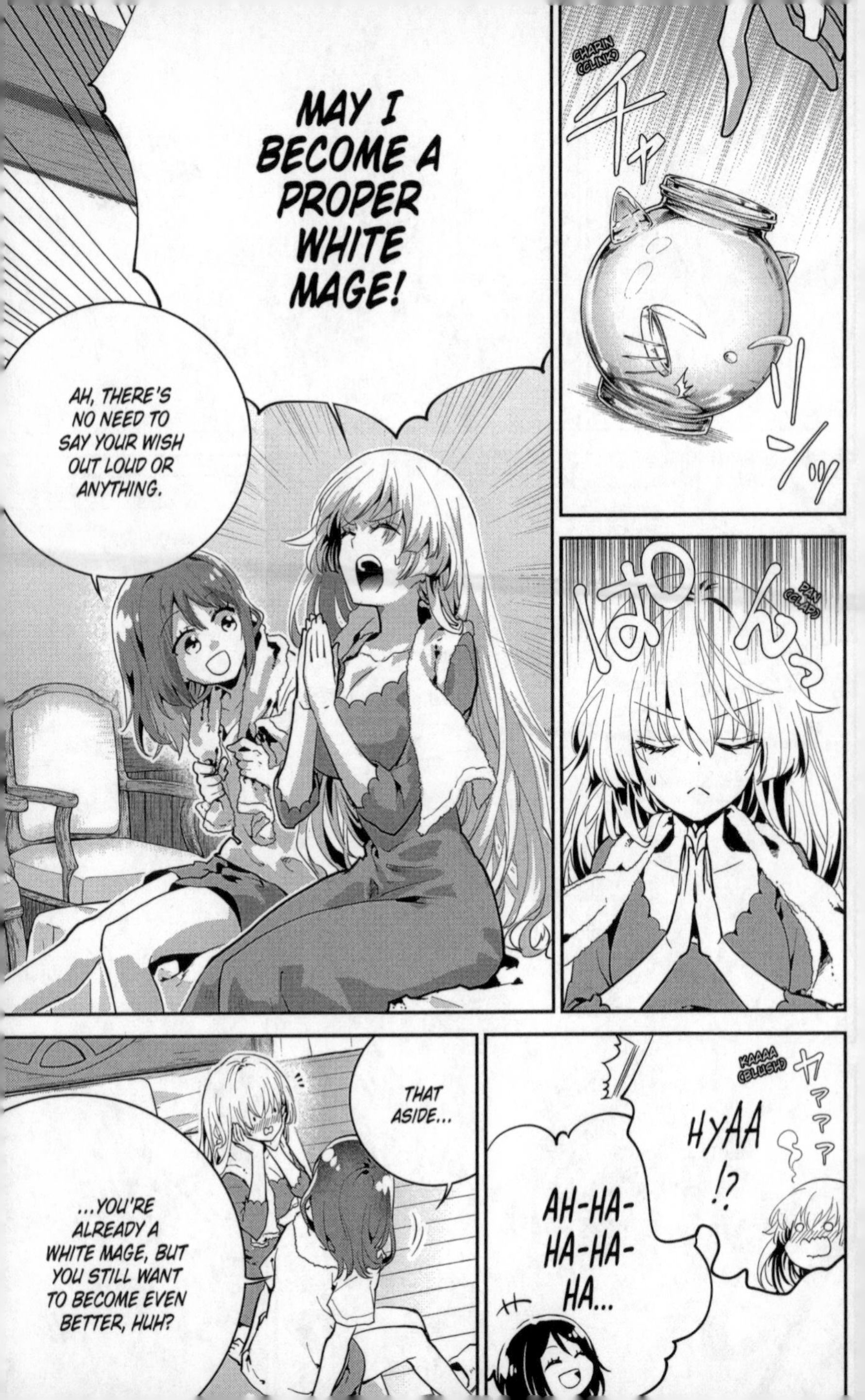
CHARIN (CLINK)
PAN (CLAP)
MAY I BECOME A PROPER WHITE MAGE!
AH, THERE'S NO NEED TO SAY YOUR WISH OUT LOUD OR ANYTHING.
KAAAA (BLUSH)
HYAA !?
AH-HA-HA-HA-HA...
THAT ASIDE...
...YOU'RE ALREADY A WHITE MAGE, BUT YOU STILL WANT TO BECOME EVEN BETTER, HUH?

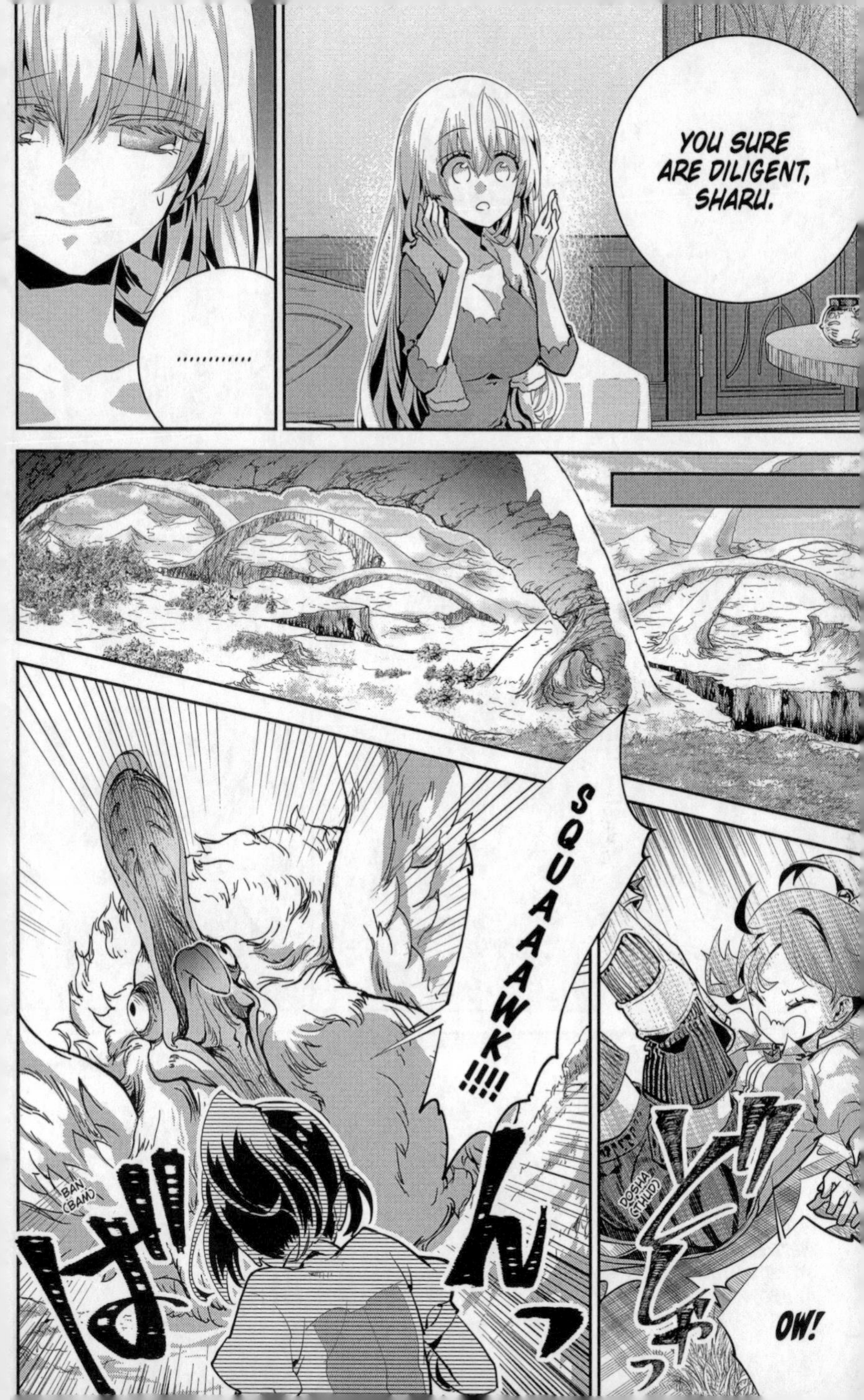
YOU SURE ARE DILIGENT, SHARU.
............
DOSHA (THUD)
OW!
SQUAAAAAWK!!!!
BAN (BAM)

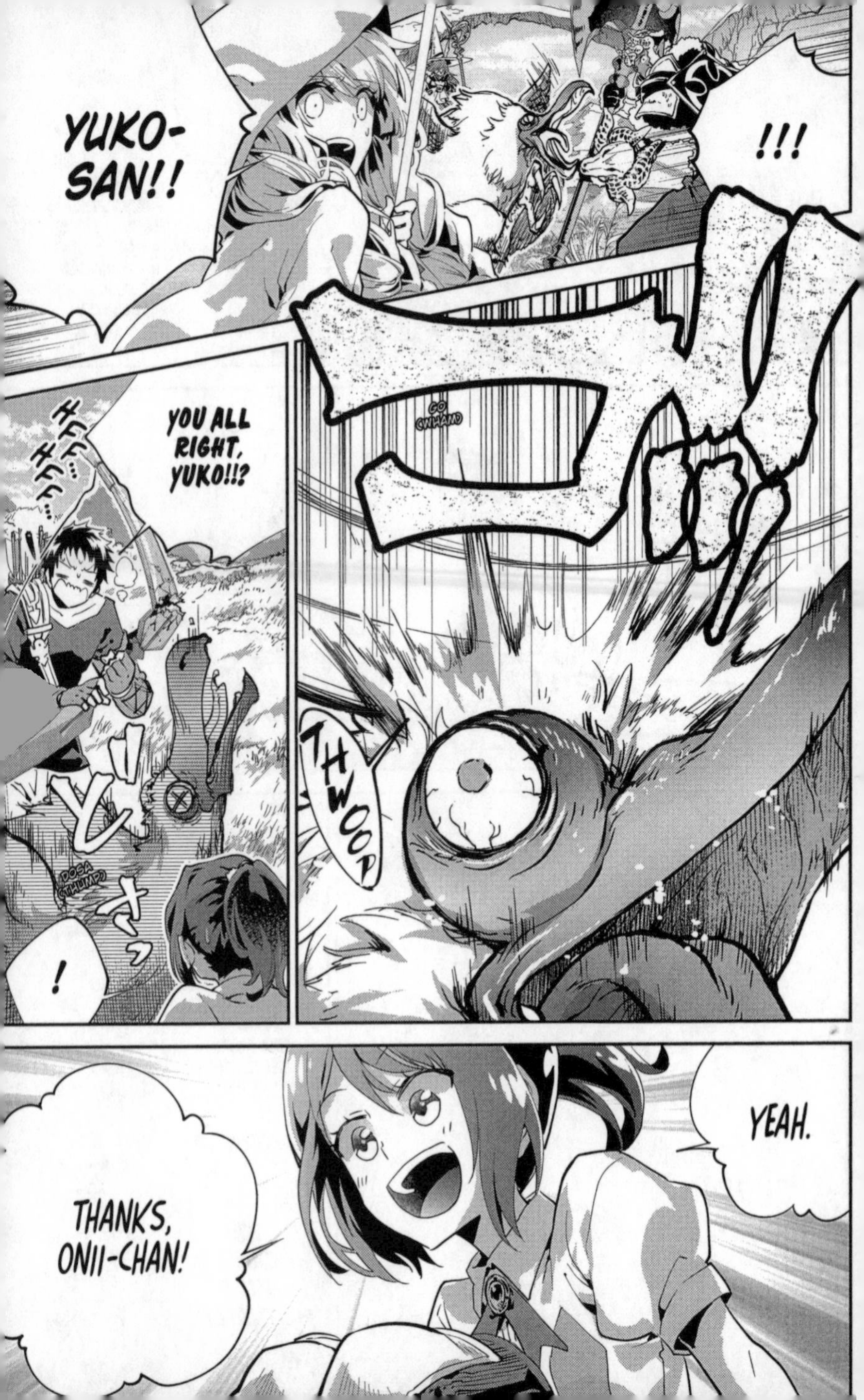
!!!
YUKO-SAN!!
GO (WHAM)
THWOOP
YOU ALL RIGHT, YUKO!!?
HFF... HFF...
DOSA (THUMP)
!
YEAH.
THANKS, ONII-CHAN!

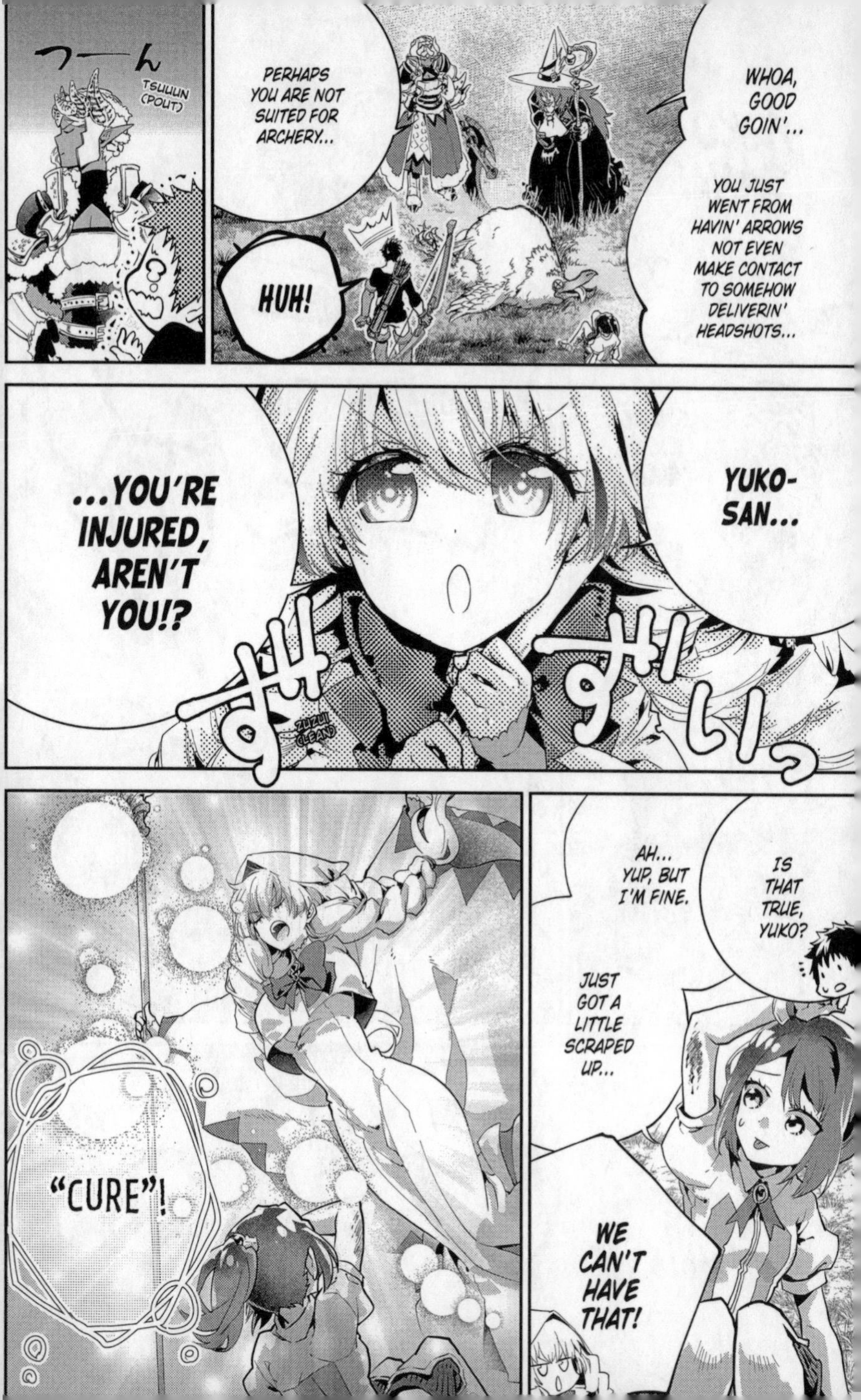
WHOA, GOOD GOIN'...
YOU JUST WENT FROM HAVIN' ARROWS NOT EVEN MAKE CONTACT TO SOMEHOW DELIVERIN' HEADSHOTS...
PERHAPS YOU ARE NOT SUITED FOR ARCHERY...
HUH!
つーん
TSUUUN (POUT)
YUKO-SAN...
...YOU'RE INJURED, AREN'T YOU!?
ずいずいっ
ZUZUI (LEAN)
IS THAT TRUE, YUKO?
AH... YUP, BUT I'M FINE.
JUST GOT A LITTLE SCRAPED UP...
WE CAN'T HAVE THAT!
"CURE"!

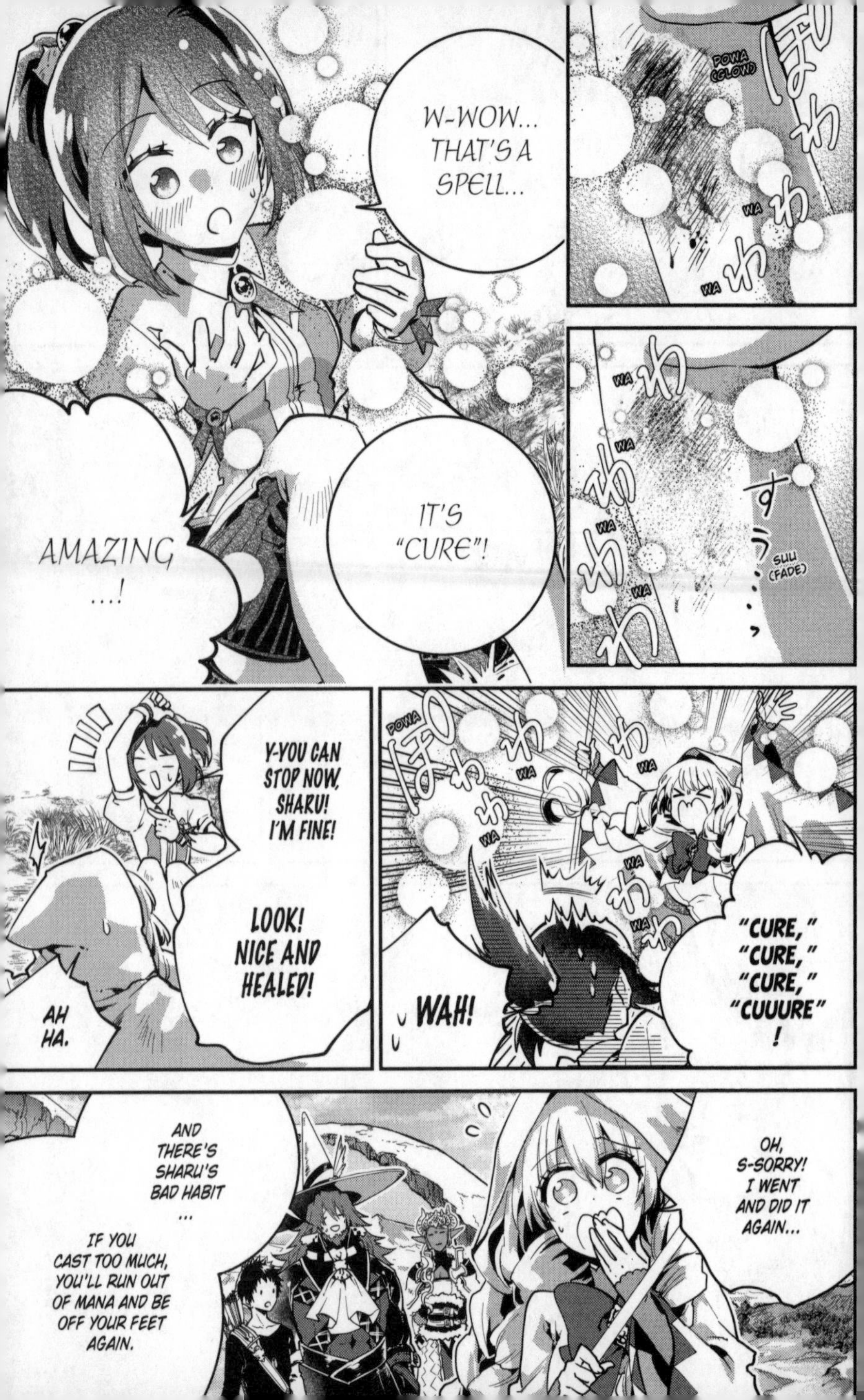
POWA (GLOW)
WA
WA
WA
WA
WA
WA
SUU (FADE)
W-WOW... THAT'S A SPELL...
IT'S "CURE"!
AMAZING ...!
POWA
WA
WA
WA
WA
WA
"CURE," "CURE," "CURE," "CUUURE" !
WAH!
Y-YOU CAN STOP NOW, SHARU! I'M FINE!
LOOK! NICE AND HEALED!
AH HA.
OH, S-SORRY! I WENT AND DID IT AGAIN...
AND THERE'S SHARU'S BAD HABIT ...
IF YOU CAST TOO MUCH, YOU'LL RUN OUT OF MANA AND BE OFF YOUR FEET AGAIN.

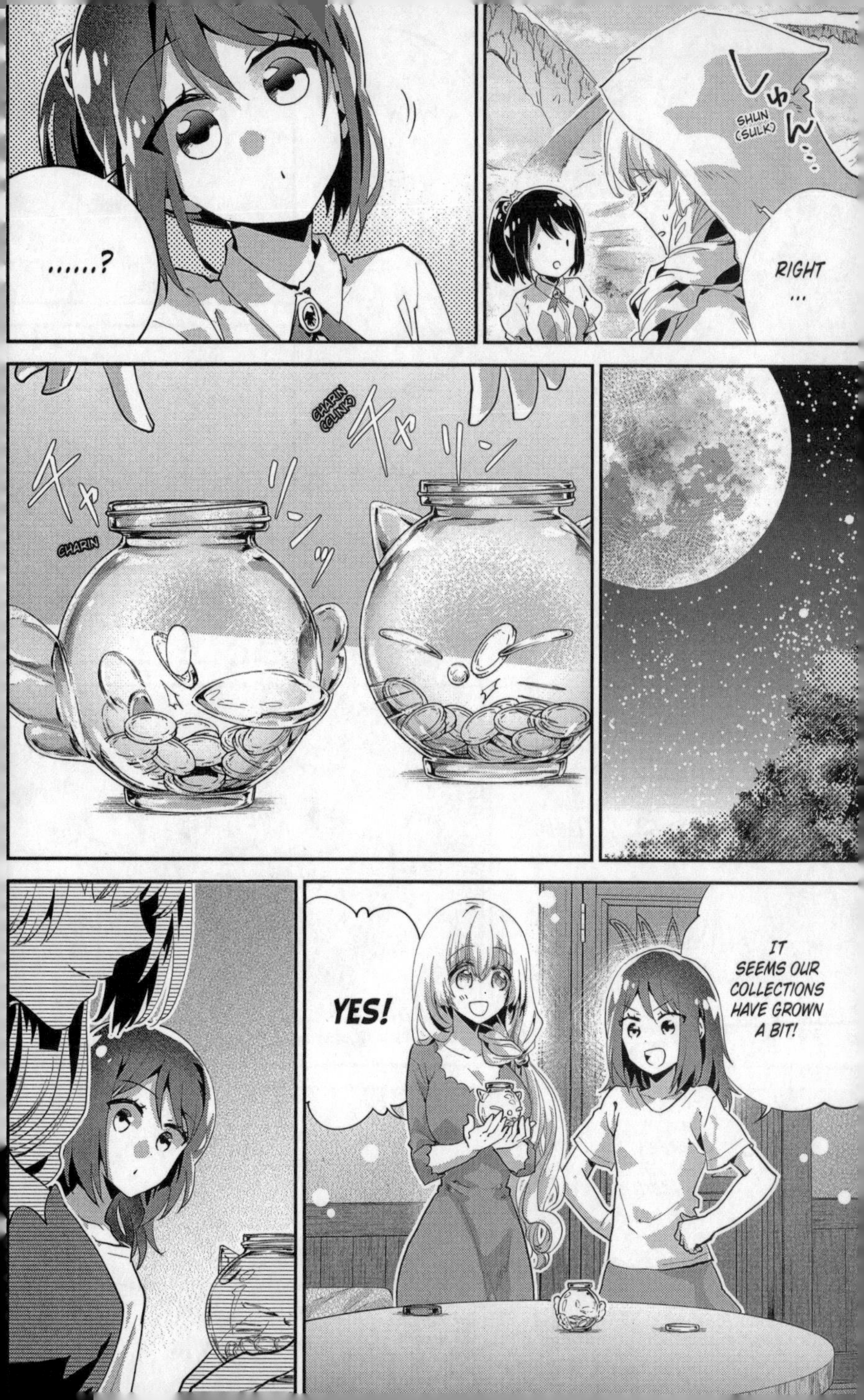

しゅん…
SHUN (SULK)
RIGHT ...
......?
キャリン
CHARIN (CLINK)
キャリンッ
CHARIN
IT SEEMS OUR COLLECTIONS HAVE GROWN A BIT!
YES!

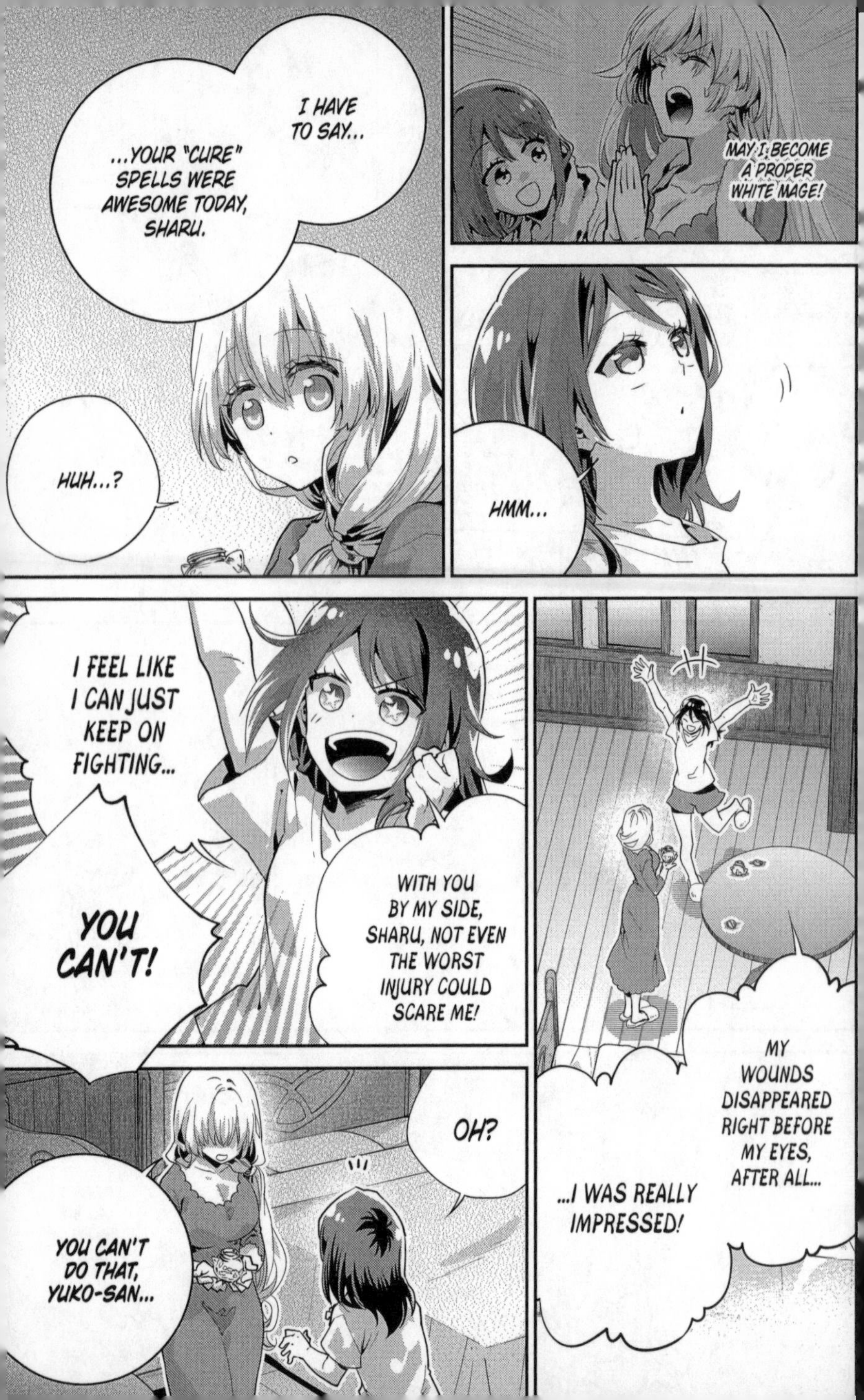
MAY I BECOME A PROPER WHITE MAGE!
HMM...
I HAVE TO SAY...
...YOUR "CURE" SPELLS WERE AWESOME TODAY, SHARU.
HUH...?
MY WOUNDS DISAPPEARED RIGHT BEFORE MY EYES, AFTER ALL...
...I WAS REALLY IMPRESSED!
WITH YOU BY MY SIDE, SHARU, NOT EVEN THE WORST INJURY COULD SCARE ME!
I FEEL LIKE I CAN JUST KEEP ON FIGHTING...
YOU CAN'T!
OH?
YOU CAN'T DO THAT, YUKO-SAN...

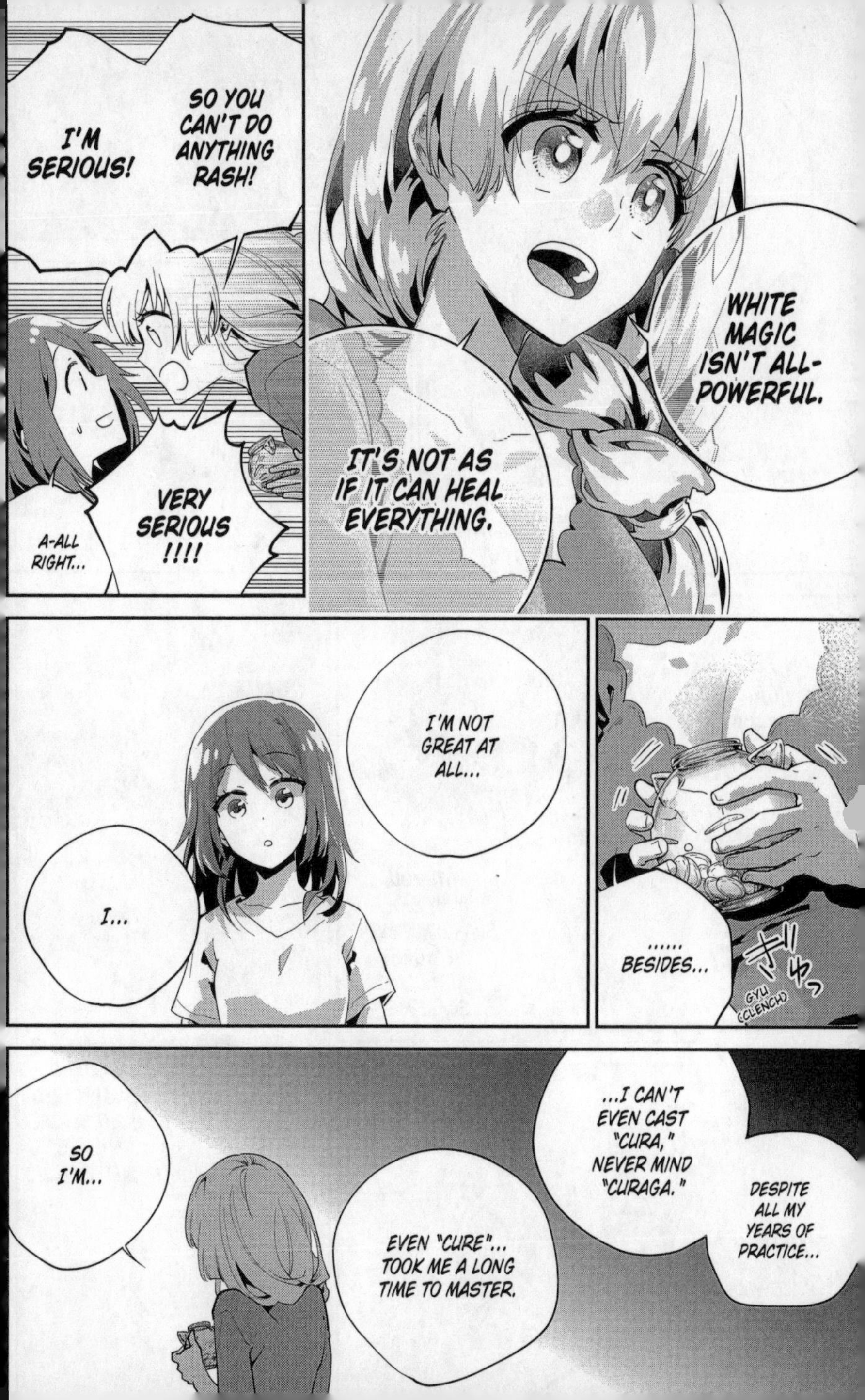
WHITE MAGIC ISN'T ALL-POWERFUL.
IT'S NOT AS IF IT CAN HEAL EVERYTHING.
SO YOU CAN'T DO ANYTHING RASH!
I'M SERIOUS!
VERY SERIOUS !!!!
A-ALL RIGHT...
...... BESIDES...
GYU (CLENCH)
I'M NOT GREAT AT ALL...
I...
DESPITE ALL MY YEARS OF PRACTICE...
...I CAN'T EVEN CAST "CURA," NEVER MIND "CURAGA."
EVEN "CURE"... TOOK ME A LONG TIME TO MASTER.
SO I'M...

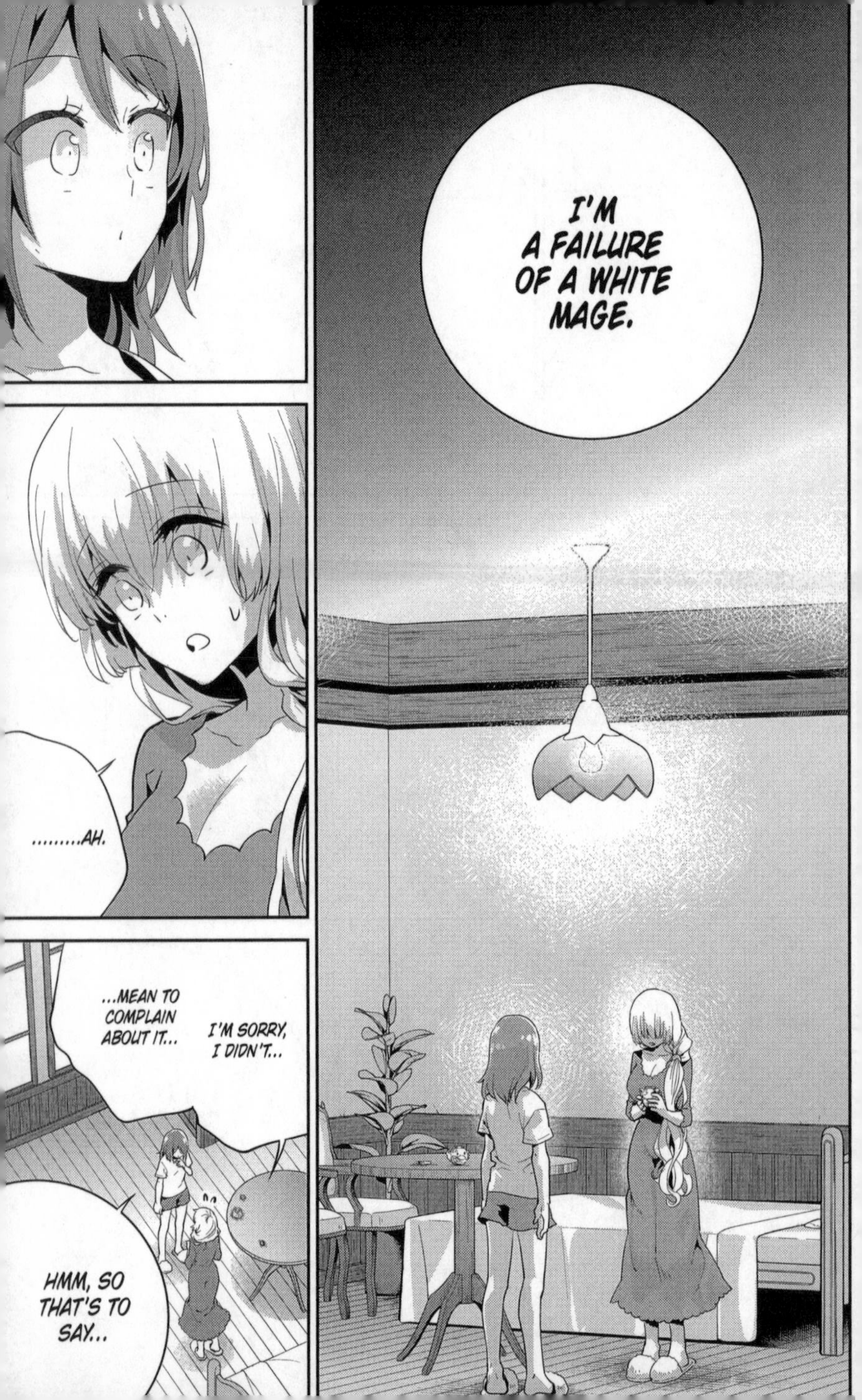
I'M A FAILURE OF A WHITE MAGE.
.........AH.
I'M SORRY, I DIDN'T...
...MEAN TO COMPLAIN ABOUT IT...
HMM, SO THAT'S TO SAY...

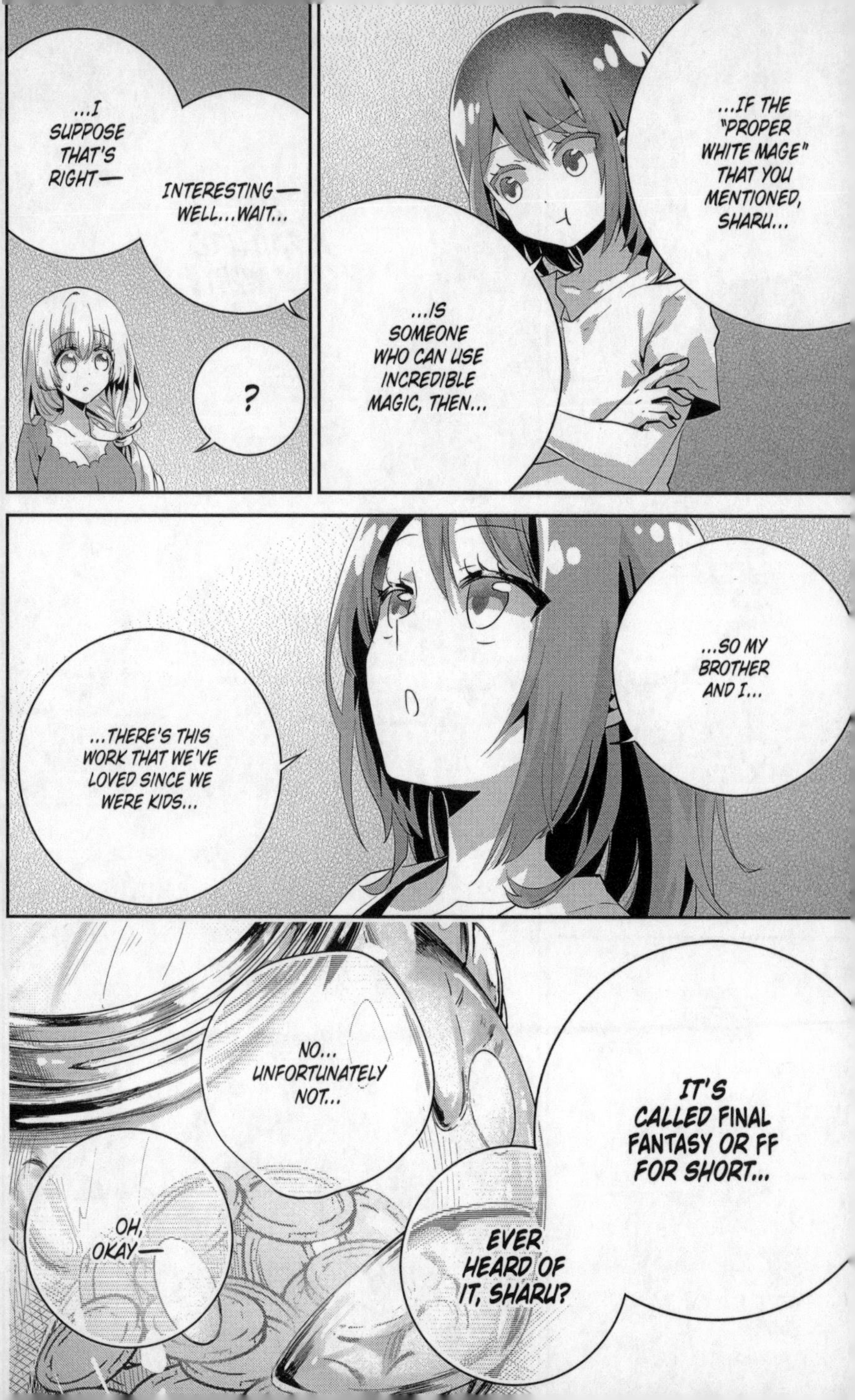
...IF THE "PROPER WHITE MAGE" THAT YOU MENTIONED, SHARU...
...IS SOMEONE WHO CAN USE INCREDIBLE MAGIC, THEN...
...I SUPPOSE THAT'S RIGHT—
INTERESTING—WELL...WAIT...
?
...SO MY BROTHER AND I...
...THERE'S THIS WORK THAT WE'VE LOVED SINCE WE WERE KIDS...
IT'S CALLED FINAL FANTASY OR FF FOR SHORT...
EVER HEARD OF IT, SHARU?
NO... UNFORTUNATELY NOT...
OH, OKAY—

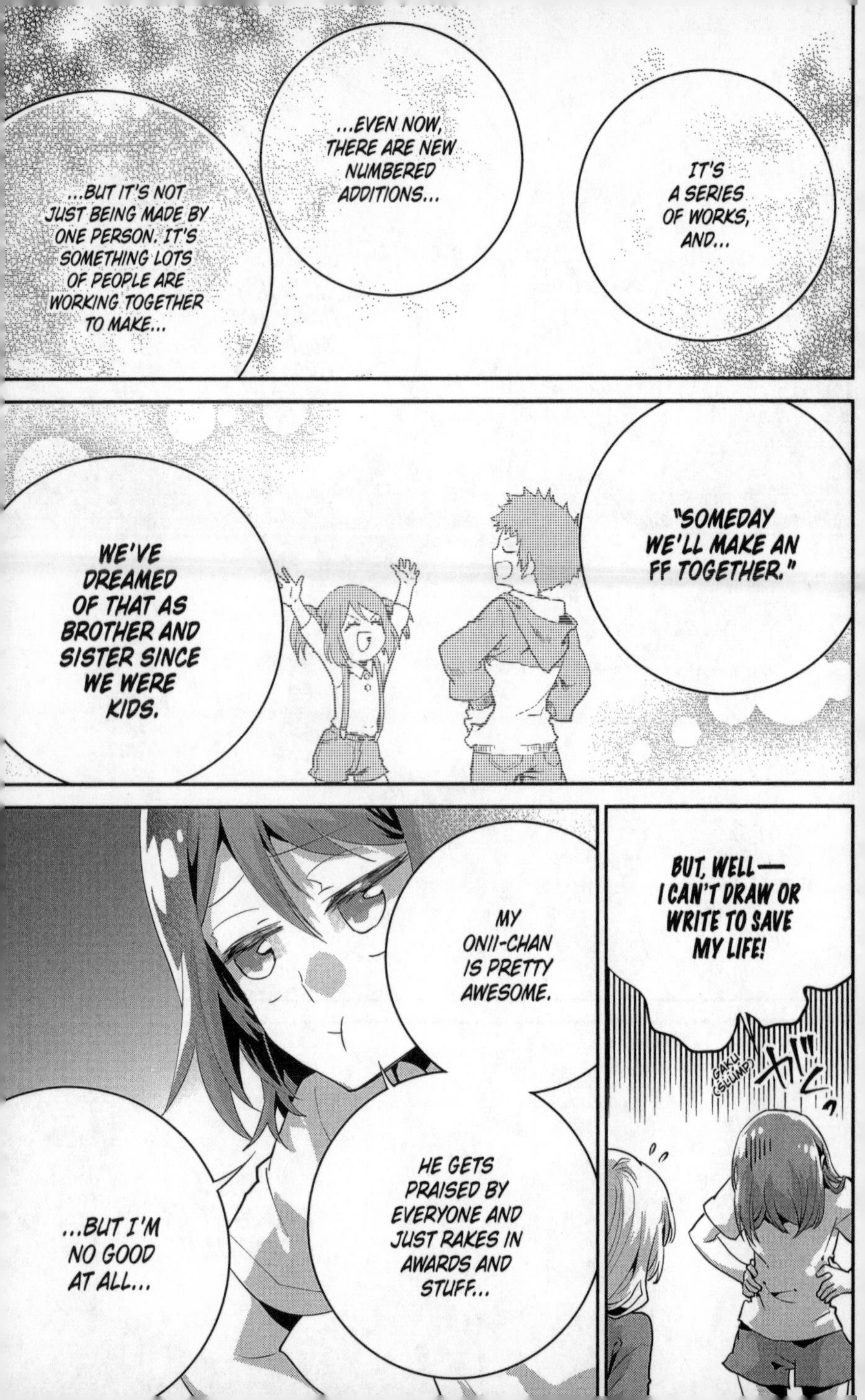
IT'S A SERIES OF WORKS, AND...
...EVEN NOW, THERE ARE NEW NUMBERED ADDITIONS...
...BUT IT'S NOT JUST BEING MADE BY ONE PERSON. IT'S SOMETHING LOTS OF PEOPLE ARE WORKING TOGETHER TO MAKE...
"SOMEDAY WE'LL MAKE AN FF TOGETHER."
WE'VE DREAMED OF THAT AS BROTHER AND SISTER SINCE WE WERE KIDS.
BUT, WELL— I CAN'T DRAW OR WRITE TO SAVE MY LIFE!
GAKU! (SLUMP)
MY ONII-CHAN IS PRETTY AWESOME.
HE GETS PRAISED BY EVERYONE AND JUST RAKES IN AWARDS AND STUFF...
...BUT I'M NO GOOD AT ALL...

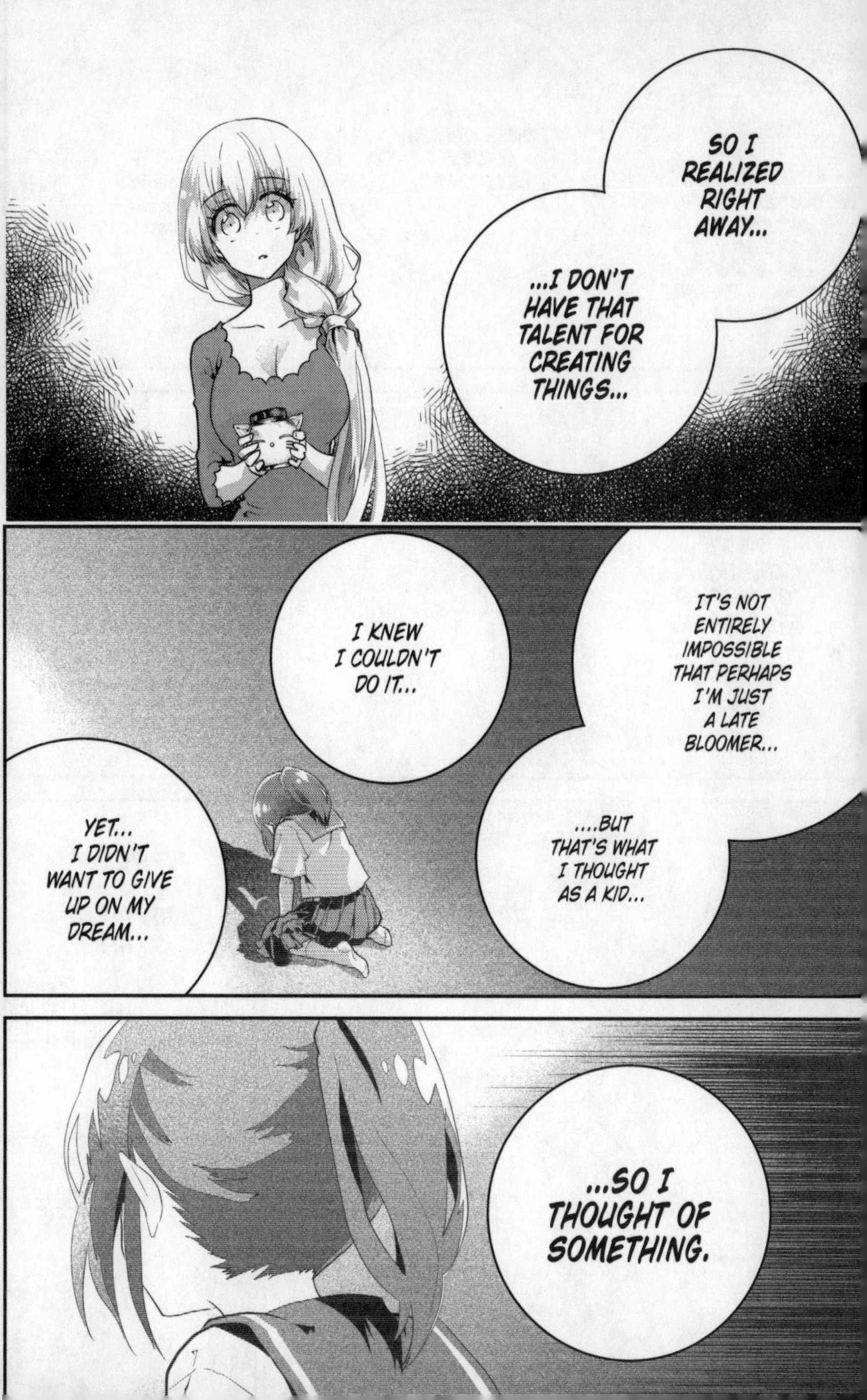
SO I REALIZED RIGHT AWAY...
...I DON'T HAVE THAT TALENT FOR CREATING THINGS...
IT'S NOT ENTIRELY IMPOSSIBLE THAT PERHAPS I'M JUST A LATE BLOOMER...
....BUT THAT'S WHAT I THOUGHT AS A KID...
I KNEW I COULDN'T DO IT...
YET... I DIDN'T WANT TO GIVE UP ON MY DREAM...
...SO I THOUGHT OF SOMETHING.

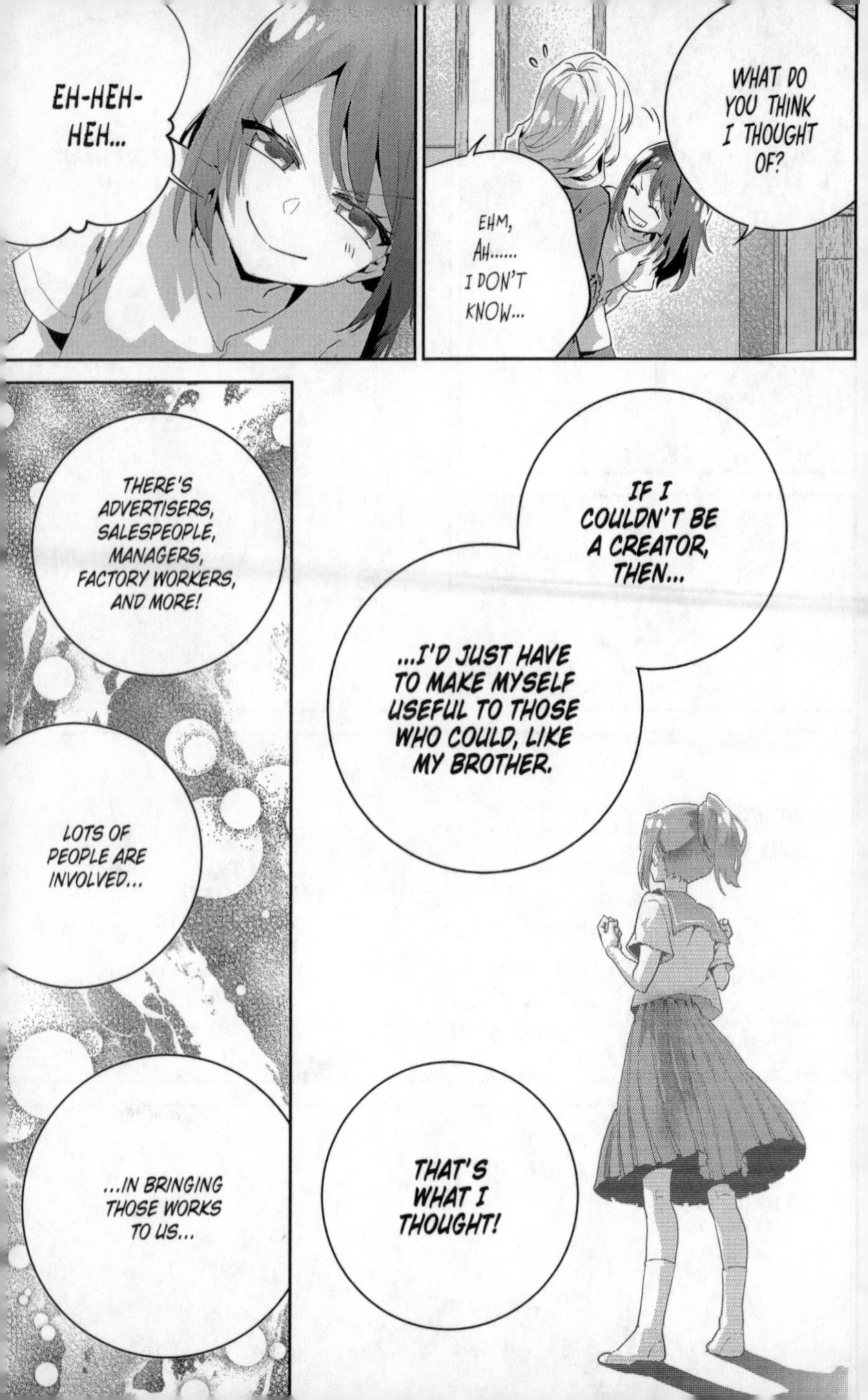
WHAT DO YOU THINK I THOUGHT OF?
EHM, AH...... I DON'T KNOW...
EH-HEH-HEH...
IF I COULDN'T BE A CREATOR, THEN...
...I'D JUST HAVE TO MAKE MYSELF USEFUL TO THOSE WHO COULD, LIKE MY BROTHER.
THAT'S WHAT I THOUGHT!
THERE'S ADVERTISERS, SALESPEOPLE, MANAGERS, FACTORY WORKERS, AND MORE!
LOTS OF PEOPLE ARE INVOLVED...
...IN BRINGING THOSE WORKS TO US...

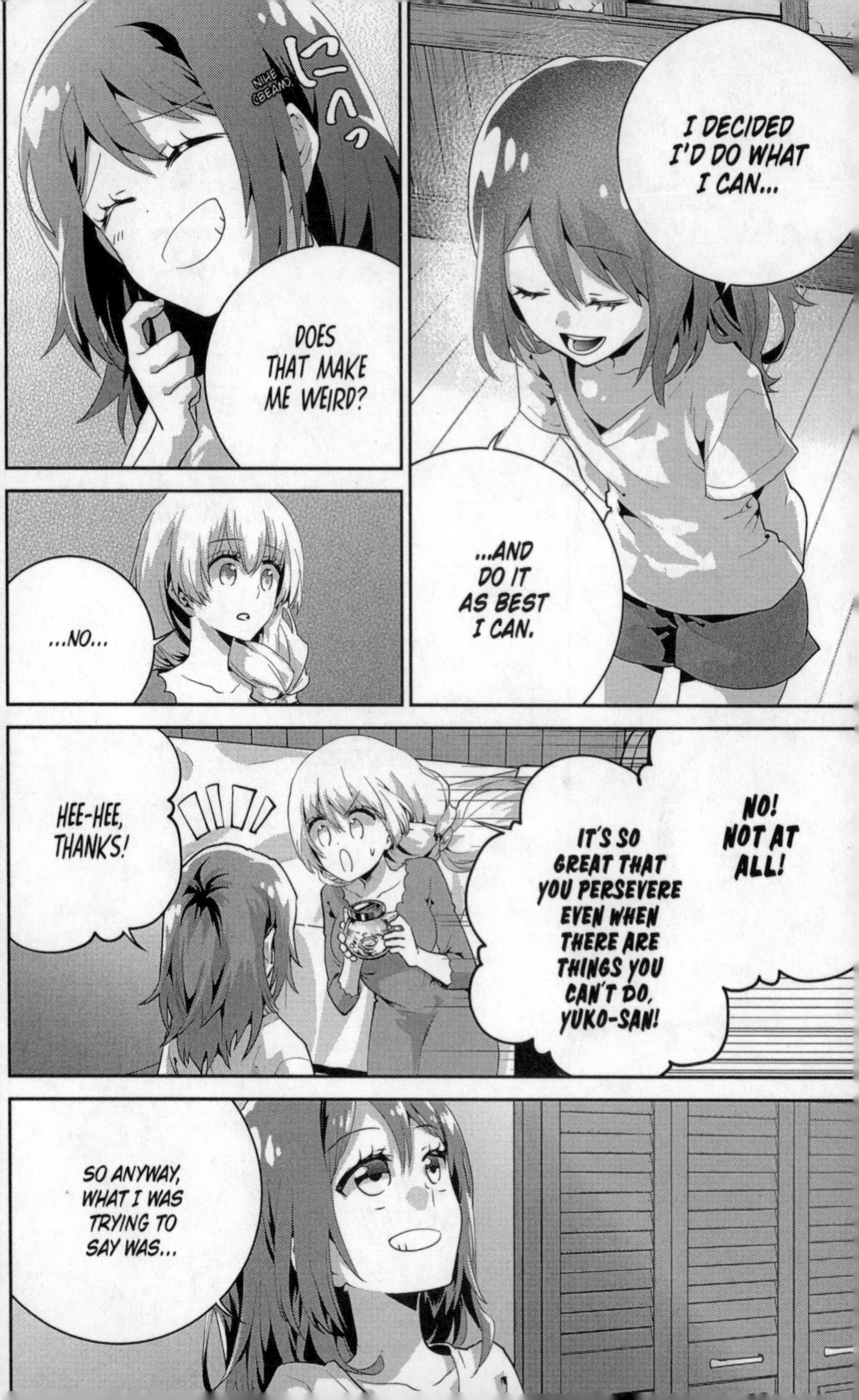
I DECIDED I'D DO WHAT I CAN...
...AND DO IT AS BEST I CAN.
NIHE (BEAM)
DOES THAT MAKE ME WEIRD?
...NO...
NO! NOT AT ALL!
IT'S SO GREAT THAT YOU PERSEVERE EVEN WHEN THERE ARE THINGS YOU CAN'T DO, YUKO-SAN!
HEE-HEE, THANKS!
SO ANYWAY, WHAT I WAS TRYING TO SAY WAS...

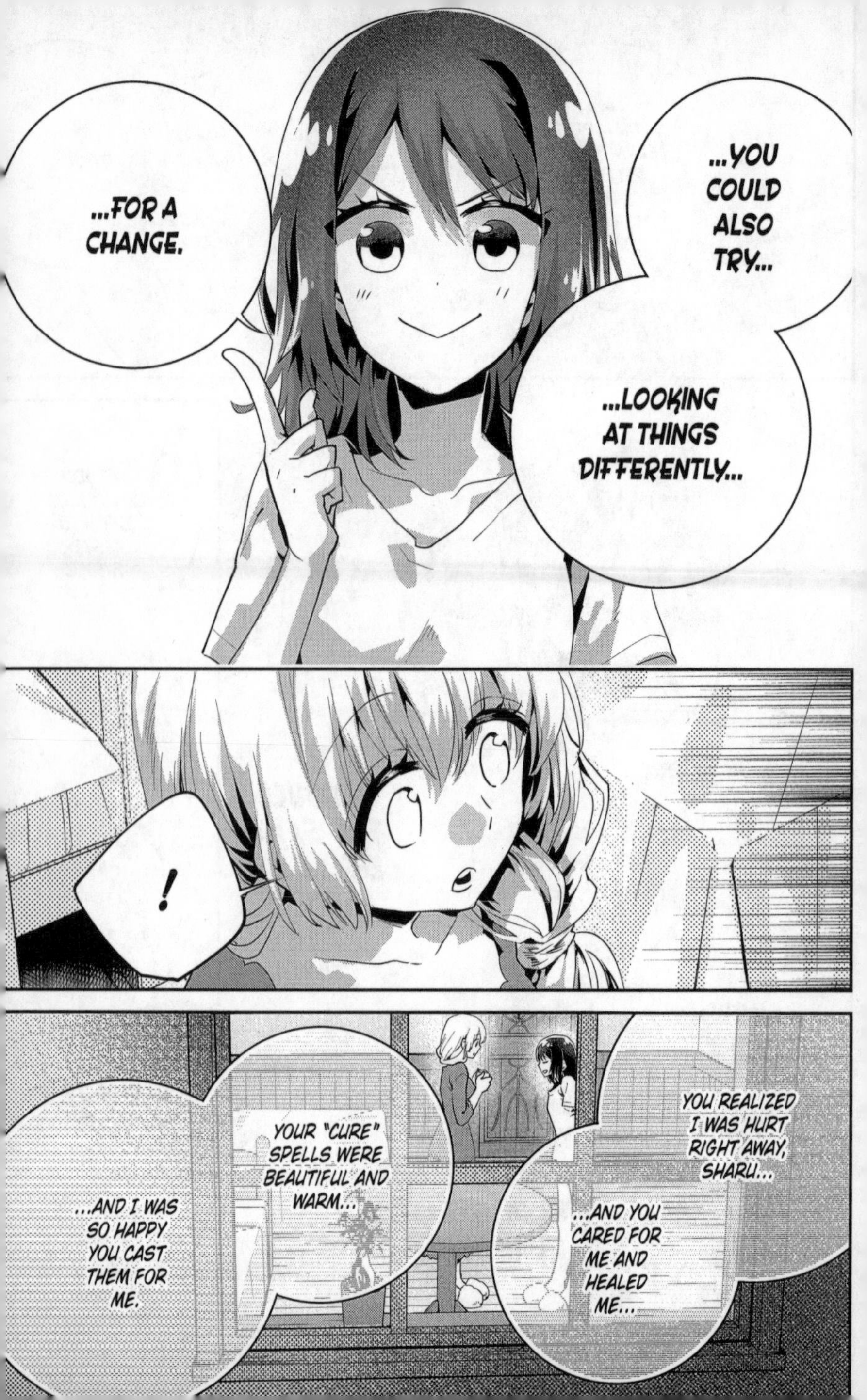
...YOU COULD ALSO TRY...
...LOOKING AT THINGS DIFFERENTLY...
...FOR A CHANGE.
!
YOU REALIZED I WAS HURT RIGHT AWAY, SHARU...
...AND YOU CARED FOR ME AND HEALED ME...
YOUR "CURE" SPELLS WERE BEAUTIFUL AND WARM...
...AND I WAS SO HAPPY YOU CAST THEM FOR ME.

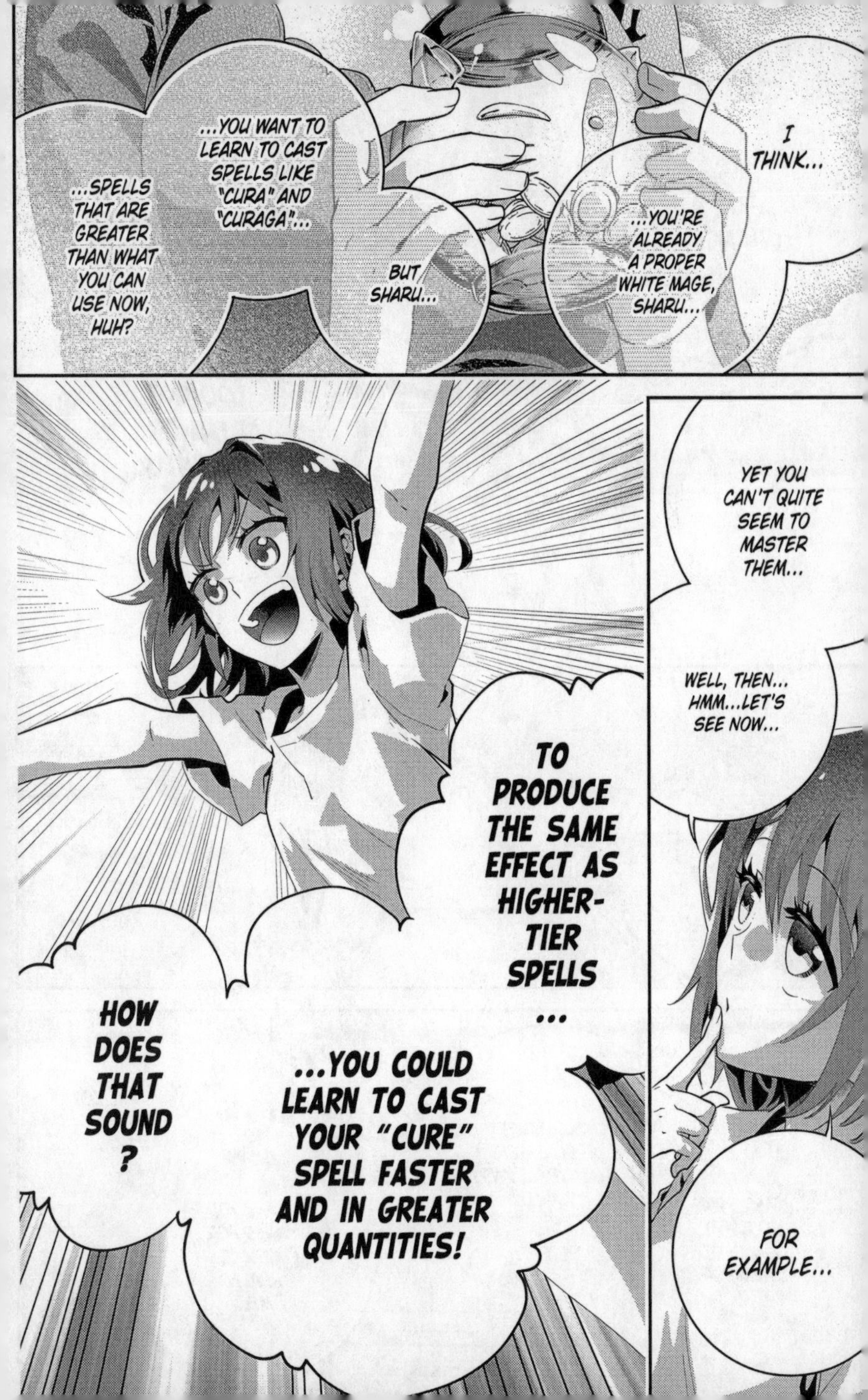
I THINK...
...YOU'RE ALREADY A PROPER WHITE MAGE, SHARU...
BUT SHARU...
...YOU WANT TO LEARN TO CAST SPELLS LIKE "CURA" AND "CURAGA"...
...SPELLS THAT ARE GREATER THAN WHAT YOU CAN USE NOW, HUH?
YET YOU CAN'T QUITE SEEM TO MASTER THEM...
WELL, THEN... HMM...LET'S SEE NOW...
FOR EXAMPLE...
TO PRODUCE THE SAME EFFECT AS HIGHER-TIER SPELLS...
...YOU COULD LEARN TO CAST YOUR "CURE" SPELL FASTER AND IN GREATER QUANTITIES!
HOW DOES THAT SOUND?

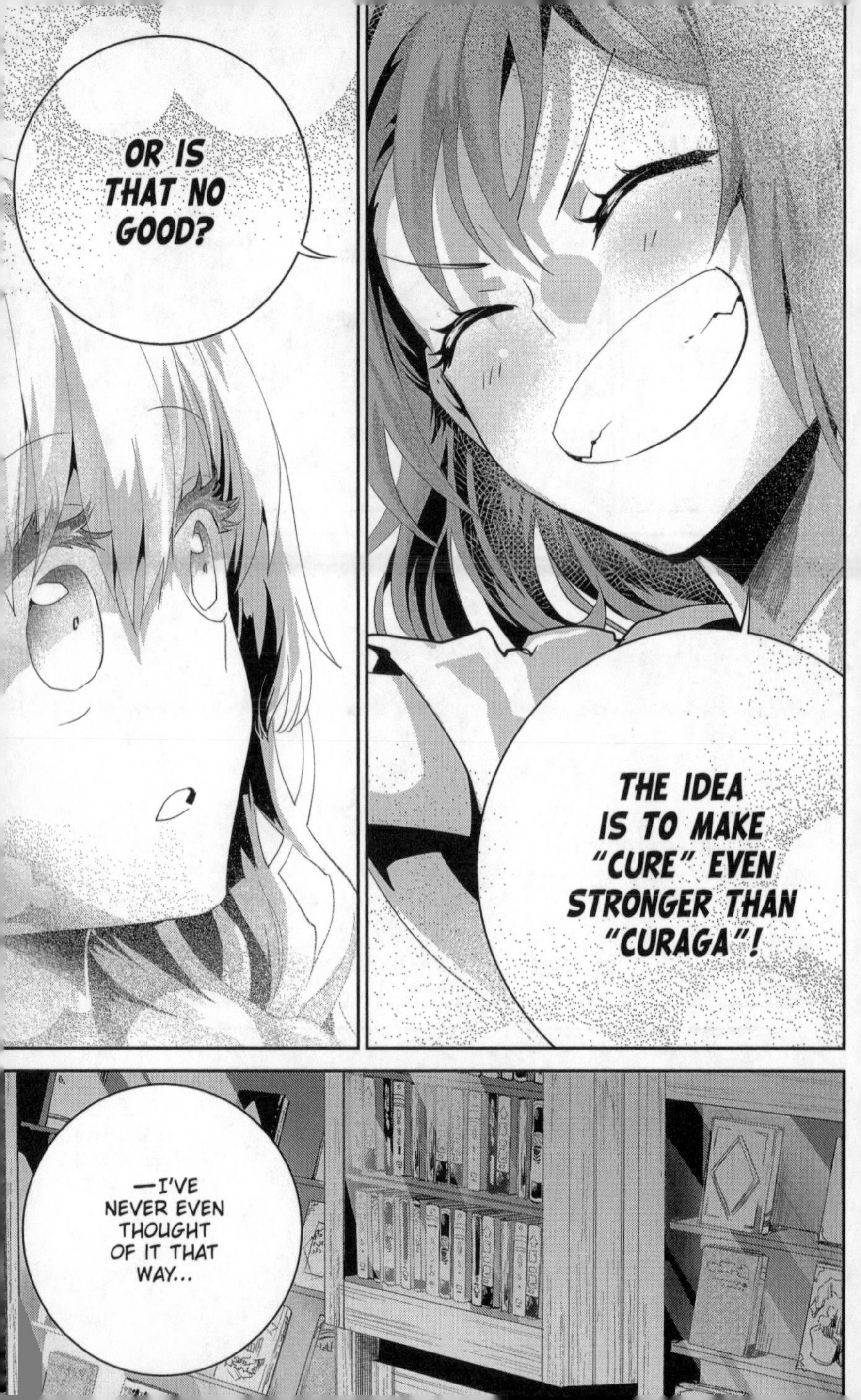
THE IDEA IS TO MAKE "CURE" EVEN STRONGER THAN "CURAGA"!
OR IS THAT NO GOOD?
—I'VE NEVER EVEN THOUGHT OF IT THAT WAY...

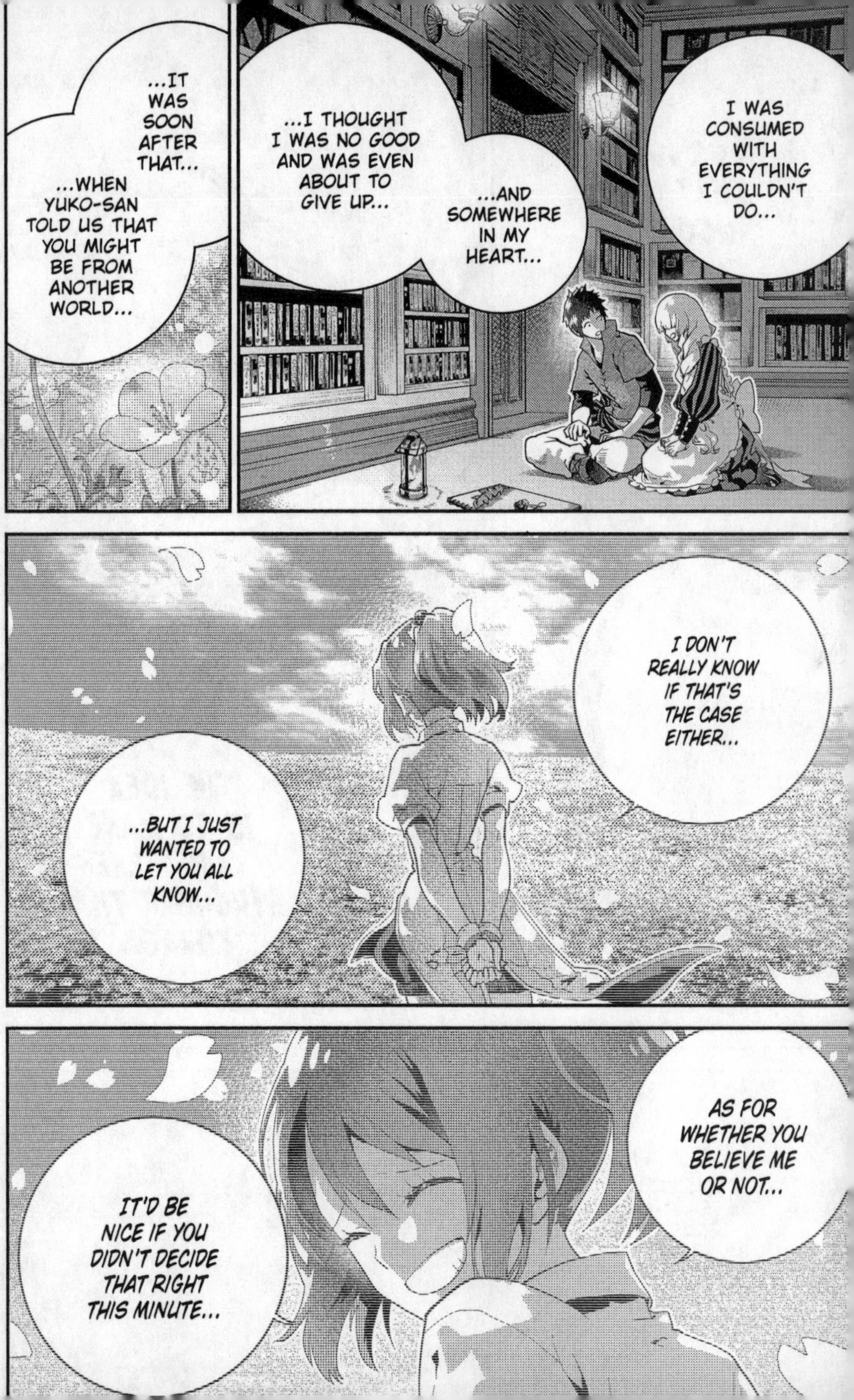
I WAS CONSUMED WITH EVERYTHING I COULDN'T DO...
...AND SOMEWHERE IN MY HEART...
...I THOUGHT I WAS NO GOOD AND WAS EVEN ABOUT TO GIVE UP...
...IT WAS SOON AFTER THAT...
...WHEN YUKO-SAN TOLD US THAT YOU MIGHT BE FROM ANOTHER WORLD...
I DON'T REALLY KNOW IF THAT'S THE CASE EITHER...
...BUT I JUST WANTED TO LET YOU ALL KNOW...
AS FOR WHETHER YOU BELIEVE ME OR NOT...
IT'D BE NICE IF YOU DIDN'T DECIDE THAT RIGHT THIS MINUTE...

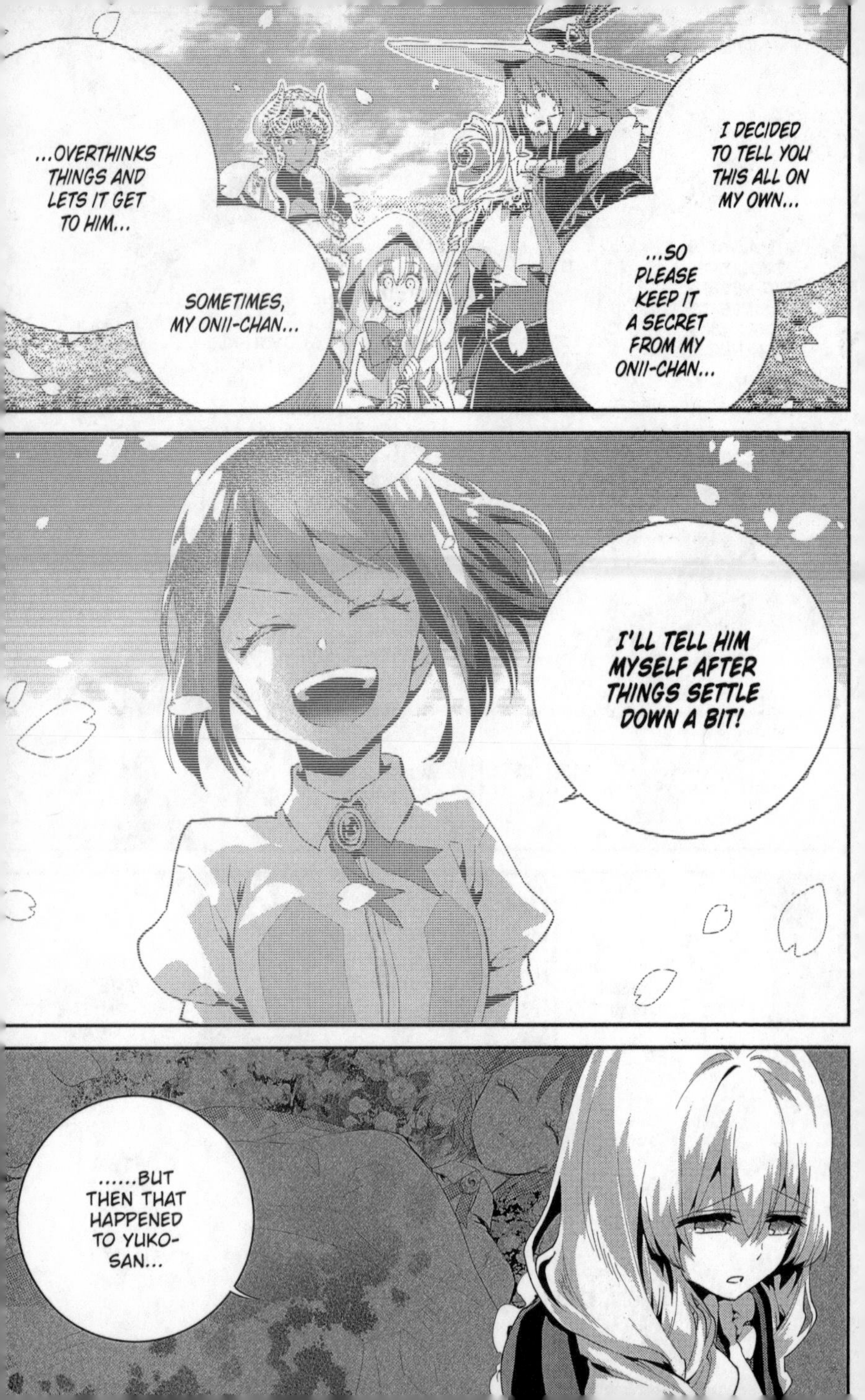

I DECIDED TO TELL YOU THIS ALL ON MY OWN...
...SO PLEASE KEEP IT A SECRET FROM MY ONII-CHAN...
SOMETIMES, MY ONII-CHAN...
...OVERTHINKS THINGS AND LETS IT GET TO HIM...
I'LL TELL HIM MYSELF AFTER THINGS SETTLE DOWN A BIT!
......BUT THEN THAT HAPPENED TO YUKO-SAN...

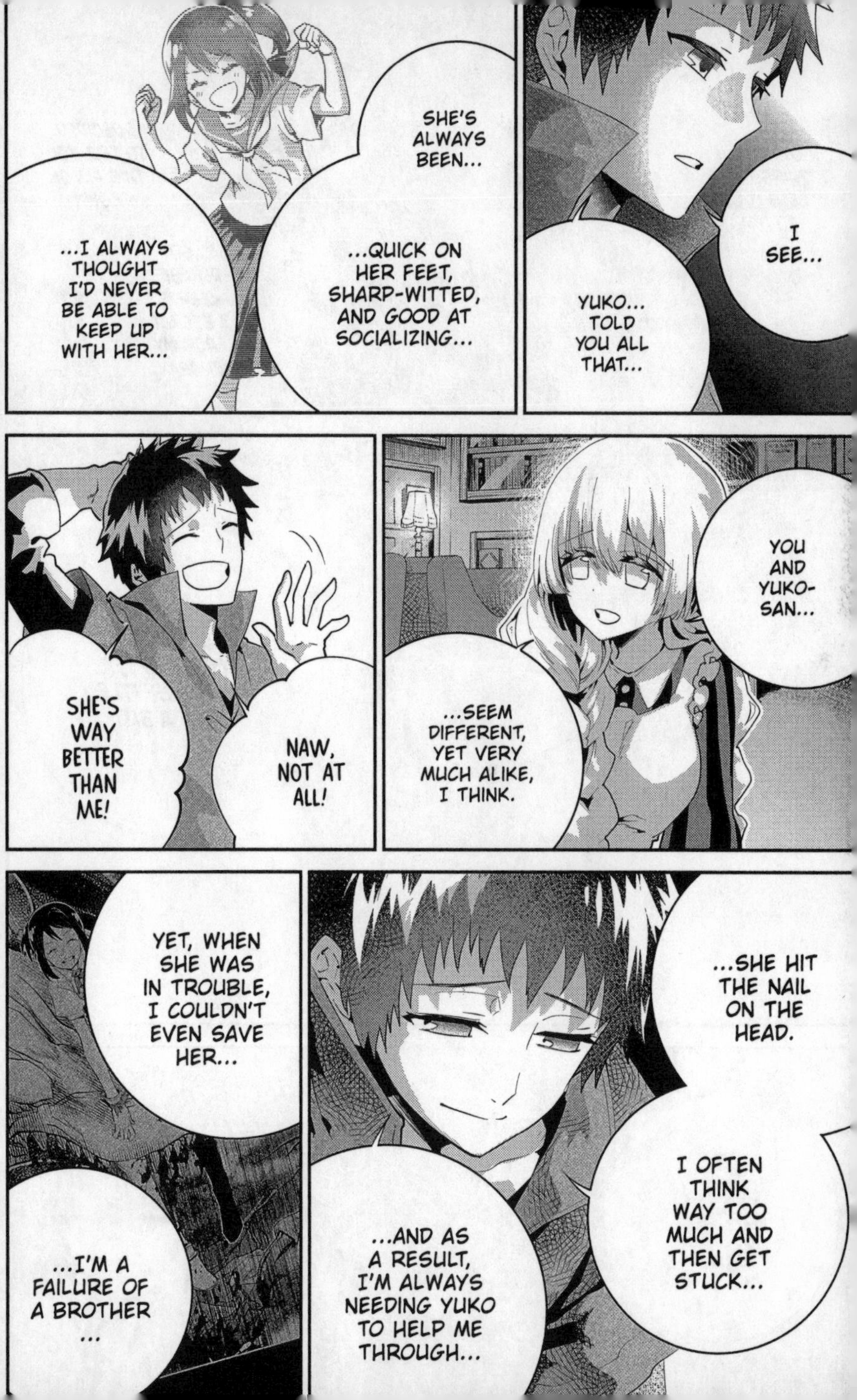
I SEE...
YUKO... TOLD YOU ALL THAT...
SHE'S ALWAYS BEEN...
...QUICK ON HER FEET, SHARP-WITTED, AND GOOD AT SOCIALIZING...
...I ALWAYS THOUGHT I'D NEVER BE ABLE TO KEEP UP WITH HER...
YOU AND YUKO-SAN...
...SEEM DIFFERENT, YET VERY MUCH ALIKE, I THINK.
NAW, NOT AT ALL!
SHE'S WAY BETTER THAN ME!
...SHE HIT THE NAIL ON THE HEAD.
I OFTEN THINK WAY TOO MUCH AND THEN GET STUCK...
...AND AS A RESULT, I'M ALWAYS NEEDING YUKO TO HELP ME THROUGH...
YET, WHEN SHE WAS IN TROUBLE, I COULDN'T EVEN SAVE HER...
...I'M A FAILURE OF A BROTHER...

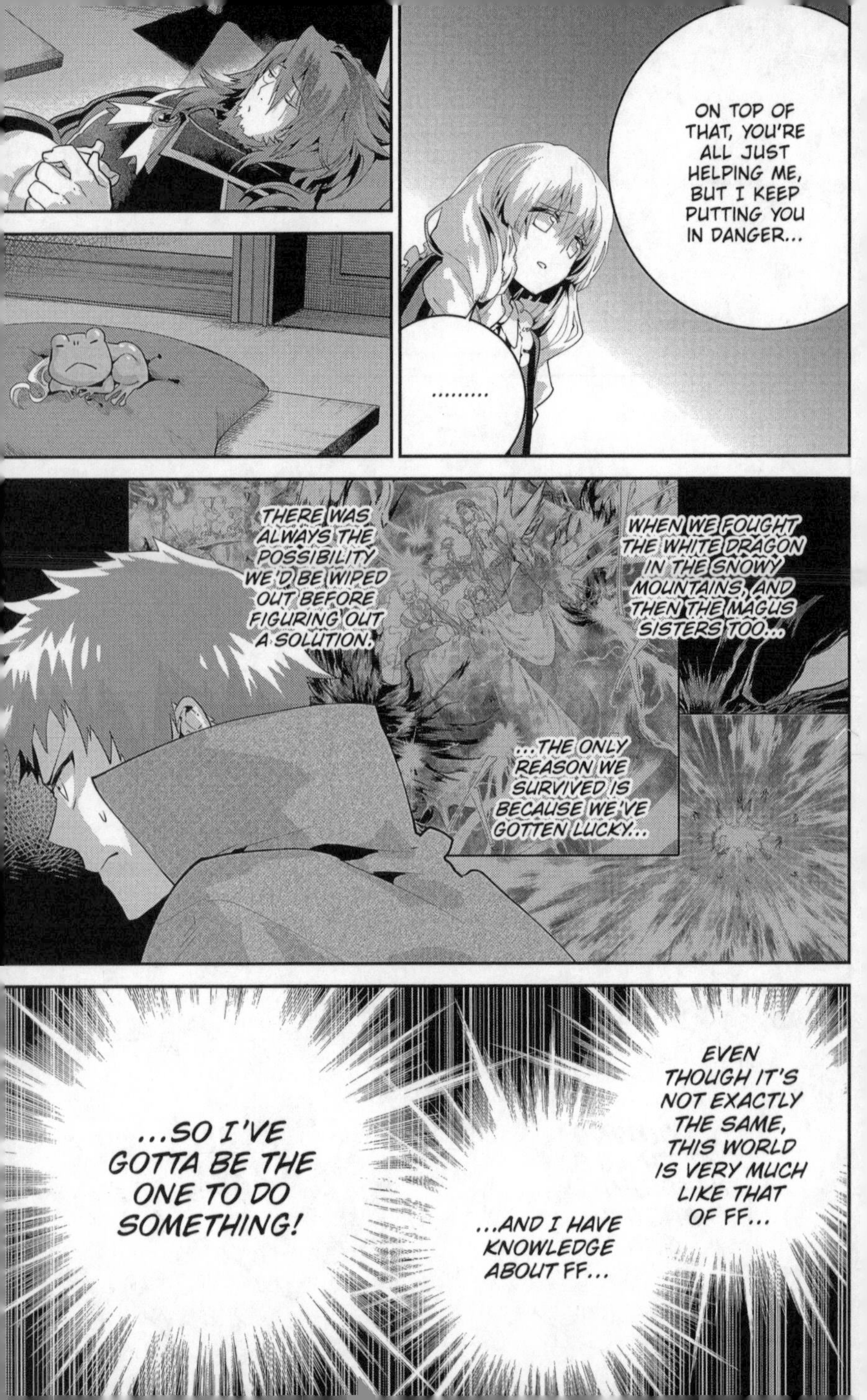
ON TOP OF THAT, YOU'RE ALL JUST HELPING ME, BUT I KEEP PUTTING YOU IN DANGER...
.........
WHEN WE FOUGHT THE WHITE DRAGON IN THE SNOWY MOUNTAINS, AND THEN THE MAGUS SISTERS TOO...
...THE ONLY REASON WE SURVIVED IS BECAUSE WE'VE GOTTEN LUCKY...
THERE WAS ALWAYS THE POSSIBILITY WE'D BE WIPED OUT BEFORE FIGURING OUT A SOLUTION.
EVEN THOUGH IT'S NOT EXACTLY THE SAME, THIS WORLD IS VERY MUCH LIKE THAT OF FF...
...AND I HAVE KNOWLEDGE ABOUT FF...
...SO I'VE GOTTA BE THE ONE TO DO SOMETHING!

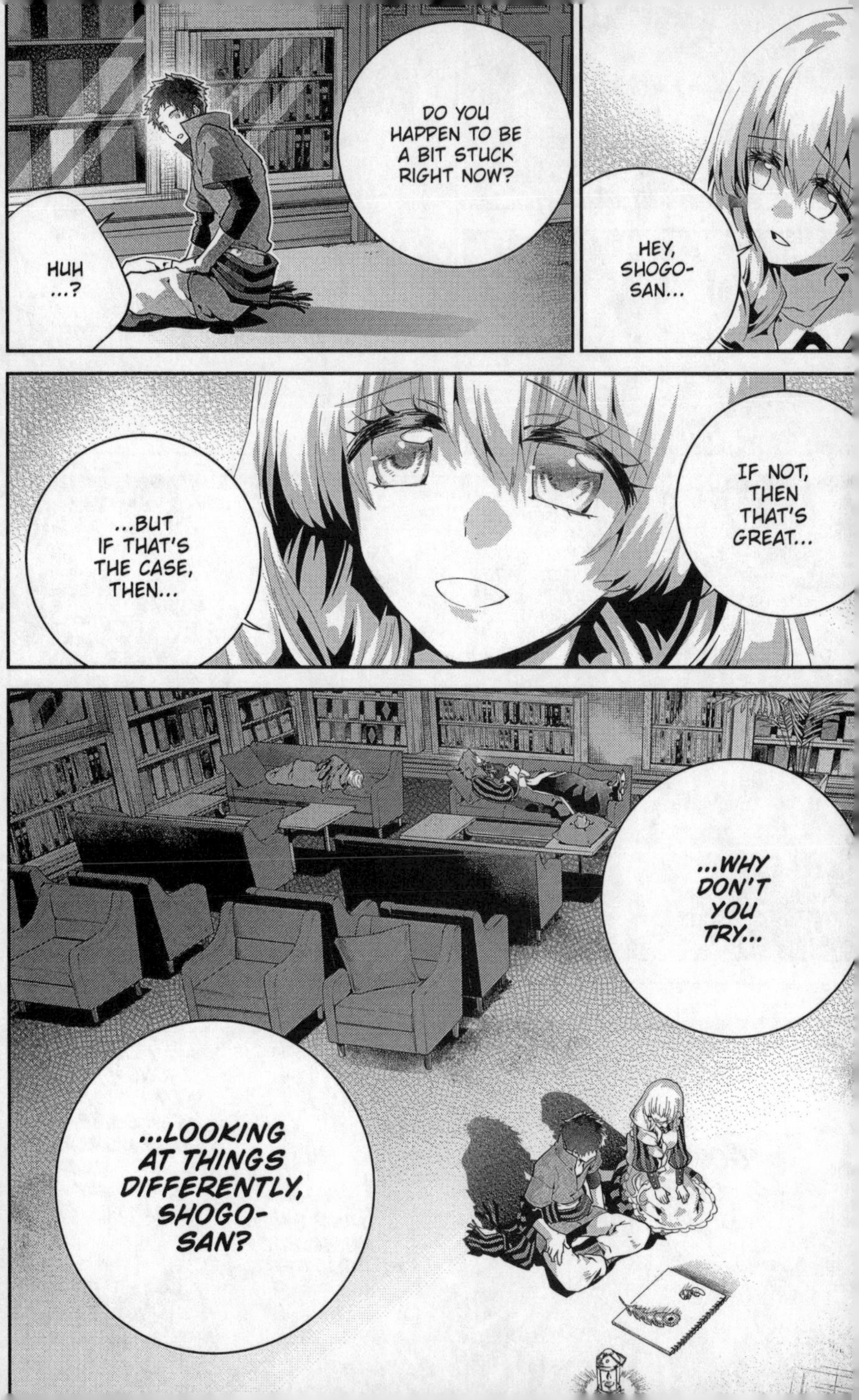
HEY, SHOGO-SAN...
DO YOU HAPPEN TO BE A BIT STUCK RIGHT NOW?
HUH...?
IF NOT, THEN THAT'S GREAT...
...BUT IF THAT'S THE CASE, THEN...
...WHY DON'T YOU TRY...
...LOOKING AT THINGS DIFFERENTLY, SHOGO-SAN?

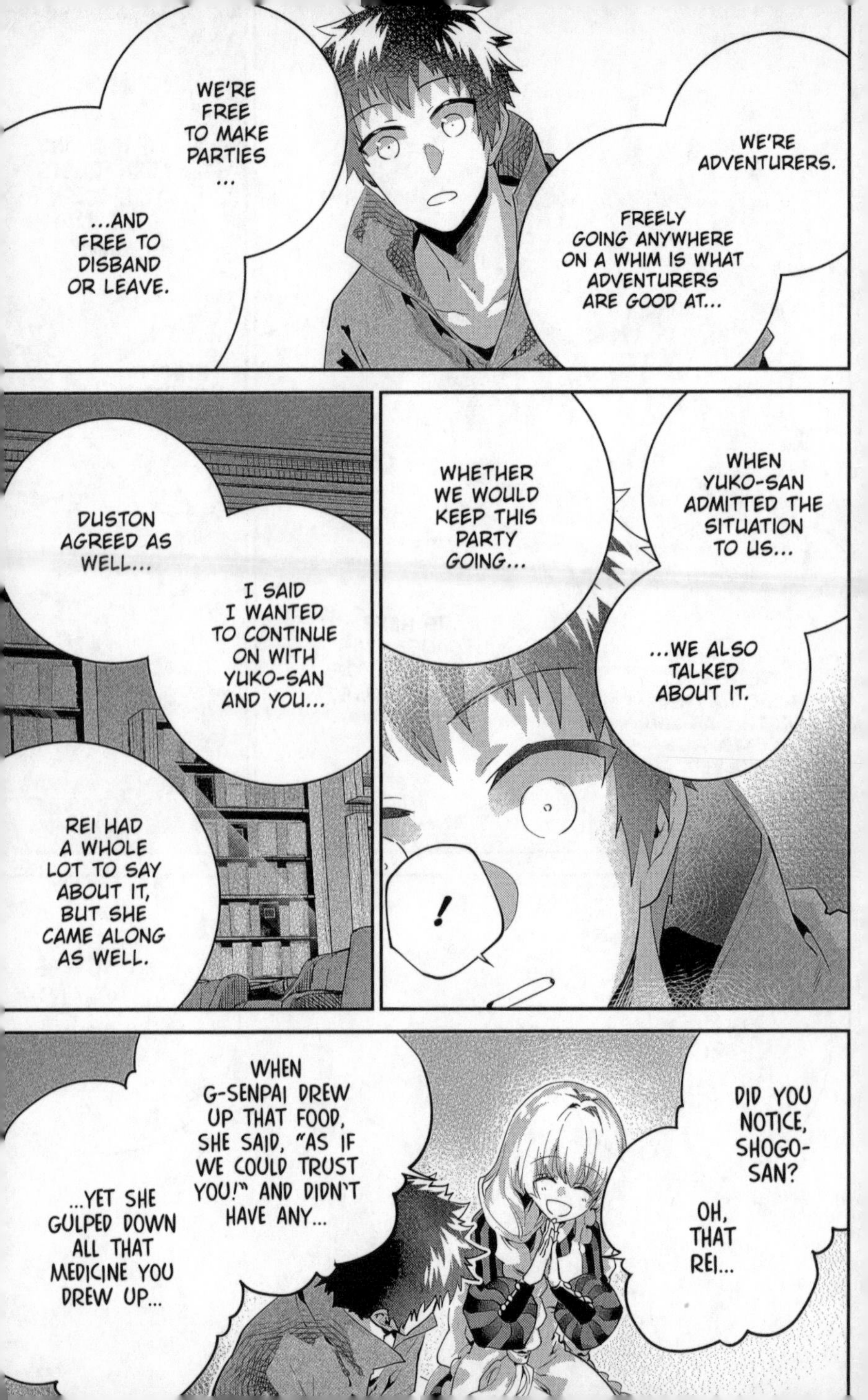
WE'RE ADVENTURERS.
FREELY GOING ANYWHERE ON A WHIM IS WHAT ADVENTURERS ARE GOOD AT...
WE'RE FREE TO MAKE PARTIES...
...AND FREE TO DISBAND OR LEAVE.
WHEN YUKO-SAN ADMITTED THE SITUATION TO US...
WHETHER WE WOULD KEEP THIS PARTY GOING...
...WE ALSO TALKED ABOUT IT.
!
I SAID I WANTED TO CONTINUE ON WITH YUKO-SAN AND YOU...
DUSTON AGREED AS WELL...
REI HAD A WHOLE LOT TO SAY ABOUT IT, BUT SHE CAME ALONG AS WELL.
DID YOU NOTICE, SHOGO-SAN?
OH, THAT REI...
WHEN G-SENPAI DREW UP THAT FOOD, SHE SAID, "AS IF WE COULD TRUST YOU!" AND DIDN'T HAVE ANY...
...YET SHE GULPED DOWN ALL THAT MEDICINE YOU DREW UP...

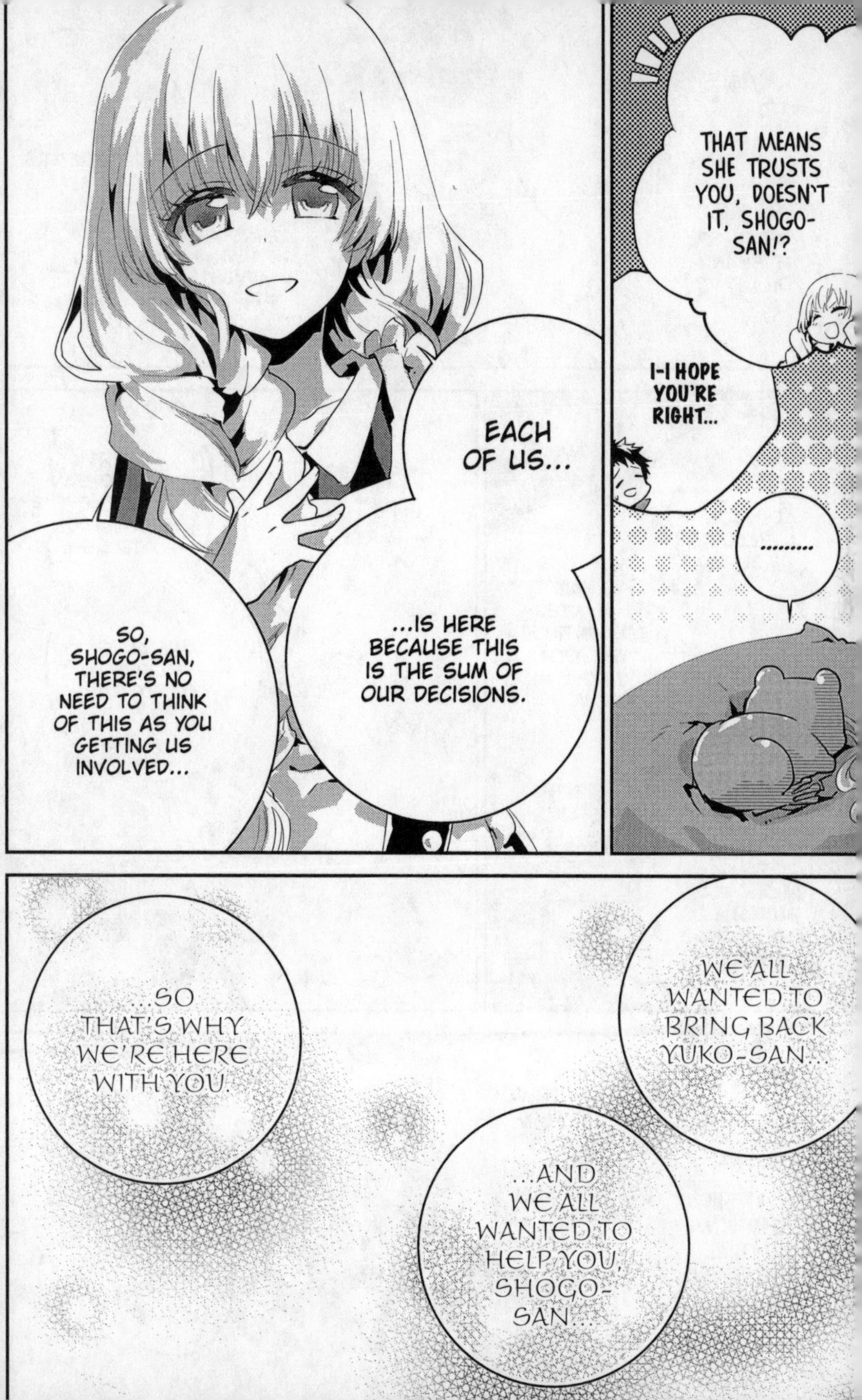
THAT MEANS SHE TRUSTS YOU, DOESN'T IT, SHOGO-SAN!?
I-I HOPE YOU'RE RIGHT...
.........
EACH OF US...
...IS HERE BECAUSE THIS IS THE SUM OF OUR DECISIONS.
SO, SHOGO-SAN, THERE'S NO NEED TO THINK OF THIS AS YOU GETTING US INVOLVED...
WE ALL WANTED TO BRING BACK YUKO-SAN...
...AND WE ALL WANTED TO HELP YOU, SHOGO-SAN...
...SO THAT'S WHY WE'RE HERE WITH YOU.

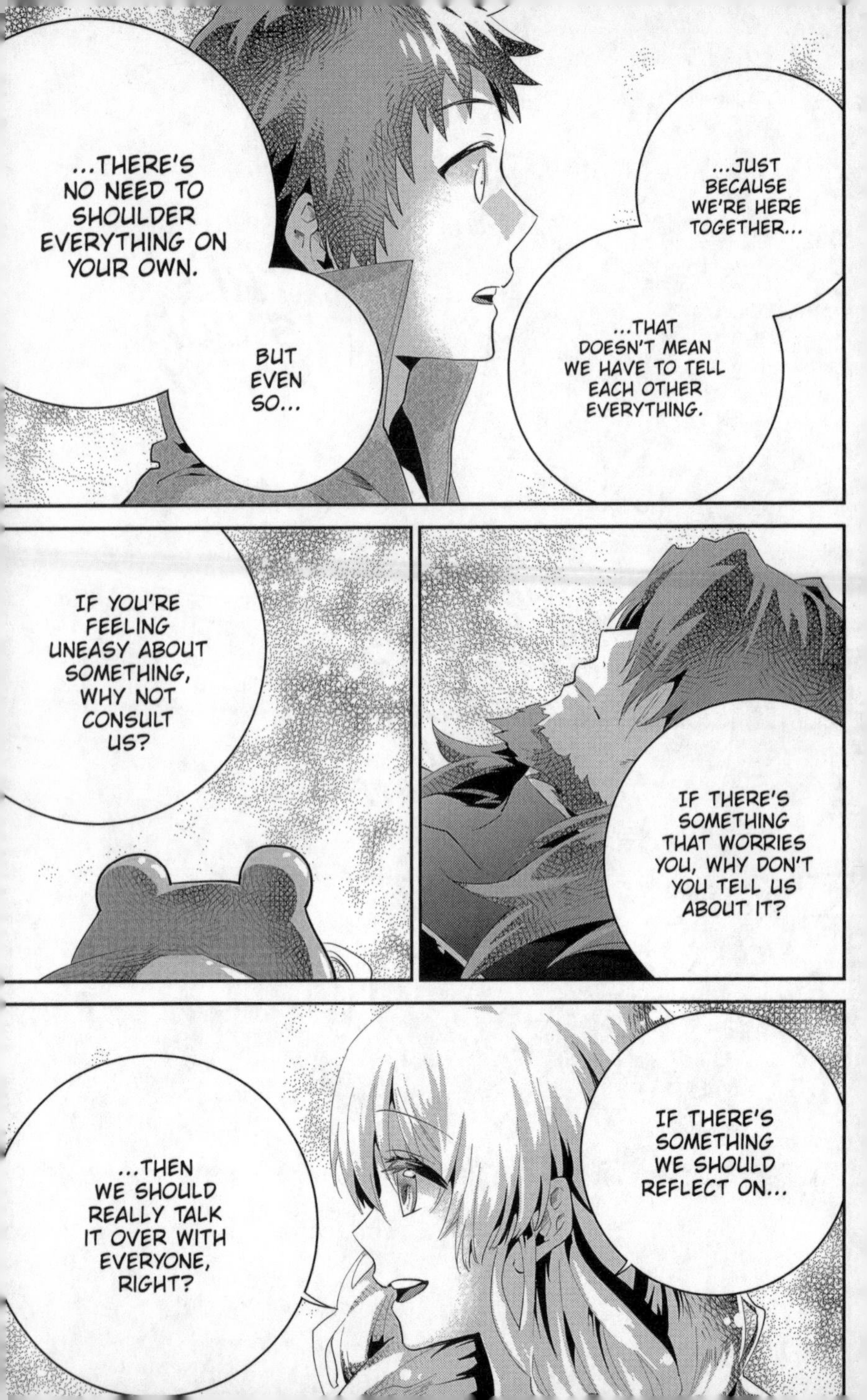
...JUST BECAUSE WE'RE HERE TOGETHER...
...THAT DOESN'T MEAN WE HAVE TO TELL EACH OTHER EVERYTHING.
BUT EVEN SO...
...THERE'S NO NEED TO SHOULDER EVERYTHING ON YOUR OWN.
IF THERE'S SOMETHING THAT WORRIES YOU, WHY DON'T YOU TELL US ABOUT IT?
IF YOU'RE FEELING UNEASY ABOUT SOMETHING, WHY NOT CONSULT US?
IF THERE'S SOMETHING WE SHOULD REFLECT ON...
...THEN WE SHOULD REALLY TALK IT OVER WITH EVERYONE, RIGHT?

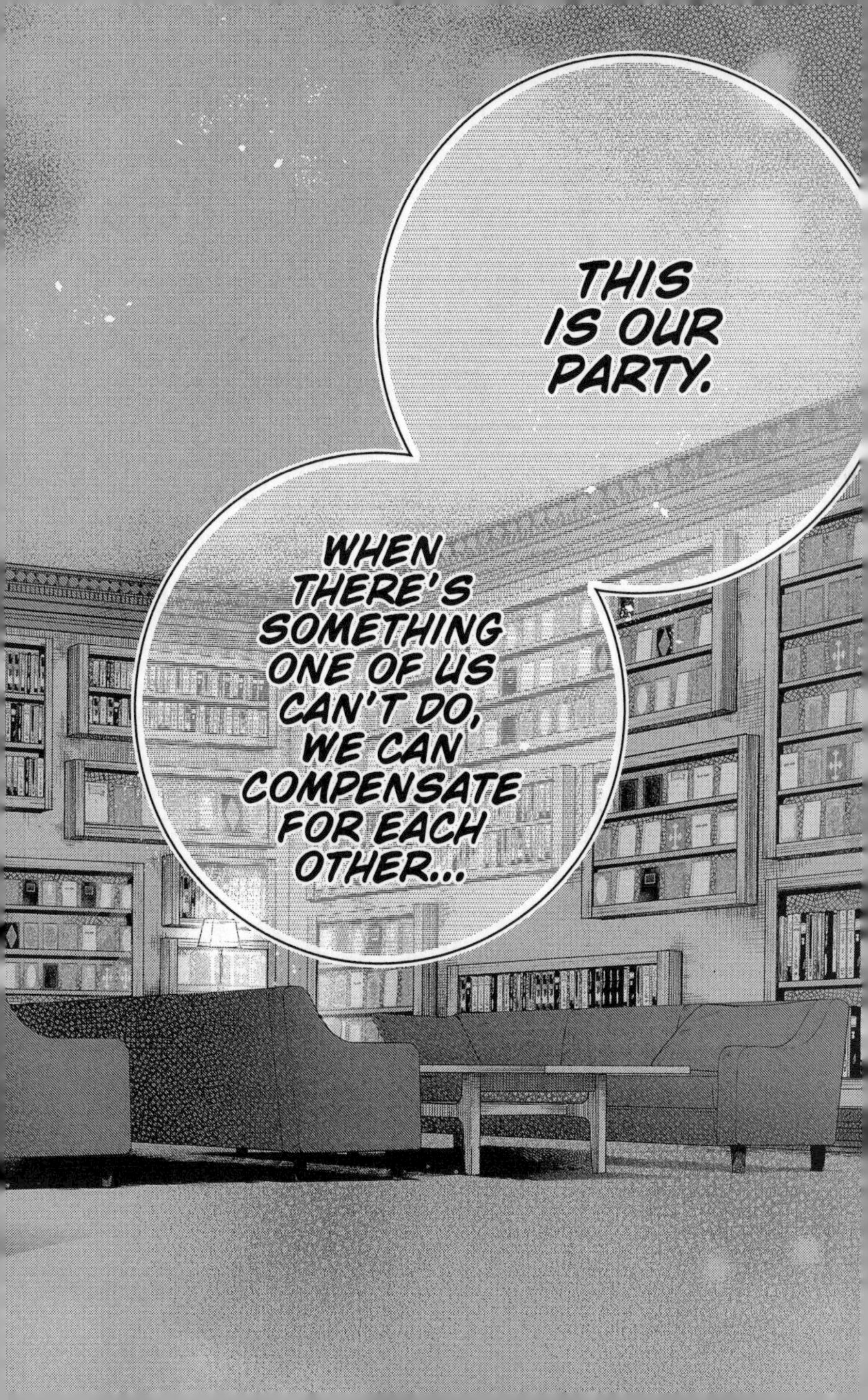
THIS IS OUR PARTY.
WHEN THERE'S SOMETHING ONE OF US CAN'T DO, WE CAN COMPENSATE FOR EACH OTHER...

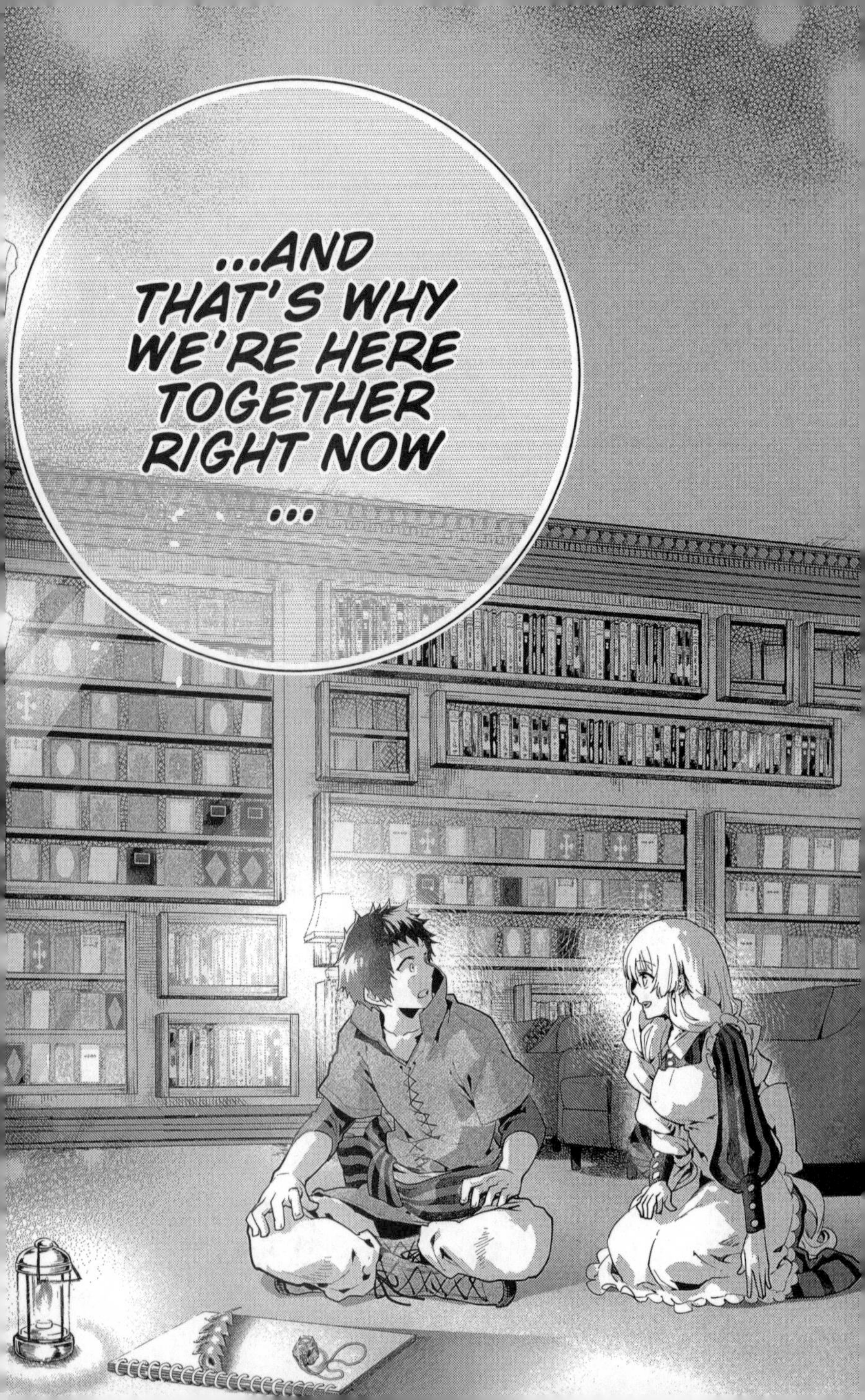
...AND THAT'S WHY WE'RE HERE TOGETHER RIGHT NOW ...

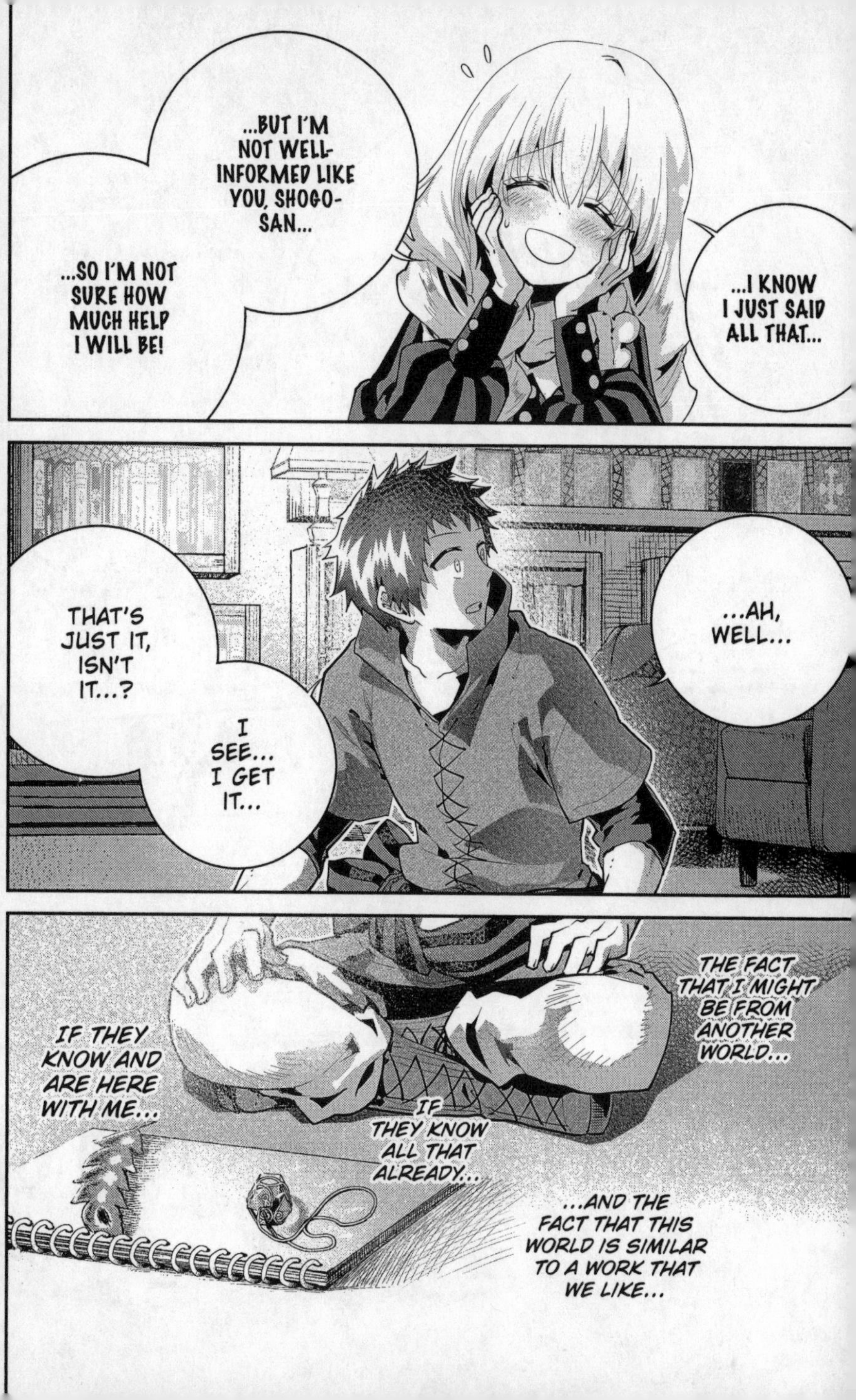
...I KNOW I JUST SAID ALL THAT...
...BUT I'M NOT WELL-INFORMED LIKE YOU, SHOGO-SAN...
...SO I'M NOT SURE HOW MUCH HELP I WILL BE!
...AH, WELL...
THAT'S JUST IT, ISN'T IT...?
I SEE... I GET IT...
THE FACT THAT I MIGHT BE FROM ANOTHER WORLD...
...AND THE FACT THAT THIS WORLD IS SIMILAR TO A WORK THAT WE LIKE...
IF THEY KNOW ALL THAT ALREADY...
IF THEY KNOW AND ARE HERE WITH ME...

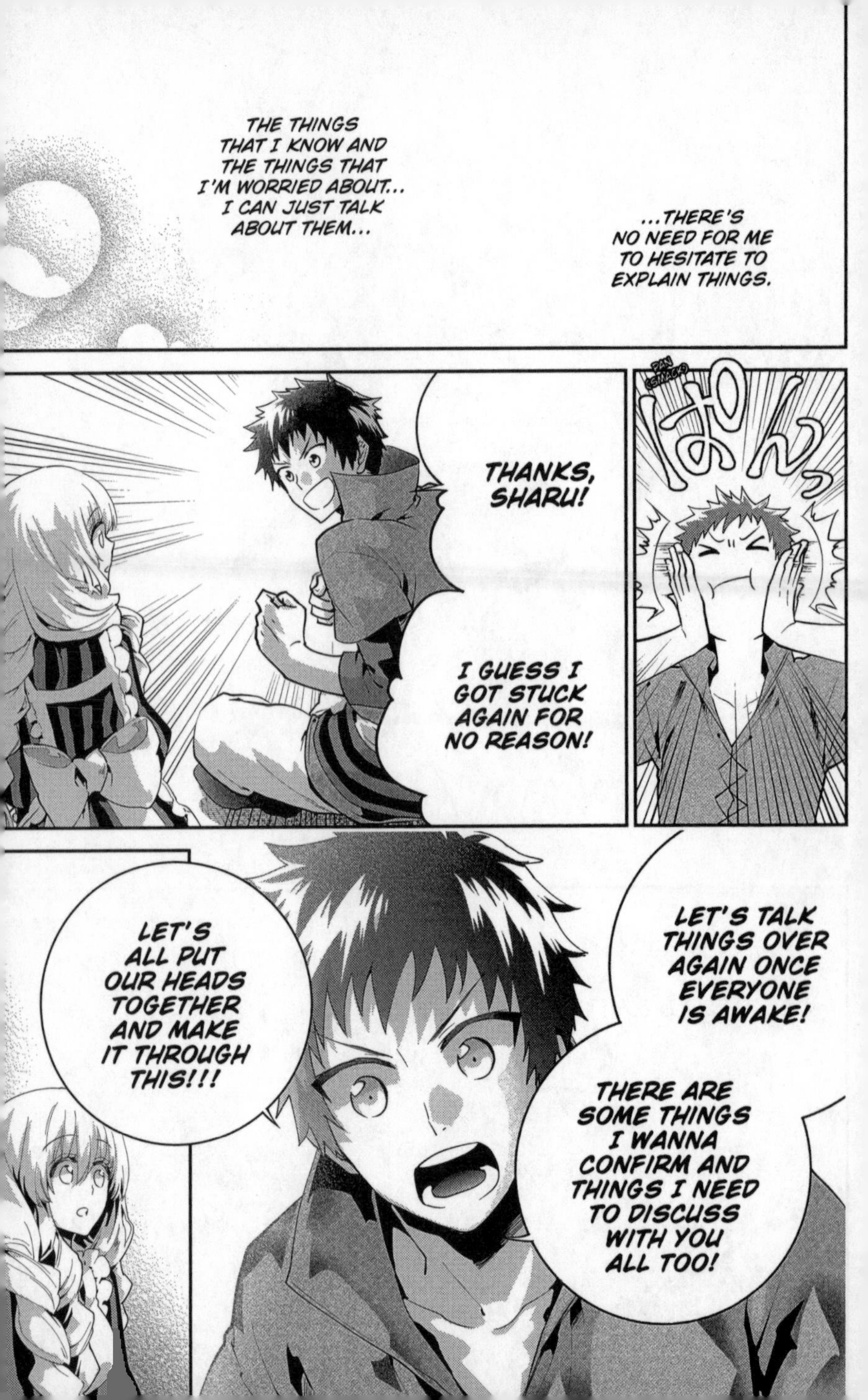
THE THINGS THAT I KNOW AND THE THINGS THAT I'M WORRIED ABOUT... I CAN JUST TALK ABOUT THEM...
...THERE'S NO NEED FOR ME TO HESITATE TO EXPLAIN THINGS.
PAN (SMACK)
ぱんっ
THANKS, SHARU!
I GUESS I GOT STUCK AGAIN FOR NO REASON!
LET'S TALK THINGS OVER AGAIN ONCE EVERYONE IS AWAKE!
THERE ARE SOME THINGS I WANNA CONFIRM AND THINGS I NEED TO DISCUSS WITH YOU ALL TOO!
LET'S ALL PUT OUR HEADS TOGETHER AND MAKE IT THROUGH THIS!!!

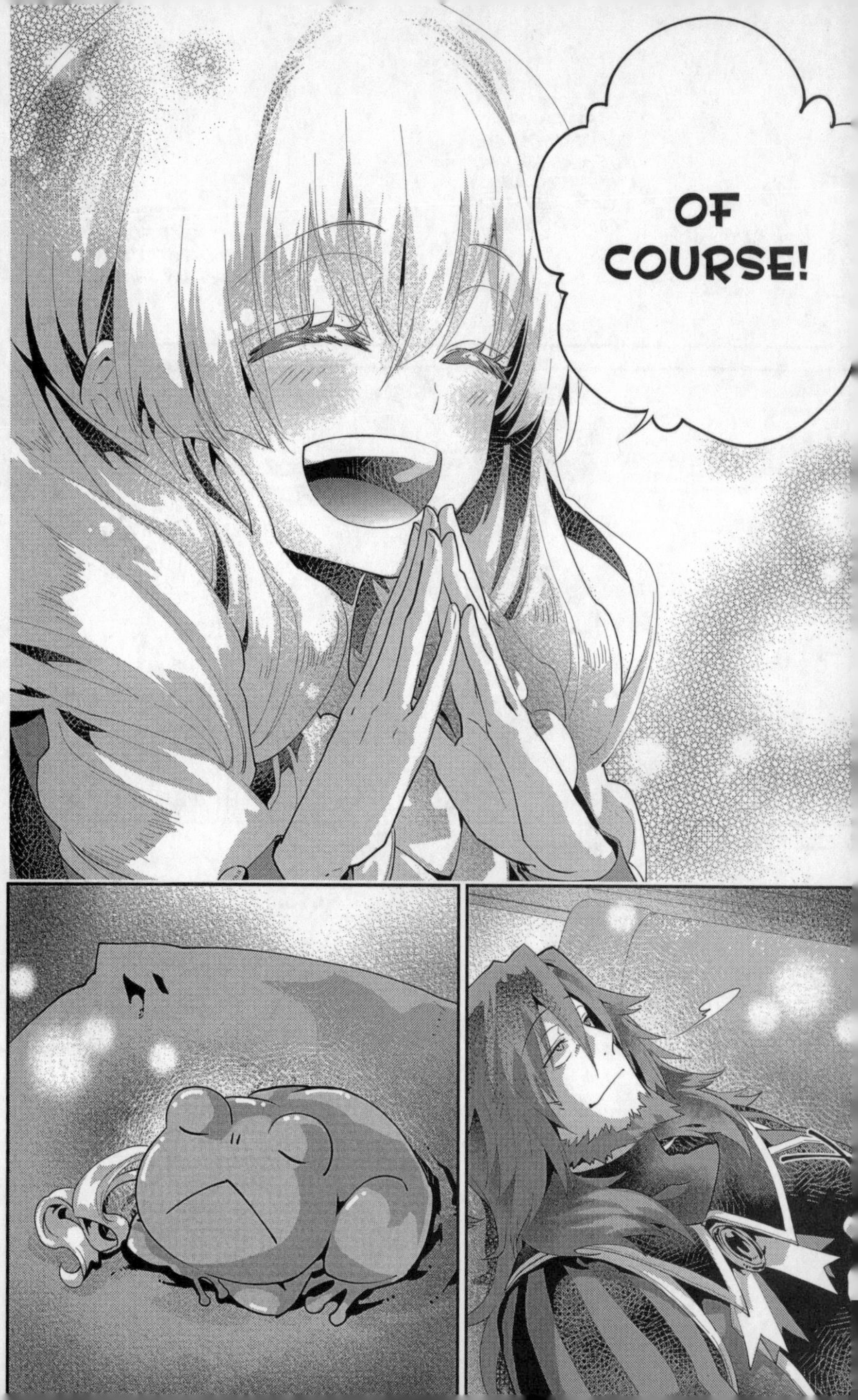
OF COURSE!

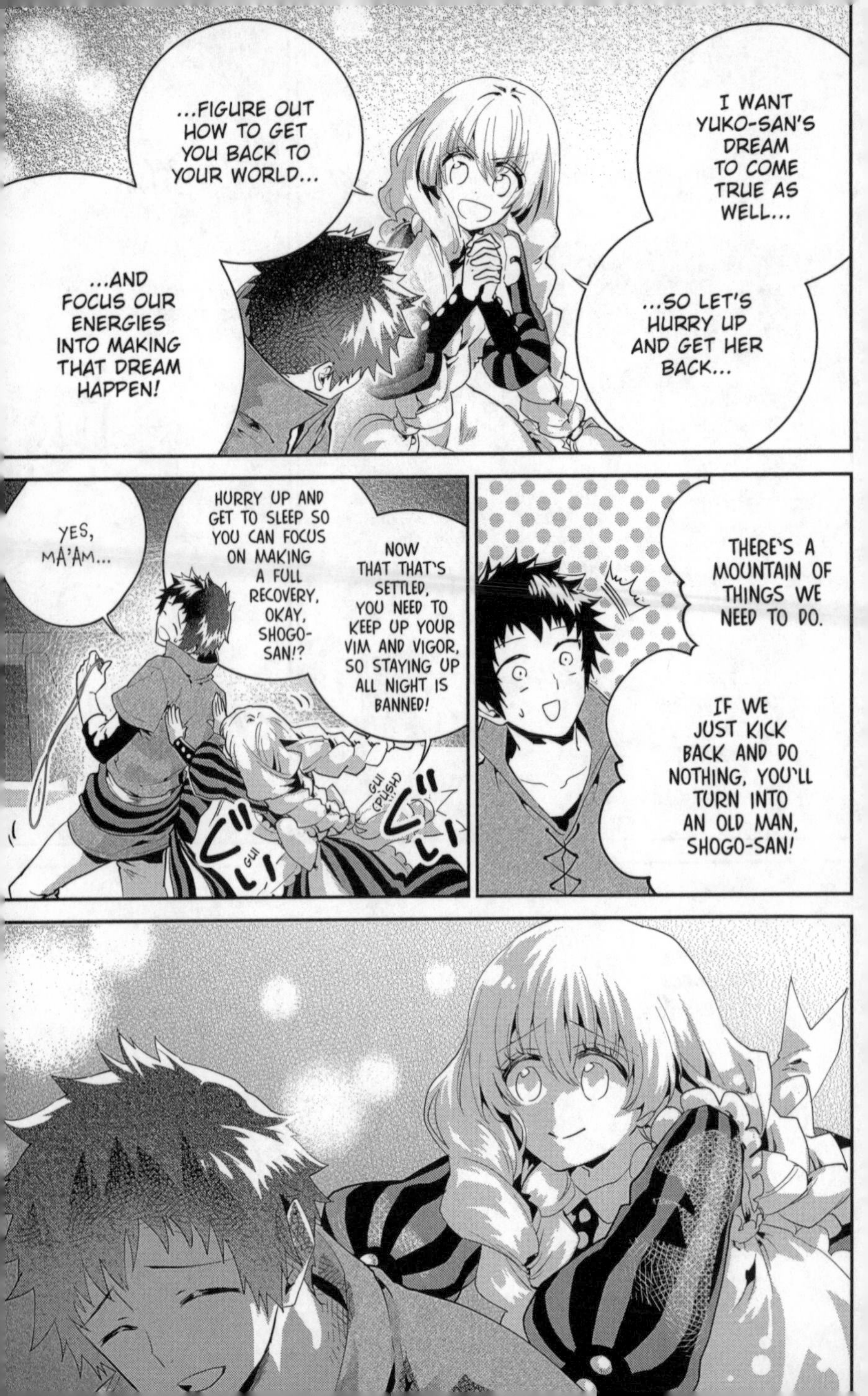
I WANT YUKO-SAN'S DREAM TO COME TRUE AS WELL...
...SO LET'S HURRY UP AND GET HER BACK...
...FIGURE OUT HOW TO GET YOU BACK TO YOUR WORLD...
...AND FOCUS OUR ENERGIES INTO MAKING THAT DREAM HAPPEN!
THERE'S A MOUNTAIN OF THINGS WE NEED TO DO.
IF WE JUST KICK BACK AND DO NOTHING, YOU'LL TURN INTO AN OLD MAN, SHOGO-SAN!
NOW THAT THAT'S SETTLED, YOU NEED TO KEEP UP YOUR VIM AND VIGOR, SO STAYING UP ALL NIGHT IS BANNED!
HURRY UP AND GET TO SLEEP SO YOU CAN FOCUS ON MAKING A FULL RECOVERY, OKAY, SHOGO-SAN!?
YES, MA'AM...
GUI (PUSH)
GUI

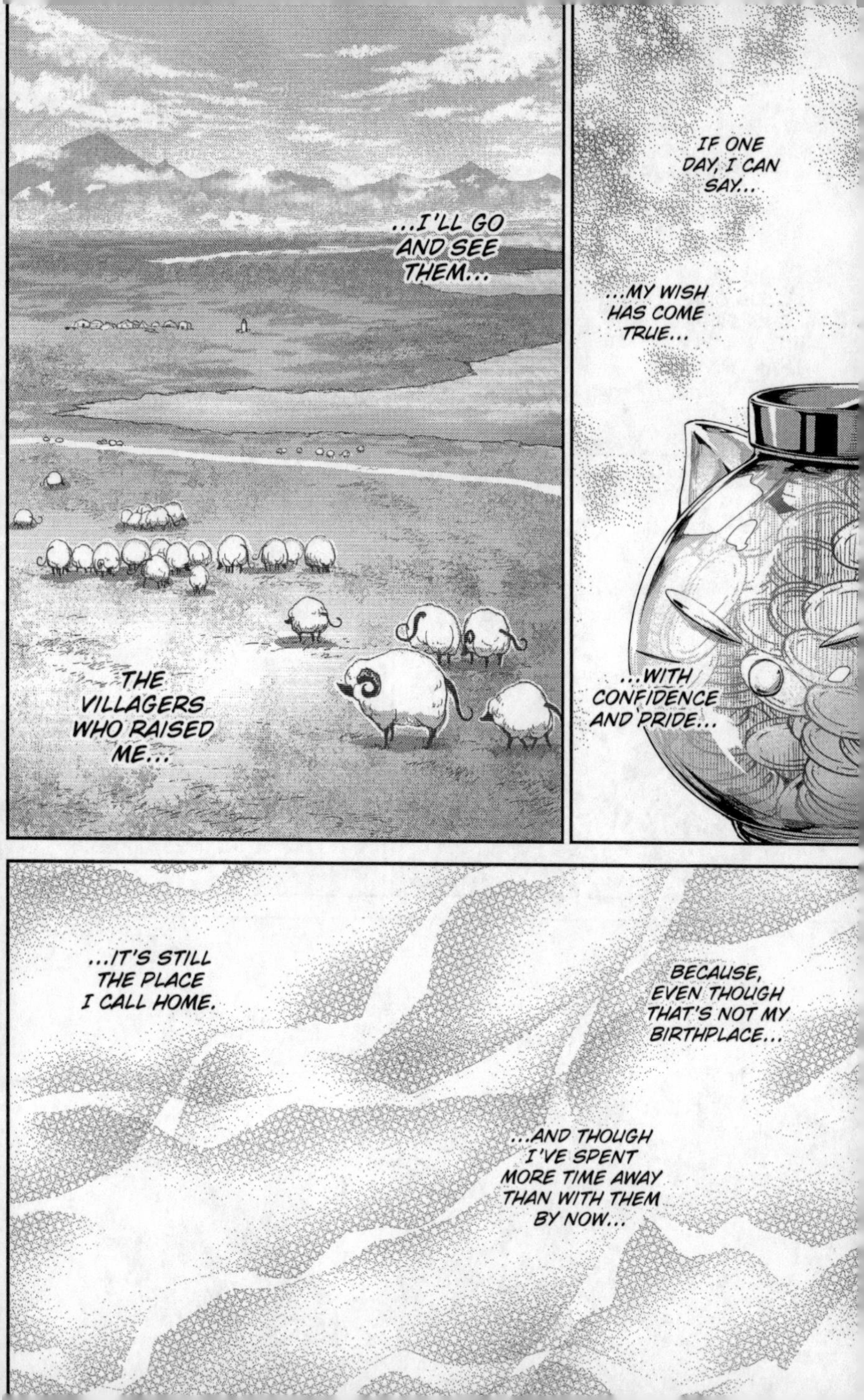
IF ONE DAY, I CAN SAY...
...MY WISH HAS COME TRUE...
...WITH CONFIDENCE AND PRIDE...
...I'LL GO AND SEE THEM...
THE VILLAGERS WHO RAISED ME...
BECAUSE, EVEN THOUGH THAT'S NOT MY BIRTHPLACE...
...AND THOUGH I'VE SPENT MORE TIME AWAY THAN WITH THEM BY NOW...
...IT'S STILL THE PLACE I CALL HOME.

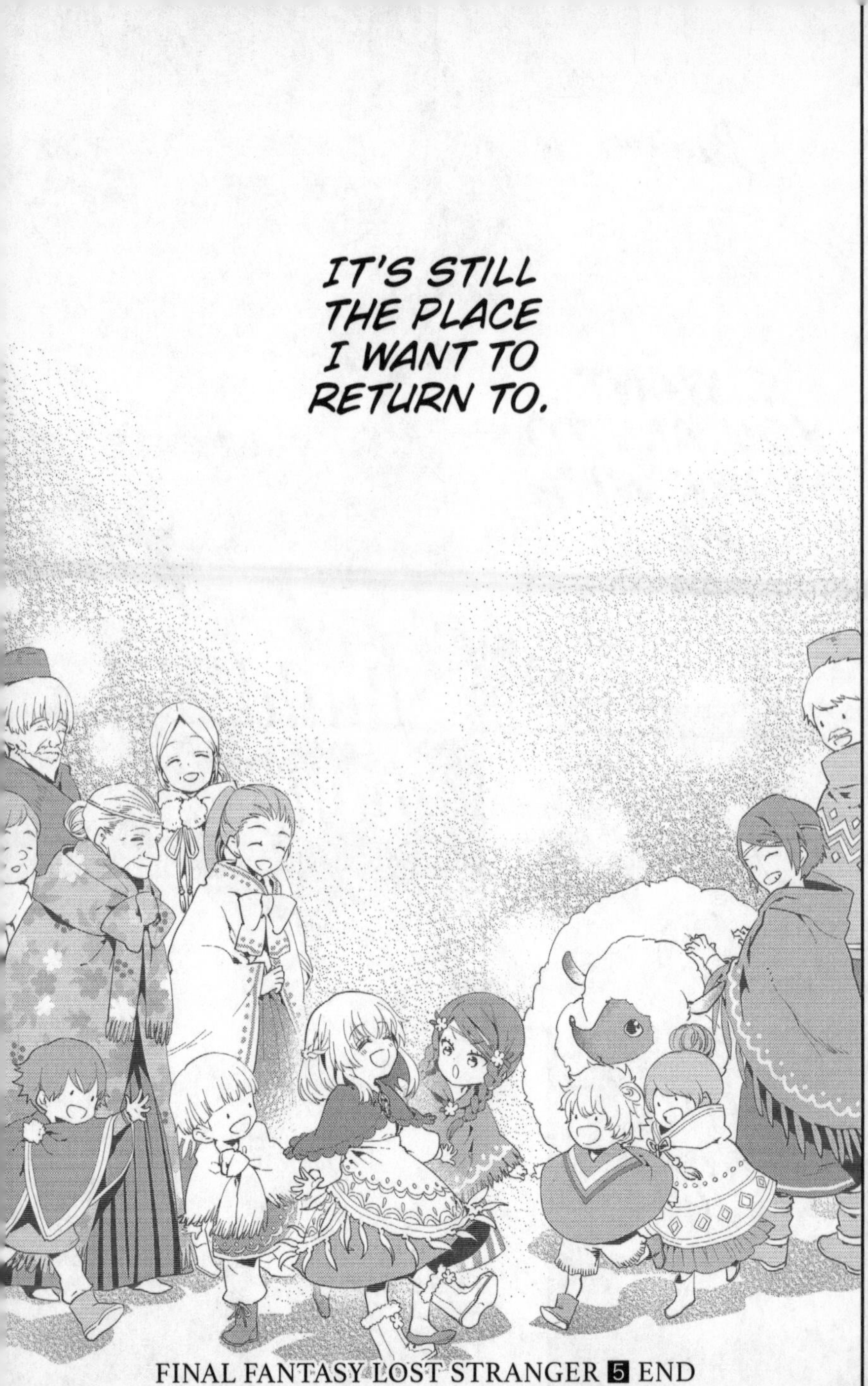
IT'S STILL THE PLACE I WANT TO RETURN TO.

FINAL FANTASY LOST STRANGER 5 END

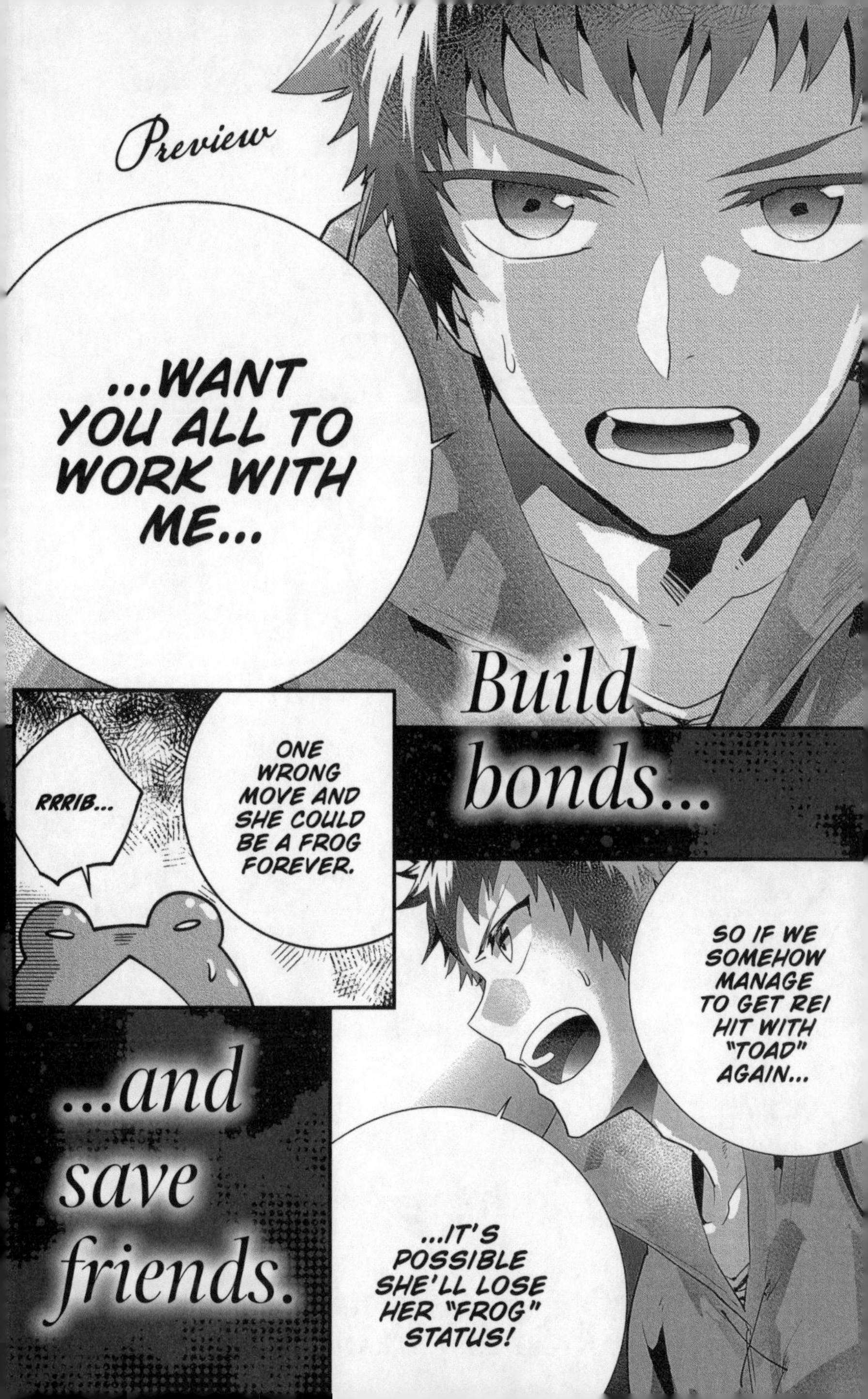
Preview
...WANT YOU ALL TO WORK WITH ME...
Build bonds...
ONE WRONG MOVE AND SHE COULD BE A FROG FOREVER.
RRRIB...
SO IF WE SOMEHOW MANAGE TO GET REI HIT WITH "TOAD" AGAIN...
...IT'S POSSIBLE SHE'LL LOSE HER "FROG" STATUS!
...and save friends.

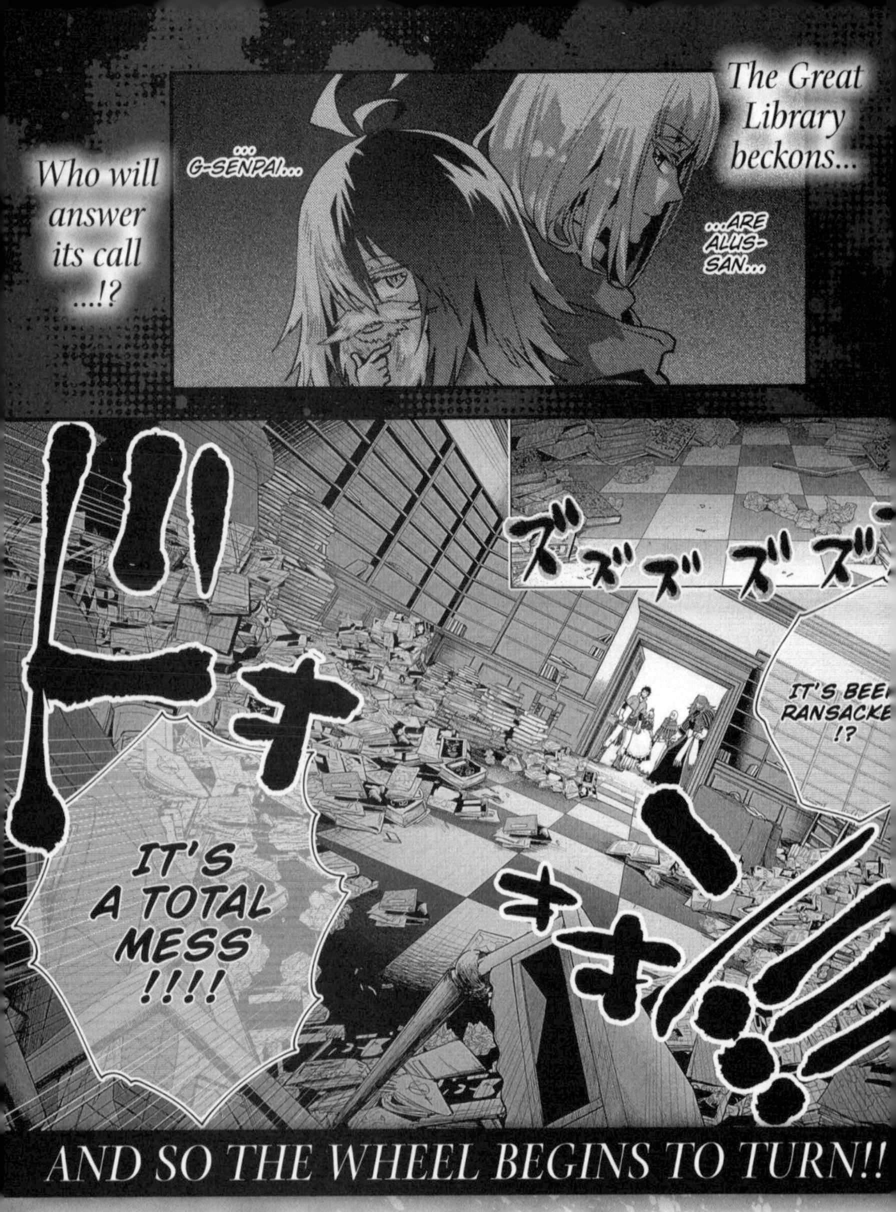
The Great Library beckons...
...ARE ALUS-SAN...
... G-SENPAI...
Who will answer its call ...!?
ズズズズズ
IT'S BEE RANSACKE !?
IT'S A TOTAL MESS !!!!
AND SO THE WHEEL BEGINS TO TURN!!

# FINAL FANTASY®
ファイナルファンタジー　ロスト・ストレンジャー
## LOST STRANGER

Volume 6 coming soon!!

# TRANSLATION NOTES

## COMMON HONORIFICS

**no honorific:** Indicates familiarity or closeness; if used without permission or reason, addressing someone in this manner would constitute an insult.

**-san:** The Japanese equivalent of Mr./Mrs./Miss. If a situation calls for politeness, this is the fail-safe honorific.

**-kun:** Used most often when referring to boys, this indicates affection or familiarity. Occasionally used by older men among their peers, but it may also be used by anyone referring to a person of lower standing.

**-chan:** An affectionate honorific indicating familiarity used mostly in reference to girls; also used in reference to cute persons or animals of either gender.

**-sensei:** A respectful term for teachers, artists, or high-level professionals.

**onii-chan:** An affectionate term used for older brothers or brother figures.

### ✦ PAGE 7
The Japanese title of this chapter translates to "Eternal Vow," but it's also the name of the *FF14* track "Promised Eternity."

### ✦ PAGE 10
**Split damage** refers to a mechanic in *FF14* in which an area-of-effect attack's total damage is split among all party members within the attack's range. Here, the other party members are rushing to their ally in order to share the damage taken, thereby saving him.

**Group-cast** refers to the act of targeting all members of a party with a spell or ability rather than a single target. This typically reduces the spell's potency significantly but can be useful in cases like the one depicted here, in which a healing spell is being group-cast on the party.

### ✦ PAGE 41
The Japanese title of this chapter translates to "Beyond the Door," but it's also the name of the *FF9* track "Behind the Door."

### ✦ PAGE 87
The Japanese title of this chapter translates to "What Burns Deep Within the Heart," but it's also the name of the *FF Crystal Chronicles* track "Something Burns in the Heart."

### ✦ PAGE 88
SOLDIER is an elite military unit that serves the Shinra Electric Power Company in *FF7*.

**PAGE 135**
The Japanese title of this chapter translates to "A Place to Return to Someday," but it's also the name of the *FF Crystal Chronicles* track "A Place to Call Home."

**PAGE 137**
"Blessing breeze, blow in energy!" is an incantation recited when casting the "Curaga" spell in *Final Fantasy Tactics*.

**PAGE 147**
A Remedy is a recurring item in *Final Fantasy* used to heal practically all status ailments.

**PAGE 148**
A *Maiden's Kiss* is a recurring item in *Final Fantasy* used to cure the "Toad" status.

**PAGE 149**
*Final Fantasy 7 International Version* was a Japan-only release that came with an extra disc with a plethora of information about the game.

**PAGE 169**
The Japanese title of this chapter translates to "If You Open Your Heart," but it's also the name of the *FF7* track "Open Your Heart."

**PAGE 177**
"If you cut your nails at night, you won't be there to see your parents die" is an old Japanese expression from a time when knives were used to cut one's nails, making the idea of doing so in the dark a very dangerous proposition.

**PAGE 223**
The Great Library is likely a nod to The Great Gubal Library, a dungeon introduced in the *Heavensward* expansion of *FF14*.

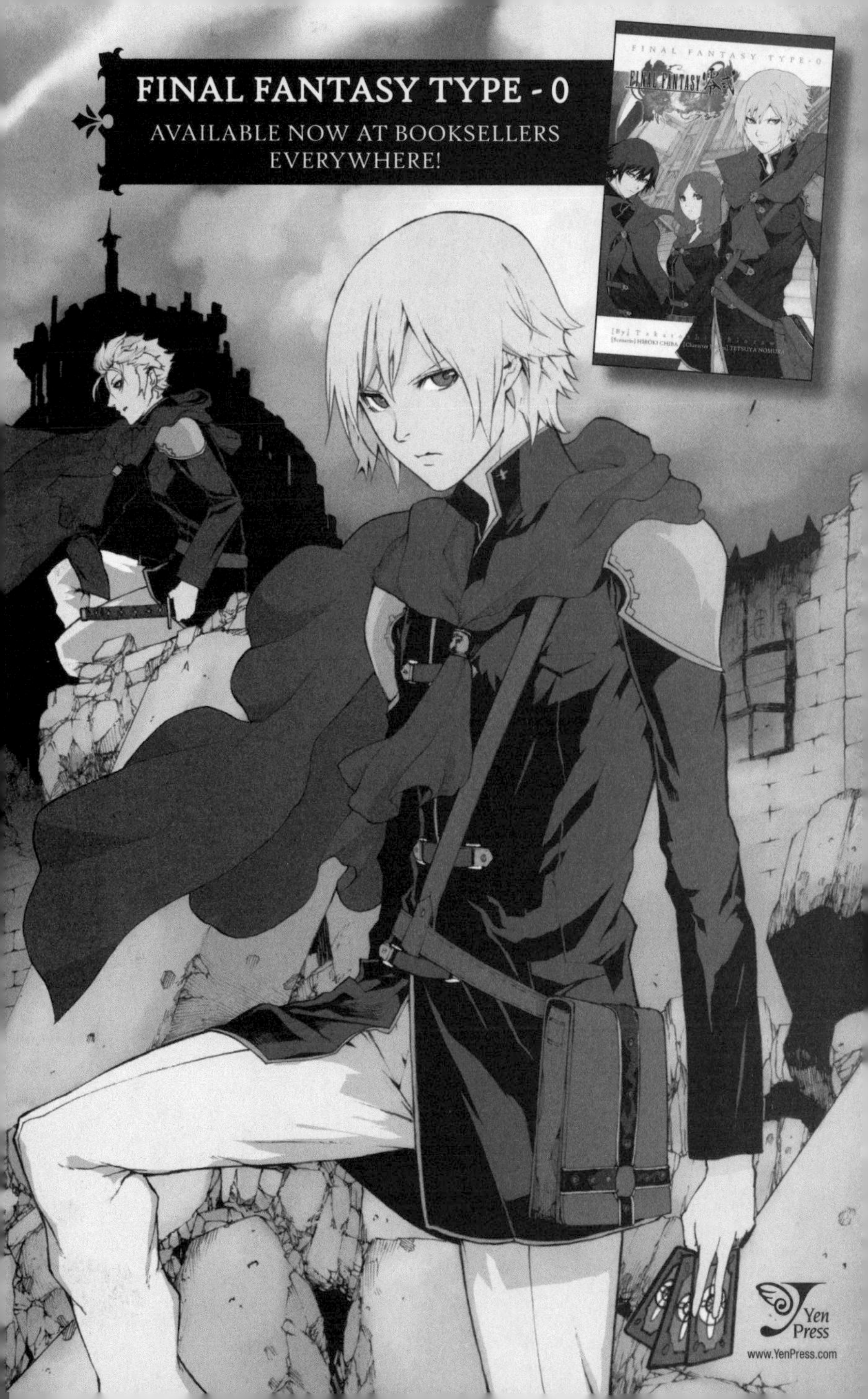
FINAL FANTASY TYPE - 0
AVAILABLE NOW AT BOOKSELLERS EVERYWHERE!
FINAL FANTASY TYPE-0
Yen Press
www.YenPress.com

# FINAL FANTASY 零式 TYPE-0™



Art: TAKATOSHI SHIOZAWA
Character Design: TETSUYA NOMURA
Scenario: HIROKI CHIBA

The cadets of Akademeia's Class Zero are legends, with strength and magic unrivaled, and crimson capes symbolizing the great Vermilion Bird of the Dominion. But will their elite training be enough to keep them alive when a war breaks out and the Class Zero cadets find themselves at the front and center of a bloody political battlefield?!

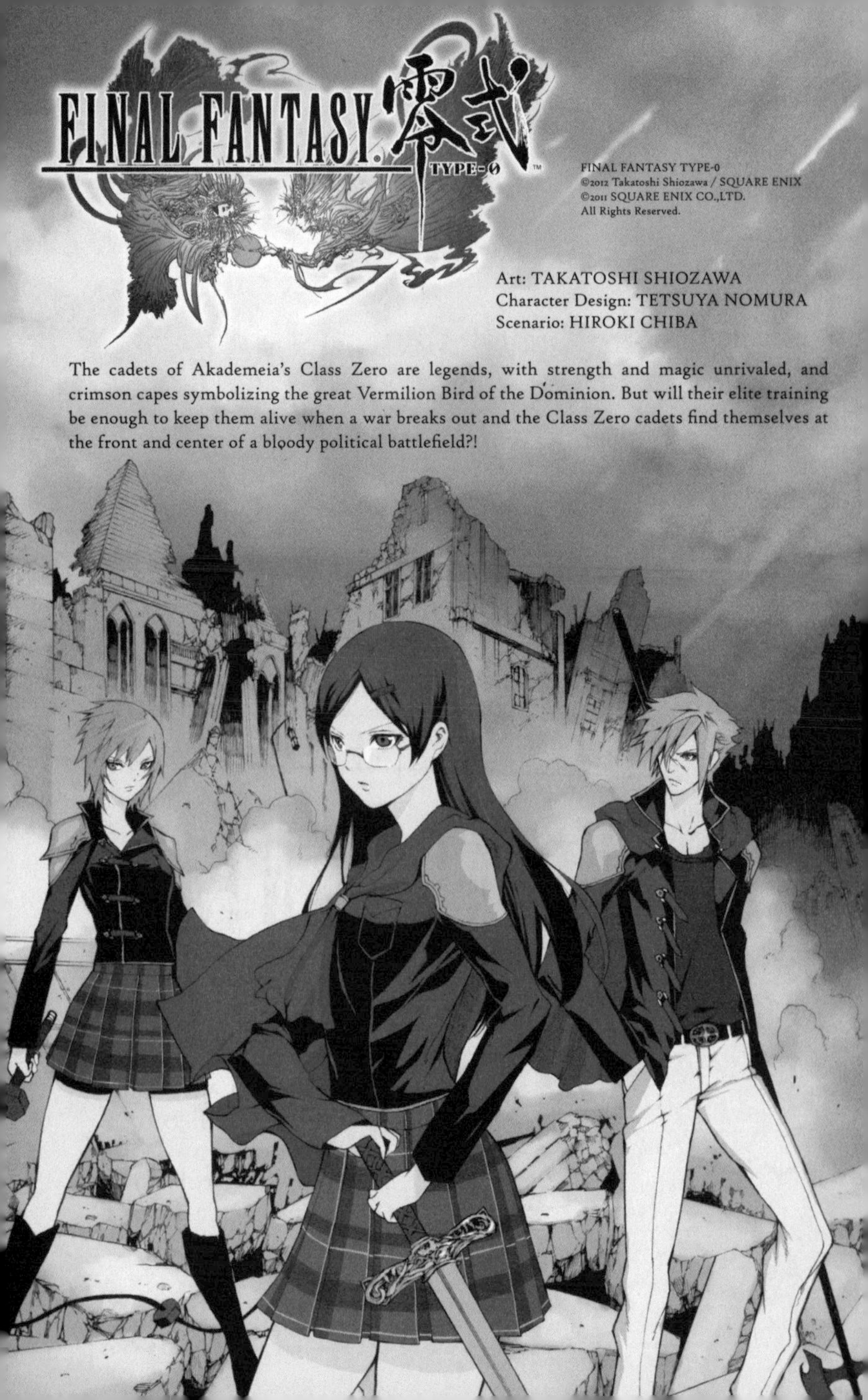

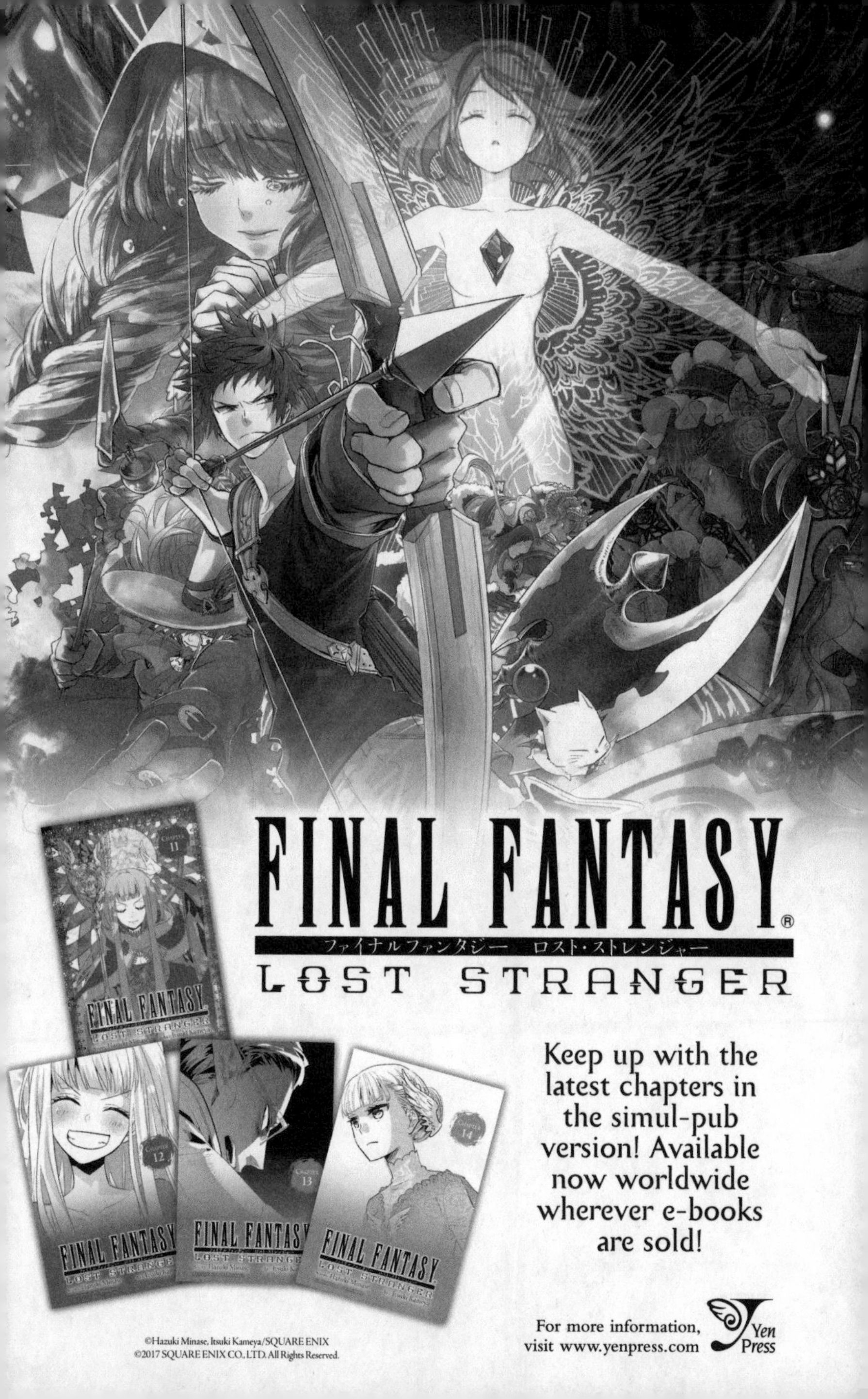
FINAL FANTASY®
ファイナルファンタジー ロスト・ストレンジャー
LOST STRANGER
Keep up with the latest chapters in the simul-pub version! Available now worldwide wherever e-books are sold!
For more information, visit www.yenpress.com
Yen Press
©Hazuki Minase, Itsuki Kameya/SQUARE ENIX
©2017 SQUARE ENIX CO., LTD. All Rights Reserved.

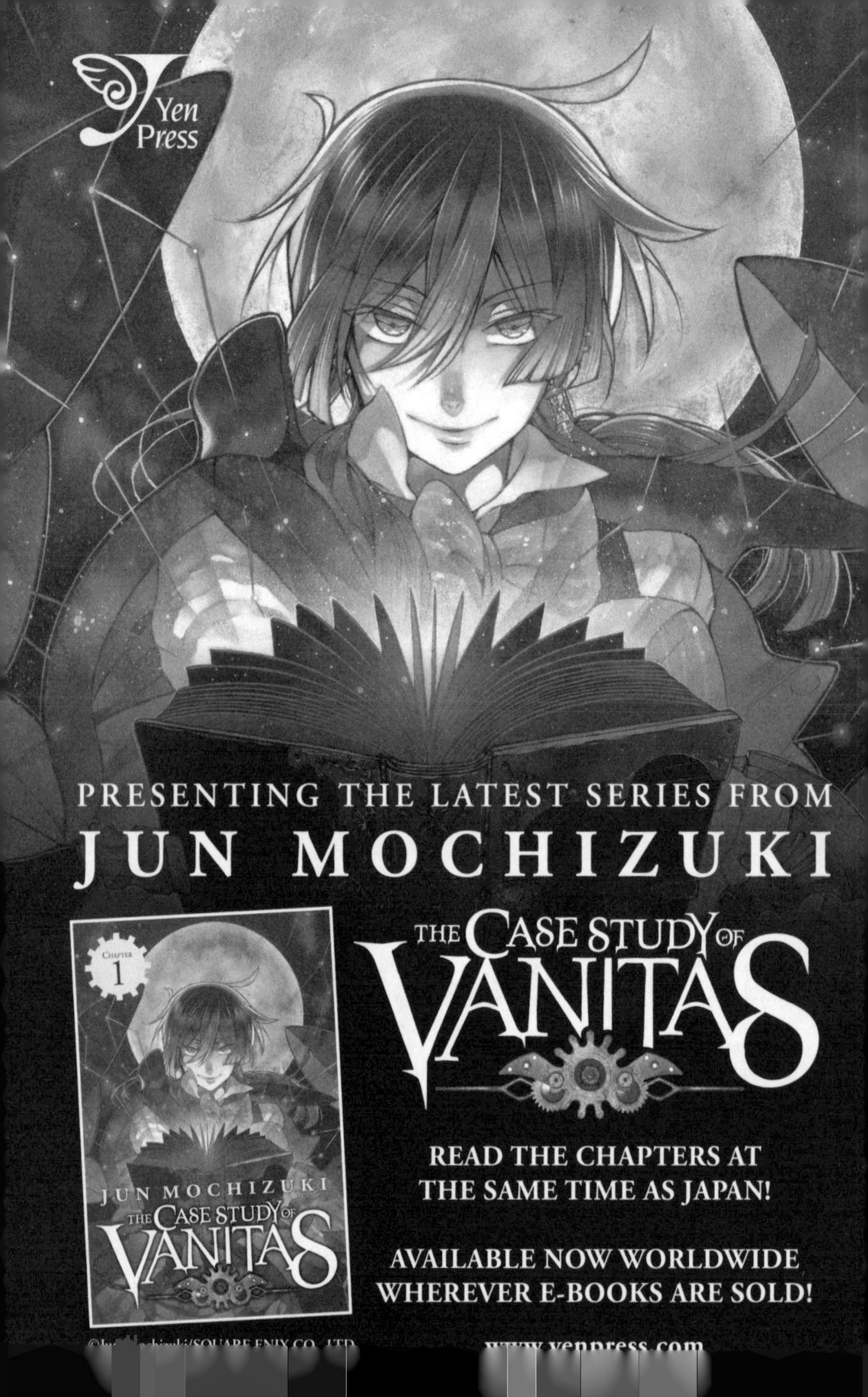
Yen Press
PRESENTING THE LATEST SERIES FROM
JUN MOCHIZUKI
CHAPTER 1
JUN MOCHIZUKI
THE CASE STUDY OF VANITAS
THE CASE STUDY OF VANITAS
READ THE CHAPTERS AT THE SAME TIME AS JAPAN!
AVAILABLE NOW WORLDWIDE WHEREVER E-BOOKS ARE SOLD!
SQUARE ENIX CO., LTD
www.yenpress.com

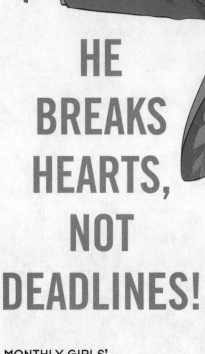

# FINAL FANTASY®

ファイナルファンタジー　ロスト・ストレンジャー

## LOST STRANGER

5

STORY: Hazuki Minase

ART: Itsuki Kameya

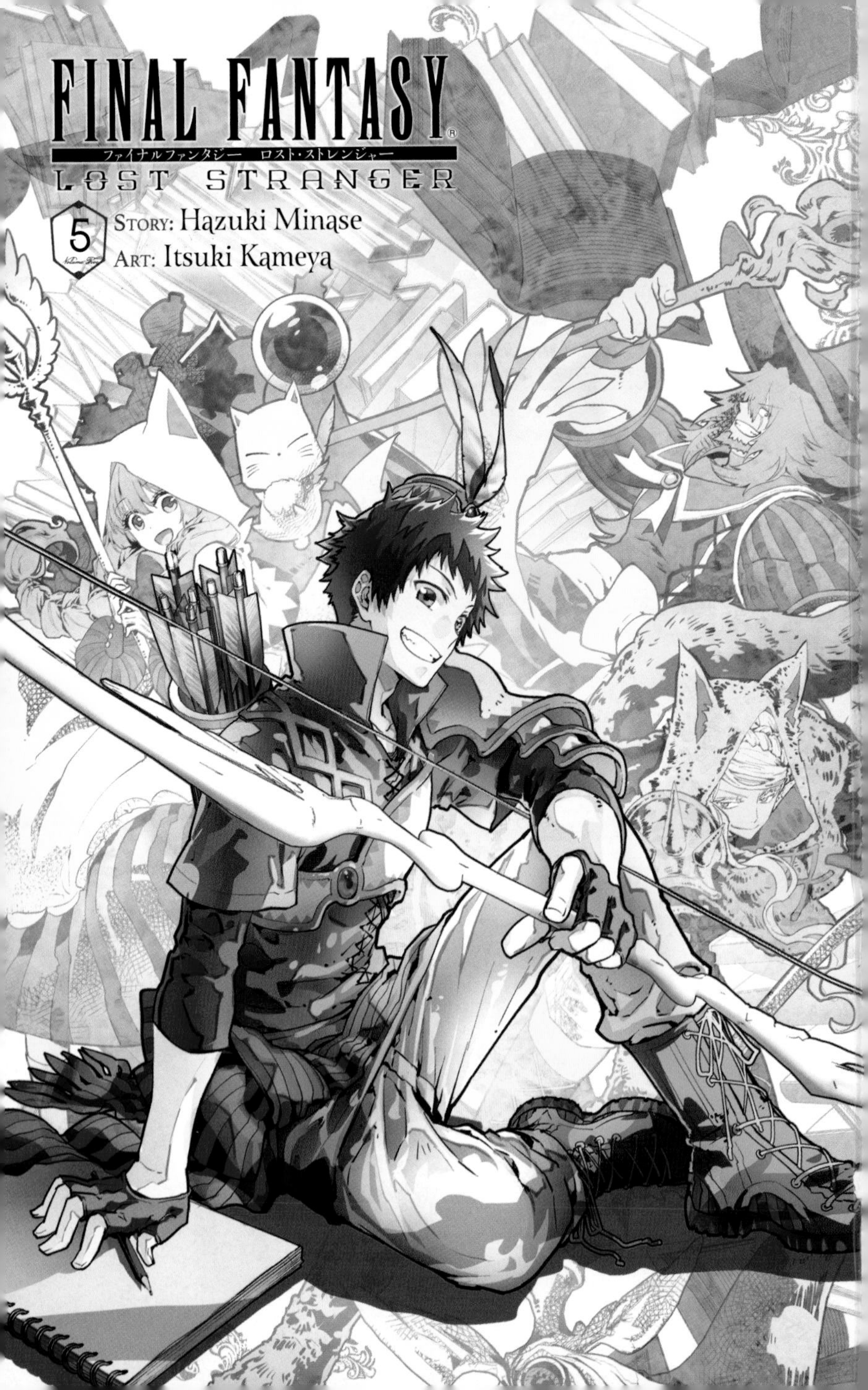

# Contents